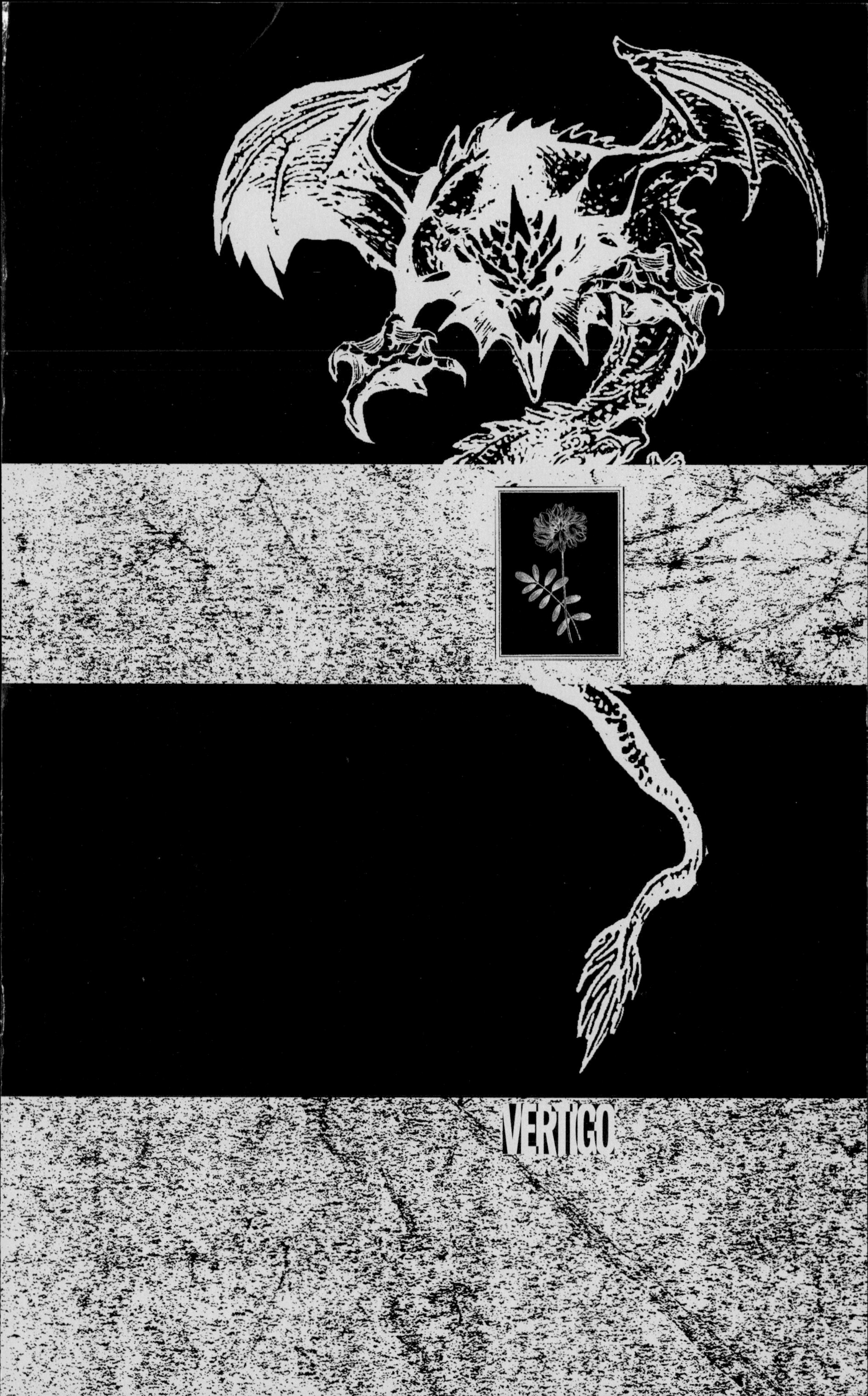
VERTIGO

THE GIR
THE DRAG
BOOK 2

ADAPTED BY DENISE MINA

ART BY LEONARDO MANCC
COLORS BY GIULIA BRUSCC
LETTERS BY STEVE WANDS
BASED ON THE NOVEL THE GIRL WITH THE

L WITH
ON TATTOO

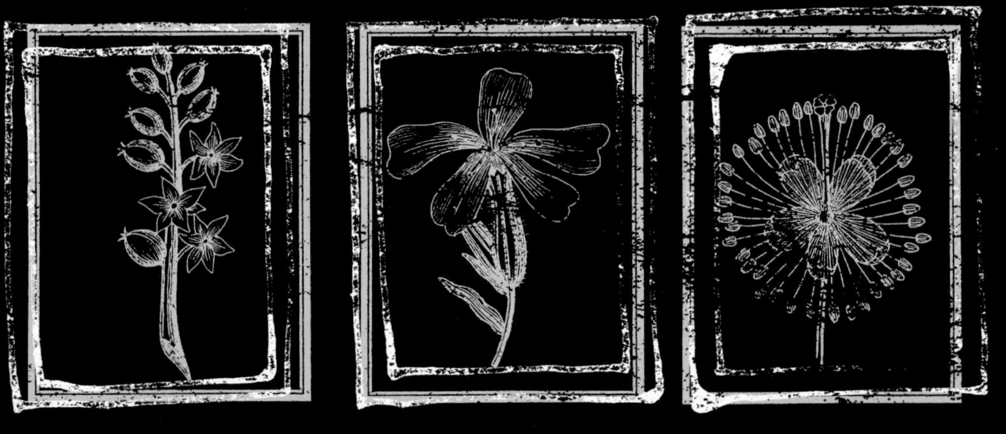

AND ANDREA MUTTI
AND PATRICIA MULVIHILL
COVER BY LEE BERMEJO
DRAGON TATTOO BY STIEG LARSSON

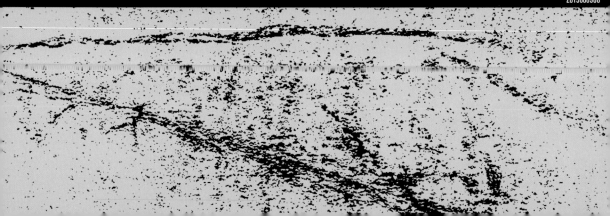

Will Dennis Editor Mark Doyle Associate Editor Sara Miller Assistant Editor Robbin Brosterman Design Director – Books Louis Prandi Publication Design

Karen Berger Senior VP – Executive Editor, Vertigo Bob Harras VP – Editor-in-Chief

Diane Nelson President Dan DiDio and Jim Lee Co-Publishers Geoff Johns Chief Creative Officer John Rood Executive VP – Sales, Marketing and Business Development
Amy Genkins Senior VP – Business and Legal Affairs Nairi Gardiner Senior VP – Finance Jeff Boison VP – Publishing Operations Mark Chiarello VP – Art Direction and Design
John Cunningham VP – Marketing Terri Cunningham VP – Talent Relations and Services Alison Gill Senior VP – Manufacturing and Operations Hank Kanalz Senior VP – Digital
Jay Kogan VP – Business and Legal Affairs, Publishing Jack Mahan VP – Business Affairs, Talent Nick Napolitano VP – Manufacturing Administration
Sue Pohja VP – Book Sales Courtney Simmons Senior VP – Publicity Bob Wayne Senior VP – Sales

Library of Congress Cataloging-in-Publication Data

Mina, Denise, author.
The girl with the dragon tattoo. Book 2 / Denise Mina, Andrea Mutti, Leonardo Manco.
pages cm
ISBN 978-1-4012-3558-1
1. Crime—Sweden—Comic books, strips, etc. 2. Graphic novels. I. Mutti, Andrea, 1973- illustrator. II. Manco, Leonardo, illustrator. III. Larsson, Stieg, 1954-2004. Girl with
the dragon tattoo. IV. Title.
PN6737.M57G58 2013
741.5'942—dc23
2013000986

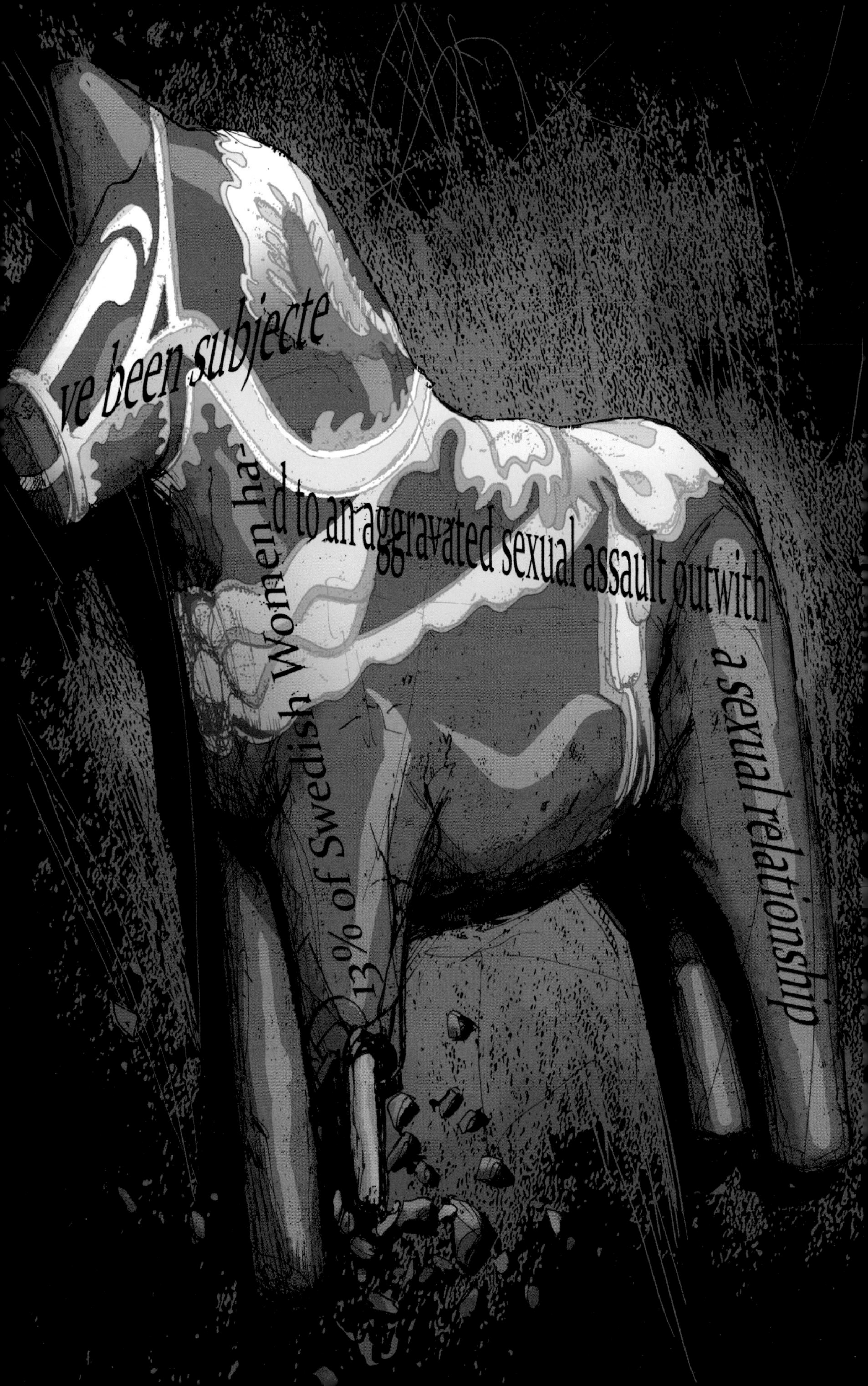
13% of Swedish Women ha-
ve been subjecte
d to an aggravated sexual assault outwith
a sexual relationship

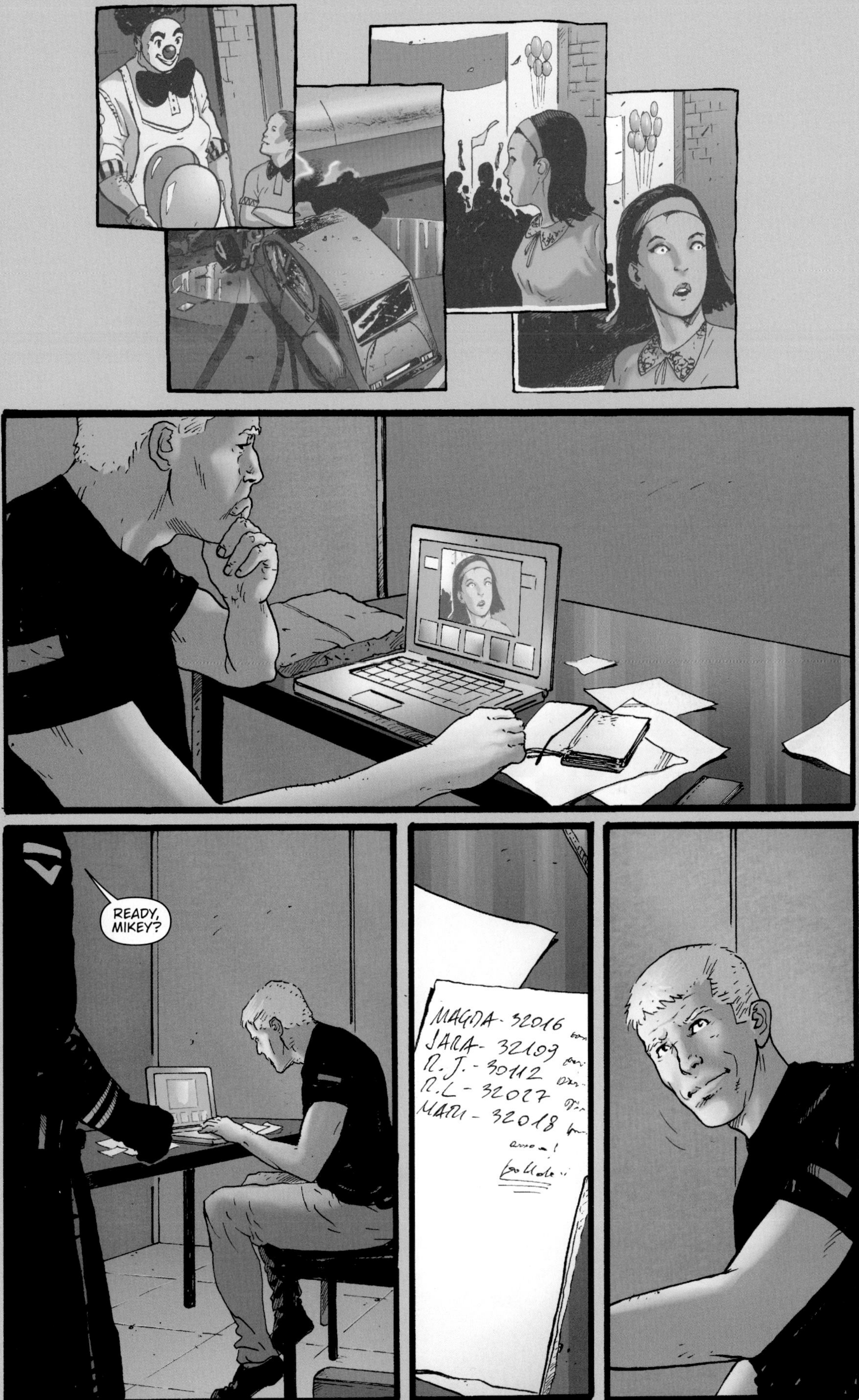
READY, MIKEY?
MAGDA - 32016
SARA - 32109
R.J. - 30112
R.L - 32027
MARI - 32018

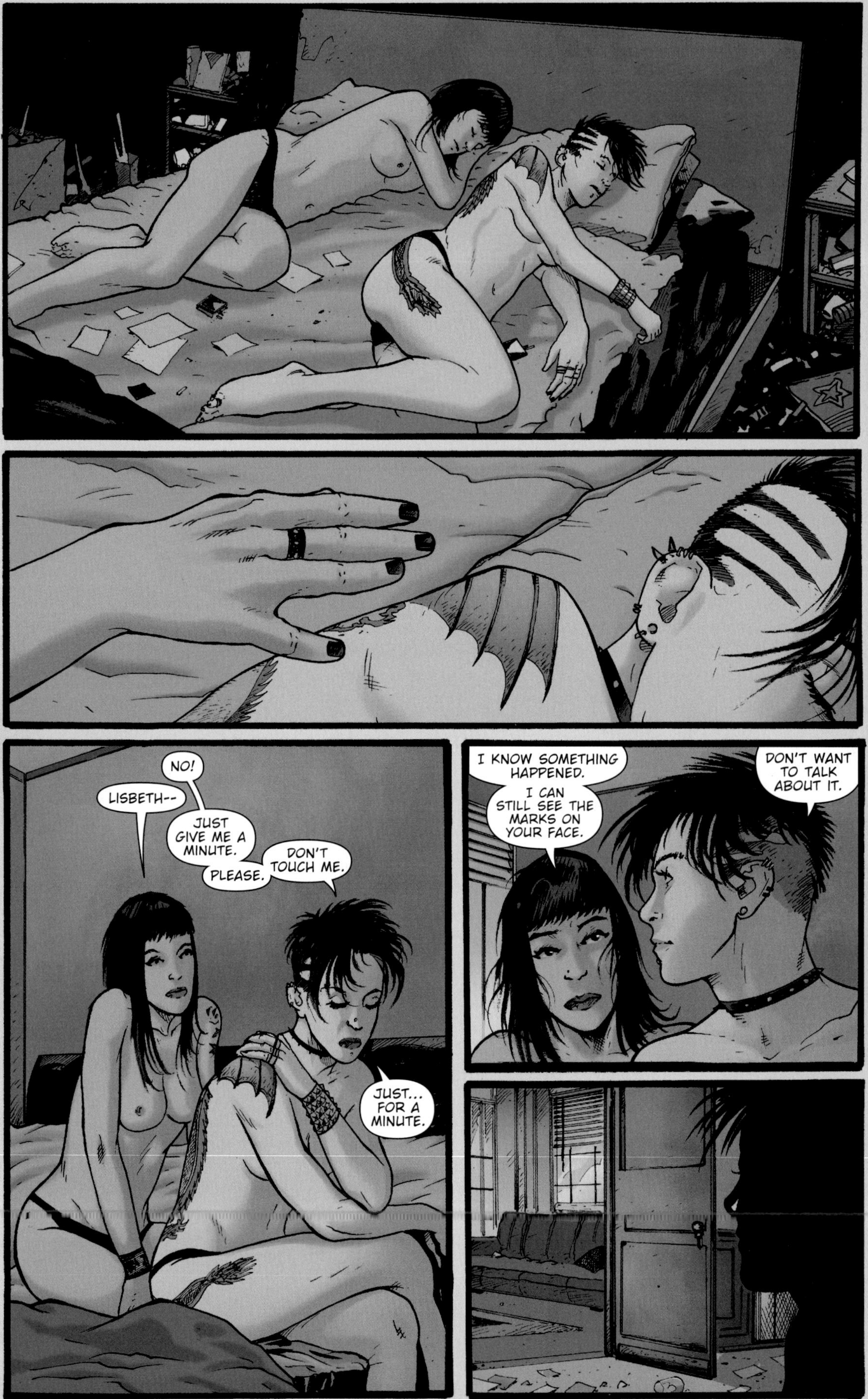
LISBETH--
NO!
JUST GIVE ME A MINUTE.
PLEASE.
DON'T TOUCH ME.
JUST... FOR A MINUTE.
I KNOW SOMETHING HAPPENED.
I CAN STILL SEE THE MARKS ON YOUR FACE.
DON'T WANT TO TALK ABOUT IT.

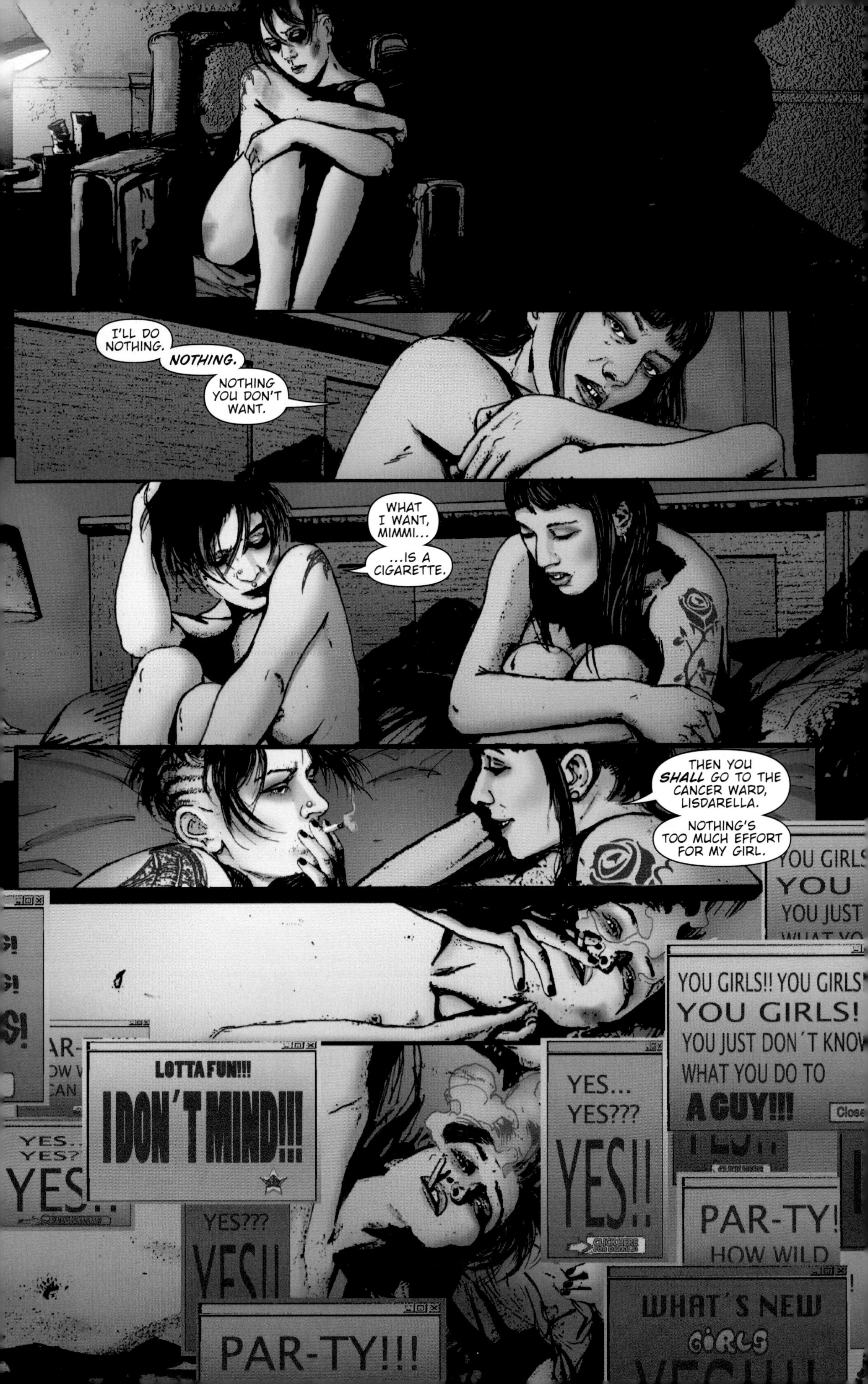

I'LL DO NOTHING.
NOTHING.
NOTHING YOU DON'T WANT.
WHAT I WANT, MIMMI...
...IS A CIGARETTE.
THEN YOU SHALL GO TO THE CANCER WARD, LISDARELLA.
NOTHING'S TOO MUCH EFFORT FOR MY GIRL.
YOU GIRLS!! YOU GIRLS!
YOU GIRLS!
YOU JUST DON'T KNOW WHAT YOU DO TO A GUY!!!
Close
LOTTA FUN!!!
I DON'T MIND!!!
YES... YES??? YES!!
YES.. YES? YES!..
YES???
PAR-TY!
HOW WILD
WHAT'S NEW
GIRLS
PAR-TY!!!

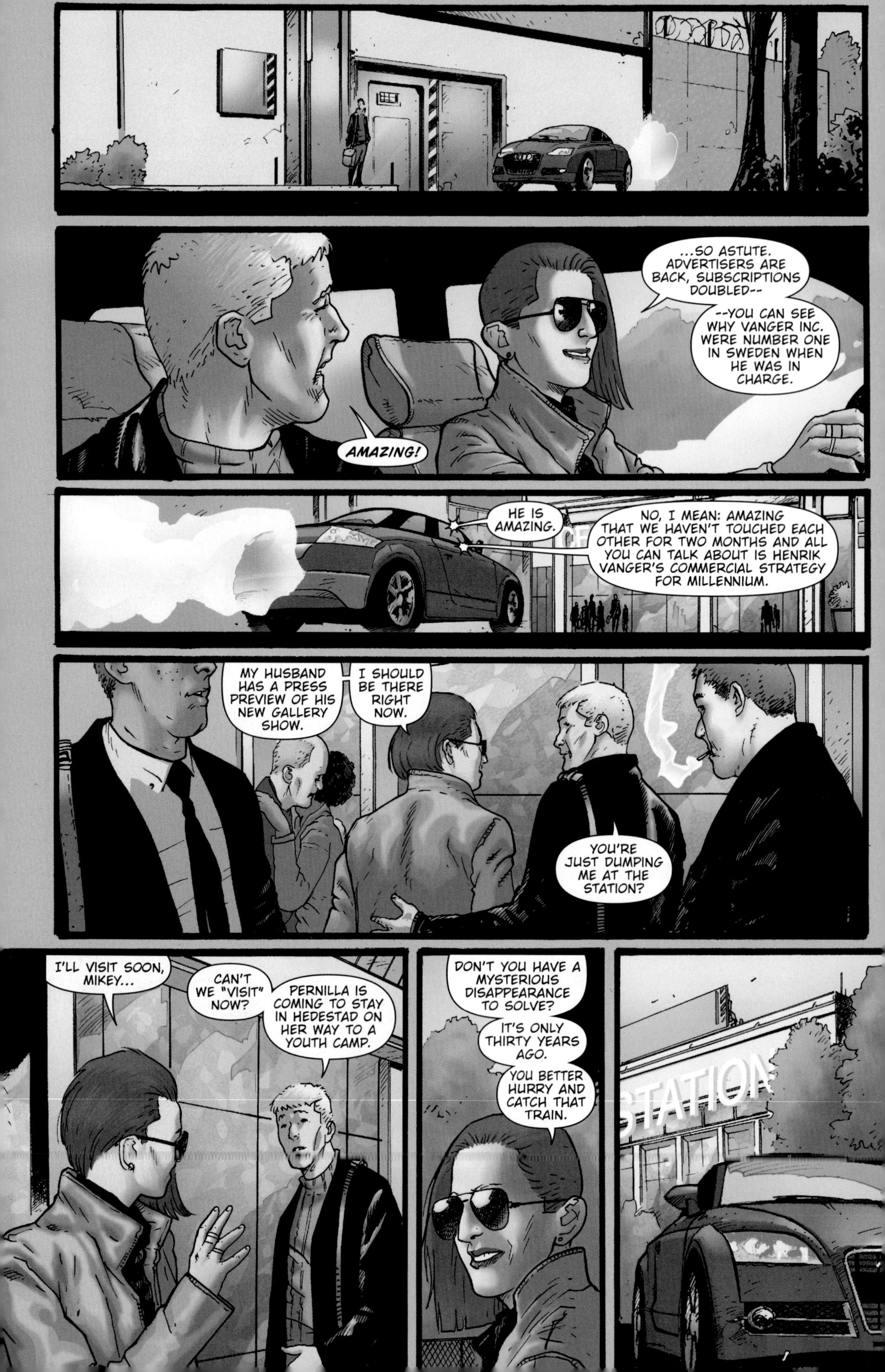
...SO ASTUTE. ADVERTISERS ARE BACK, SUBSCRIPTIONS DOUBLED--
--YOU CAN SEE WHY VANGER INC. WERE NUMBER ONE IN SWEDEN WHEN HE WAS IN CHARGE.
AMAZING!
HE IS AMAZING.
NO, I MEAN: AMAZING THAT WE HAVEN'T TOUCHED EACH OTHER FOR TWO MONTHS AND ALL YOU CAN TALK ABOUT IS HENRIK VANGER'S COMMERCIAL STRATEGY FOR MILLENNIUM.
MY HUSBAND HAS A PRESS PREVIEW OF HIS NEW GALLERY SHOW.
I SHOULD BE THERE RIGHT NOW.
YOU'RE JUST DUMPING ME AT THE STATION?
I'LL VISIT SOON, MIKEY...
CAN'T WE "VISIT" NOW?
PERNILLA IS COMING TO STAY IN HEDESTAD ON HER WAY TO A YOUTH CAMP.
DON'T YOU HAVE A MYSTERIOUS DISAPPEARANCE TO SOLVE?
IT'S ONLY THIRTY YEARS AGO.
YOU BETTER HURRY AND CATCH THAT TRAIN.
STATION

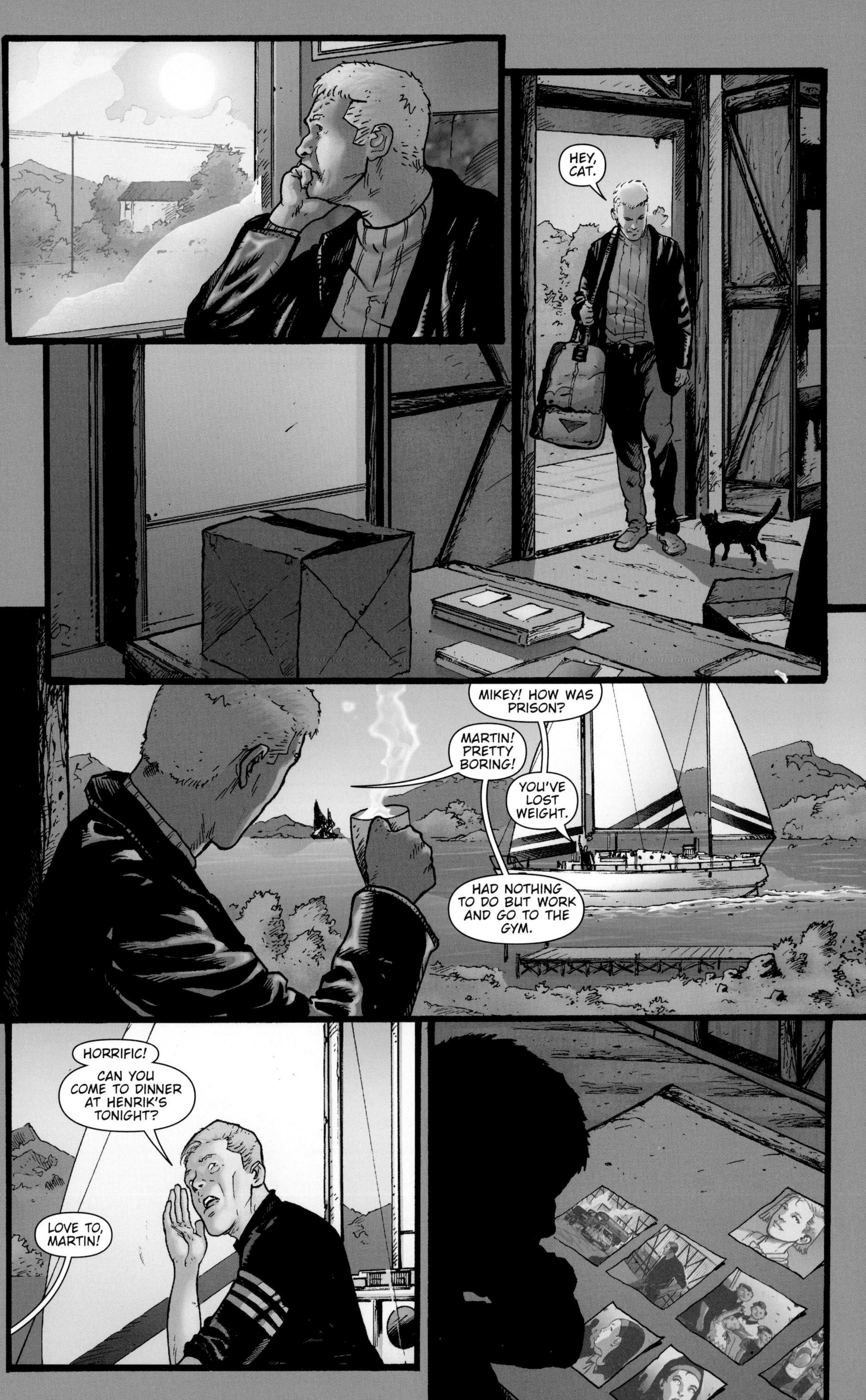
HEY, CAT.
MIKEY! HOW WAS PRISON?
MARTIN! PRETTY BORING!
YOU'VE LOST WEIGHT.
HAD NOTHING TO DO BUT WORK AND GO TO THE GYM.
HORRIFIC!
CAN YOU COME TO DINNER AT HENRIK'S TONIGHT?
LOVE TO, MARTIN!

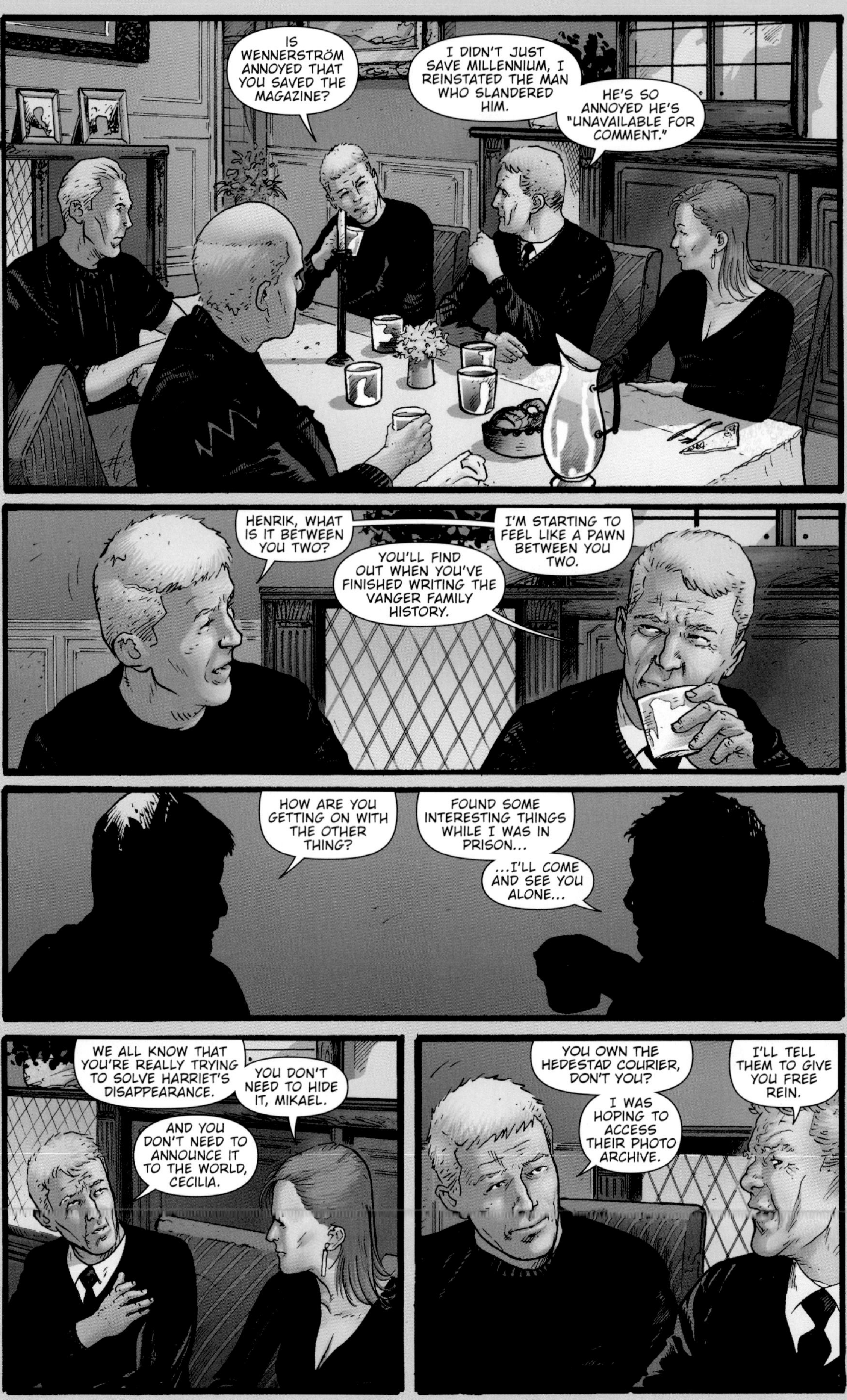
IS WENNERSTRÖM ANNOYED THAT YOU SAVED THE MAGAZINE?
I DIDN'T JUST SAVE MILLENNIUM, I REINSTATED THE MAN WHO SLANDERED HIM.
HE'S SO ANNOYED HE'S "UNAVAILABLE FOR COMMENT."
HENRIK, WHAT IS IT BETWEEN YOU TWO?
I'M STARTING TO FEEL LIKE A PAWN BETWEEN YOU TWO.
YOU'LL FIND OUT WHEN YOU'VE FINISHED WRITING THE VANGER FAMILY HISTORY.
HOW ARE YOU GETTING ON WITH THE OTHER THING?
FOUND SOME INTERESTING THINGS WHILE I WAS IN PRISON...
...I'LL COME AND SEE YOU ALONE...
WE ALL KNOW THAT YOU'RE REALLY TRYING TO SOLVE HARRIET'S DISAPPEARANCE.
YOU DON'T NEED TO HIDE IT, MIKAEL.
AND YOU DON'T NEED TO ANNOUNCE IT TO THE WORLD, CECILIA.
YOU OWN THE HEDESTAD COURIER, DON'T YOU?
I WAS HOPING TO ACCESS THEIR PHOTO ARCHIVE.
I'LL TELL THEM TO GIVE YOU FREE REIN.

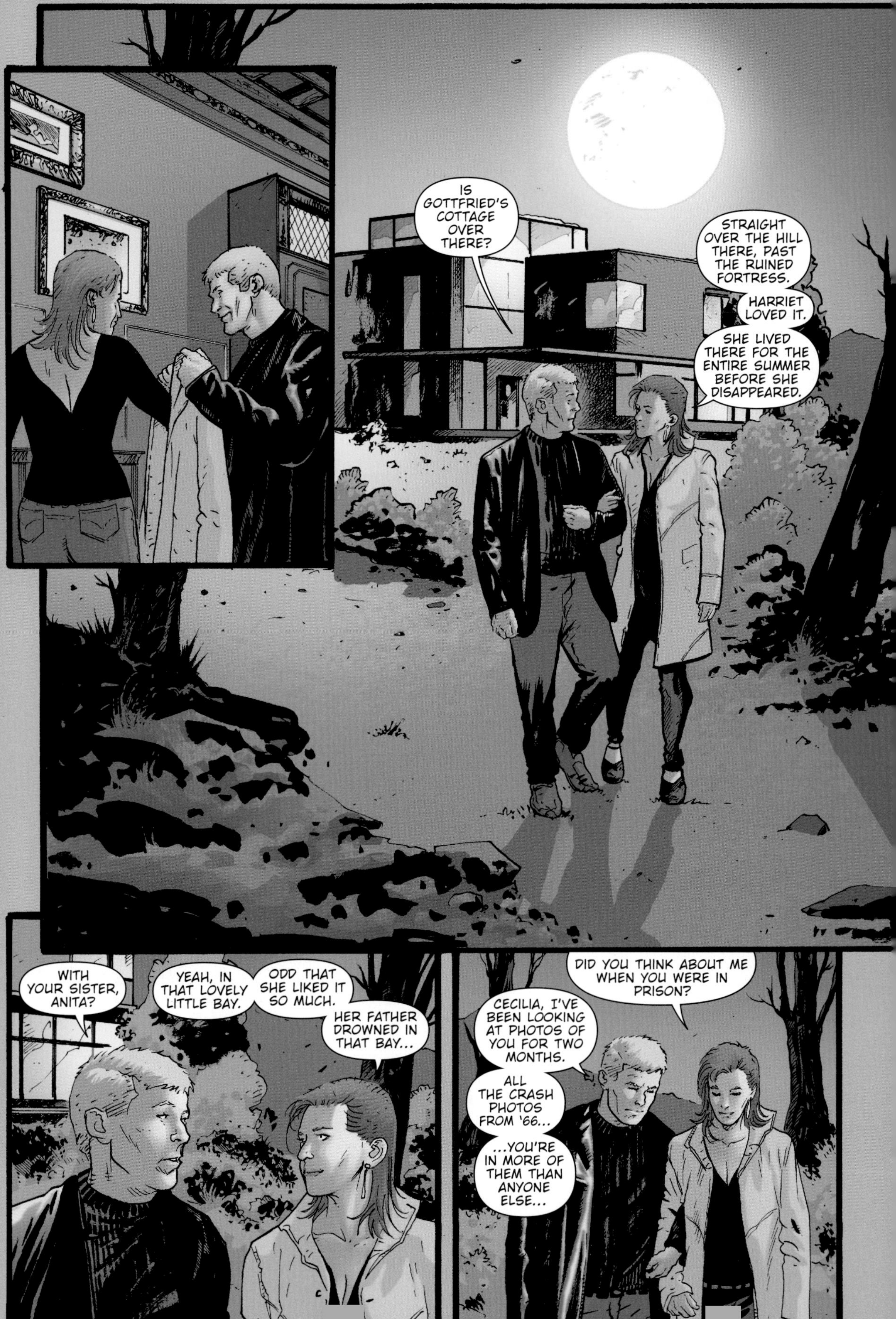
IS GOTTFRIED'S COTTAGE OVER THERE?
STRAIGHT OVER THE HILL THERE, PAST THE RUINED FORTRESS.
HARRIET LOVED IT.
SHE LIVED THERE FOR THE ENTIRE SUMMER BEFORE SHE DISAPPEARED.
WITH YOUR SISTER, ANITA?
YEAH, IN THAT LOVELY LITTLE BAY.
ODD THAT SHE LIKED IT SO MUCH.
HER FATHER DROWNED IN THAT BAY...
DID YOU THINK ABOUT ME WHEN YOU WERE IN PRISON?
CECILIA, I'VE BEEN LOOKING AT PHOTOS OF YOU FOR TWO MONTHS.
ALL THE CRASH PHOTOS FROM '66...
...YOU'RE IN MORE OF THEM THAN ANYONE ELSE...

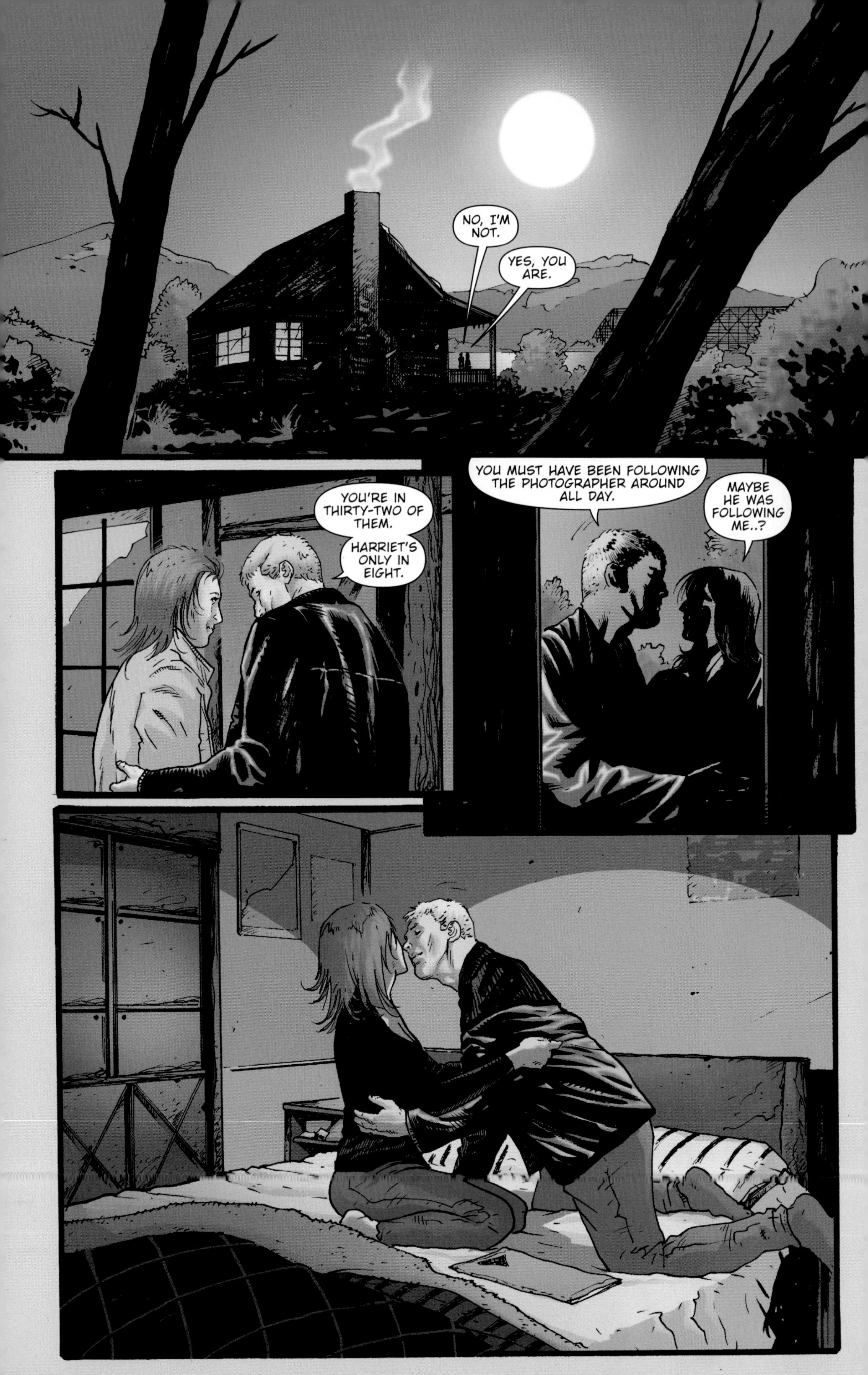
NO, I'M NOT.
YES, YOU ARE.
YOU'RE IN THIRTY-TWO OF THEM.
HARRIET'S ONLY IN EIGHT.
YOU MUST HAVE BEEN FOLLOWING THE PHOTOGRAPHER AROUND ALL DAY.
MAYBE HE WAS FOLLOWING ME..?

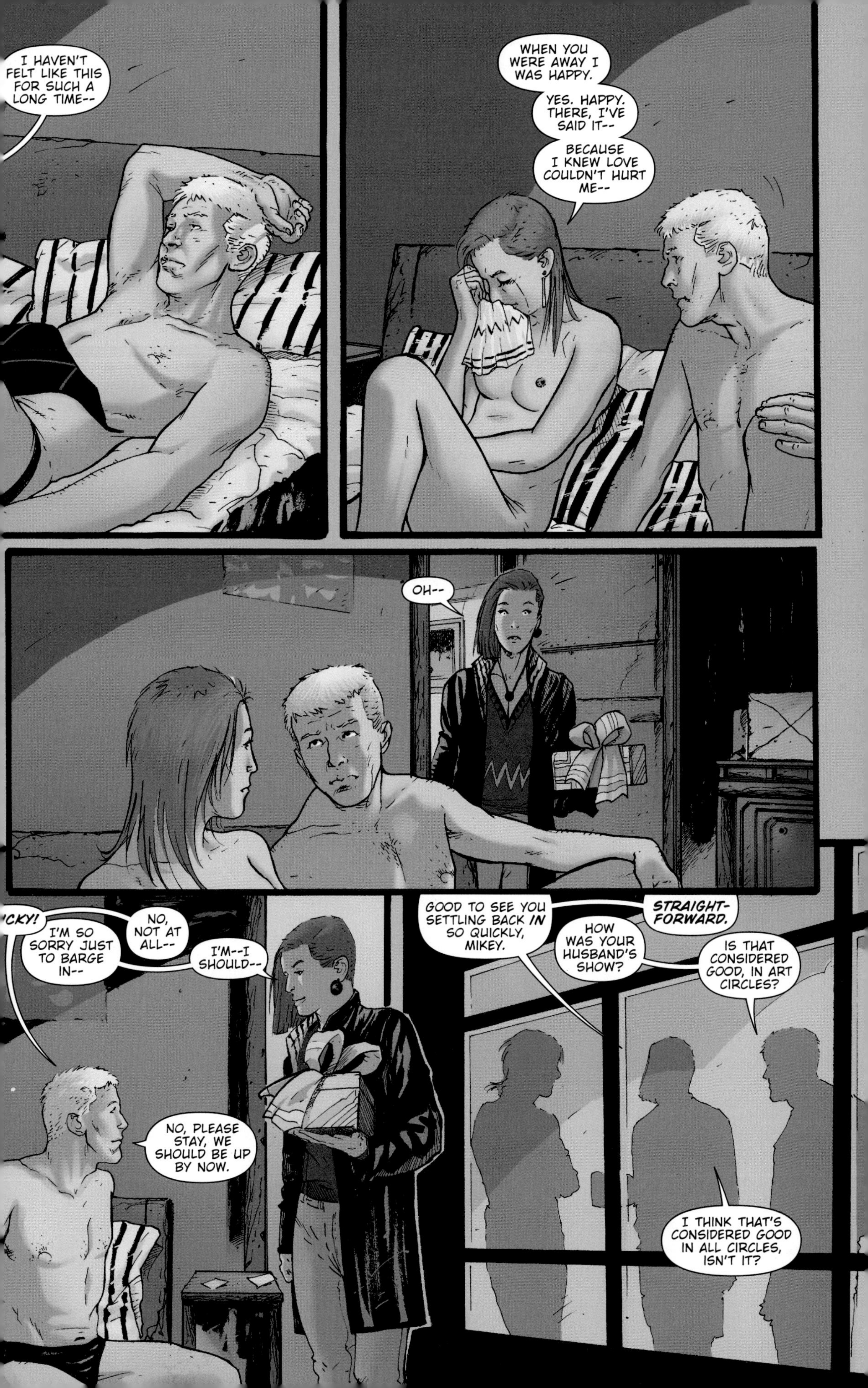
I HAVEN'T FELT LIKE THIS FOR SUCH A LONG TIME--
WHEN YOU WERE AWAY I WAS HAPPY.
YES. HAPPY. THERE, I'VE SAID IT--
BECAUSE I KNEW LOVE COULDN'T HURT ME--
OH--
CKY!
I'M SO SORRY JUST TO BARGE IN--
NO, NOT AT ALL--
I'M--I SHOULD--
NO, PLEASE STAY, WE SHOULD BE UP BY NOW.
GOOD TO SEE YOU SETTLING BACK *IN* SO QUICKLY, MIKEY.
STRAIGHT-FORWARD.
HOW WAS YOUR HUSBAND'S SHOW?
IS THAT CONSIDERED GOOD, IN ART CIRCLES?
I THINK THAT'S CONSIDERED GOOD IN ALL CIRCLES, ISN'T IT?

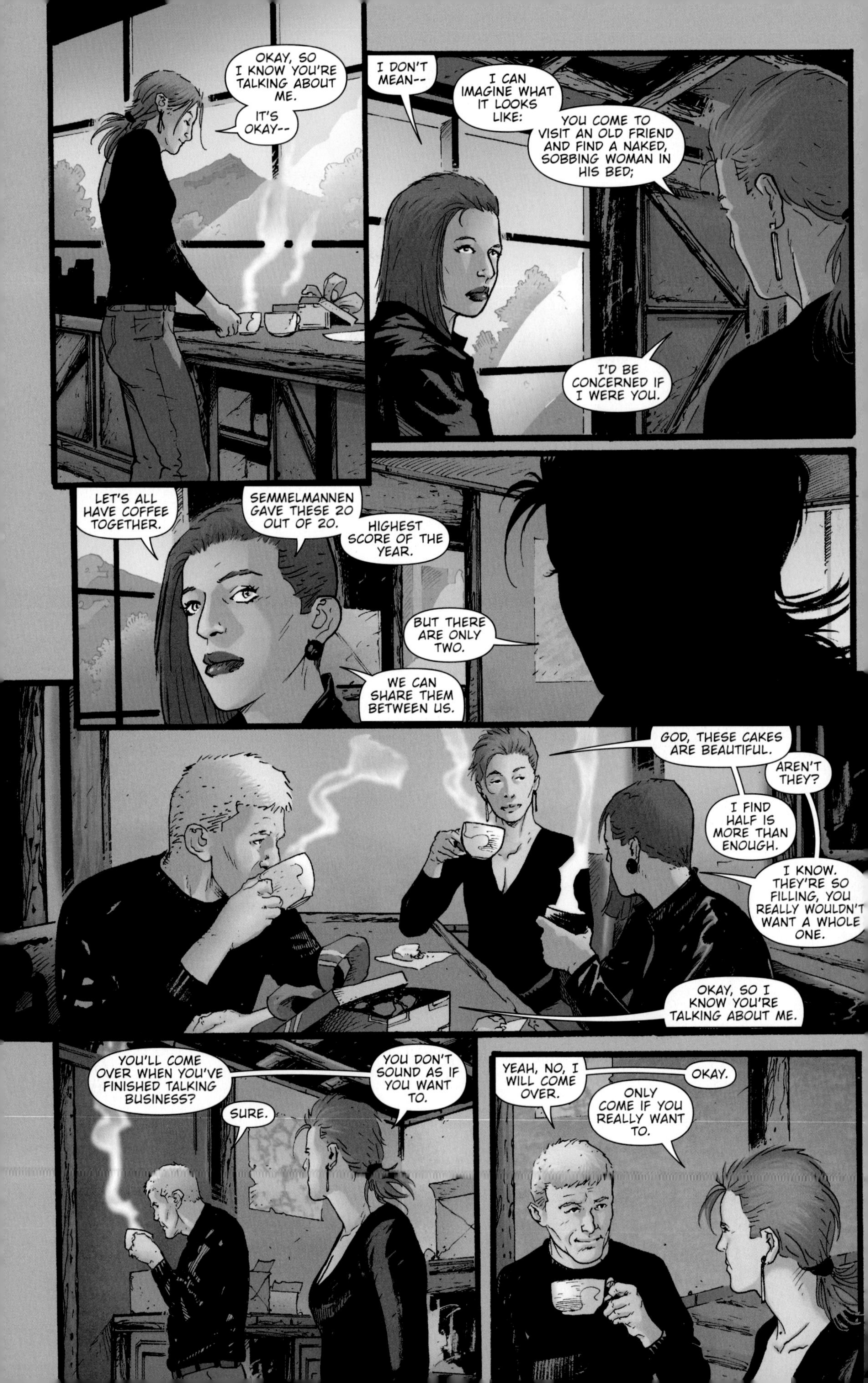
OKAY, SO I KNOW YOU'RE TALKING ABOUT ME.
IT'S OKAY--
I DON'T MEAN--
I CAN IMAGINE WHAT IT LOOKS LIKE:
YOU COME TO VISIT AN OLD FRIEND AND FIND A NAKED, SOBBING WOMAN IN HIS BED;
I'D BE CONCERNED IF I WERE YOU.
LET'S ALL HAVE COFFEE TOGETHER.
SEMMELMANNEN GAVE THESE 20 OUT OF 20.
HIGHEST SCORE OF THE YEAR.
BUT THERE ARE ONLY TWO.
WE CAN SHARE THEM BETWEEN US.
GOD, THESE CAKES ARE BEAUTIFUL.
AREN'T THEY?
I FIND HALF IS MORE THAN ENOUGH.
I KNOW. THEY'RE SO FILLING, YOU REALLY WOULDN'T WANT A WHOLE ONE.
OKAY, SO I KNOW YOU'RE TALKING ABOUT ME.
YOU'LL COME OVER WHEN YOU'VE FINISHED TALKING BUSINESS?
SURE.
YOU DON'T SOUND AS IF YOU WANT TO.
YEAH, NO, I WILL COME OVER.
OKAY.
ONLY COME IF YOU REALLY WANT TO.

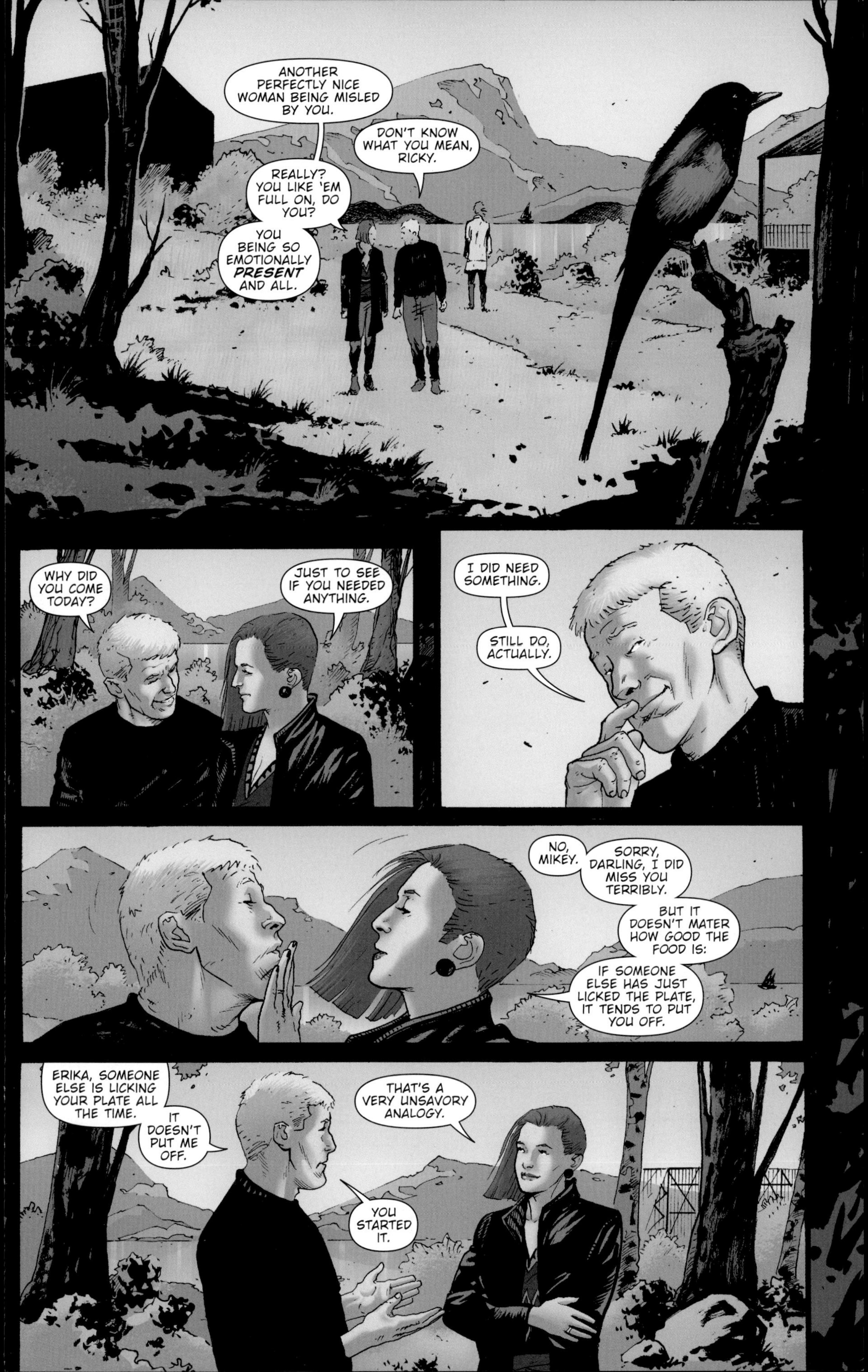
ANOTHER PERFECTLY NICE WOMAN BEING MISLED BY YOU.
DON'T KNOW WHAT YOU MEAN, RICKY.
REALLY? YOU LIKE 'EM FULL ON, DO YOU?
YOU BEING SO EMOTIONALLY *PRESENT* AND ALL.
WHY DID YOU COME TODAY?
JUST TO SEE IF YOU NEEDED ANYTHING.
I DID NEED SOMETHING.
STILL DO, ACTUALLY.
NO, MIKEY.
SORRY, DARLING, I DID MISS YOU TERRIBLY.
BUT IT DOESN'T MATER HOW GOOD THE FOOD IS:
IF SOMEONE ELSE HAS JUST LICKED THE PLATE, IT TENDS TO PUT YOU OFF.
ERIKA, SOMEONE ELSE IS LICKING YOUR PLATE ALL THE TIME.
IT DOESN'T PUT ME OFF.
THAT'S A VERY UNSAVORY ANALOGY.
YOU STARTED IT.

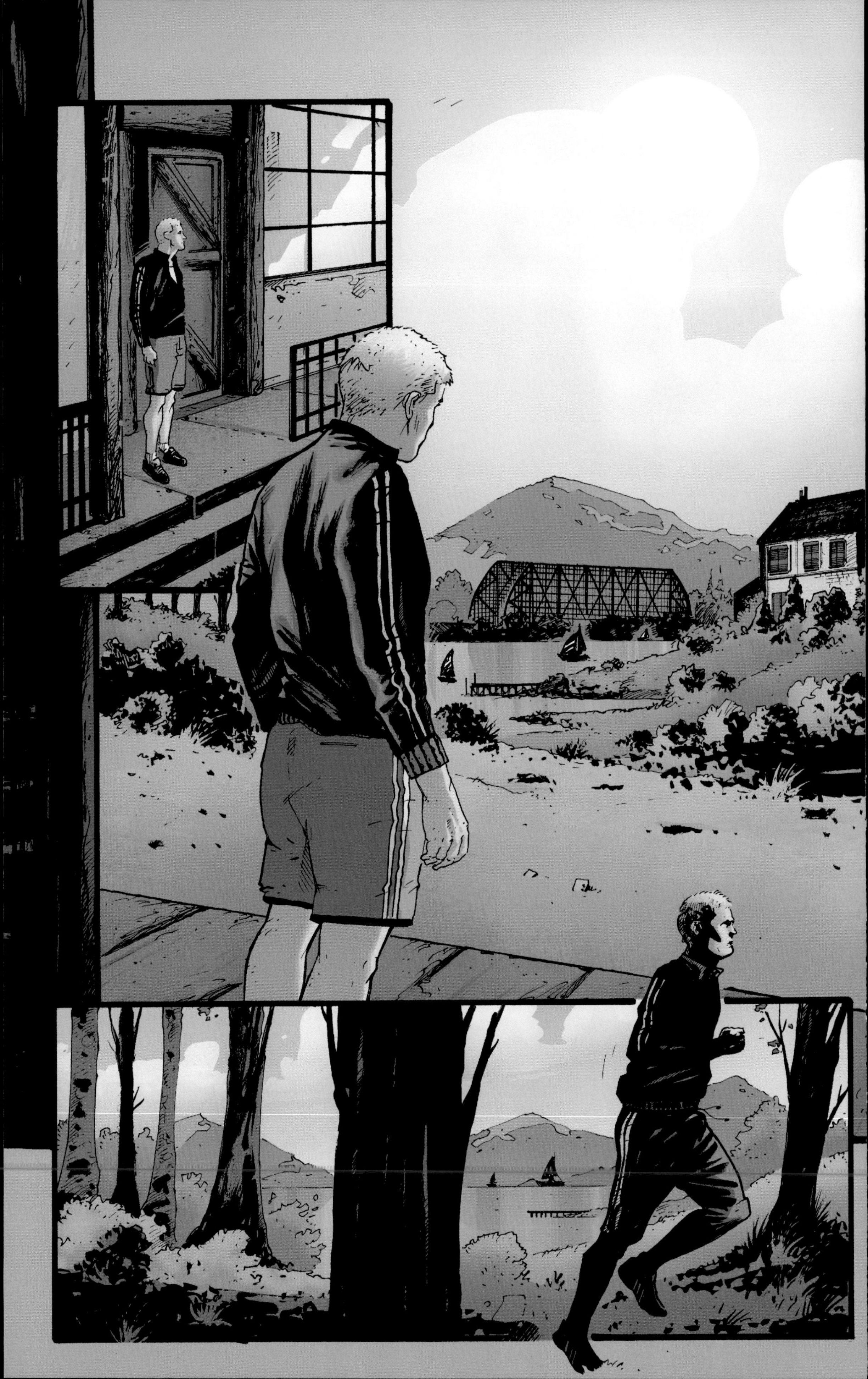

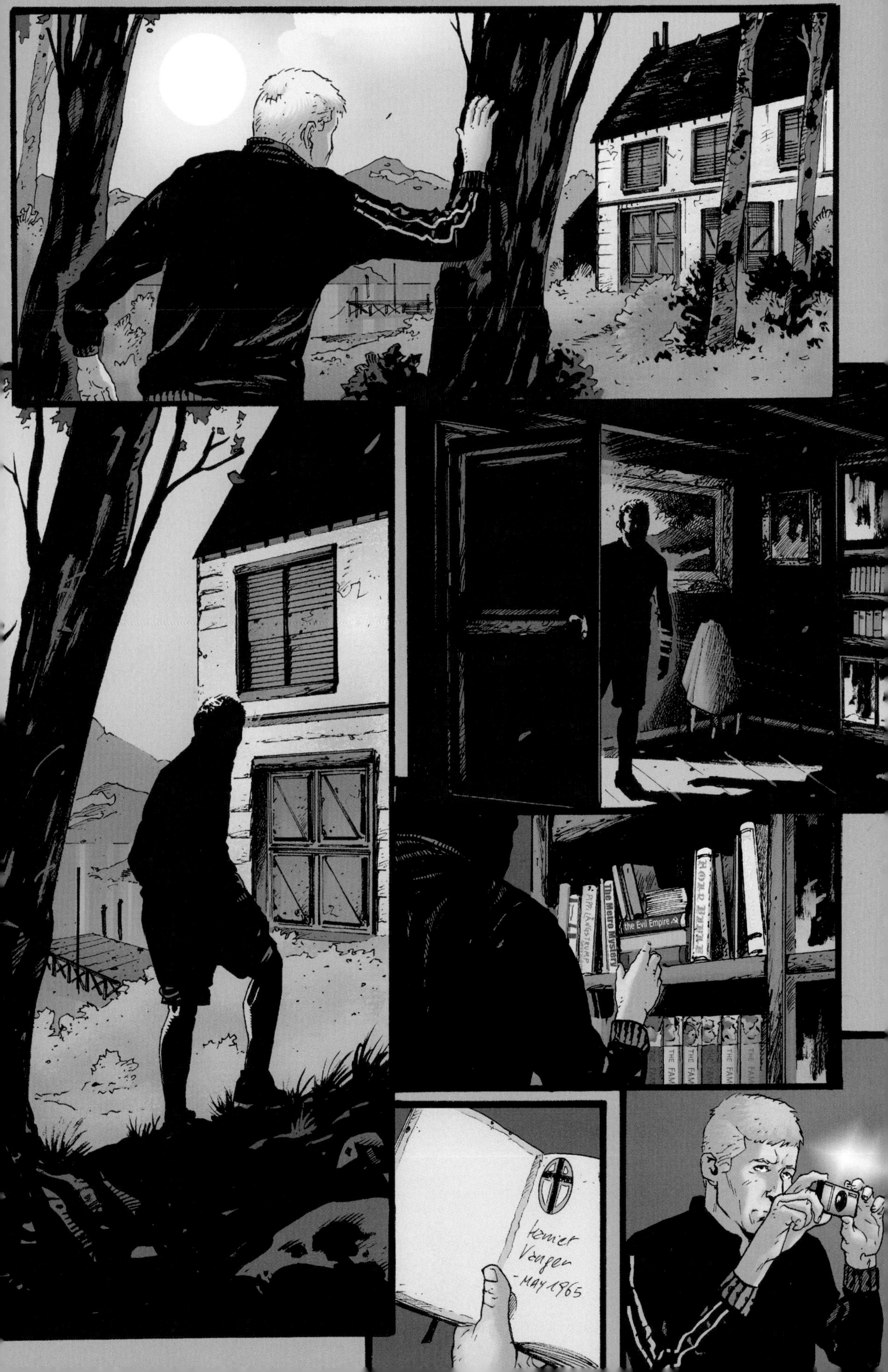
Pippi Långstrump
The Metro Mystery
the Evil Empire
Harriet Vanger
- MAY 1965

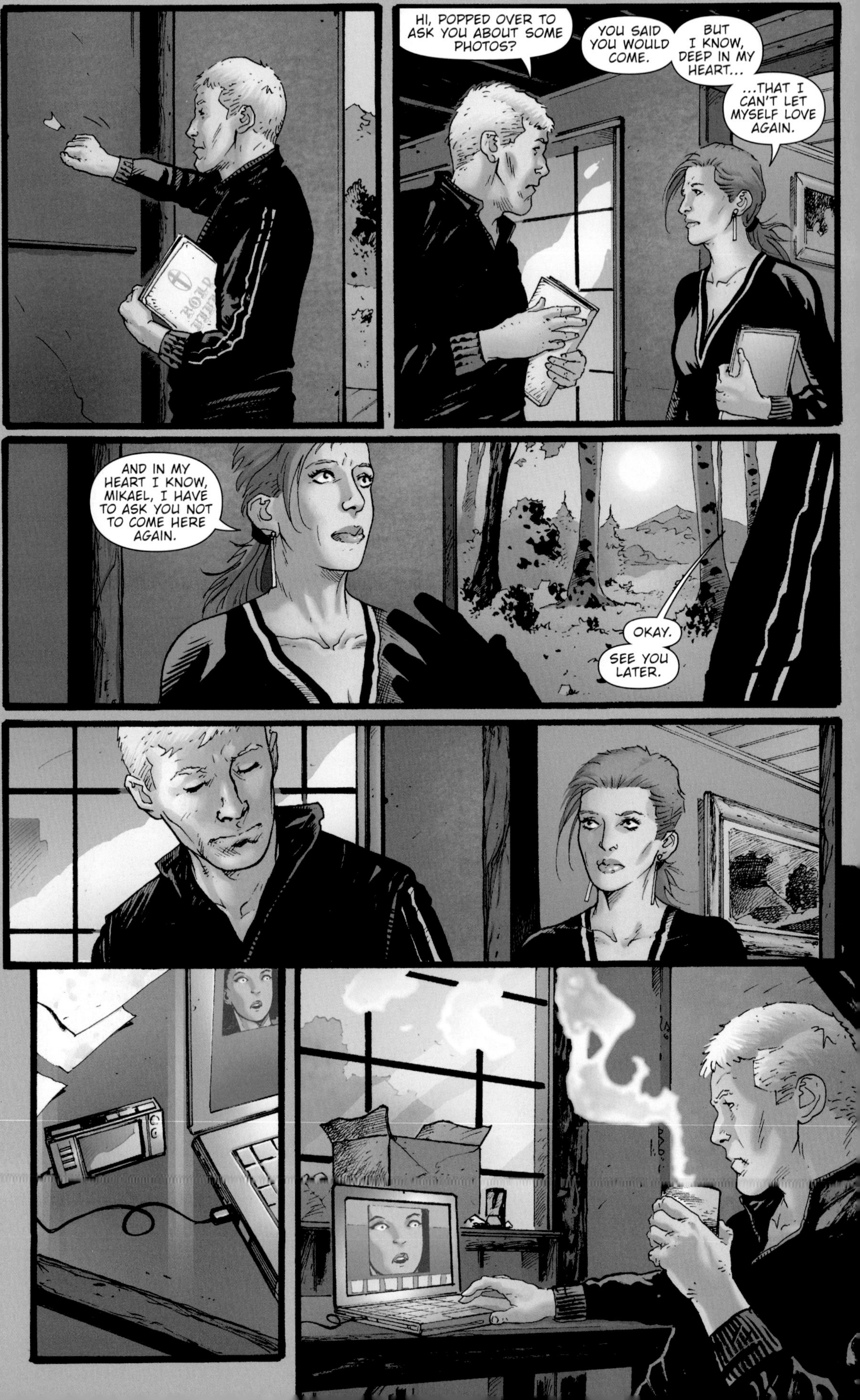
HI, POPPED OVER TO ASK YOU ABOUT SOME PHOTOS?
YOU SAID YOU WOULD COME.
BUT I KNOW, DEEP IN MY HEART...
...THAT I CAN'T LET MYSELF LOVE AGAIN.
AND IN MY HEART I KNOW, MIKAEL, I HAVE TO ASK YOU NOT TO COME HERE AGAIN.
OKAY.
SEE YOU LATER.

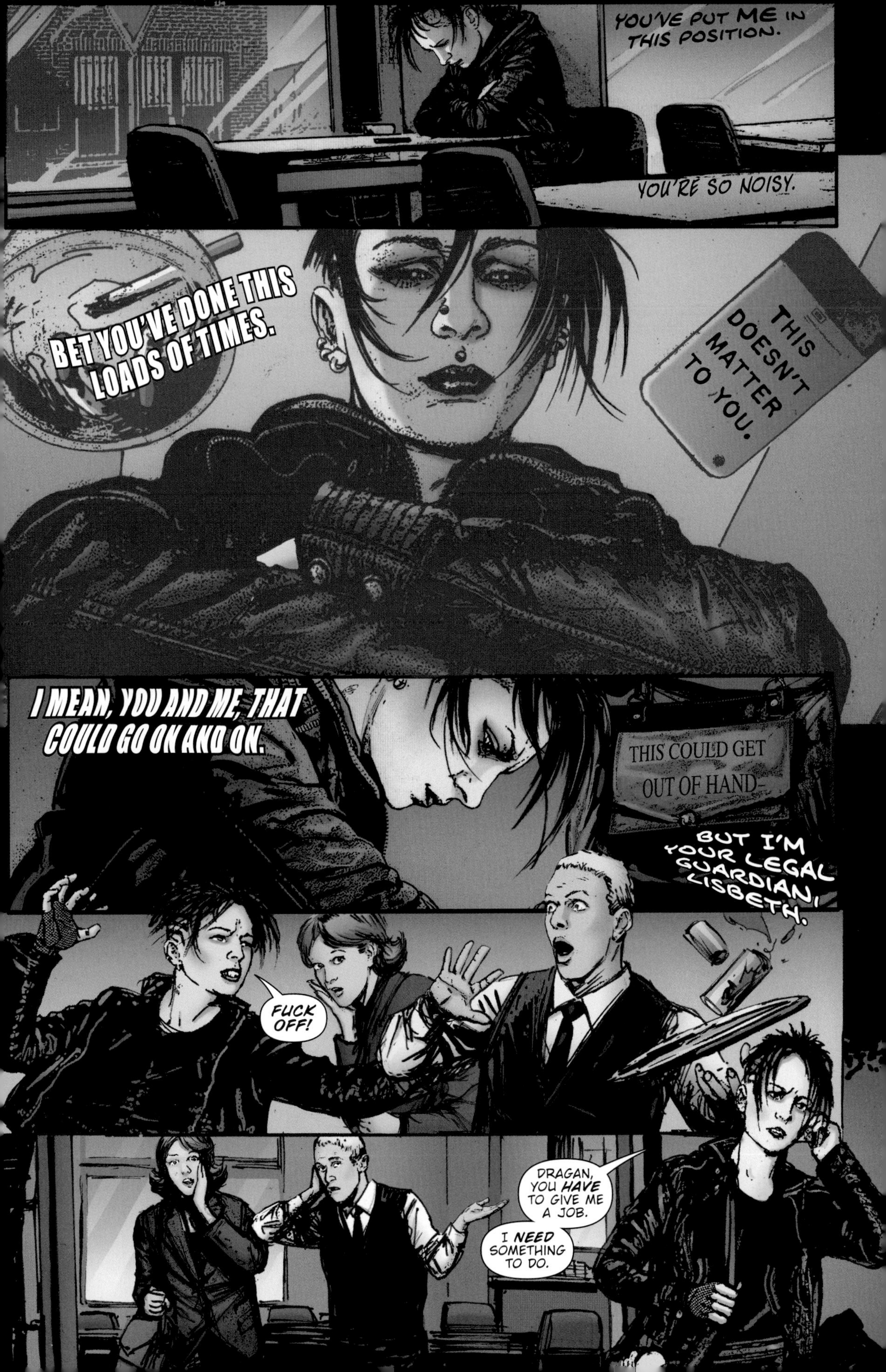
YOU'VE PUT ME IN THIS POSITION.
YOU'RE SO NOISY.
BET YOU'VE DONE THIS LOADS OF TIMES.
THIS DOESN'T MATTER TO YOU.
I MEAN, YOU AND ME, THAT COULD GO ON AND ON.
THIS COULD GET OUT OF HAND
BUT I'M YOUR LEGAL GUARDIAN, LISBETH.
FUCK OFF!
DRAGAN, YOU HAVE TO GIVE ME A JOB.
I NEED SOMETHING TO DO.

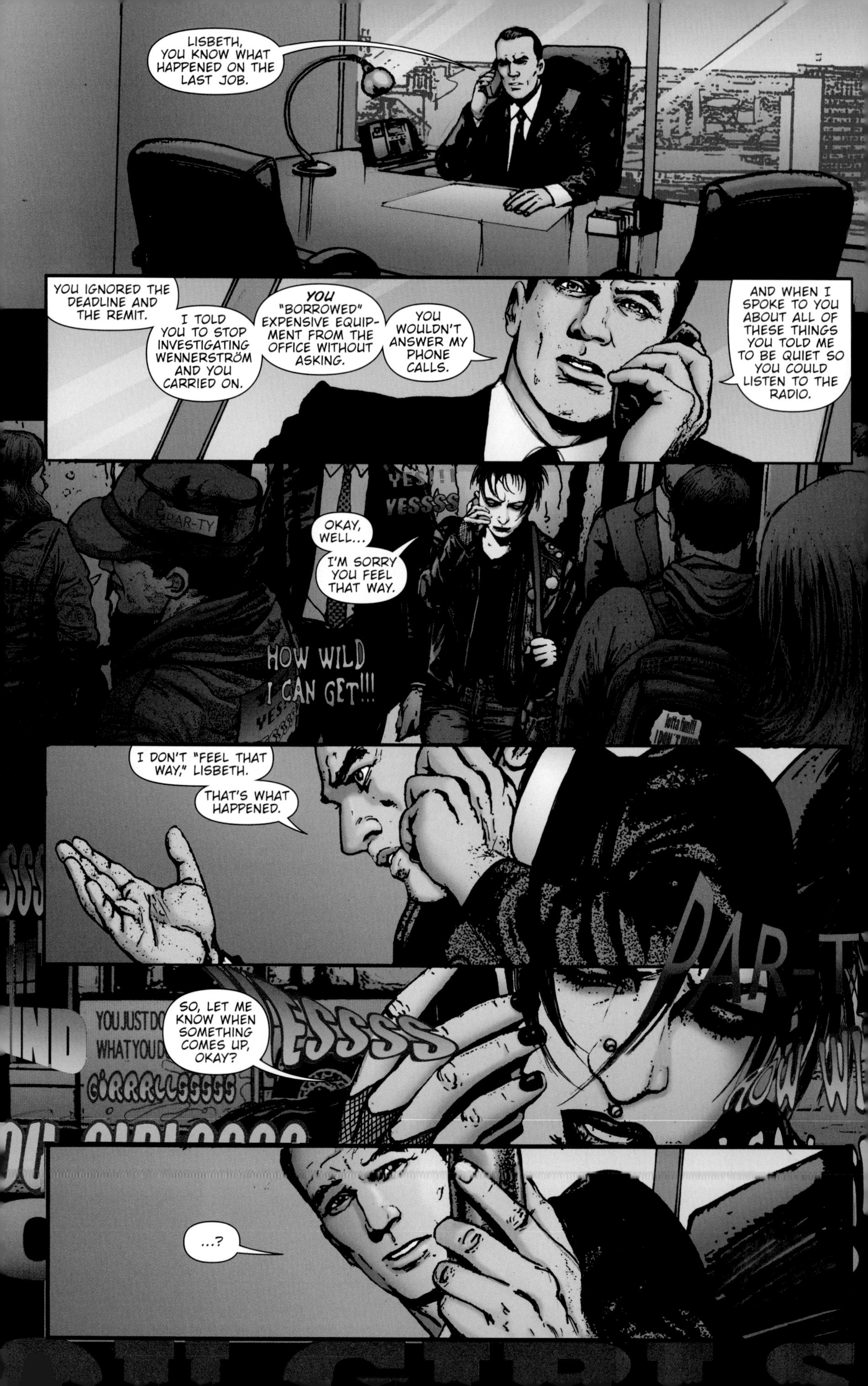
LISBETH, YOU KNOW WHAT HAPPENED ON THE LAST JOB.
YOU IGNORED THE DEADLINE AND THE REMIT.
I TOLD YOU TO STOP INVESTIGATING WENNERSTRÖM AND YOU CARRIED ON.
YOU "BORROWED" EXPENSIVE EQUIPMENT FROM THE OFFICE WITHOUT ASKING.
YOU WOULDN'T ANSWER MY PHONE CALLS.
AND WHEN I SPOKE TO YOU ABOUT ALL OF THESE THINGS YOU TOLD ME TO BE QUIET SO YOU COULD LISTEN TO THE RADIO.
PAR-TY
YESSSS
OKAY, WELL...
I'M SORRY YOU FEEL THAT WAY.
HOW WILD I CAN GET!!!
I DON'T "FEEL THAT WAY," LISBETH.
THAT'S WHAT HAPPENED.
PAR-T
YOU JUST DO
WHAT YOU D
GIRRRLLSSSSS
SO, LET ME KNOW WHEN SOMETHING COMES UP, OKAY?
YESSSS
...?

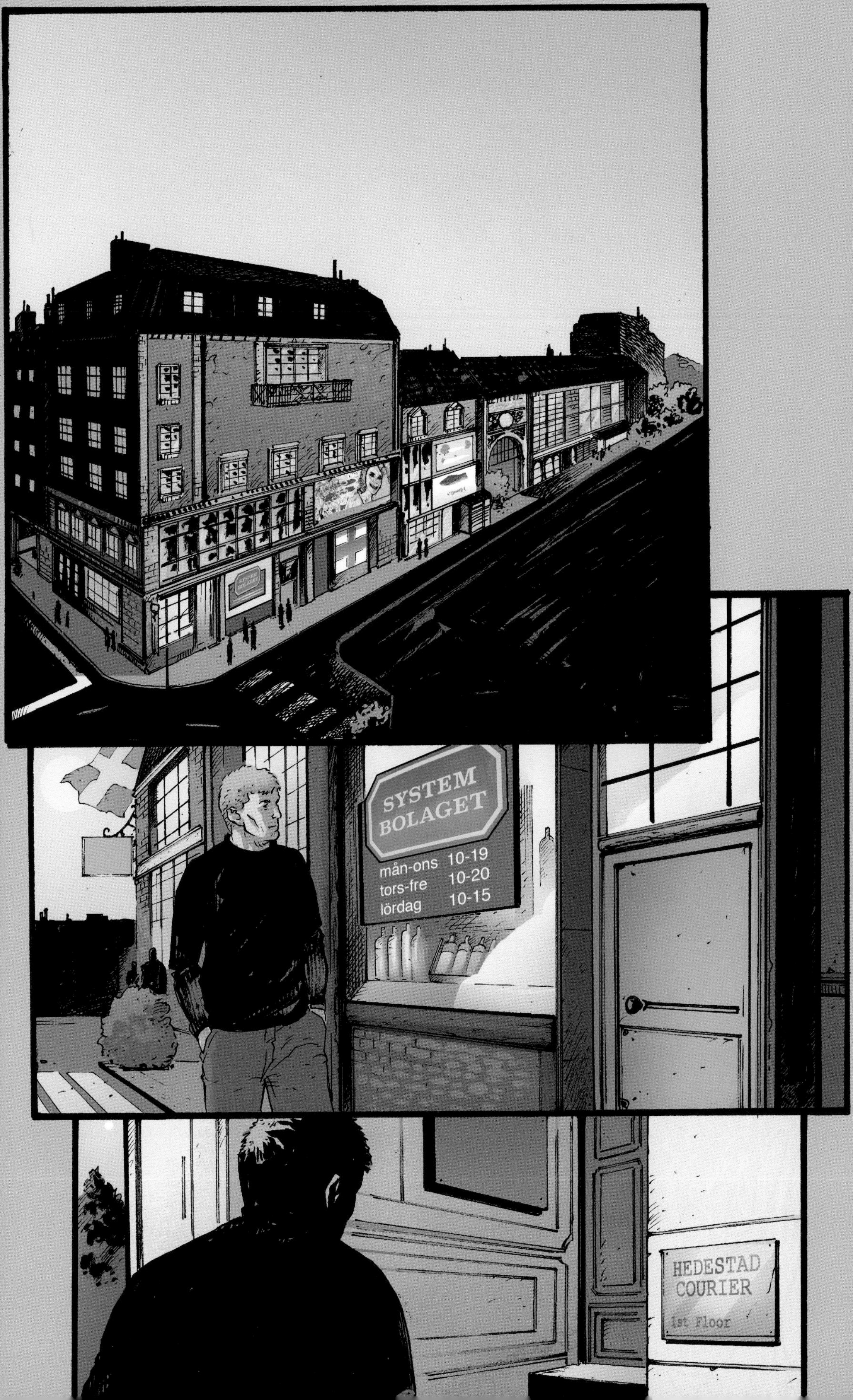
SYSTEM BOLAGET
mån-ons 10-19
tors-fre 10-20
lördag 10-15
HEDESTAD COURIER
1st Floor

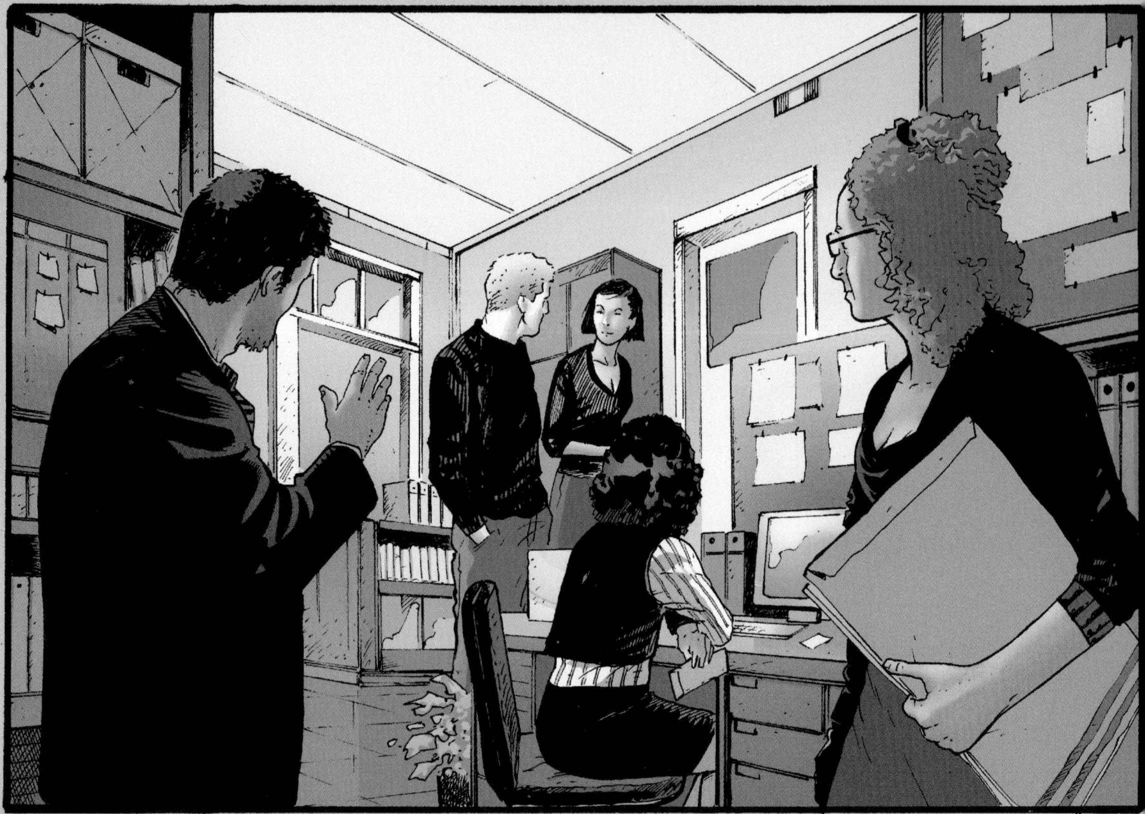
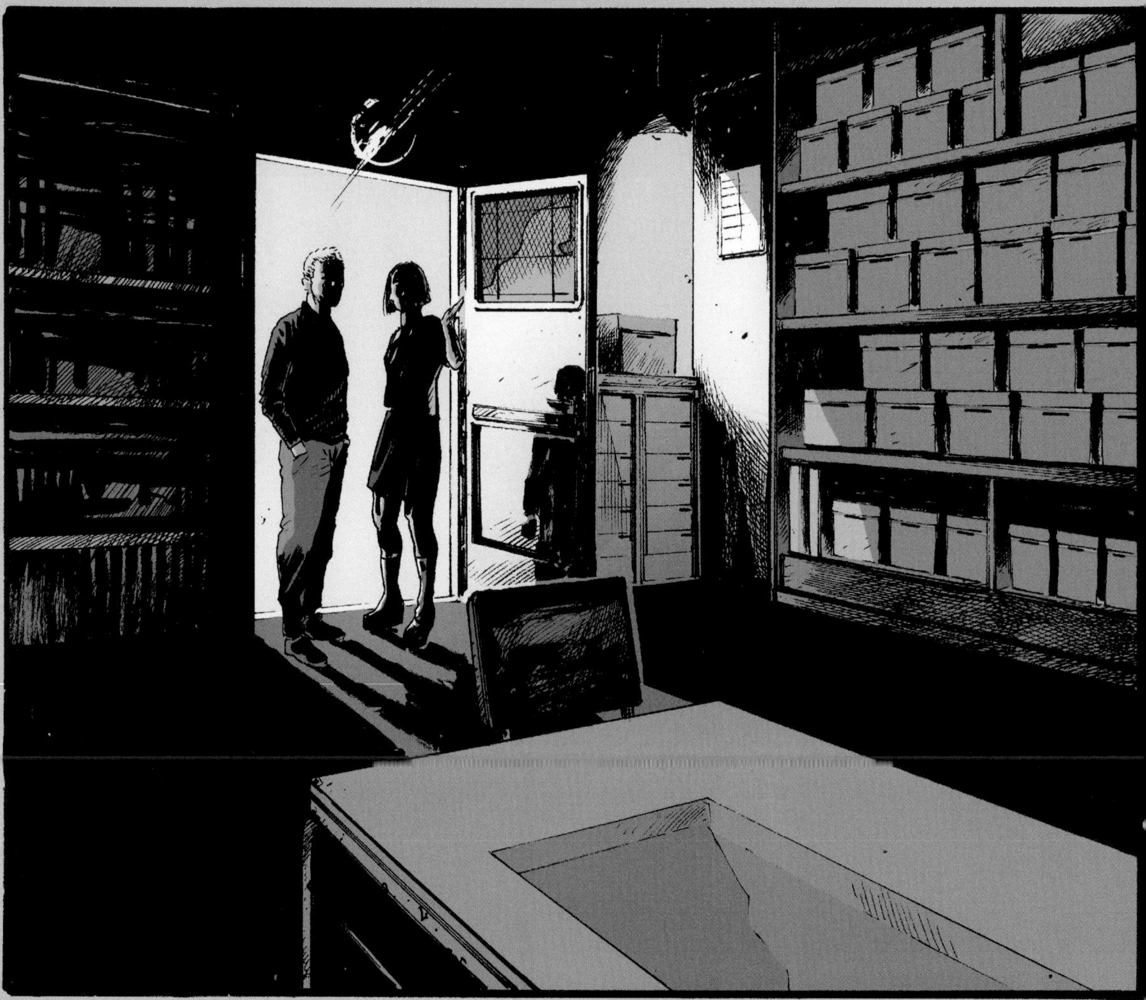

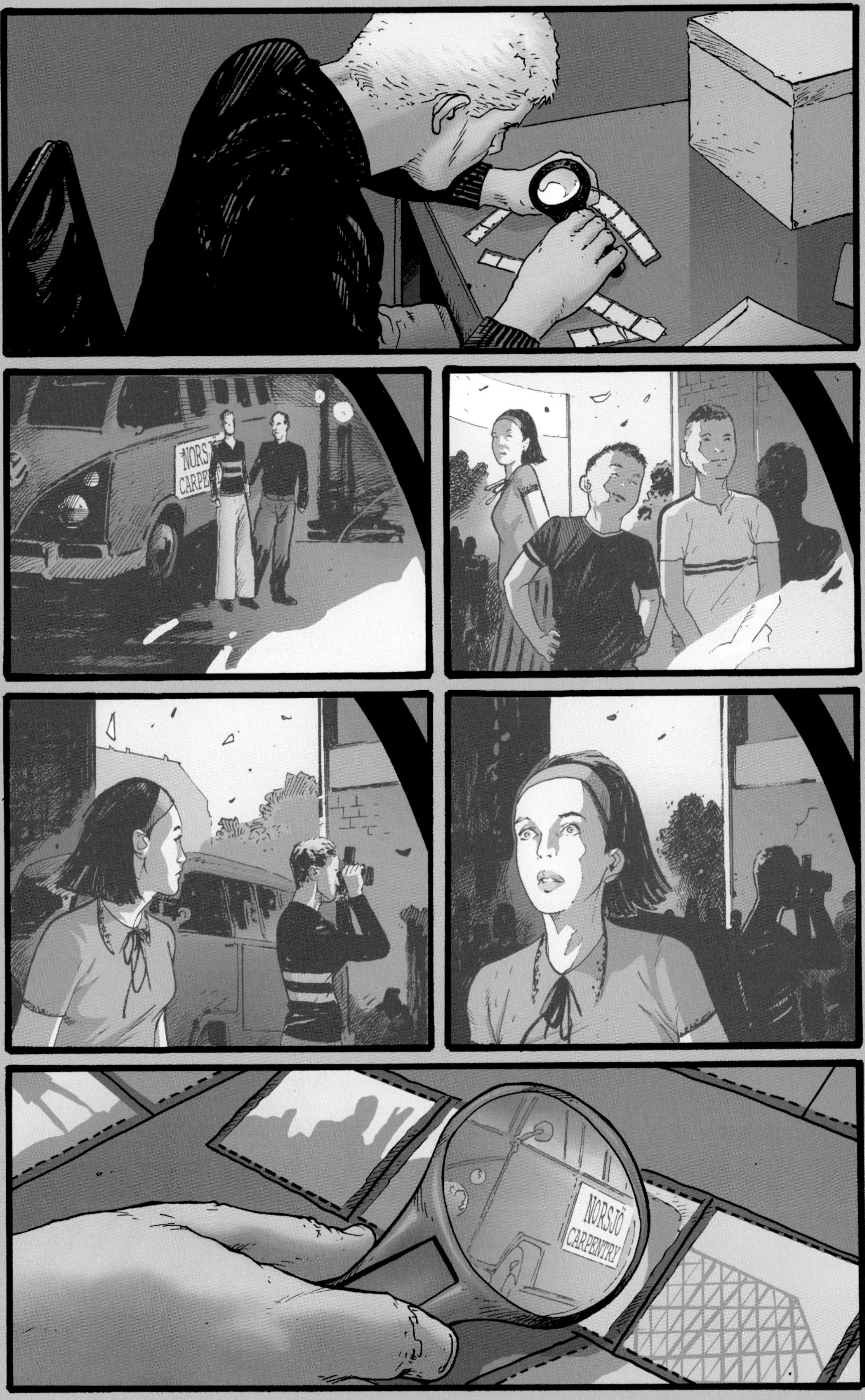
NORSJÖ
CARPENTRY

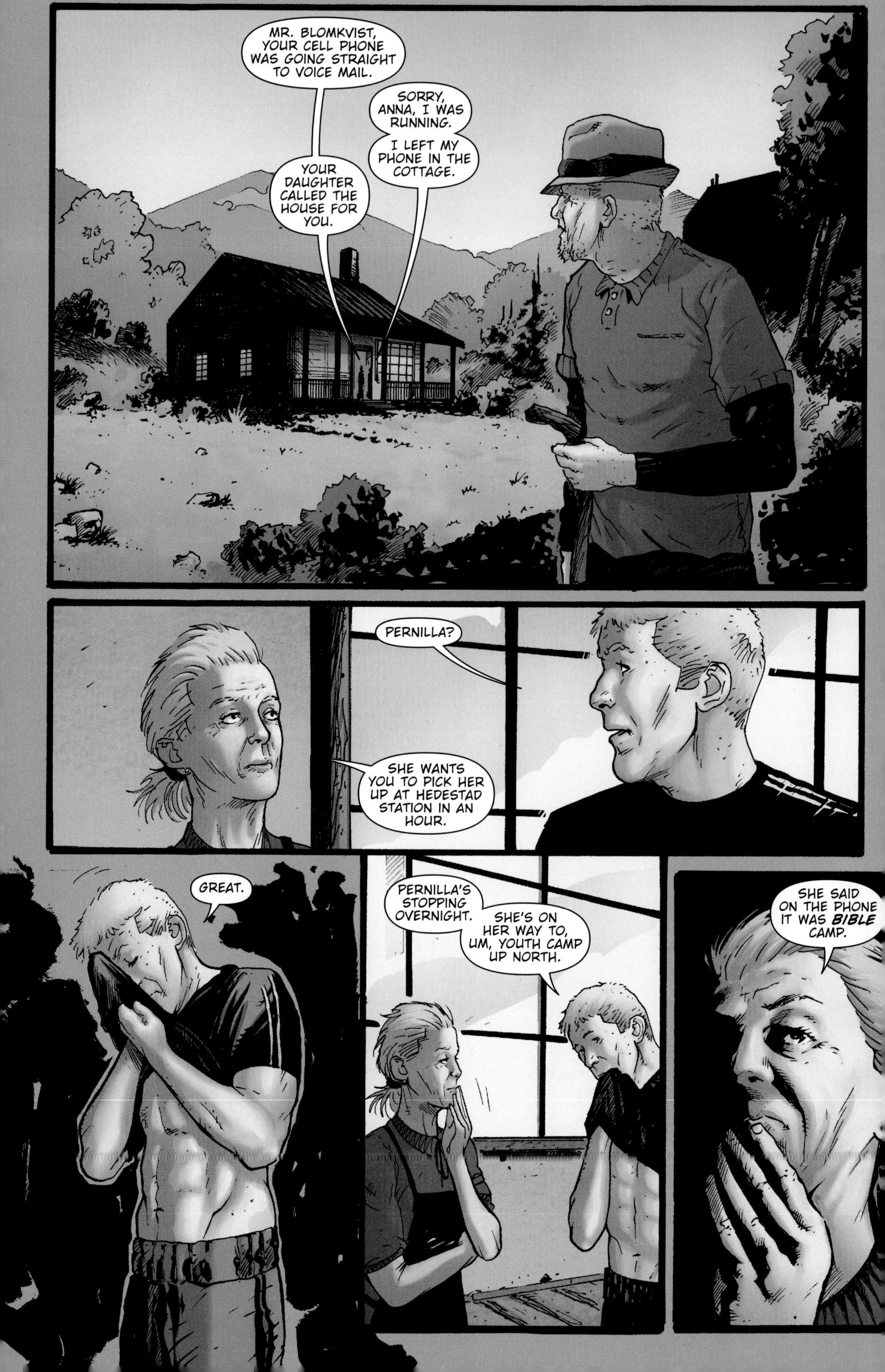
MR. BLOMKVIST, YOUR CELL PHONE WAS GOING STRAIGHT TO VOICE MAIL.
YOUR DAUGHTER CALLED THE HOUSE FOR YOU.
SORRY, ANNA, I WAS RUNNING.
I LEFT MY PHONE IN THE COTTAGE.
PERNILLA?
SHE WANTS YOU TO PICK HER UP AT HEDESTAD STATION IN AN HOUR.
GREAT.
PERNILLA'S STOPPING OVERNIGHT.
SHE'S ON HER WAY TO, UM, YOUTH CAMP UP NORTH.
SHE SAID ON THE PHONE IT WAS *BIBLE* CAMP.

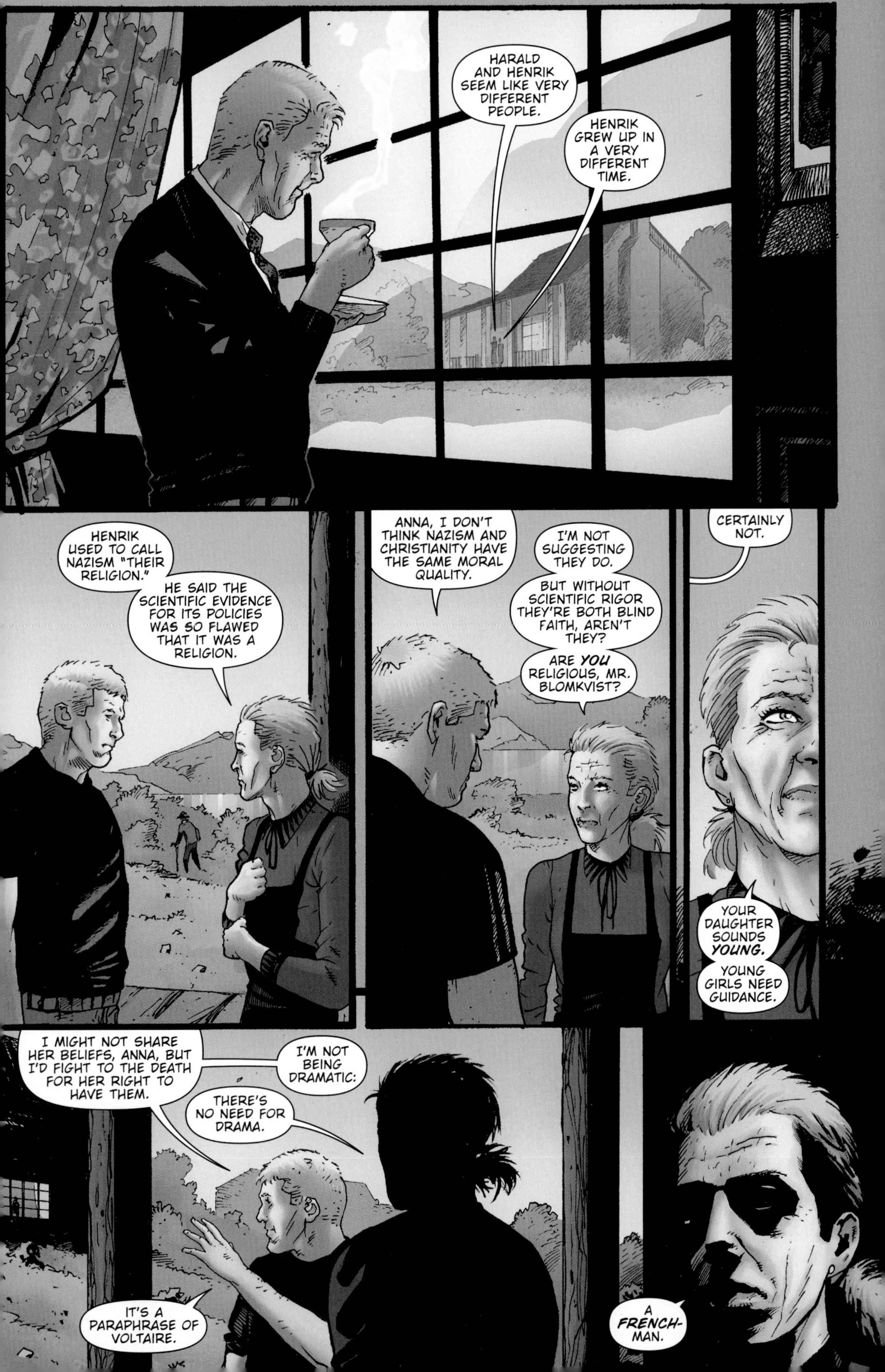
HARALD AND HENRIK SEEM LIKE VERY DIFFERENT PEOPLE.
HENRIK GREW UP IN A VERY DIFFERENT TIME.
HENRIK USED TO CALL NAZISM "THEIR RELIGION."
HE SAID THE SCIENTIFIC EVIDENCE FOR ITS POLICIES WAS SO FLAWED THAT IT WAS A RELIGION.
ANNA, I DON'T THINK NAZISM AND CHRISTIANITY HAVE THE SAME MORAL QUALITY.
I'M NOT SUGGESTING THEY DO.
BUT WITHOUT SCIENTIFIC RIGOR THEY'RE BOTH BLIND FAITH, AREN'T THEY?
ARE YOU RELIGIOUS, MR. BLOMKVIST?
CERTAINLY NOT.
YOUR DAUGHTER SOUNDS YOUNG.
YOUNG GIRLS NEED GUIDANCE.
I MIGHT NOT SHARE HER BELIEFS, ANNA, BUT I'D FIGHT TO THE DEATH FOR HER RIGHT TO HAVE THEM.
I'M NOT BEING DRAMATIC:
THERE'S NO NEED FOR DRAMA.
IT'S A PARAPHRASE OF VOLTAIRE.
A FRENCH-MAN.

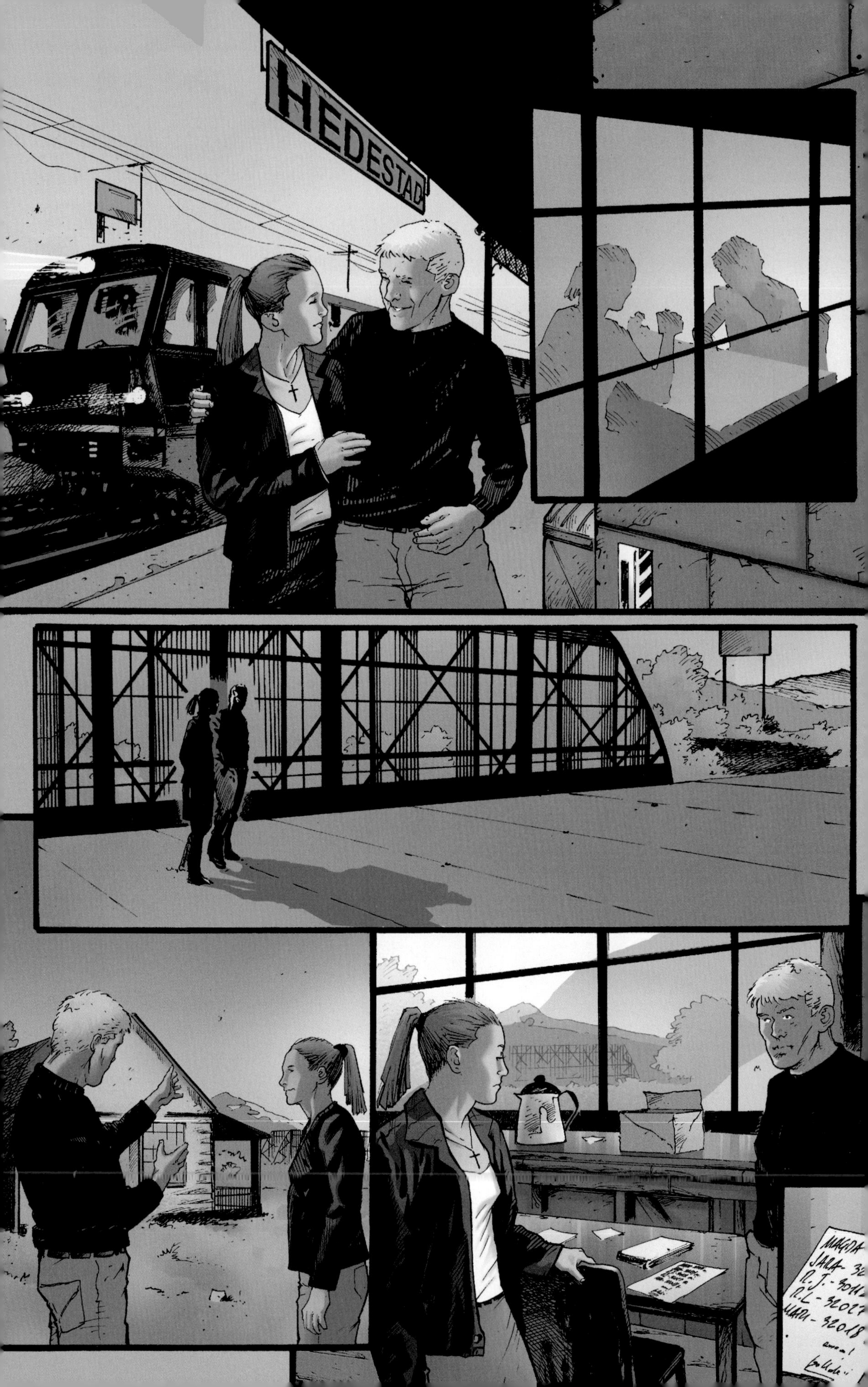

HEDESTAD
MAGDA
SARA
R.J.
R.L - 32027
MARI - 32018

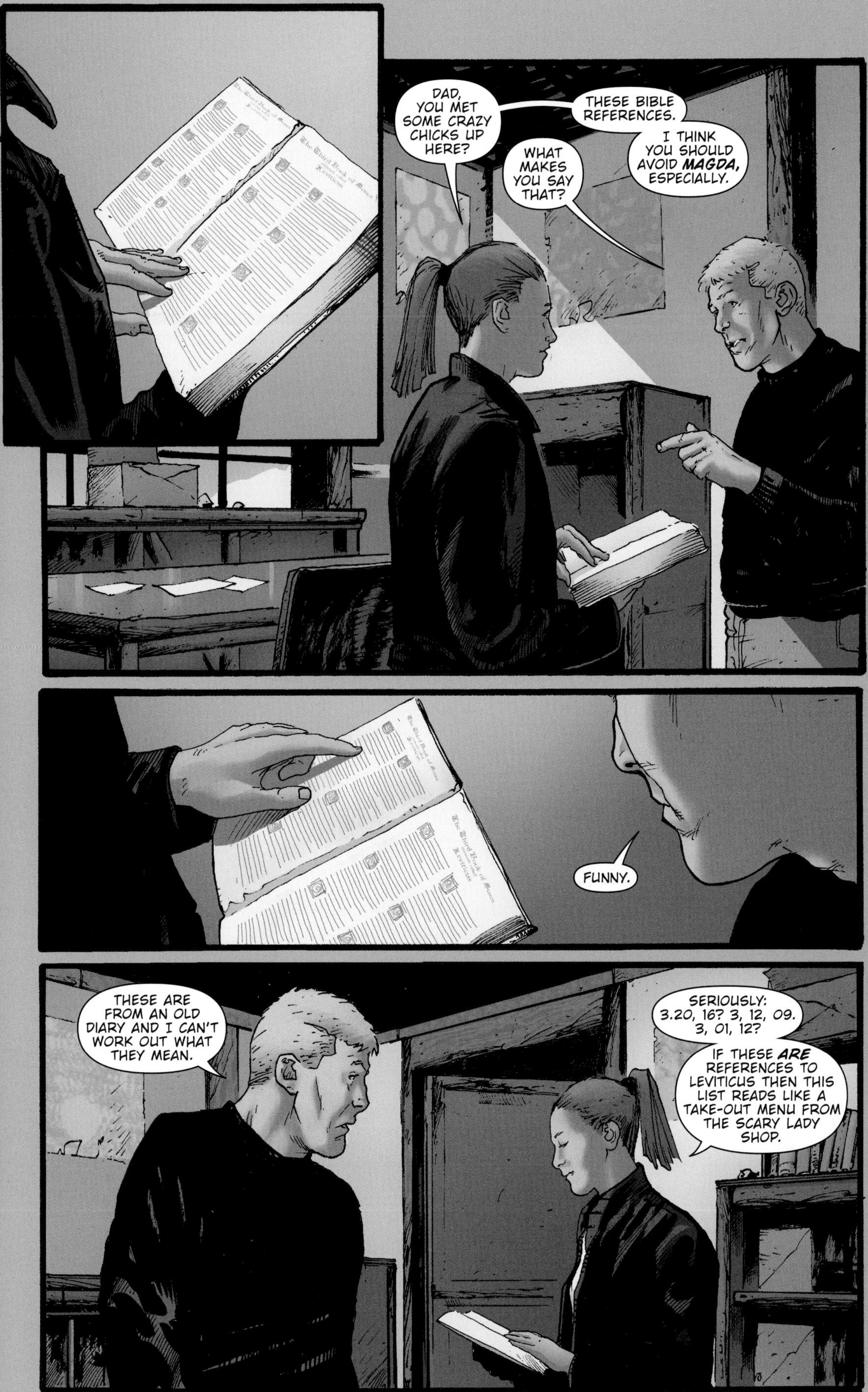
DAD, YOU MET SOME CRAZY CHICKS UP HERE?
THESE BIBLE REFERENCES.
I THINK YOU SHOULD AVOID MAGDA, ESPECIALLY.
WHAT MAKES YOU SAY THAT?
FUNNY.
THESE ARE FROM AN OLD DIARY AND I CAN'T WORK OUT WHAT THEY MEAN.
SERIOUSLY: 3.20, 16? 3, 12, 09. 3, 01, 12?
IF THESE ARE REFERENCES TO LEVITICUS THEN THIS LIST READS LIKE A TAKE-OUT MENU FROM THE SCARY LADY SHOP.

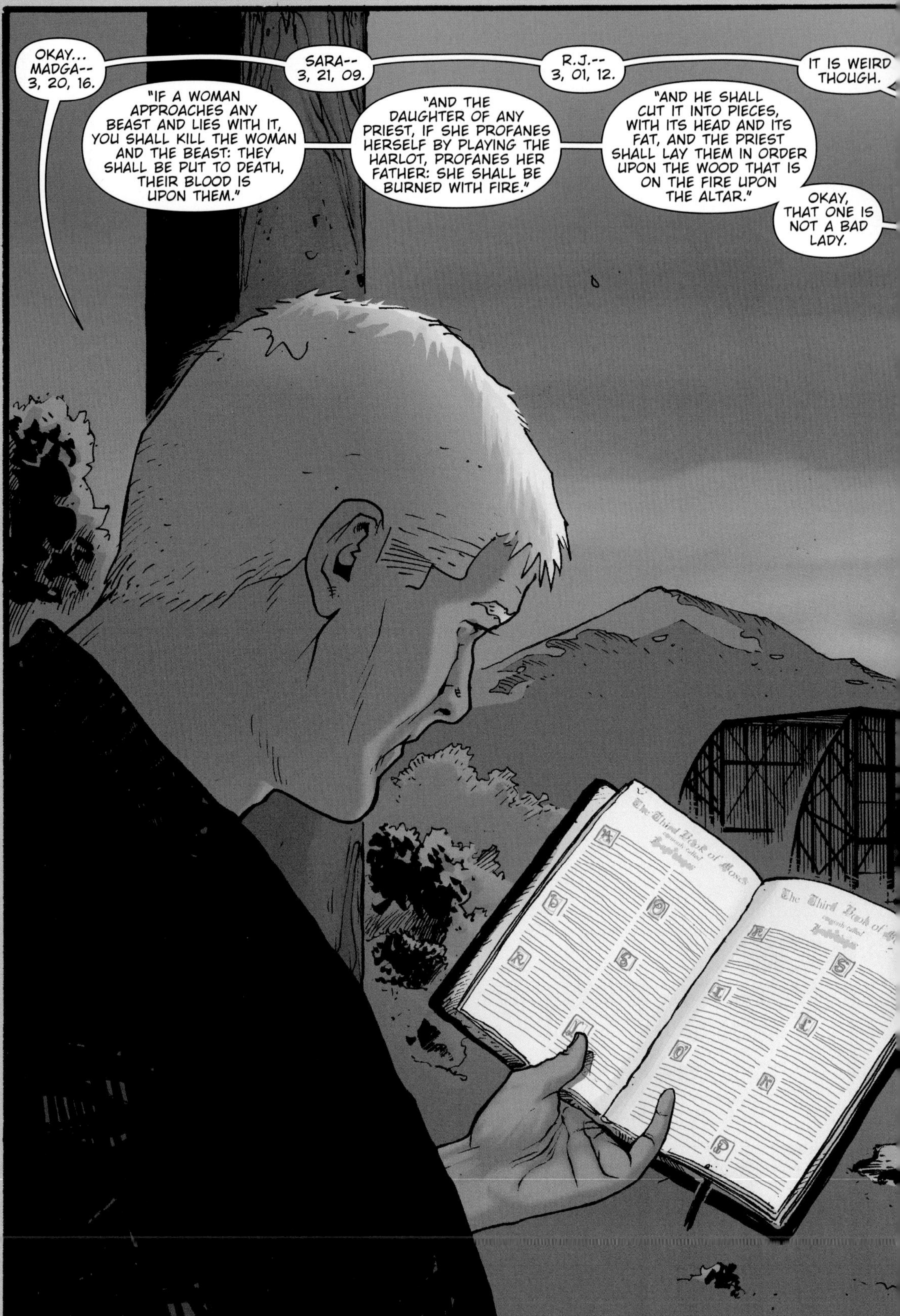
OKAY... MADGA-- 3, 20, 16.
"IF A WOMAN APPROACHES ANY BEAST AND LIES WITH IT, YOU SHALL KILL THE WOMAN AND THE BEAST: THEY SHALL BE PUT TO DEATH, THEIR BLOOD IS UPON THEM."
SARA-- 3, 21, 09.
"AND THE DAUGHTER OF ANY PRIEST, IF SHE PROFANES HERSELF BY PLAYING THE HARLOT, PROFANES HER FATHER: SHE SHALL BE BURNED WITH FIRE."
R.J.-- 3, 01, 12.
"AND HE SHALL CUT IT INTO PIECES, WITH ITS HEAD AND ITS FAT, AND THE PRIEST SHALL LAY THEM IN ORDER UPON THE WOOD THAT IS ON THE FIRE UPON THE ALTAR."
OKAY, THAT ONE IS NOT A BAD LADY.
IT IS WEIRD THOUGH.
The Third Book of Moses

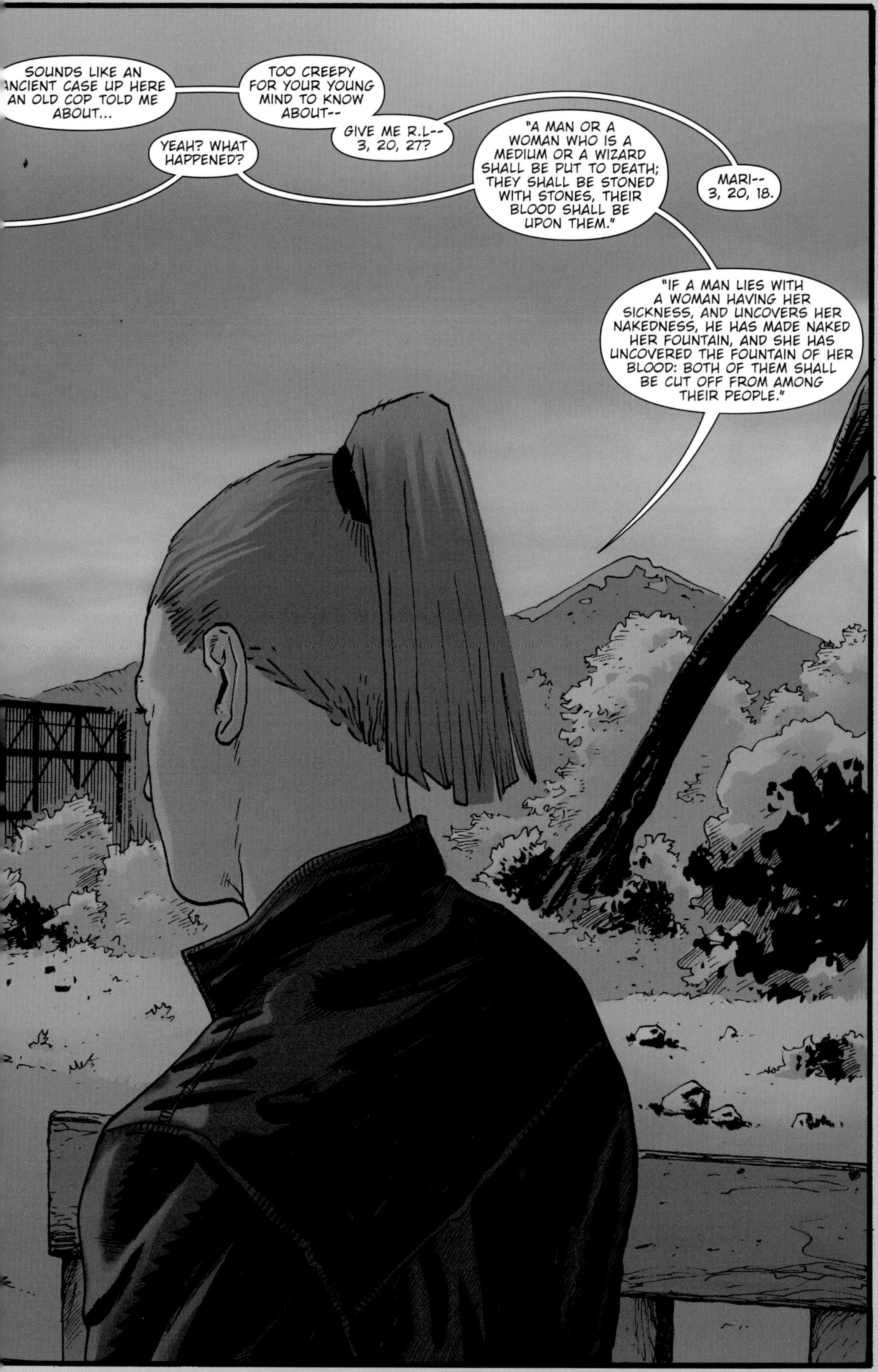
SOUNDS LIKE AN ANCIENT CASE UP HERE AN OLD COP TOLD ME ABOUT...
TOO CREEPY FOR YOUR YOUNG MIND TO KNOW ABOUT--
YEAH? WHAT HAPPENED?
GIVE ME R.L-- 3, 20, 27?
"A MAN OR A WOMAN WHO IS A MEDIUM OR A WIZARD SHALL BE PUT TO DEATH; THEY SHALL BE STONED WITH STONES, THEIR BLOOD SHALL BE UPON THEM."
MARI-- 3, 20, 18.
"IF A MAN LIES WITH A WOMAN HAVING HER SICKNESS, AND UNCOVERS HER NAKEDNESS, HE HAS MADE NAKED HER FOUNTAIN, AND SHE HAS UNCOVERED THE FOUNTAIN OF HER BLOOD: BOTH OF THEM SHALL BE CUT OFF FROM AMONG THEIR PEOPLE."

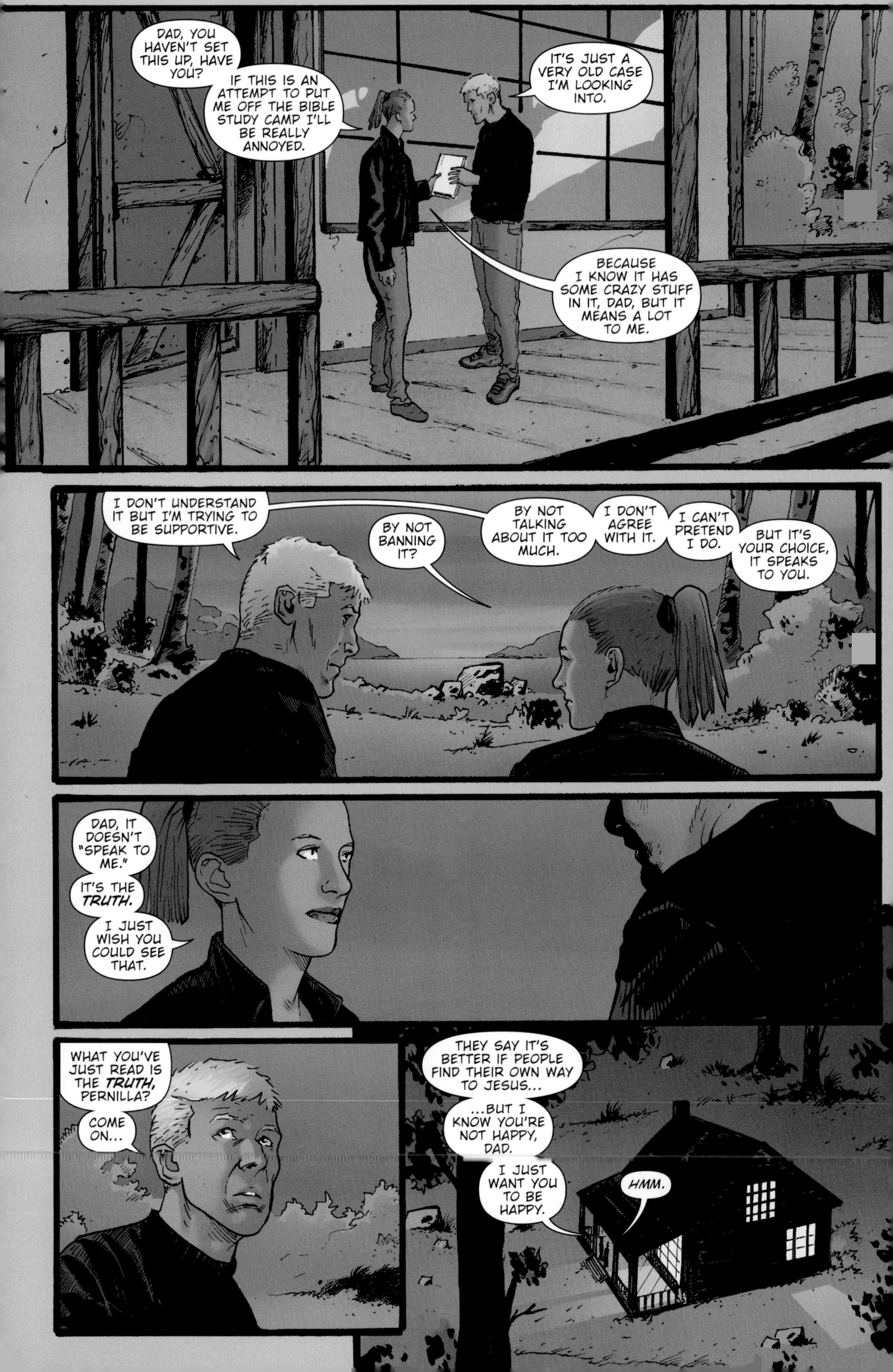
DAD, YOU HAVEN'T SET THIS UP, HAVE YOU?
IF THIS IS AN ATTEMPT TO PUT ME OFF THE BIBLE STUDY CAMP I'LL BE REALLY ANNOYED.
IT'S JUST A VERY OLD CASE I'M LOOKING INTO.
BECAUSE I KNOW IT HAS SOME CRAZY STUFF IN IT, DAD, BUT IT MEANS A LOT TO ME.
I DON'T UNDERSTAND IT BUT I'M TRYING TO BE SUPPORTIVE.
BY NOT BANNING IT?
BY NOT TALKING ABOUT IT TOO MUCH.
I DON'T AGREE WITH IT.
I CAN'T PRETEND I DO.
BUT IT'S YOUR CHOICE, IT SPEAKS TO YOU.
DAD, IT DOESN'T "SPEAK TO ME."
IT'S THE TRUTH.
I JUST WISH YOU COULD SEE THAT.
WHAT YOU'VE JUST READ IS THE TRUTH, PERNILLA?
COME ON...
THEY SAY IT'S BETTER IF PEOPLE FIND THEIR OWN WAY TO JESUS...
...BUT I KNOW YOU'RE NOT HAPPY, DAD.
I JUST WANT YOU TO BE HAPPY.
HMM.

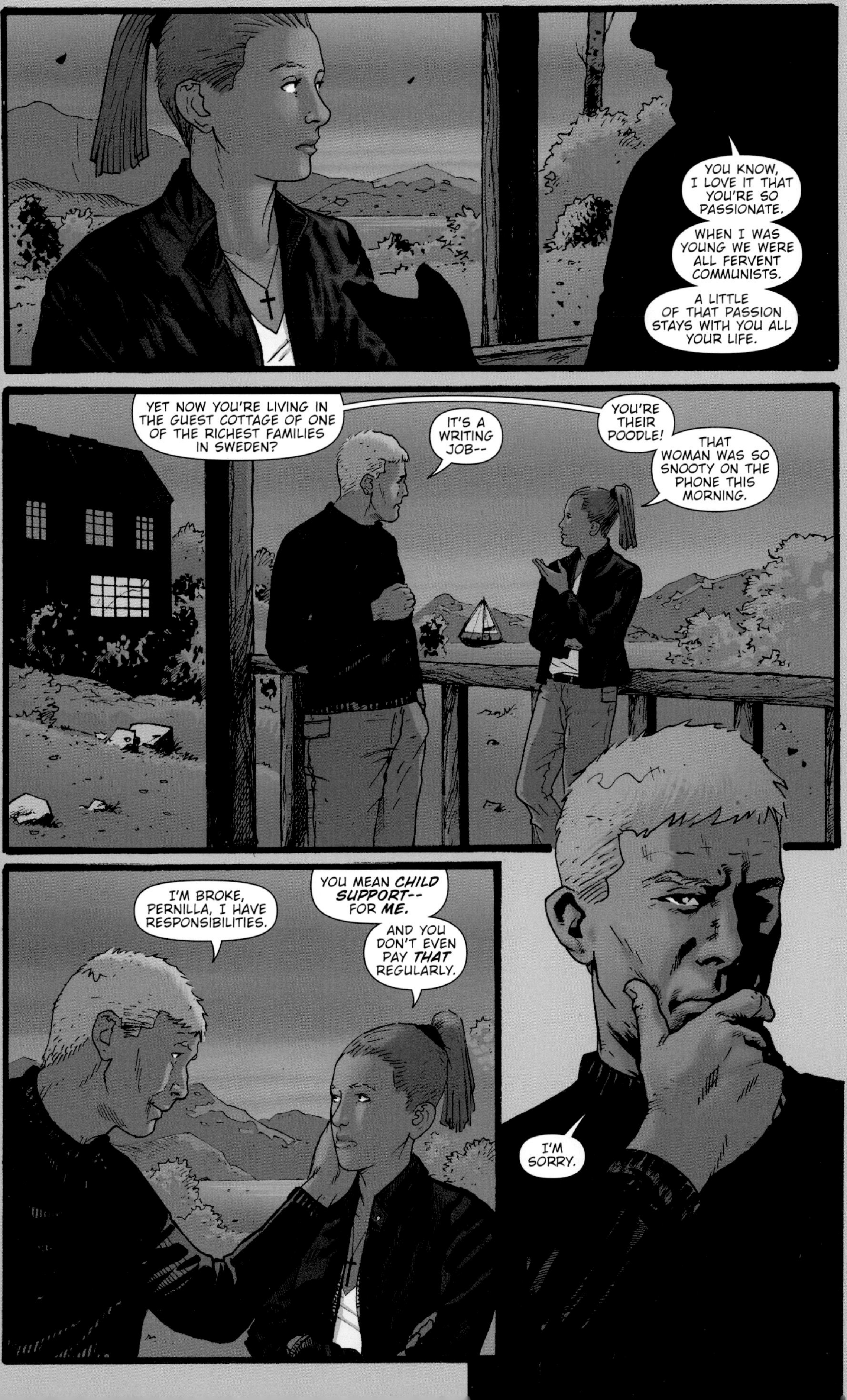
YOU KNOW, I LOVE IT THAT YOU'RE SO PASSIONATE.
WHEN I WAS YOUNG WE WERE ALL FERVENT COMMUNISTS.
A LITTLE OF THAT PASSION STAYS WITH YOU ALL YOUR LIFE.
YET NOW YOU'RE LIVING IN THE GUEST COTTAGE OF ONE OF THE RICHEST FAMILIES IN SWEDEN?
IT'S A WRITING JOB--
YOU'RE THEIR POODLE!
THAT WOMAN WAS SO SNOOTY ON THE PHONE THIS MORNING.
I'M BROKE, PERNILLA, I HAVE RESPONSIBILITIES.
YOU MEAN CHILD SUPPORT-- FOR ME.
AND YOU DON'T EVEN PAY THAT REGULARLY.
I'M SORRY.

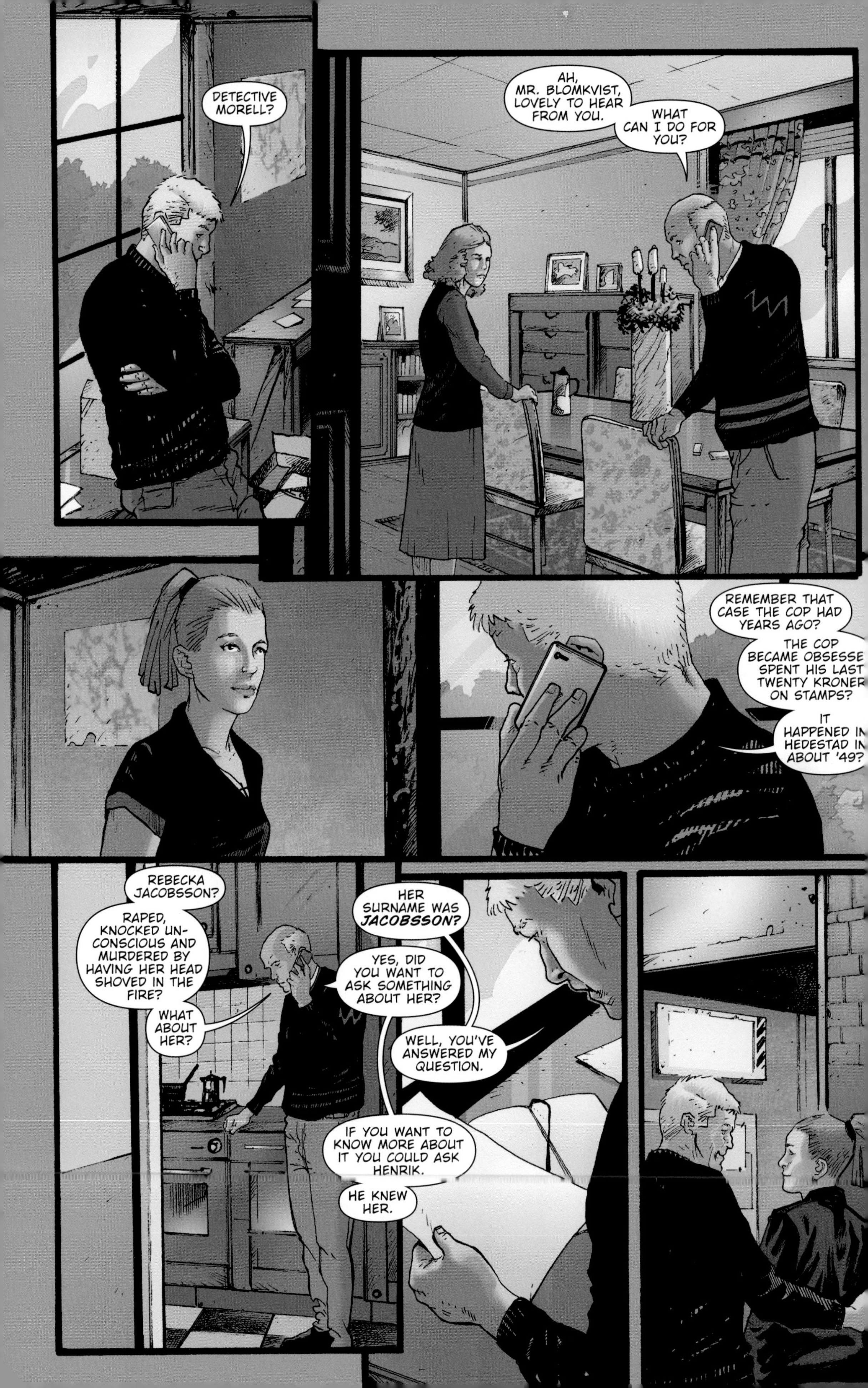
DETECTIVE MORELL?
AH, MR. BLOMKVIST, LOVELY TO HEAR FROM YOU.
WHAT CAN I DO FOR YOU?
REMEMBER THAT CASE THE COP HAD YEARS AGO?
THE COP BECAME OBSESSE SPENT HIS LAST TWENTY KRONER ON STAMPS?
IT HAPPENED IN HEDESTAD IN ABOUT '49?
REBECKA JACOBSSON?
RAPED, KNOCKED UN-CONSCIOUS AND MURDERED BY HAVING HER HEAD SHOVED IN THE FIRE?
WHAT ABOUT HER?
HER SURNAME WAS ***JACOBSSON?***
YES, DID YOU WANT TO ASK SOMETHING ABOUT HER?
WELL, YOU'VE ANSWERED MY QUESTION.
IF YOU WANT TO KNOW MORE ABOUT IT YOU COULD ASK HENRIK.
HE KNEW HER.

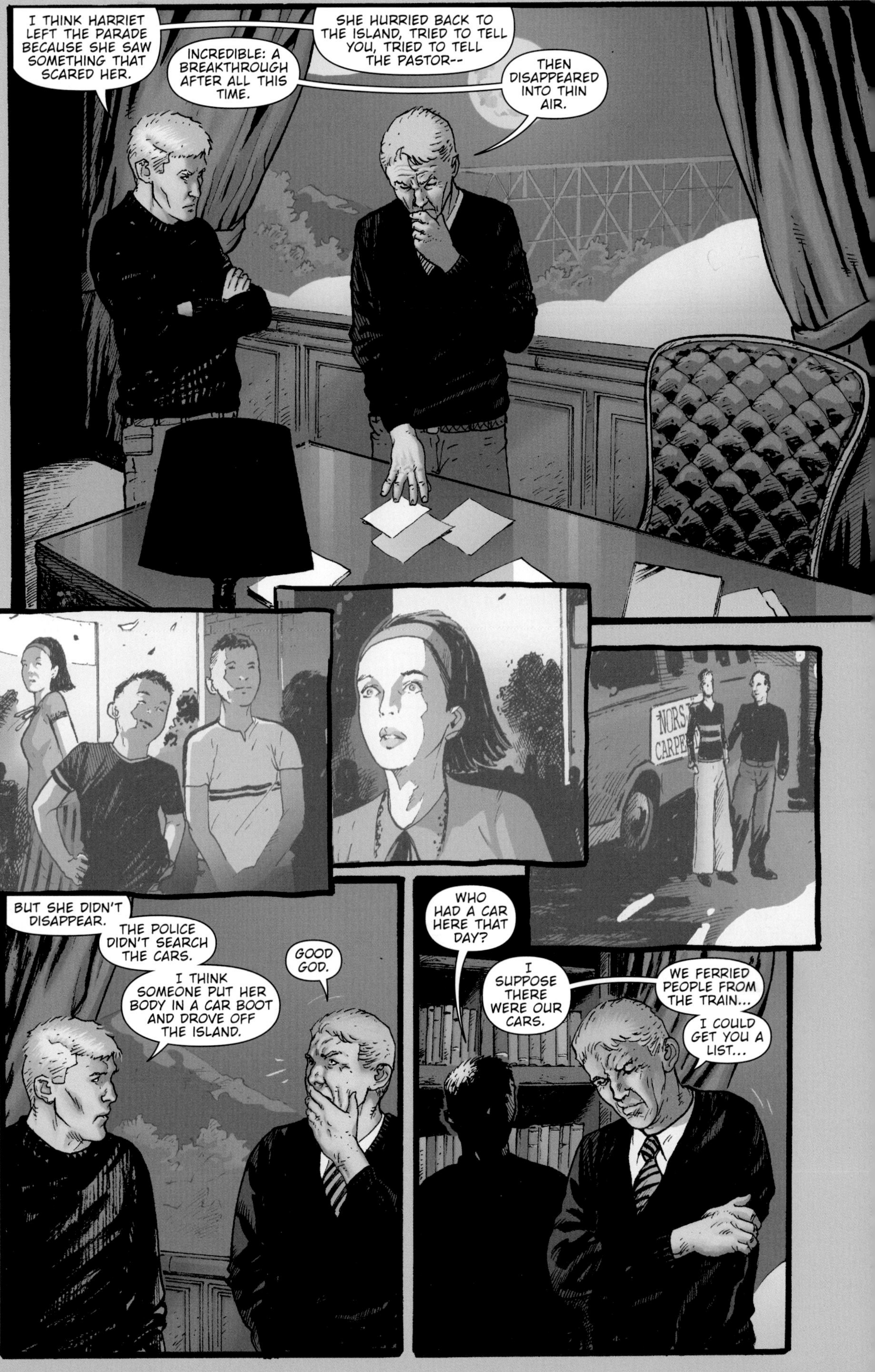

I THINK HARRIET LEFT THE PARADE BECAUSE SHE SAW SOMETHING THAT SCARED HER.
SHE HURRIED BACK TO THE ISLAND, TRIED TO TELL YOU, TRIED TO TELL THE PASTOR--
INCREDIBLE: A BREAKTHROUGH AFTER ALL THIS TIME.
THEN DISAPPEARED INTO THIN AIR.
NORS
CARPE
BUT SHE DIDN'T DISAPPEAR.
THE POLICE DIDN'T SEARCH THE CARS.
I THINK SOMEONE PUT HER BODY IN A CAR BOOT AND DROVE OFF THE ISLAND.
GOOD GOD.
WHO HAD A CAR HERE THAT DAY?
I SUPPOSE THERE WERE OUR CARS.
WE FERRIED PEOPLE FROM THE TRAIN...
I COULD GET YOU A LIST...

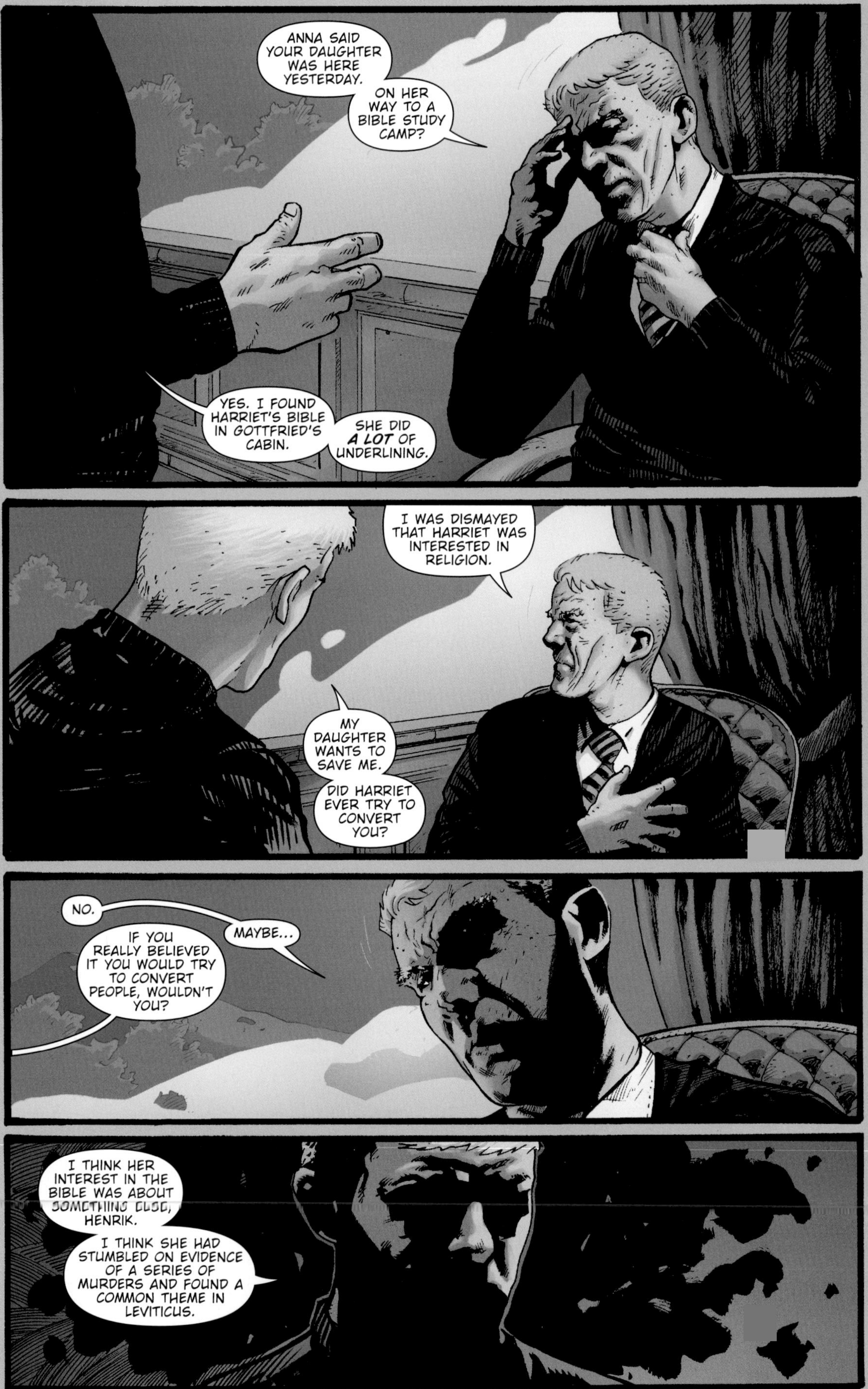
ANNA SAID YOUR DAUGHTER WAS HERE YESTERDAY.
ON HER WAY TO A BIBLE STUDY CAMP?
YES. I FOUND HARRIET'S BIBLE IN GOTTFRIED'S CABIN.
SHE DID *A LOT* OF UNDERLINING.
I WAS DISMAYED THAT HARRIET WAS INTERESTED IN RELIGION.
MY DAUGHTER WANTS TO SAVE ME.
DID HARRIET EVER TRY TO CONVERT YOU?
NO.
MAYBE...
IF YOU REALLY BELIEVED IT YOU WOULD TRY TO CONVERT PEOPLE, WOULDN'T YOU?
I THINK HER INTEREST IN THE BIBLE WAS ABOUT SOMETHING ELSE, HENRIK.
I THINK SHE HAD STUMBLED ON EVIDENCE OF A SERIES OF MURDERS AND FOUND A COMMON THEME IN LEVITICUS.

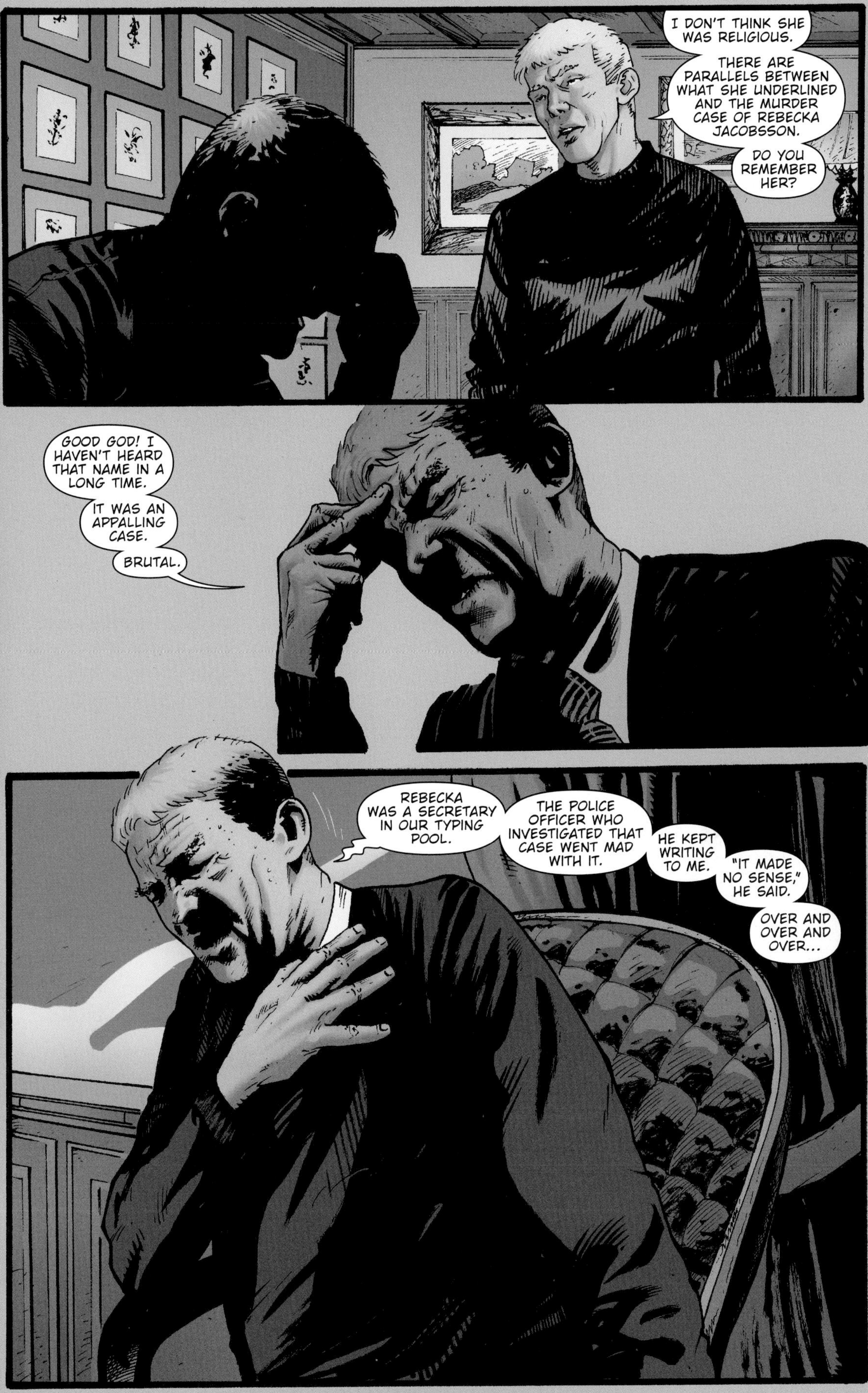
I DON'T THINK SHE WAS RELIGIOUS.
THERE ARE PARALLELS BETWEEN WHAT SHE UNDERLINED AND THE MURDER CASE OF REBECKA JACOBSSON.
DO YOU REMEMBER HER?
GOOD GOD! I HAVEN'T HEARD THAT NAME IN A LONG TIME.
IT WAS AN APPALLING CASE.
BRUTAL.
REBECKA WAS A SECRETARY IN OUR TYPING POOL.
THE POLICE OFFICER WHO INVESTIGATED THAT CASE WENT MAD WITH IT.
HE KEPT WRITING TO ME.
"IT MADE NO SENSE," HE SAID.
OVER AND OVER AND OVER...

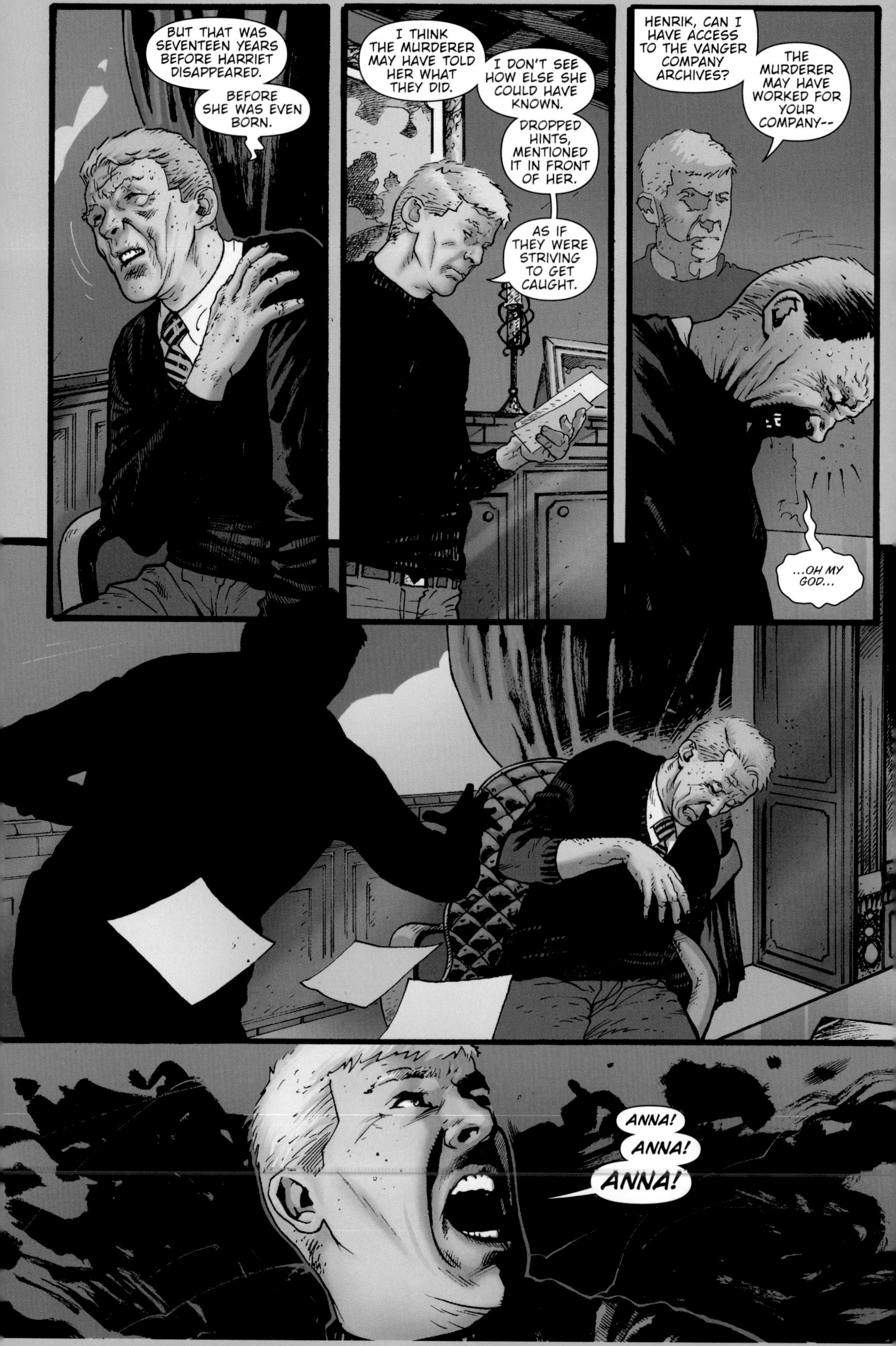
BUT THAT WAS SEVENTEEN YEARS BEFORE HARRIET DISAPPEARED.
BEFORE SHE WAS EVEN BORN.
I THINK THE MURDERER MAY HAVE TOLD HER WHAT THEY DID.
I DON'T SEE HOW ELSE SHE COULD HAVE KNOWN.
DROPPED HINTS, MENTIONED IT IN FRONT OF HER.
AS IF THEY WERE STRIVING TO GET CAUGHT.
HENRIK, CAN I HAVE ACCESS TO THE VANGER COMPANY ARCHIVES?
THE MURDERER MAY HAVE WORKED FOR YOUR COMPANY--
...OH MY GOD...
ANNA!
ANNA!
ANNA!

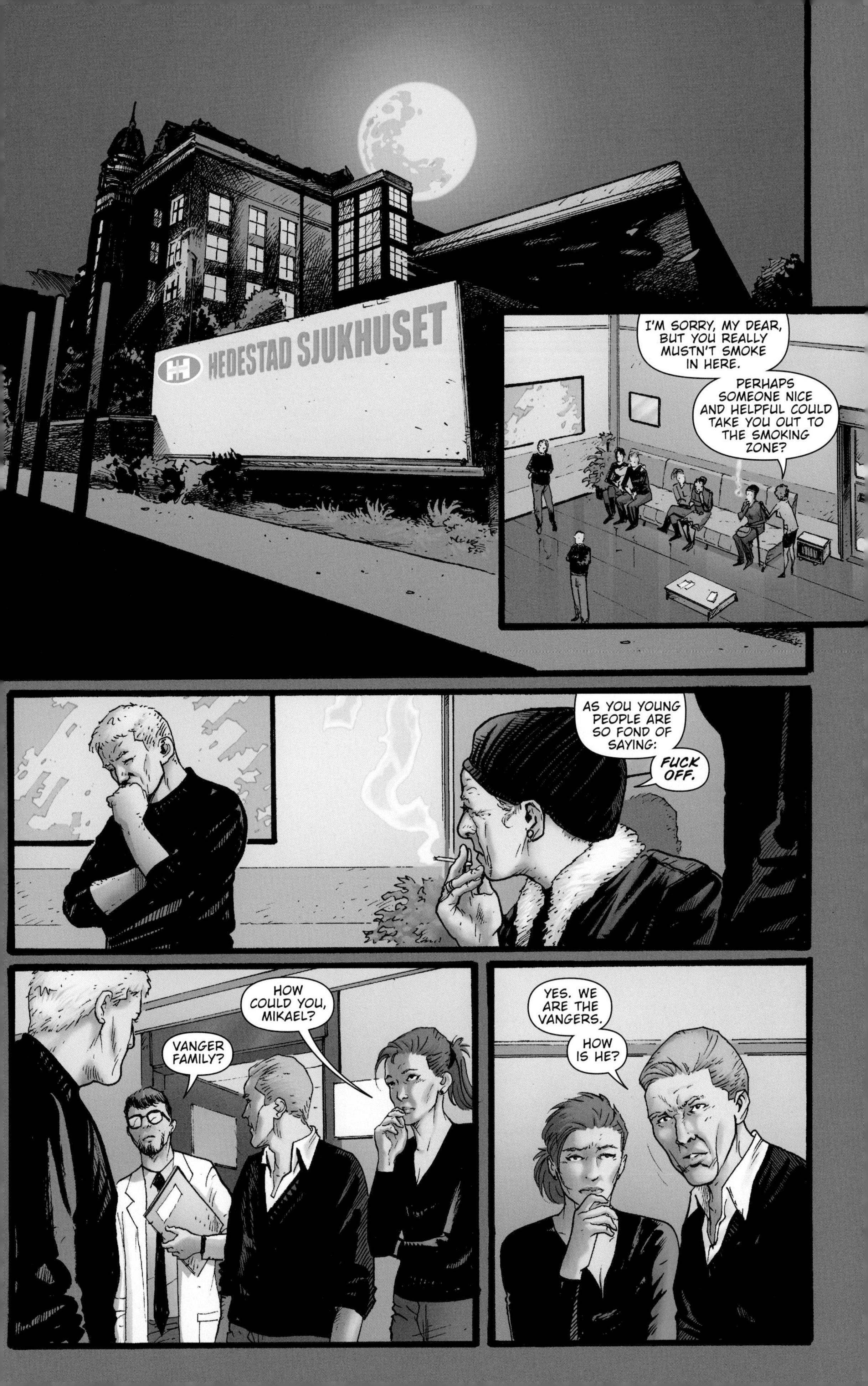
HEDESTAD SJUKHUSET
I'M SORRY, MY DEAR, BUT YOU REALLY MUSTN'T SMOKE IN HERE.
PERHAPS SOMEONE NICE AND HELPFUL COULD TAKE YOU OUT TO THE SMOKING ZONE?
AS YOU YOUNG PEOPLE ARE SO FOND OF SAYING:
FUCK OFF.
HOW COULD YOU, MIKAEL?
VANGER FAMILY?
YES. WE ARE THE VANGERS.
HOW IS HE?

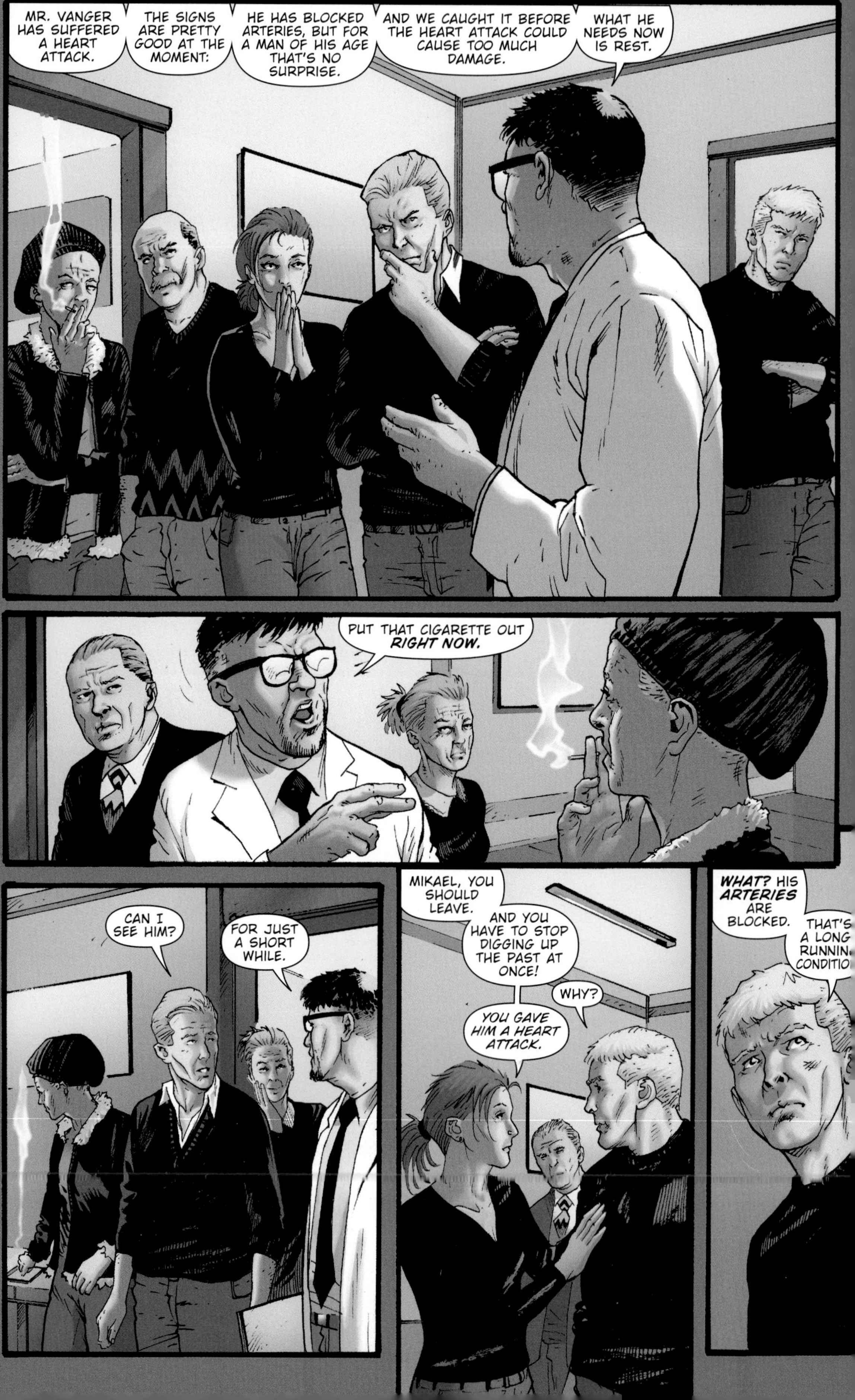
MR. VANGER HAS SUFFERED A HEART ATTACK.
THE SIGNS ARE PRETTY GOOD AT THE MOMENT:
HE HAS BLOCKED ARTERIES, BUT FOR A MAN OF HIS AGE THAT'S NO SURPRISE.
AND WE CAUGHT IT BEFORE THE HEART ATTACK COULD CAUSE TOO MUCH DAMAGE.
WHAT HE NEEDS NOW IS REST.
PUT THAT CIGARETTE OUT ***RIGHT NOW.***
CAN I SEE HIM?
FOR JUST A SHORT WHILE.
MIKAEL, YOU SHOULD LEAVE.
AND YOU HAVE TO STOP DIGGING UP THE PAST AT ONCE!
WHY?
YOU GAVE HIM A HEART ATTACK.
WHAT? HIS ***ARTERIES*** ARE BLOCKED.
THAT'S A LONG RUNNIN CONDITIO

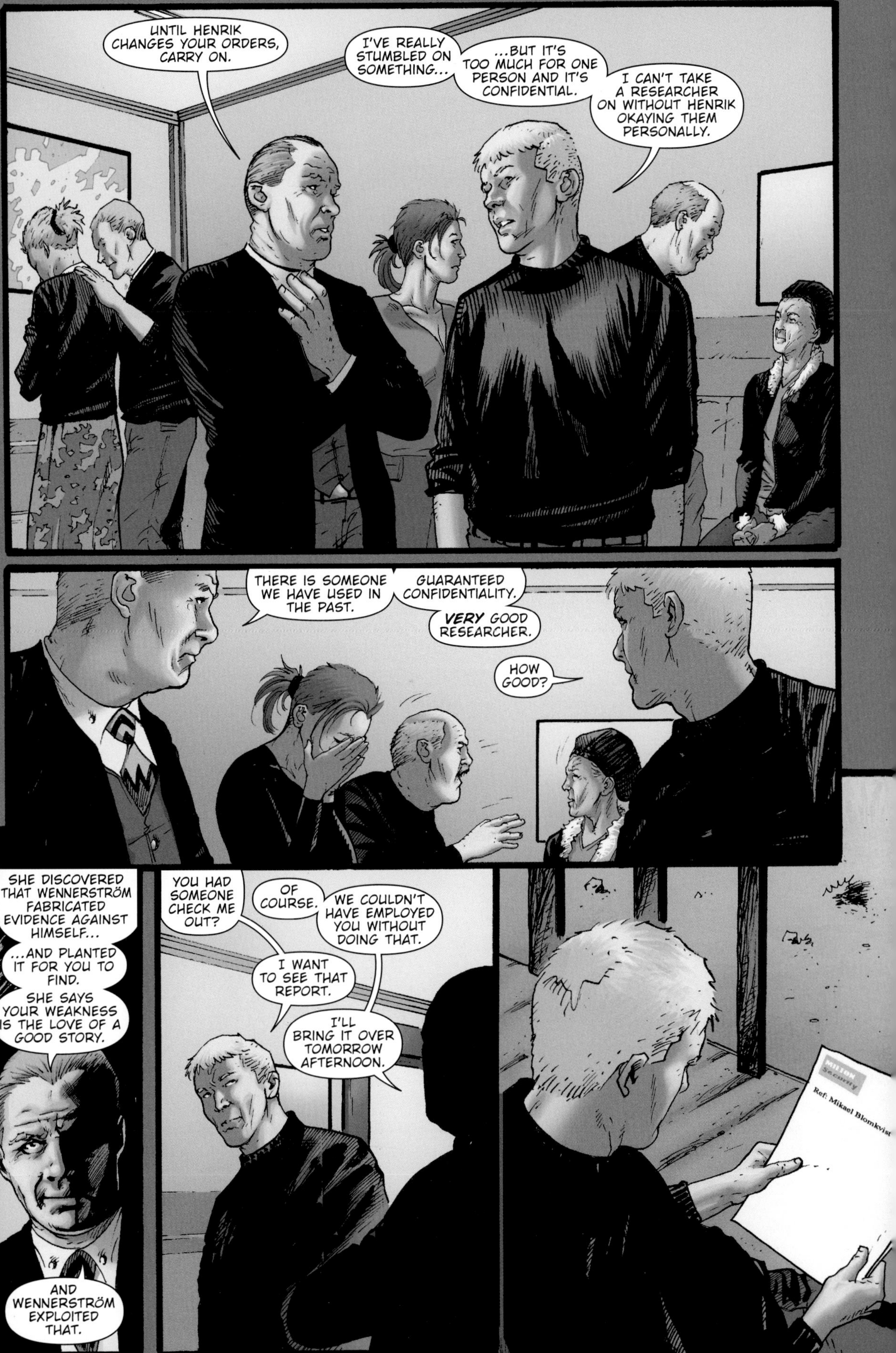
UNTIL HENRIK CHANGES YOUR ORDERS, CARRY ON.
I'VE REALLY STUMBLED ON SOMETHING...
...BUT IT'S TOO MUCH FOR ONE PERSON AND IT'S CONFIDENTIAL.
I CAN'T TAKE A RESEARCHER ON WITHOUT HENRIK OKAYING THEM PERSONALLY.
THERE IS SOMEONE WE HAVE USED IN THE PAST.
GUARANTEED CONFIDENTIALITY.
VERY GOOD RESEARCHER.
HOW GOOD?
SHE DISCOVERED THAT WENNERSTRÖM FABRICATED EVIDENCE AGAINST HIMSELF...
...AND PLANTED IT FOR YOU TO FIND.
SHE SAYS YOUR WEAKNESS IS THE LOVE OF A GOOD STORY.
AND WENNERSTRÖM EXPLOITED THAT.
YOU HAD SOMEONE CHECK ME OUT?
OF COURSE.
WE COULDN'T HAVE EMPLOYED YOU WITHOUT DOING THAT.
I WANT TO SEE THAT REPORT.
I'LL BRING IT OVER TOMORROW AFTERNOON.
MILTON Security
Ref: Mikael Blomkvist

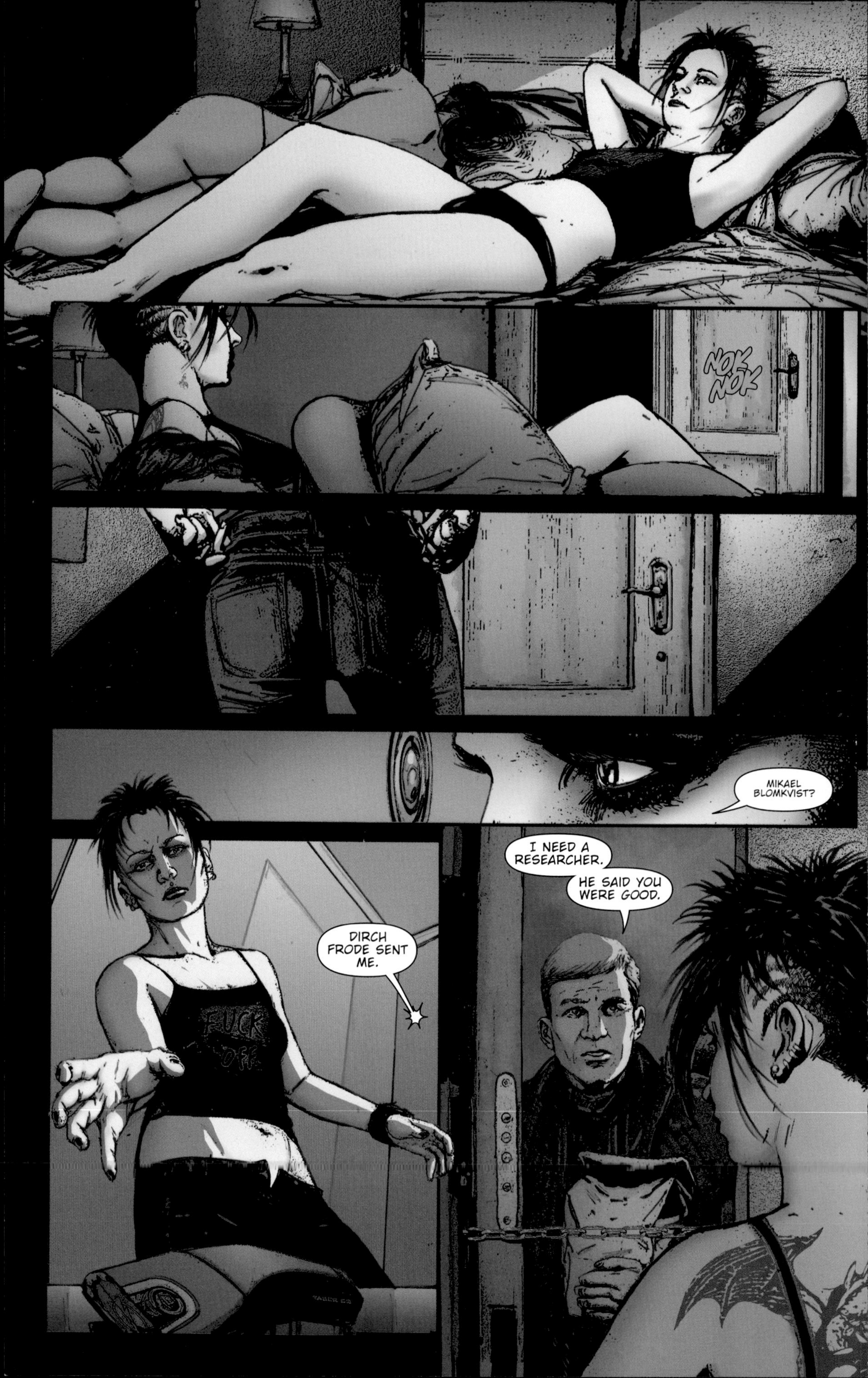
NOK NOK
MIKAEL BLOMKVIST?
DIRCH FRODE SENT ME.
I NEED A RESEARCHER.
HE SAID YOU WERE GOOD.
FUCK OFF

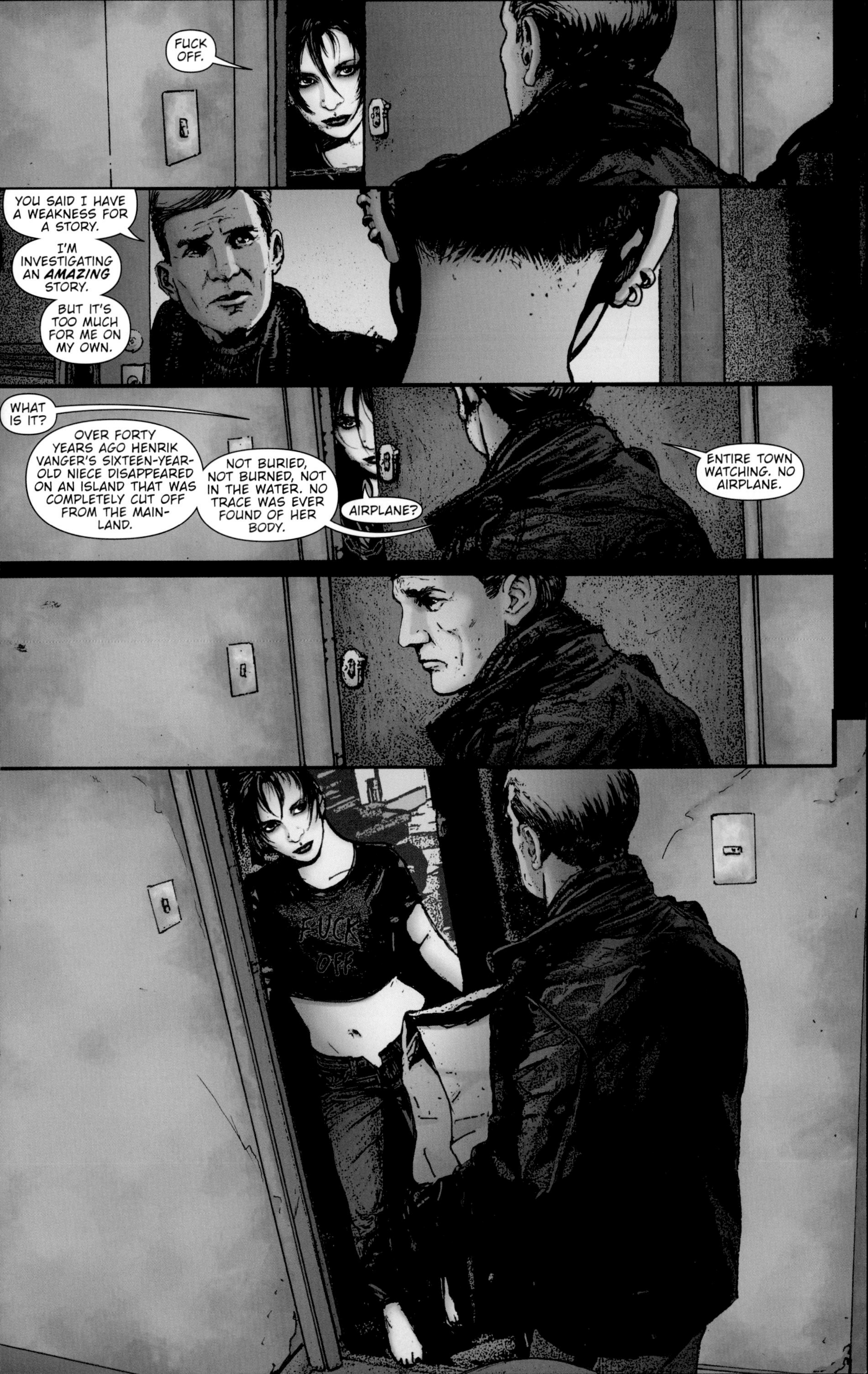
FUCK OFF.
YOU SAID I HAVE A WEAKNESS FOR A STORY.
I'M INVESTIGATING AN ***AMAZING*** STORY.
BUT IT'S TOO MUCH FOR ME ON MY OWN.
WHAT IS IT?
OVER FORTY YEARS AGO HENRIK VANGER'S SIXTEEN-YEAR-OLD NIECE DISAPPEARED ON AN ISLAND THAT WAS COMPLETELY CUT OFF FROM THE MAIN-LAND.
NOT BURIED, NOT BURNED, NOT IN THE WATER. NO TRACE WAS EVER FOUND OF HER BODY.
AIRPLANE?
ENTIRE TOWN WATCHING. NO AIRPLANE.
FUCK OFF

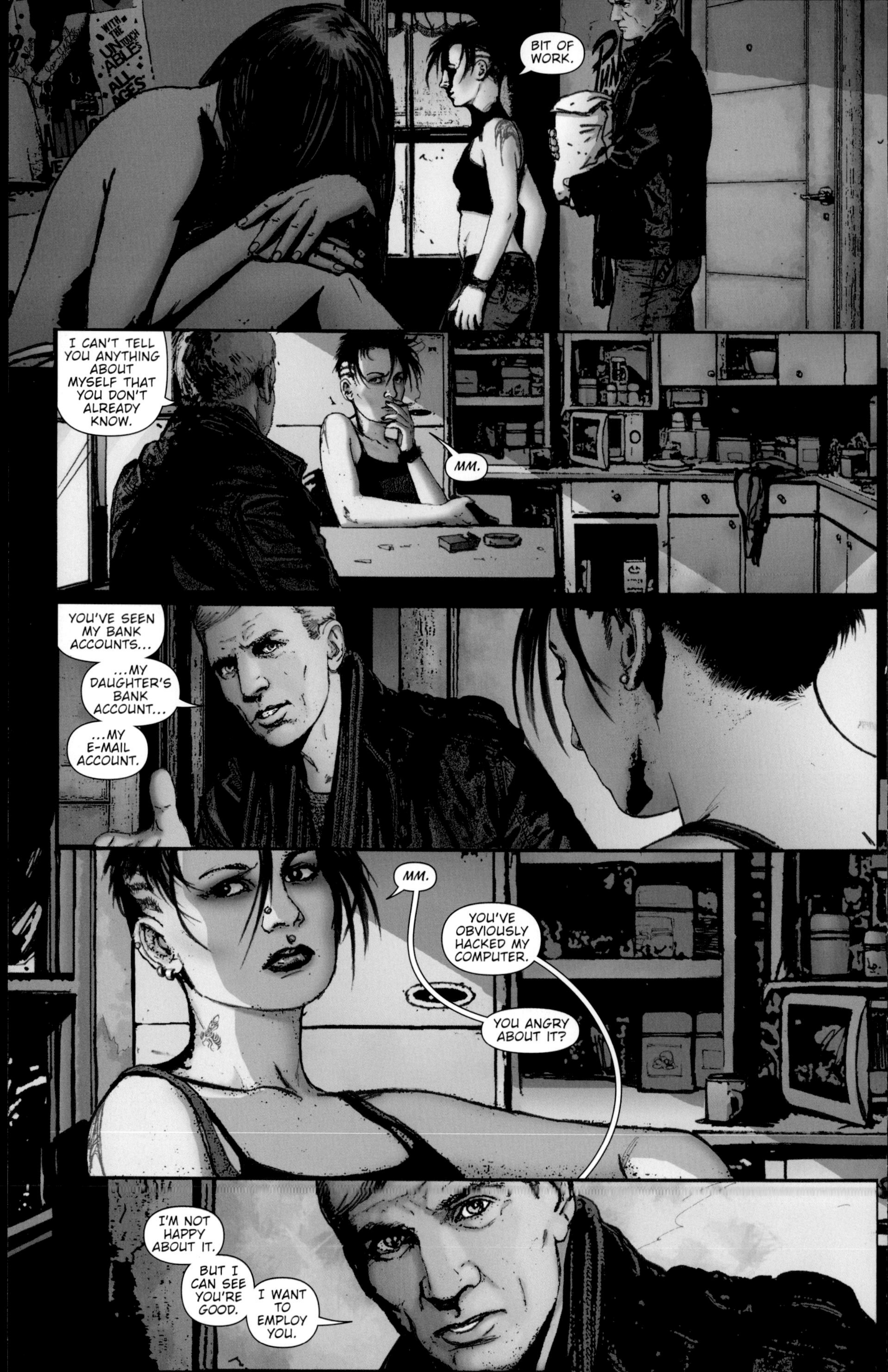
BIT OF WORK.
I CAN'T TELL YOU ANYTHING ABOUT MYSELF THAT YOU DON'T ALREADY KNOW.
MM.
YOU'VE SEEN MY BANK ACCOUNTS...
...MY DAUGHTER'S BANK ACCOUNT...
...MY E-MAIL ACCOUNT.
MM.
YOU'VE OBVIOUSLY HACKED MY COMPUTER.
YOU ANGRY ABOUT IT?
I'M NOT HAPPY ABOUT IT.
BUT I CAN SEE YOU'RE GOOD.
I WANT TO EMPLOY YOU.

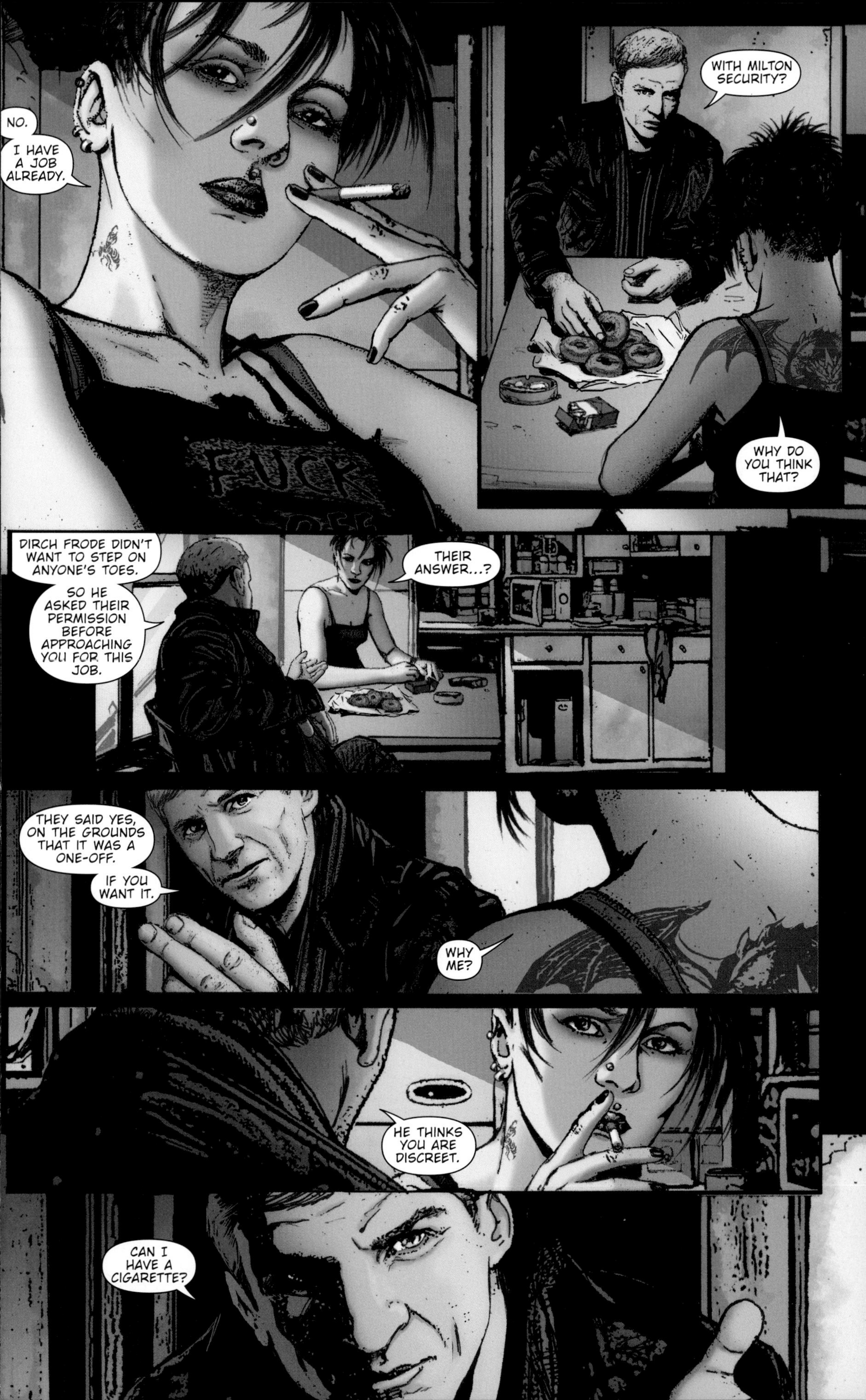
NO.
I HAVE A JOB ALREADY.
WITH MILTON SECURITY?
WHY DO YOU THINK THAT?
DIRCH FRODE DIDN'T WANT TO STEP ON ANYONE'S TOES.
SO HE ASKED THEIR PERMISSION BEFORE APPROACHING YOU FOR THIS JOB.
THEIR ANSWER...?
THEY SAID YES, ON THE GROUNDS THAT IT WAS A ONE-OFF.
IF YOU WANT IT.
WHY ME?
HE THINKS YOU ARE DISCREET.
CAN I HAVE A CIGARETTE?

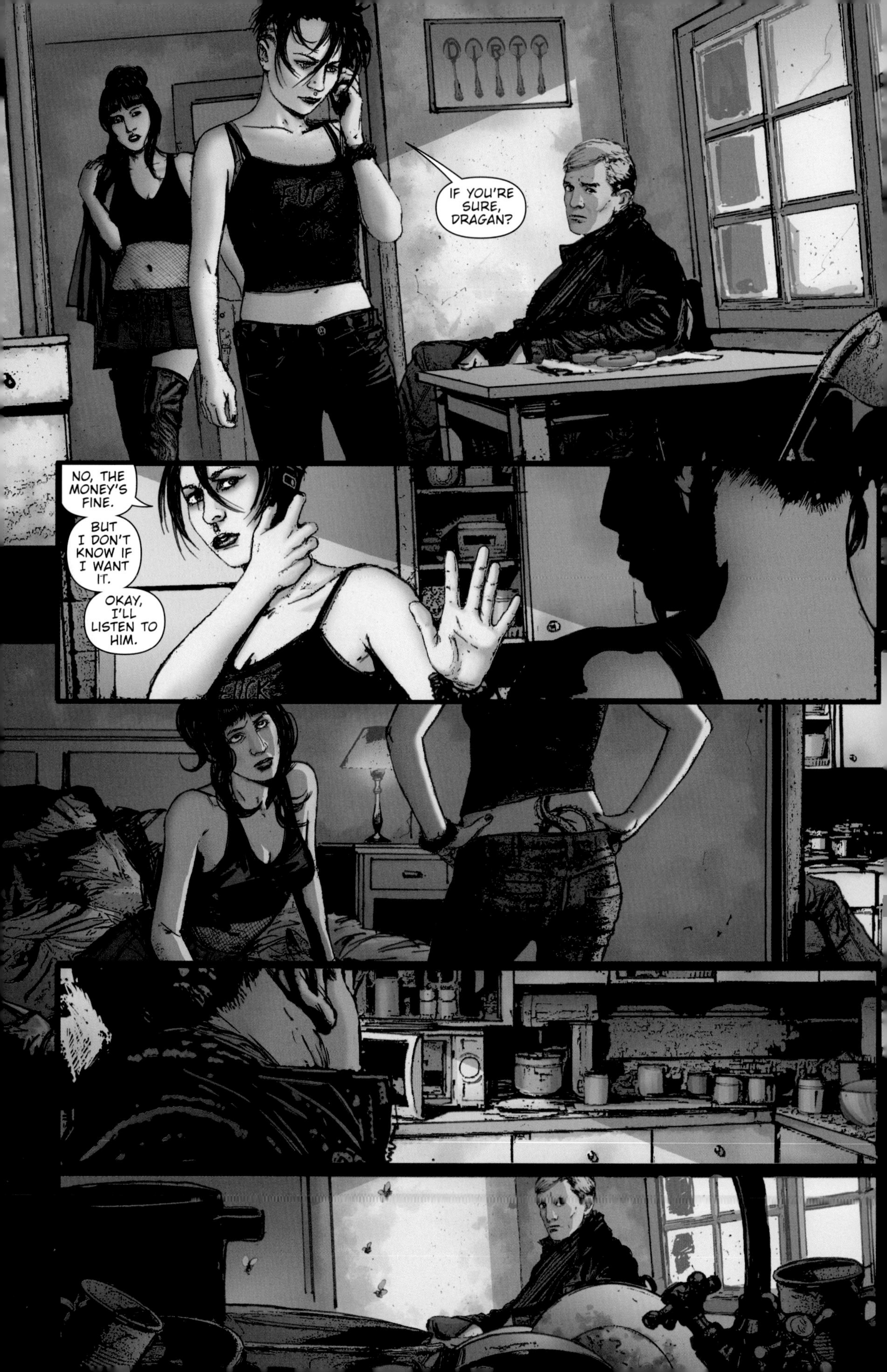
DIRTY
IF YOU'RE SURE, DRAGAN?
NO, THE MONEY'S FINE.
BUT I DON'T KNOW IF I WANT IT.
OKAY, I'LL LISTEN TO HIM.

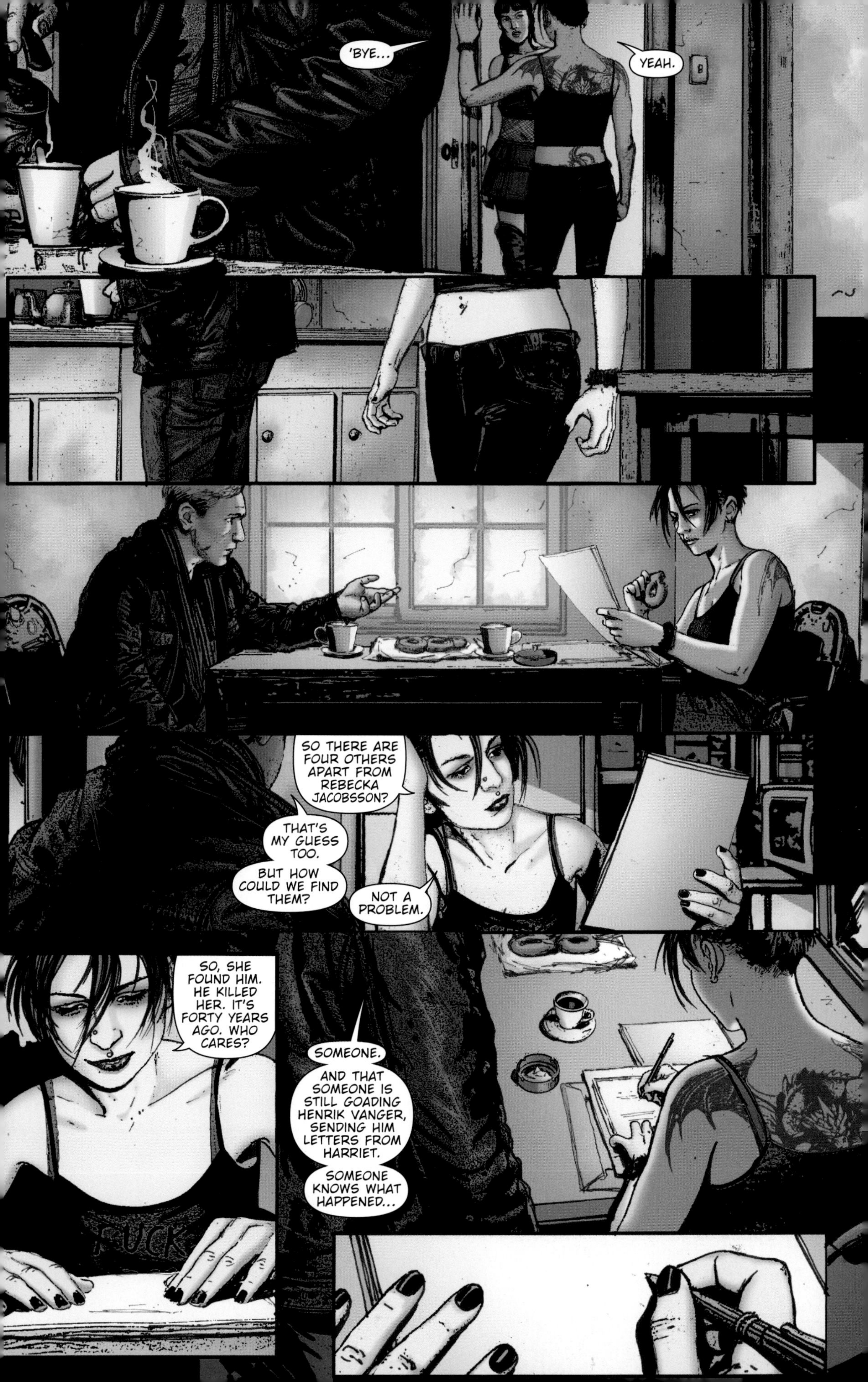
'BYE...
YEAH.
SO THERE ARE FOUR OTHERS APART FROM REBECKA JACOBSSON?
THAT'S MY GUESS TOO.
BUT HOW COULD WE FIND THEM?
NOT A PROBLEM.
SO, SHE FOUND HIM. HE KILLED HER. IT'S FORTY YEARS AGO. WHO CARES?
SOMEONE.
AND THAT SOMEONE IS STILL GOADING HENRIK VANGER, SENDING HIM LETTERS FROM HARRIET.
SOMEONE KNOWS WHAT HAPPENED...

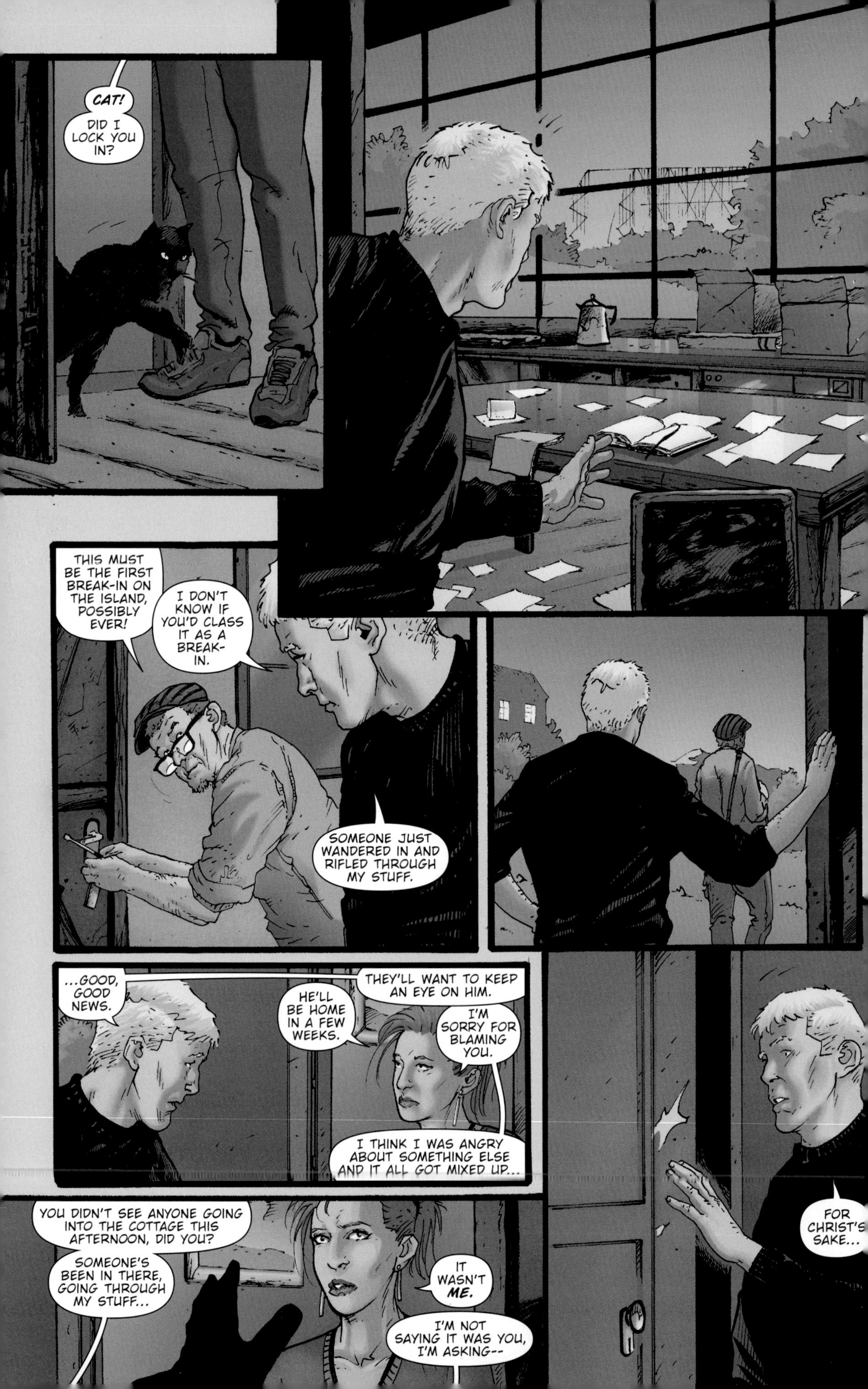
CAT! DID I LOCK YOU IN?
THIS MUST BE THE FIRST BREAK-IN ON THE ISLAND, POSSIBLY EVER!
I DON'T KNOW IF YOU'D CLASS IT AS A BREAK-IN.
SOMEONE JUST WANDERED IN AND RIFLED THROUGH MY STUFF.
...GOOD, GOOD NEWS.
THEY'LL WANT TO KEEP AN EYE ON HIM.
HE'LL BE HOME IN A FEW WEEKS.
I'M SORRY FOR BLAMING YOU.
I THINK I WAS ANGRY ABOUT SOMETHING ELSE AND IT ALL GOT MIXED UP...
FOR CHRIST'S SAKE...
YOU DIDN'T SEE ANYONE GOING INTO THE COTTAGE THIS AFTERNOON, DID YOU?
SOMEONE'S BEEN IN THERE, GOING THROUGH MY STUFF...
IT WASN'T ME.
I'M NOT SAYING IT WAS YOU, I'M ASKING--

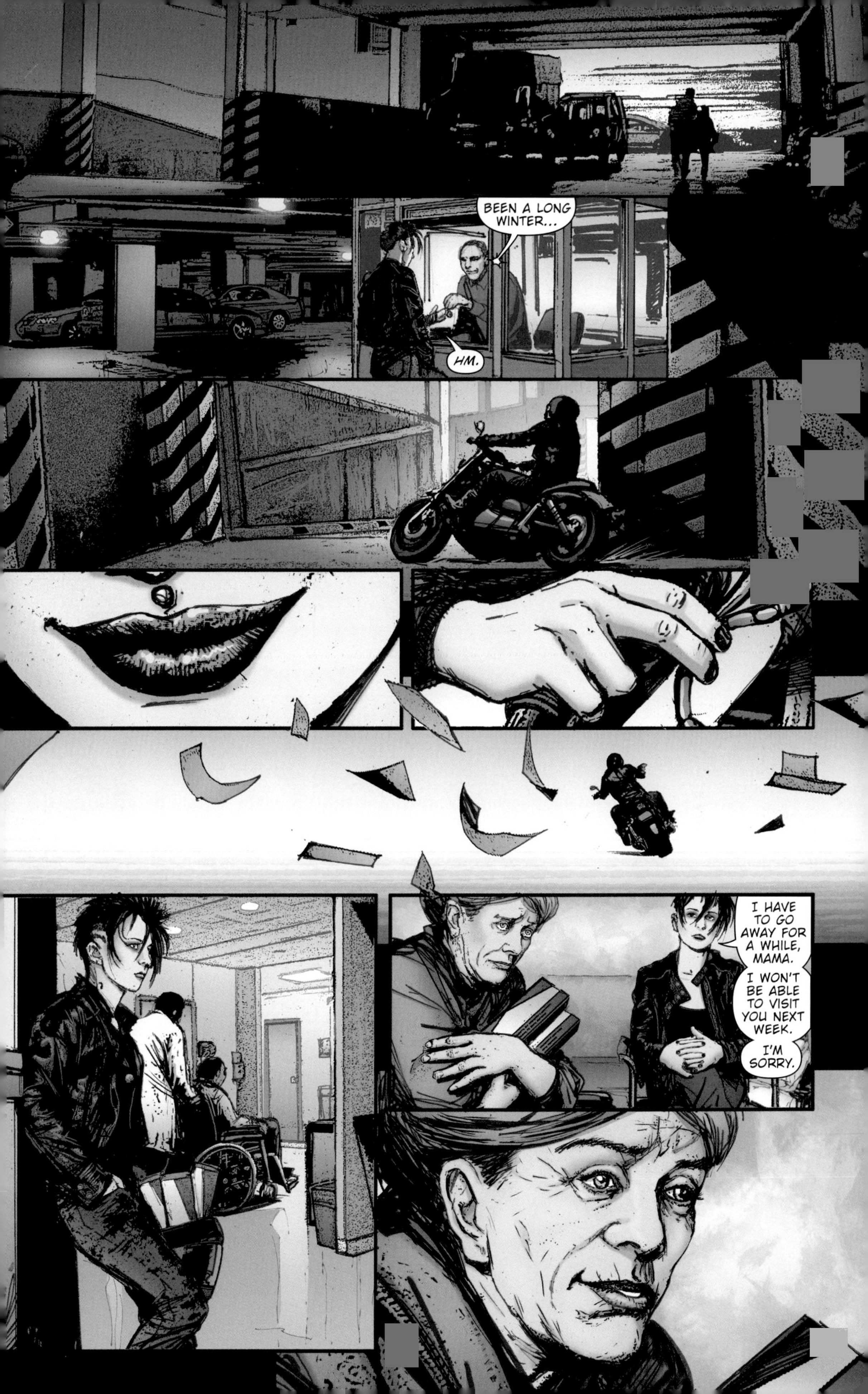
BEEN A LONG WINTER...
HM.
I HAVE TO GO AWAY FOR A WHILE, MAMA.
I WON'T BE ABLE TO VISIT YOU NEXT WEEK.
I'M SORRY.

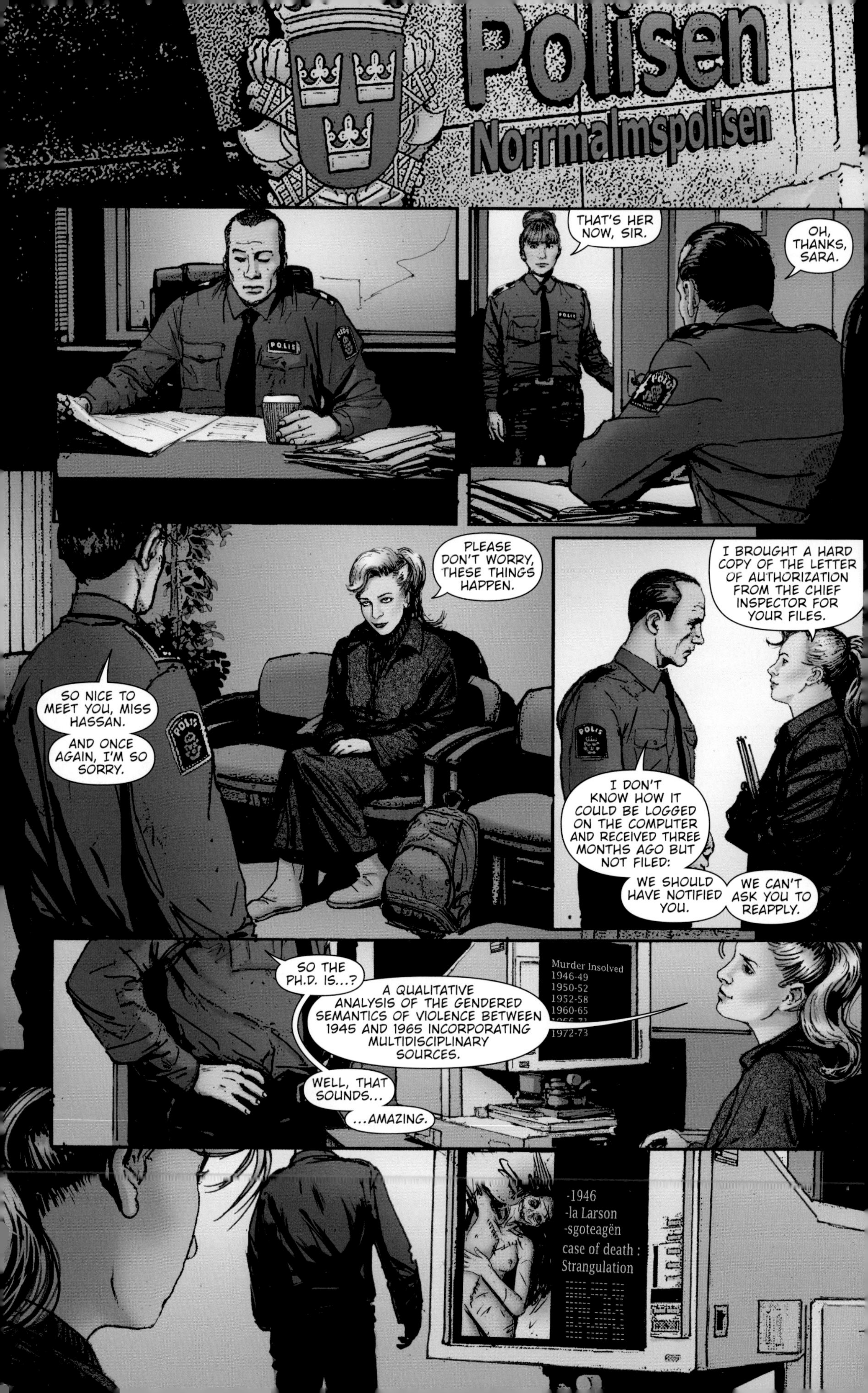
Polisen
Norrmalmspolisen
THAT'S HER NOW, SIR.
OH, THANKS, SARA.
PLEASE DON'T WORRY, THESE THINGS HAPPEN.
SO NICE TO MEET YOU, MISS HASSAN.
AND ONCE AGAIN, I'M SO SORRY.
I BROUGHT A HARD COPY OF THE LETTER OF AUTHORIZATION FROM THE CHIEF INSPECTOR FOR YOUR FILES.
I DON'T KNOW HOW IT COULD BE LOGGED ON THE COMPUTER AND RECEIVED THREE MONTHS AGO BUT NOT FILED:
WE SHOULD HAVE NOTIFIED YOU.
WE CAN'T ASK YOU TO REAPPLY.
SO THE PH.D. IS...?
A QUALITATIVE ANALYSIS OF THE GENDERED SEMANTICS OF VIOLENCE BETWEEN 1945 AND 1965 INCORPORATING MULTIDISCIPLINARY SOURCES.
WELL, THAT SOUNDS...
...AMAZING.
Murder Insolved
1946-49
1950-52
1952-58
1960-65
1972-73
-1946
-la Larson
-sgoteagën
case of death :
Strangulation

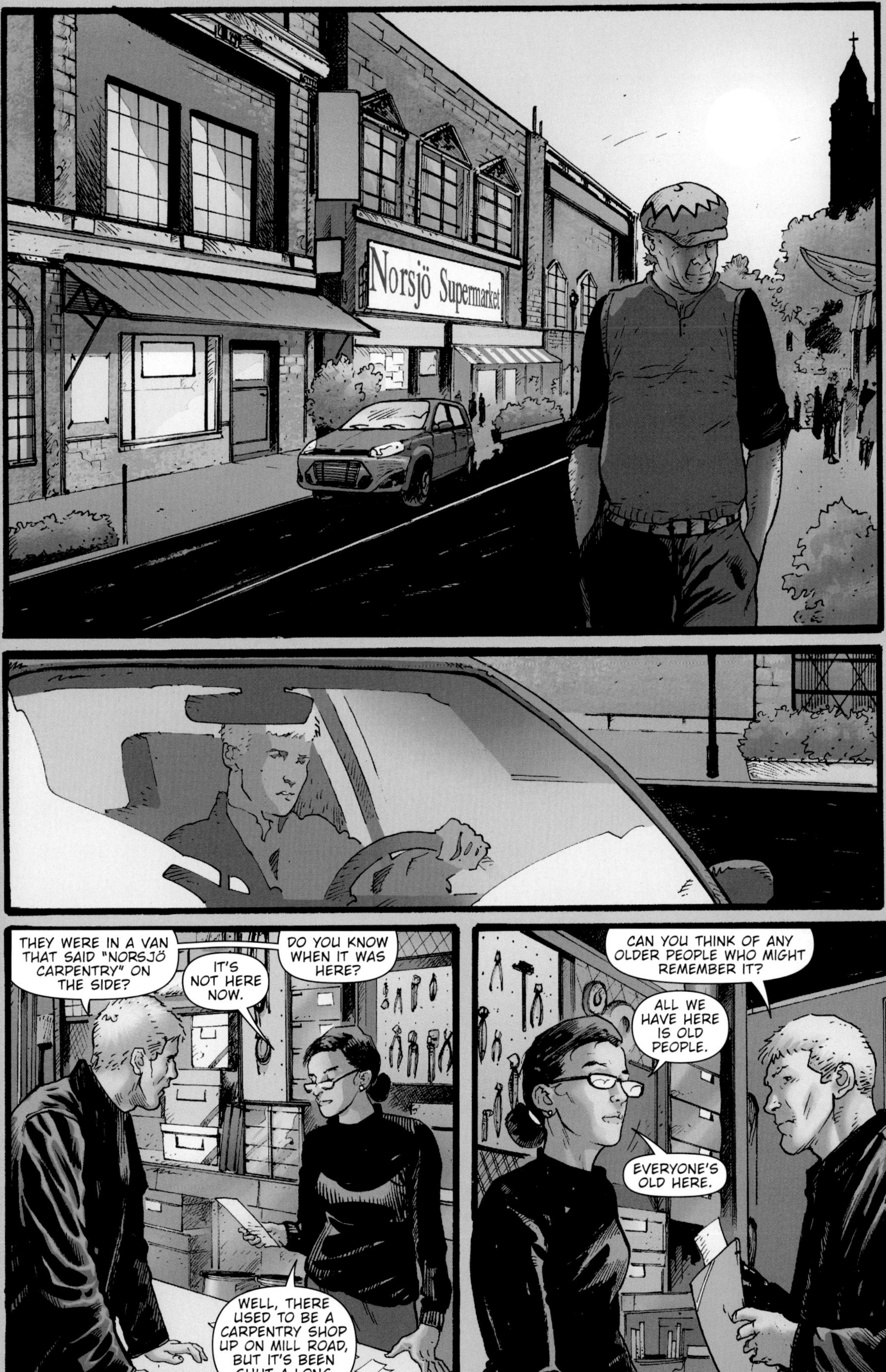
Norsjö Supermarket
THEY WERE IN A VAN THAT SAID "NORSJÖ CARPENTRY" ON THE SIDE?
IT'S NOT HERE NOW.
DO YOU KNOW WHEN IT WAS HERE?
WELL, THERE USED TO BE A CARPENTRY SHOP UP ON MILL ROAD, BUT IT'S BEEN SHUT A LONG TIME.
CAN YOU THINK OF ANY OLDER PEOPLE WHO MIGHT REMEMBER IT?
ALL WE HAVE HERE IS OLD PEOPLE.
EVERYONE'S OLD HERE.

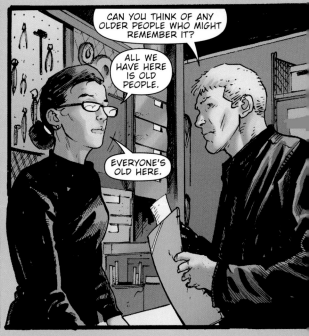

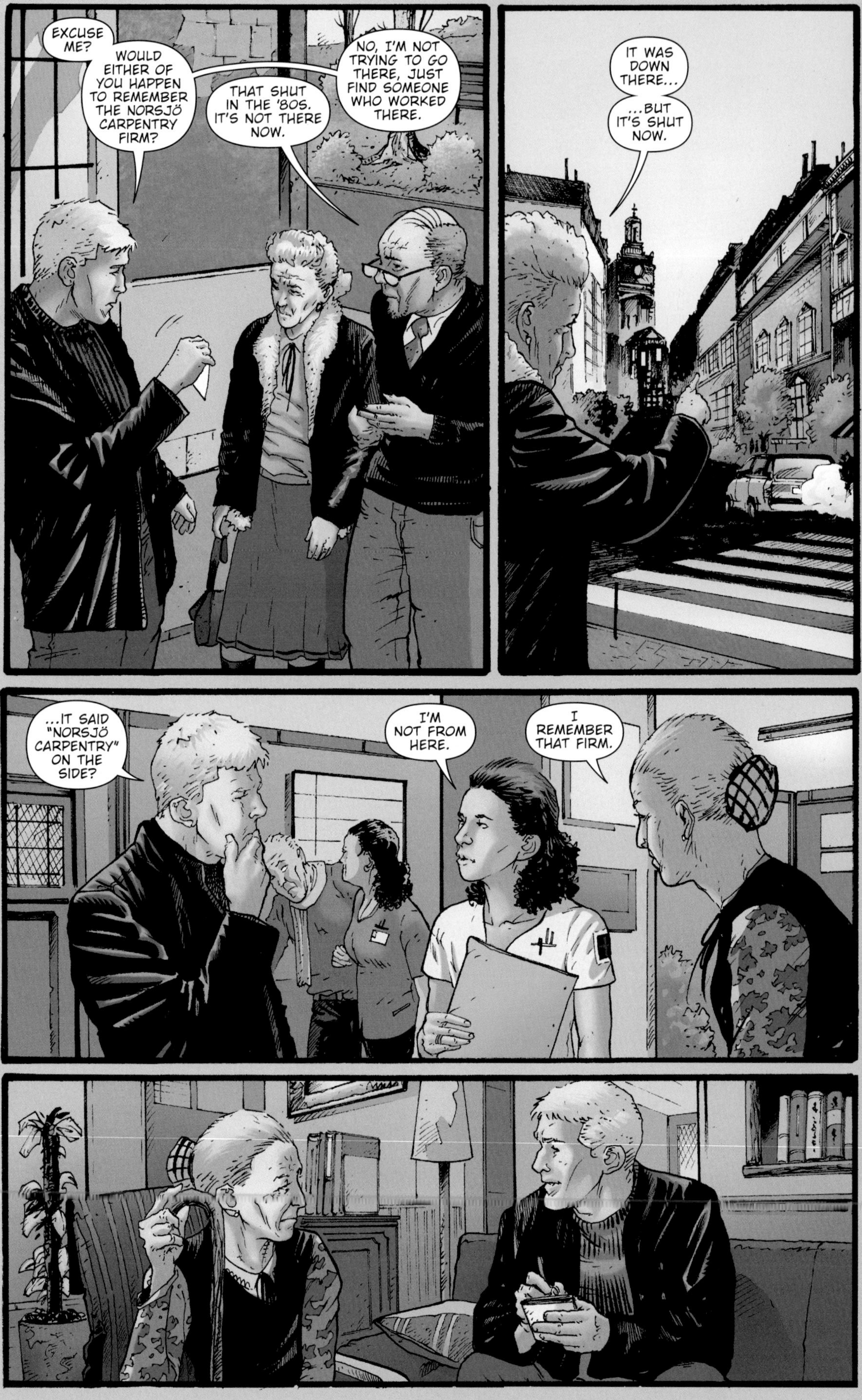
EXCUSE ME?
WOULD EITHER OF YOU HAPPEN TO REMEMBER THE NORSJÖ CARPENTRY FIRM?
THAT SHUT IN THE '80S. IT'S NOT THERE NOW.
NO, I'M NOT TRYING TO GO THERE, JUST FIND SOMEONE WHO WORKED THERE.
IT WAS DOWN THERE...
...BUT IT'S SHUT NOW.
...IT SAID "NORSJÖ CARPENTRY" ON THE SIDE?
I'M NOT FROM HERE.
I REMEMBER THAT FIRM.

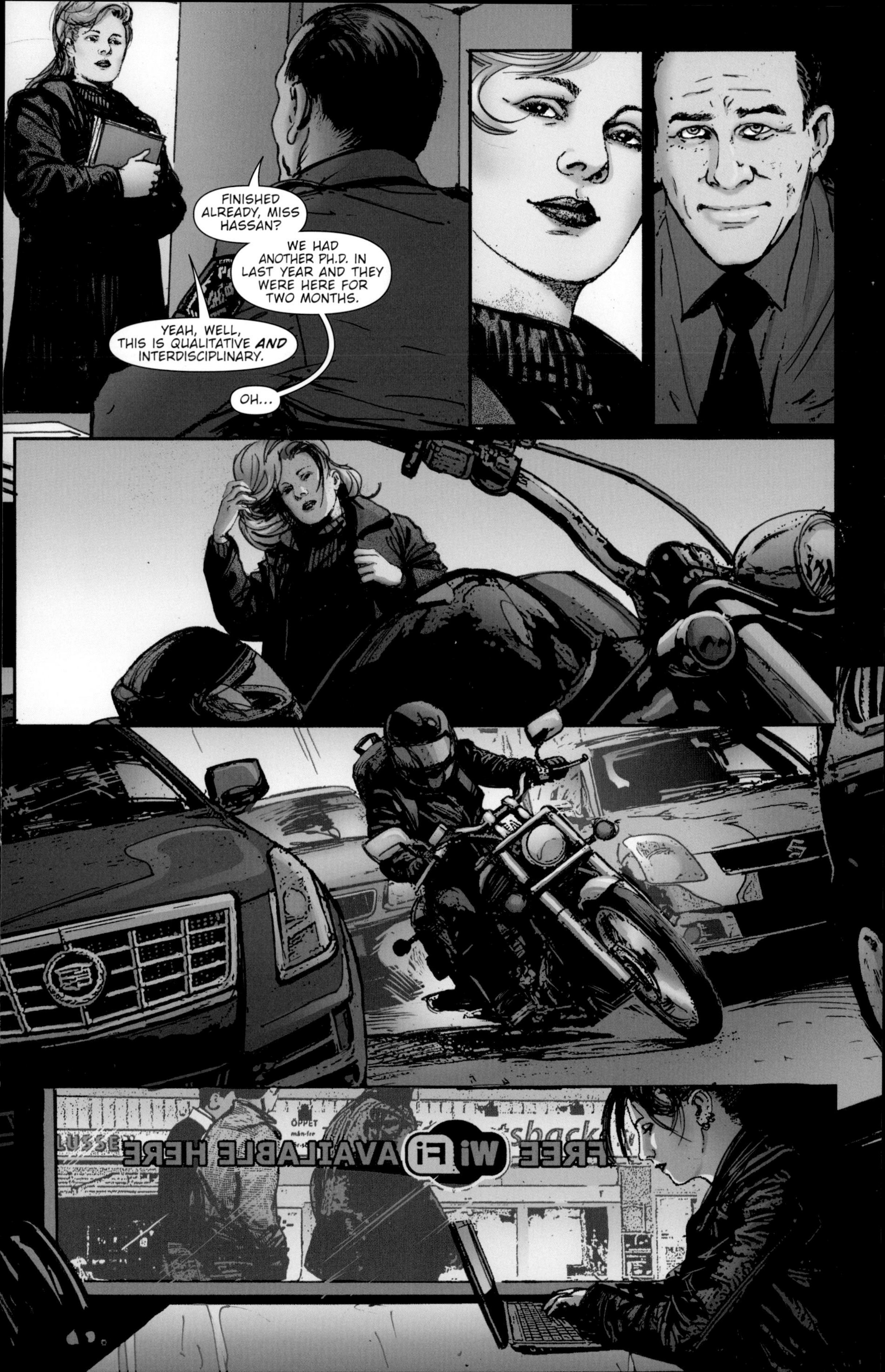
FINISHED ALREADY, MISS HASSAN?
WE HAD ANOTHER PH.D. IN LAST YEAR AND THEY WERE HERE FOR TWO MONTHS.
YEAH, WELL, THIS IS QUALITATIVE **AND** INTERDISCIPLINARY.
OH...
FREE WiFi AVAILABLE HERE
ÖPPET

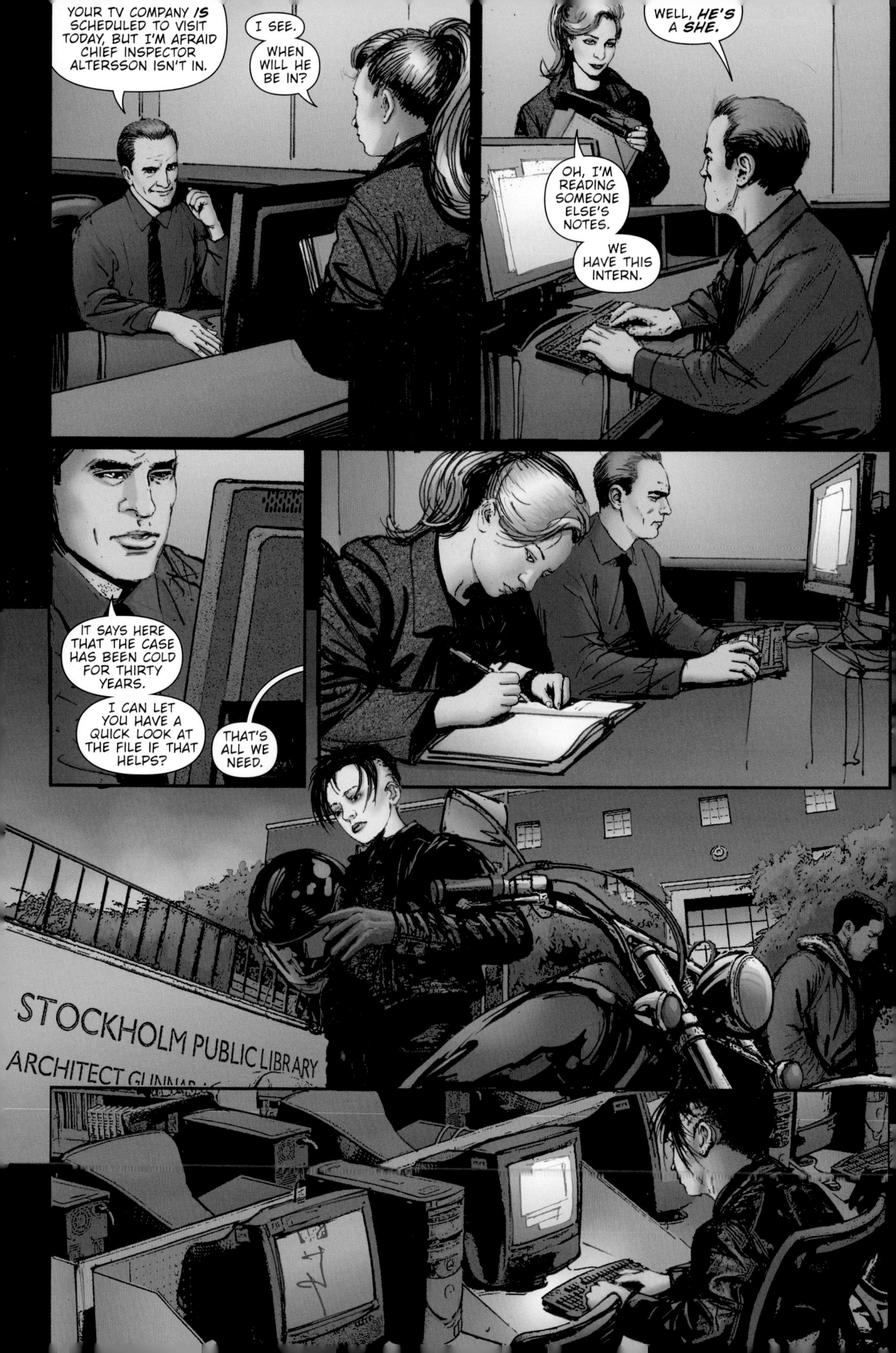
YOUR TV COMPANY *IS* SCHEDULED TO VISIT TODAY, BUT I'M AFRAID CHIEF INSPECTOR ALTERSSON ISN'T IN.
I SEE.
WHEN WILL HE BE IN?
WELL, *HE'S* A *SHE.*
OH, I'M READING SOMEONE ELSE'S NOTES.
WE HAVE THIS INTERN.
IT SAYS HERE THAT THE CASE HAS BEEN COLD FOR THIRTY YEARS.
I CAN LET YOU HAVE A QUICK LOOK AT THE FILE IF THAT HELPS?
THAT'S ALL WE NEED.
STOCKHOLM PUBLIC LIBRARY
ARCHITECT GUNNAR

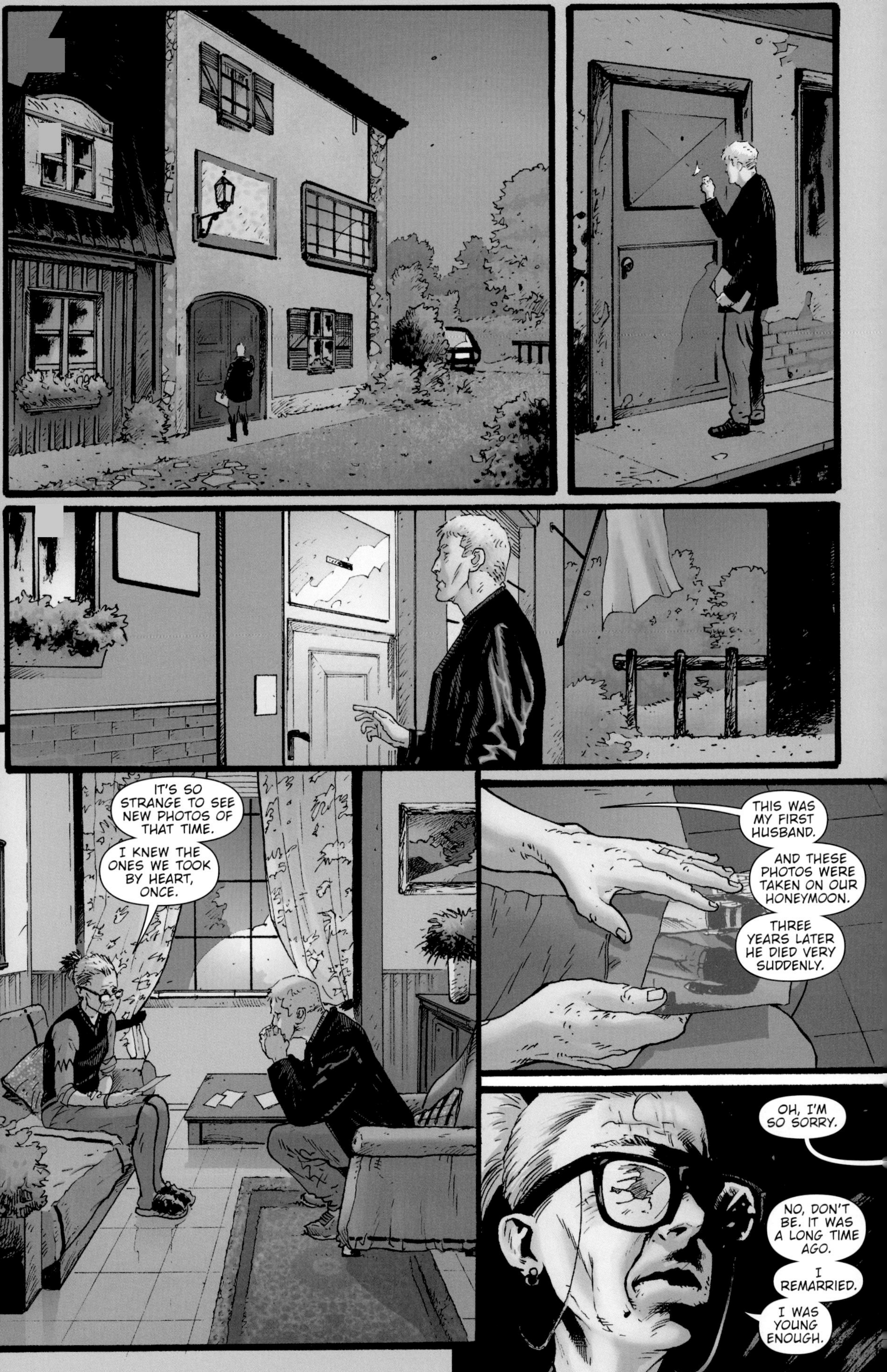
IT'S SO STRANGE TO SEE NEW PHOTOS OF THAT TIME.
I KNEW THE ONES WE TOOK BY HEART, ONCE.
THIS WAS MY FIRST HUSBAND.
AND THESE PHOTOS WERE TAKEN ON OUR HONEYMOON.
THREE YEARS LATER HE DIED VERY SUDDENLY.
OH, I'M SO SORRY.
NO, DON'T BE. IT WAS A LONG TIME AGO.
I REMARRIED.
I WAS YOUNG ENOUGH.

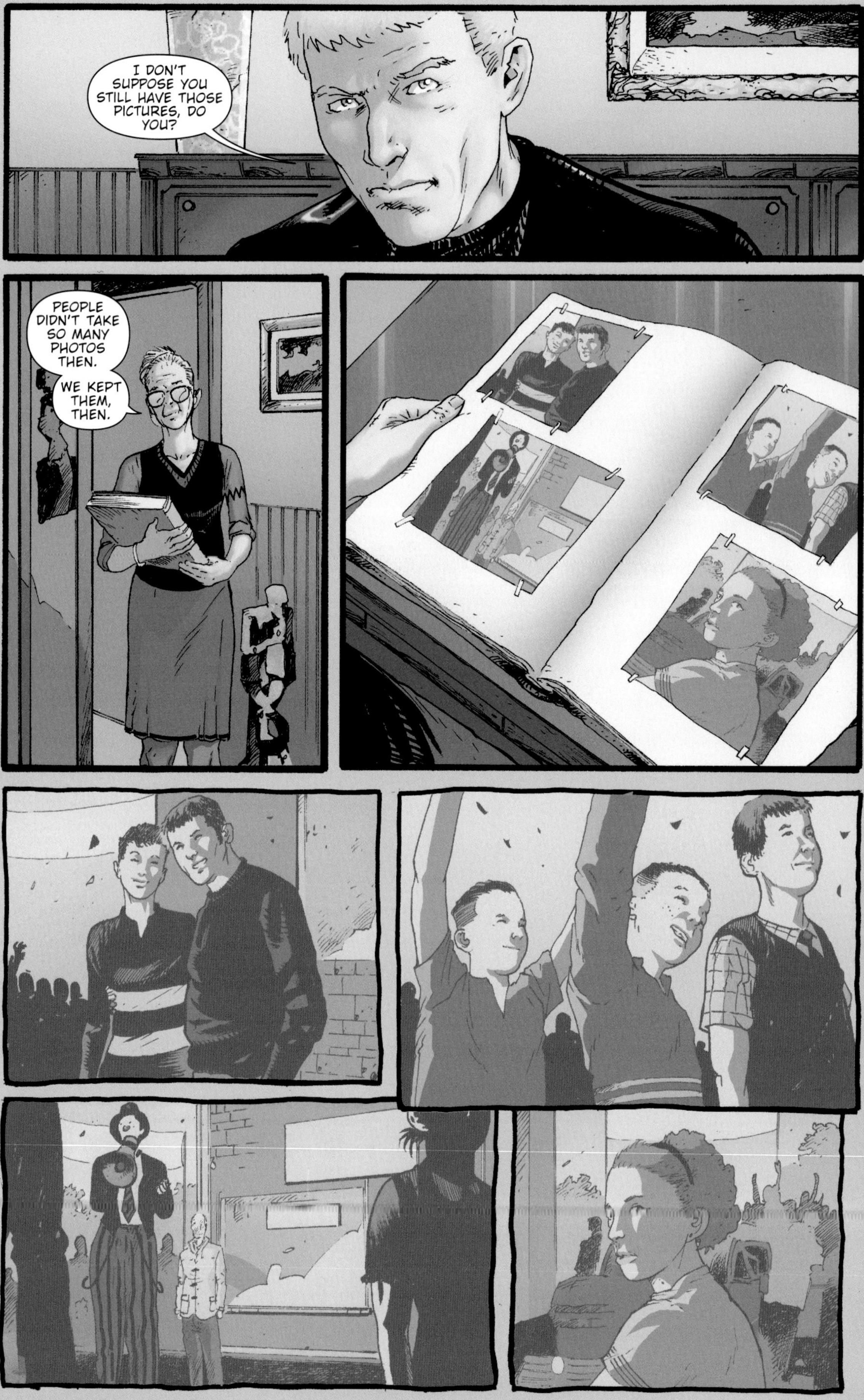
I DON'T SUPPOSE YOU STILL HAVE THOSE PICTURES, DO YOU?
PEOPLE DIDN'T TAKE SO MANY PHOTOS THEN.
WE KEPT THEM, THEN.

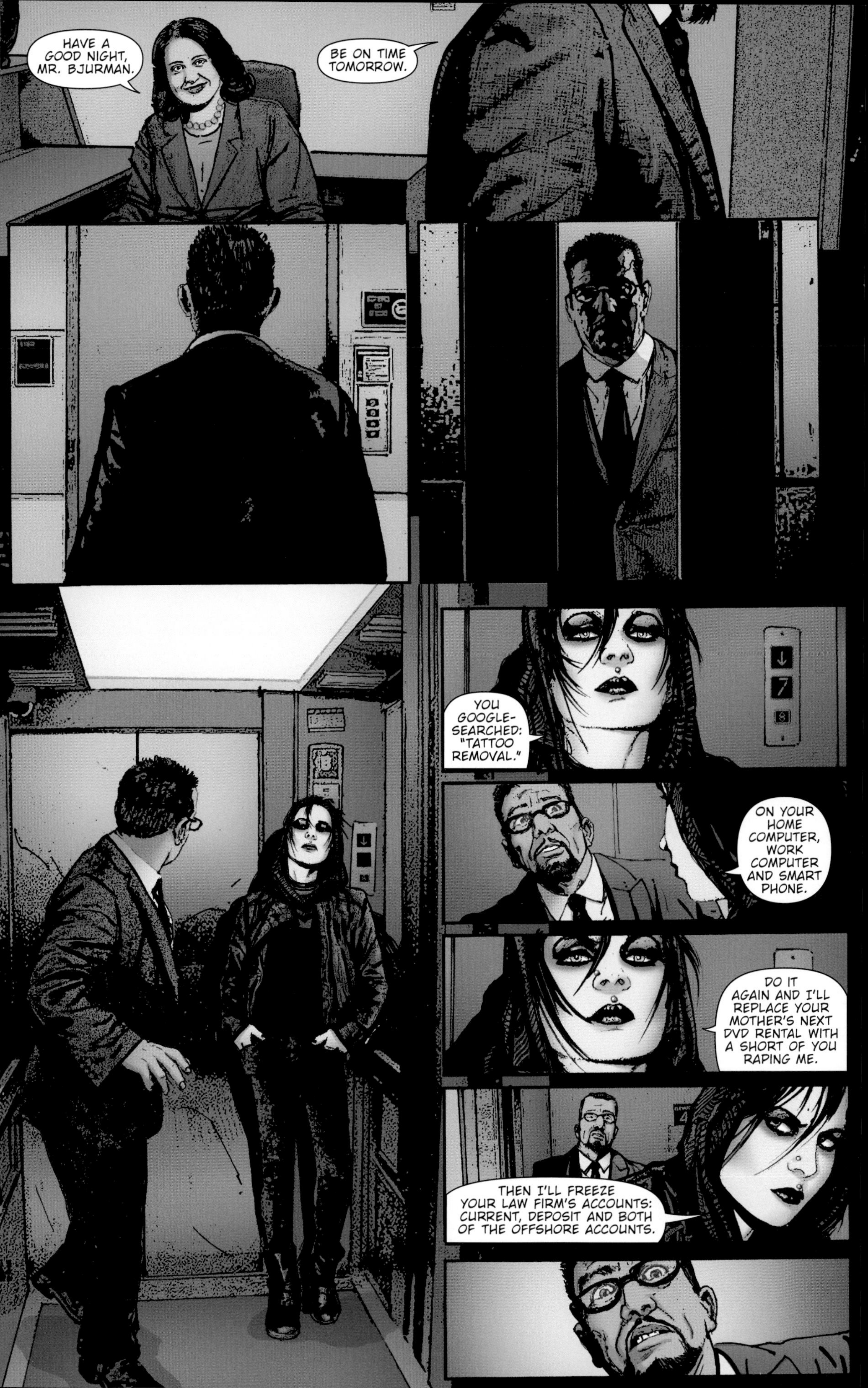
HAVE A GOOD NIGHT, MR. BJURMAN.
BE ON TIME TOMORROW.
YOU GOOGLE-SEARCHED: "TATTOO REMOVAL."
ON YOUR HOME COMPUTER, WORK COMPUTER AND SMART PHONE.
DO IT AGAIN AND I'LL REPLACE YOUR MOTHER'S NEXT DVD RENTAL WITH A SHORT OF YOU RAPING ME.
THEN I'LL FREEZE YOUR LAW FIRM'S ACCOUNTS: CURRENT, DEPOSIT AND BOTH OF THE OFFSHORE ACCOUNTS.

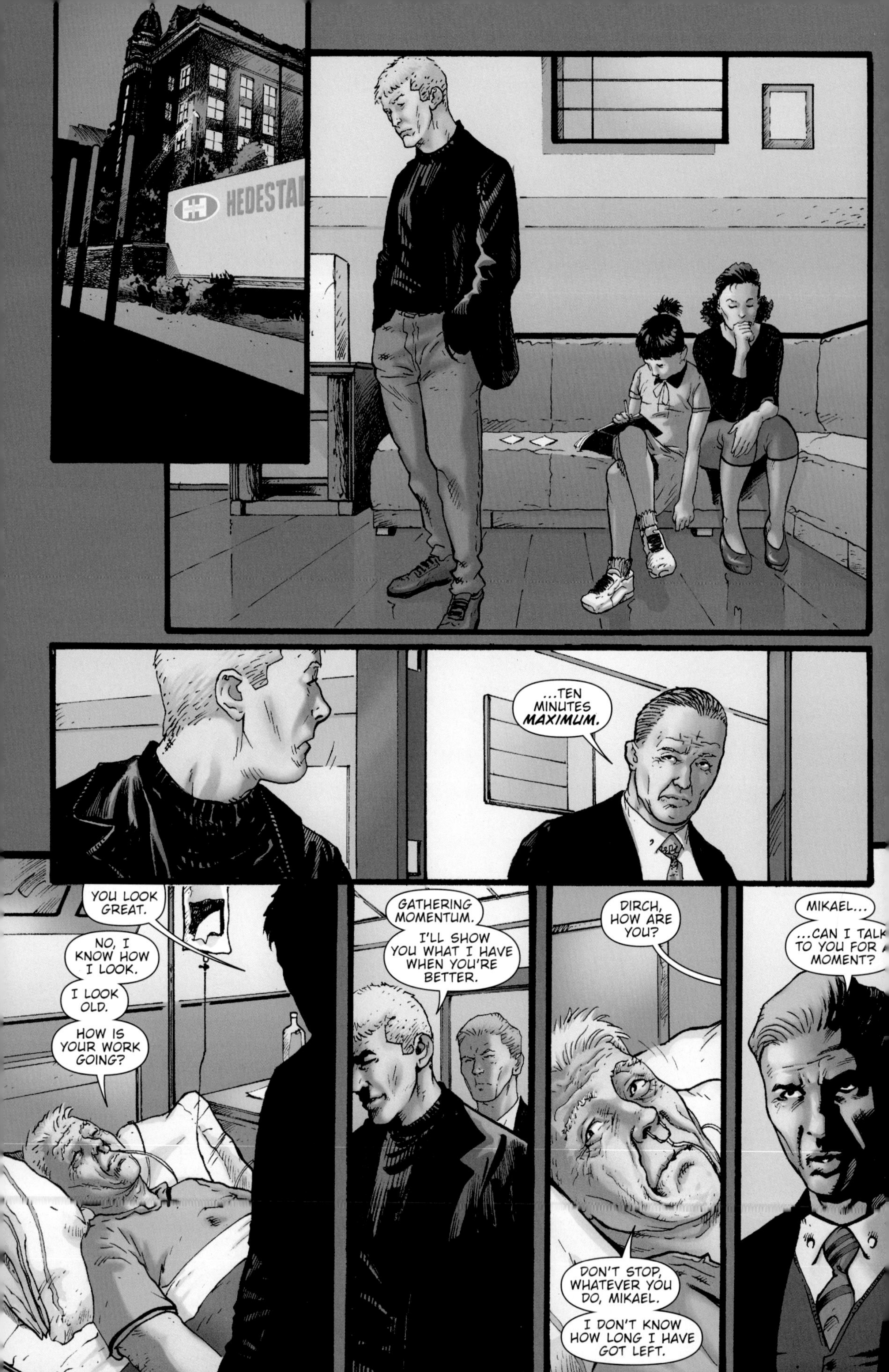
HEDESTAD
...TEN MINUTES MAXIMUM.
YOU LOOK GREAT.
NO, I KNOW HOW I LOOK.
I LOOK OLD.
HOW IS YOUR WORK GOING?
GATHERING MOMENTUM.
I'LL SHOW YOU WHAT I HAVE WHEN YOU'RE BETTER.
DIRCH, HOW ARE YOU?
DON'T STOP, WHATEVER YOU DO, MIKAEL.
I DON'T KNOW HOW LONG I HAVE GOT LEFT.
MIKAEL...
...CAN I TALK TO YOU FOR A MOMENT?

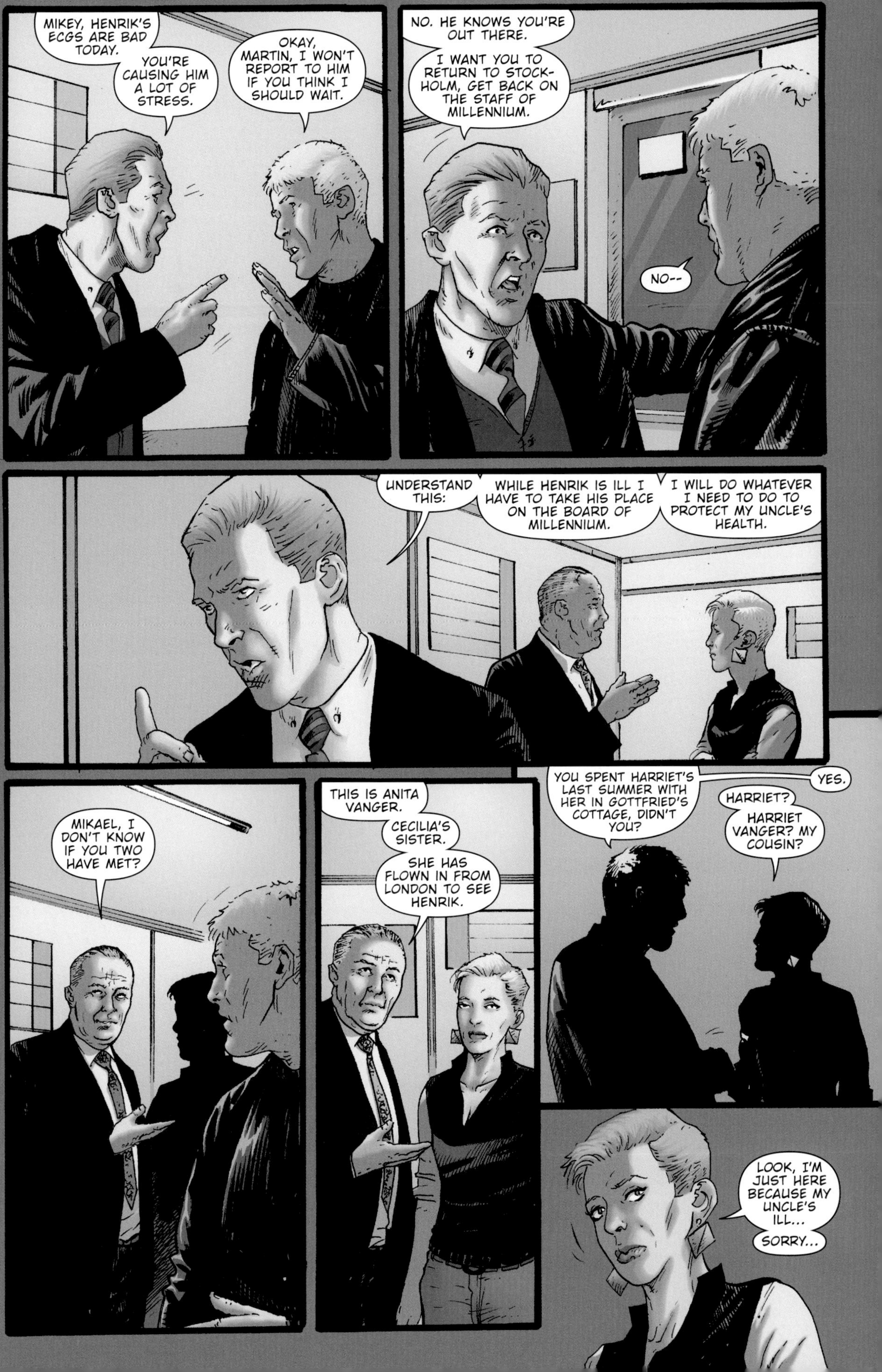
MIKEY, HENRIK'S ECGS ARE BAD TODAY.
YOU'RE CAUSING HIM A LOT OF STRESS.
OKAY, MARTIN, I WON'T REPORT TO HIM IF YOU THINK I SHOULD WAIT.
NO. HE KNOWS YOU'RE OUT THERE.
I WANT YOU TO RETURN TO STOCKHOLM, GET BACK ON THE STAFF OF MILLENNIUM.
NO--
UNDERSTAND THIS:
WHILE HENRIK IS ILL I HAVE TO TAKE HIS PLACE ON THE BOARD OF MILLENNIUM.
I WILL DO WHATEVER I NEED TO DO TO PROTECT MY UNCLE'S HEALTH.
MIKAEL, I DON'T KNOW IF YOU TWO HAVE MET?
THIS IS ANITA VANGER.
CECILIA'S SISTER.
SHE HAS FLOWN IN FROM LONDON TO SEE HENRIK.
YOU SPENT HARRIET'S LAST SUMMER WITH HER IN GOTTFRIED'S COTTAGE, DIDN'T YOU?
YES.
HARRIET?
HARRIET VANGER? MY COUSIN?
LOOK, I'M JUST HERE BECAUSE MY UNCLE'S ILL...
SORRY...

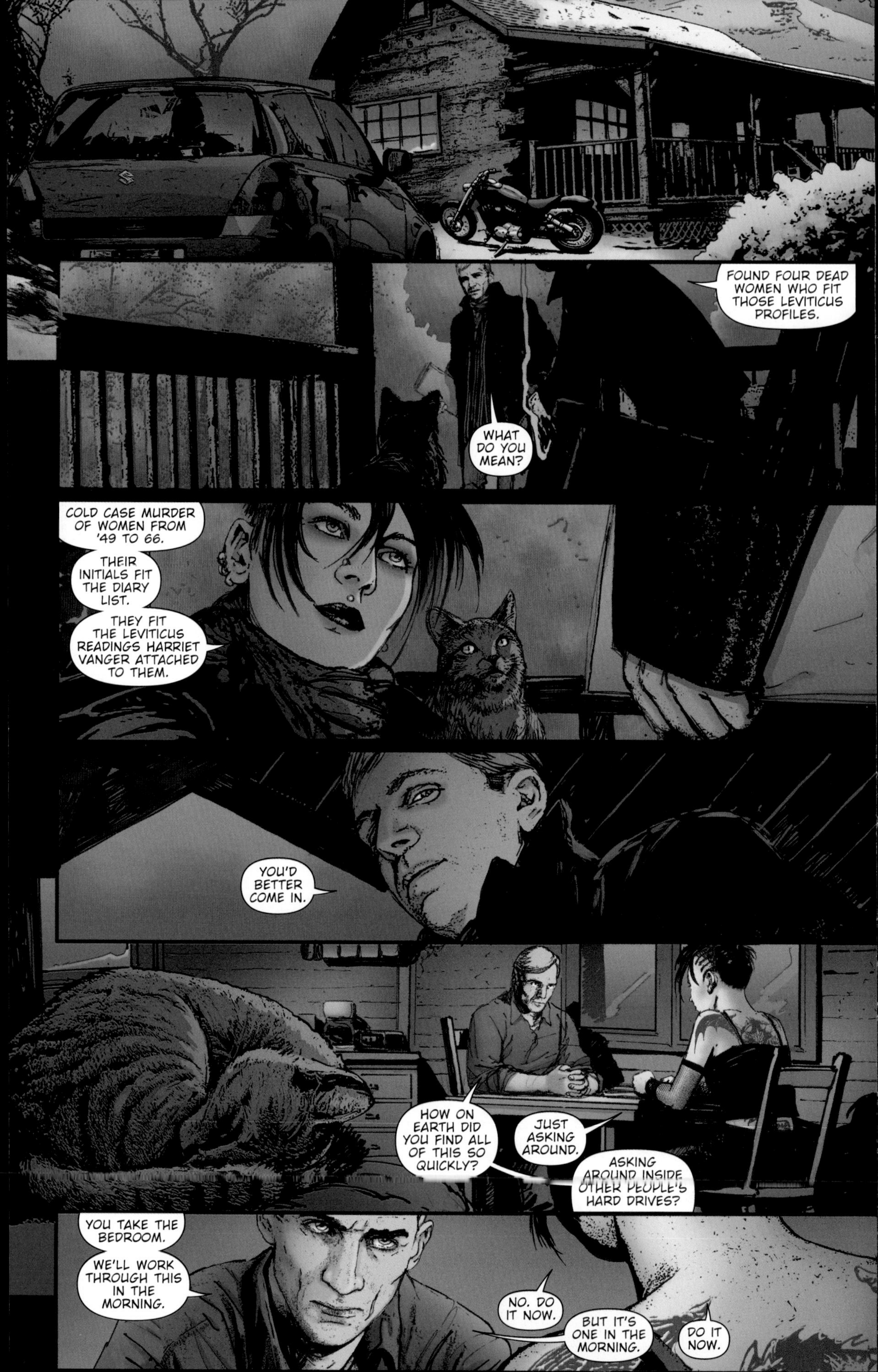

FOUND FOUR DEAD WOMEN WHO FIT THOSE LEVITICUS PROFILES.
WHAT DO YOU MEAN?
COLD CASE MURDER OF WOMEN FROM '49 TO 66.
THEIR INITIALS FIT THE DIARY LIST.
THEY FIT THE LEVITICUS READINGS HARRIET VANGER ATTACHED TO THEM.
YOU'D BETTER COME IN.
HOW ON EARTH DID YOU FIND ALL OF THIS SO QUICKLY?
JUST ASKING AROUND.
ASKING AROUND INSIDE OTHER PEOPLE'S HARD DRIVES?
YOU TAKE THE BEDROOM.
WE'LL WORK THROUGH THIS IN THE MORNING.
NO. DO IT NOW.
BUT IT'S ONE IN THE MORNING.
DO IT NOW.

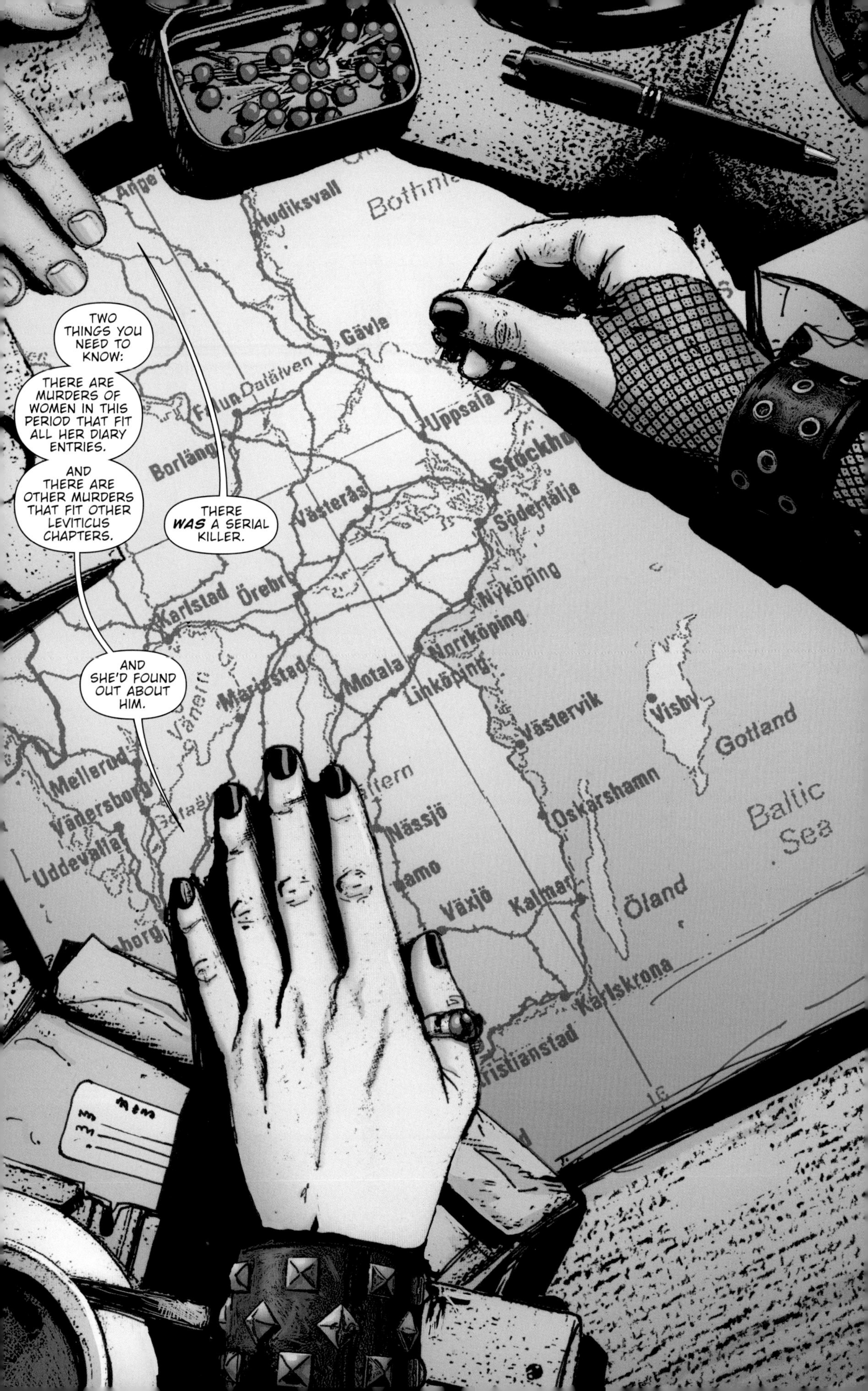
TWO THINGS YOU NEED TO KNOW:
THERE ARE MURDERS OF WOMEN IN THIS PERIOD THAT FIT ALL HER DIARY ENTRIES.
AND THERE ARE OTHER MURDERS THAT FIT OTHER LEVITICUS CHAPTERS.
THERE *WAS* A SERIAL KILLER.
AND SHE'D FOUND OUT ABOUT HIM.
Hudiksvall
Gävle
Dalälven
Falun
Uppsala
Västerås
Södertälje
Karlstad
Nyköping
Norrköping
Mariestad
Motala
Linköping
Mellerud
Vänersborg
Uddevalla
Nässjö
Västervik
Visby
Gotland
Oskarshamn
Baltic Sea
Växjö
Kalmar
Öland
Karlskrona

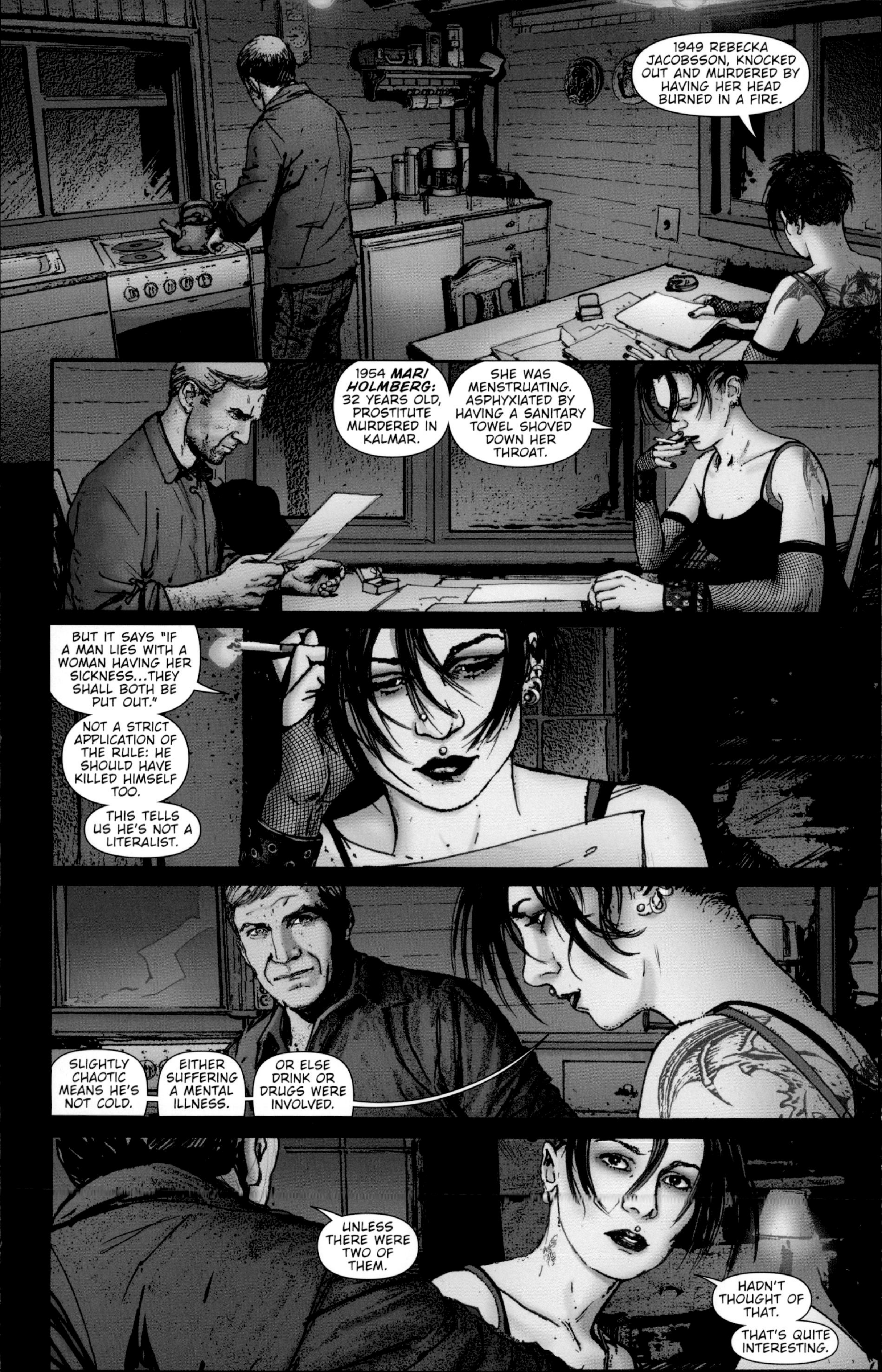
1949 REBECKA JACOBSSON, KNOCKED OUT AND MURDERED BY HAVING HER HEAD BURNED IN A FIRE.
1954 MARI HOLMBERG: 32 YEARS OLD, PROSTITUTE MURDERED IN KALMAR.
SHE WAS MENSTRUATING. ASPHYXIATED BY HAVING A SANITARY TOWEL SHOVED DOWN HER THROAT.
BUT IT SAYS "IF A MAN LIES WITH A WOMAN HAVING HER SICKNESS...THEY SHALL BOTH BE PUT OUT."
NOT A STRICT APPLICATION OF THE RULE: HE SHOULD HAVE KILLED HIMSELF TOO.
THIS TELLS US HE'S NOT A LITERALIST.
SLIGHTLY CHAOTIC MEANS HE'S NOT COLD.
EITHER SUFFERING A MENTAL ILLNESS.
OR ELSE DRINK OR DRUGS WERE INVOLVED.
UNLESS THERE WERE TWO OF THEM.
HADN'T THOUGHT OF THAT.
THAT'S QUITE INTERESTING.

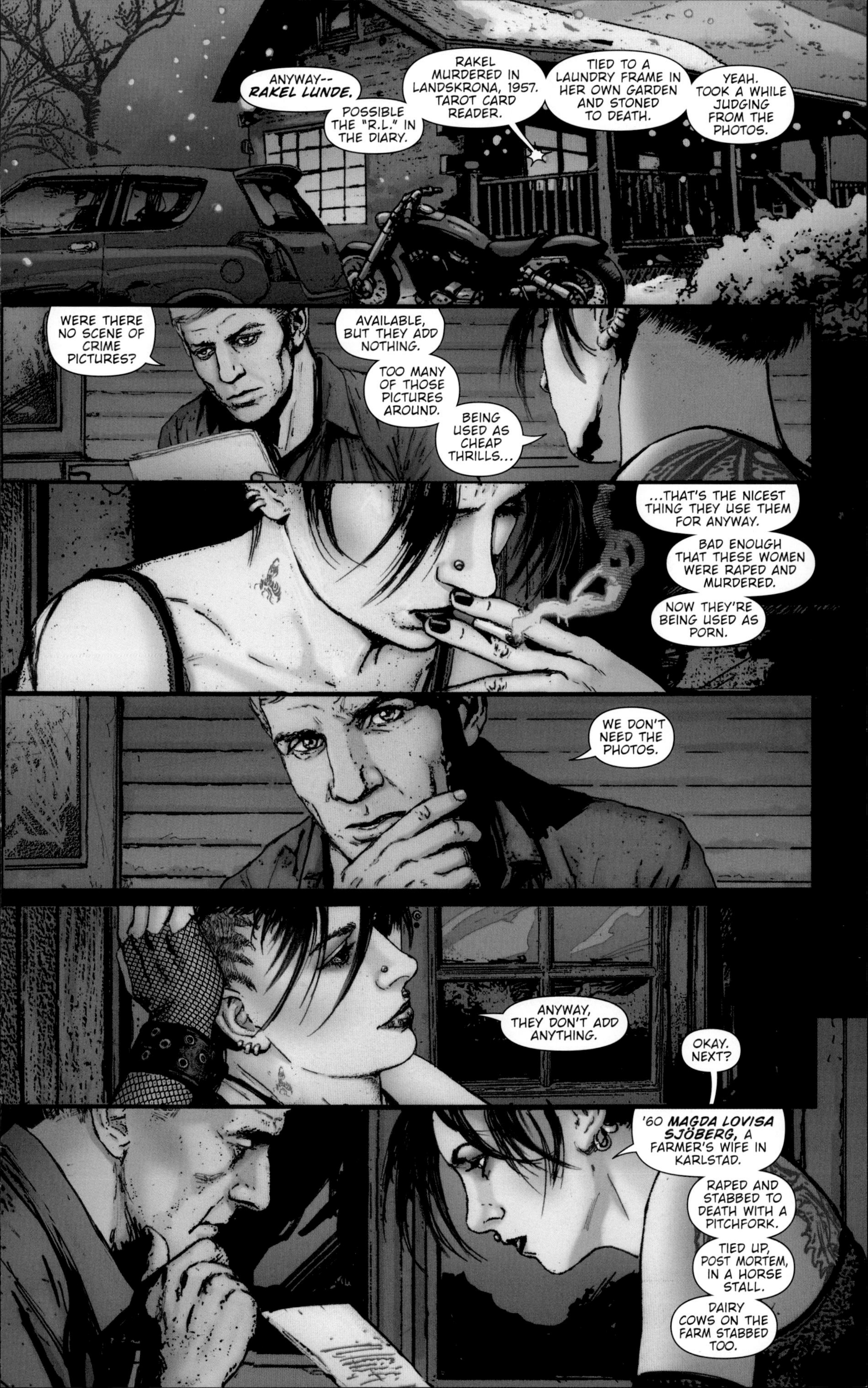
ANYWAY-- RAKEL LUNDE.
POSSIBLE THE "R.L." IN THE DIARY.
RAKEL MURDERED IN LANDSKRONA, 1957. TAROT CARD READER.
TIED TO A LAUNDRY FRAME IN HER OWN GARDEN AND STONED TO DEATH.
YEAH. TOOK A WHILE JUDGING FROM THE PHOTOS.
WERE THERE NO SCENE OF CRIME PICTURES?
AVAILABLE, BUT THEY ADD NOTHING.
TOO MANY OF THOSE PICTURES AROUND.
BEING USED AS CHEAP THRILLS...
...THAT'S THE NICEST THING THEY USE THEM FOR ANYWAY.
BAD ENOUGH THAT THESE WOMEN WERE RAPED AND MURDERED.
NOW THEY'RE BEING USED AS PORN.
WE DON'T NEED THE PHOTOS.
ANYWAY, THEY DON'T ADD ANYTHING.
OKAY. NEXT?
'60 MAGDA LOVISA SJÖBERG, A FARMER'S WIFE IN KARLSTAD.
RAPED AND STABBED TO DEATH WITH A PITCHFORK.
TIED UP, POST MORTEM, IN A HORSE STALL.
DAIRY COWS ON THE FARM STABBED TOO.

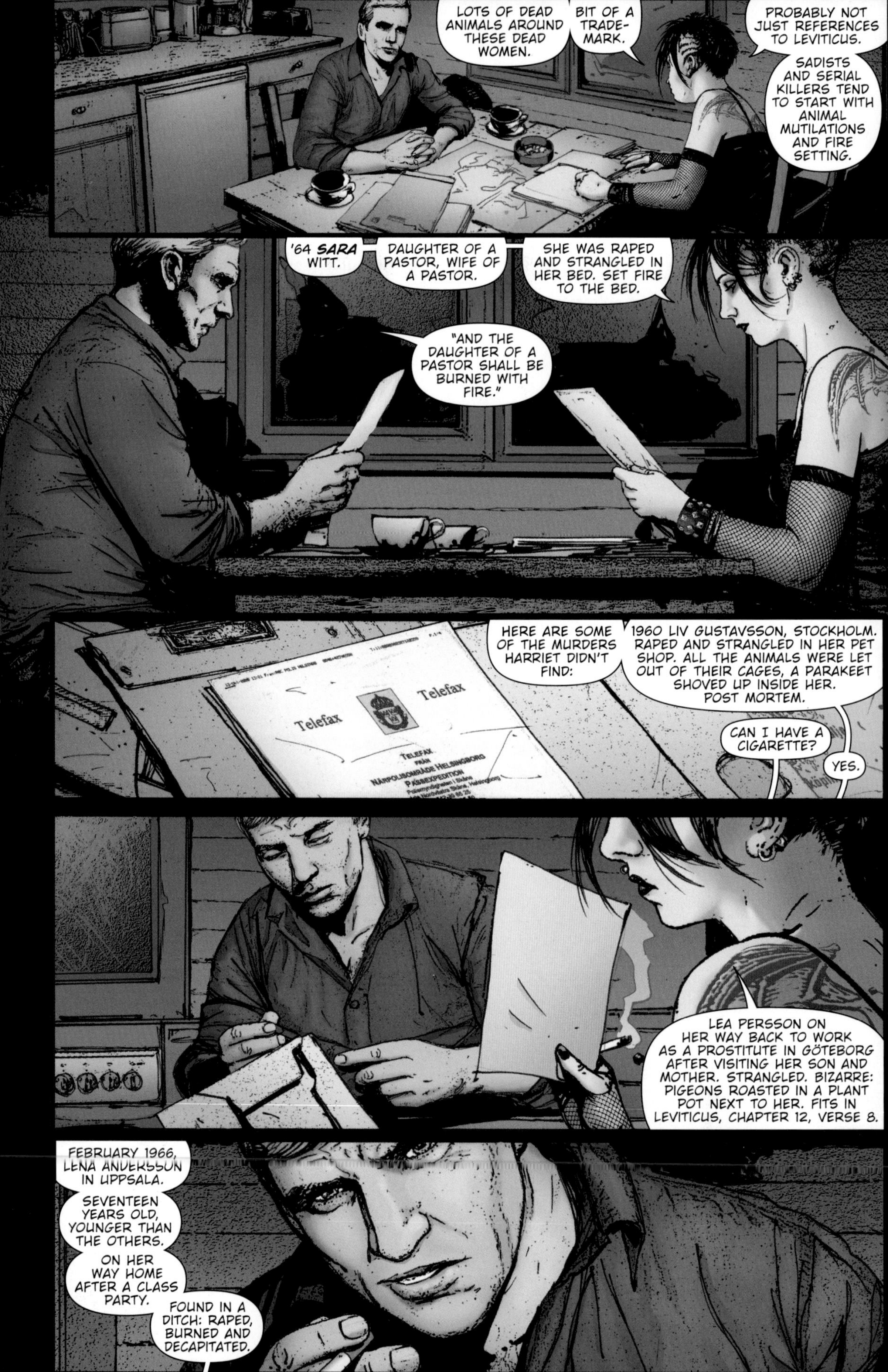
LOTS OF DEAD ANIMALS AROUND THESE DEAD WOMEN.
BIT OF A TRADE-MARK.
PROBABLY NOT JUST REFERENCES TO LEVITICUS.
SADISTS AND SERIAL KILLERS TEND TO START WITH ANIMAL MUTILATIONS AND FIRE SETTING.
'64 SARA WITT.
DAUGHTER OF A PASTOR, WIFE OF A PASTOR.
SHE WAS RAPED AND STRANGLED IN HER BED. SET FIRE TO THE BED.
"AND THE DAUGHTER OF A PASTOR SHALL BE BURNED WITH FIRE."
Telefax
Telefax
Telefax
HERE ARE SOME OF THE MURDERS HARRIET DIDN'T FIND:
1960 LIV GUSTAVSSON, STOCKHOLM. RAPED AND STRANGLED IN HER PET SHOP. ALL THE ANIMALS WERE LET OUT OF THEIR CAGES, A PARAKEET SHOVED UP INSIDE HER. POST MORTEM.
CAN I HAVE A CIGARETTE?
YES.
LEA PERSSON ON HER WAY BACK TO WORK AS A PROSTITUTE IN GÖTEBORG AFTER VISITING HER SON AND MOTHER. STRANGLED. BIZARRE: PIGEONS ROASTED IN A PLANT POT NEXT TO HER. FITS IN LEVITICUS, CHAPTER 12, VERSE 8.
FEBRUARY 1966, LENA ANDERSSON IN UPPSALA.
SEVENTEEN YEARS OLD, YOUNGER THAN THE OTHERS.
ON HER WAY HOME AFTER A CLASS PARTY.
FOUND IN A DITCH: RAPED, BURNED AND DECAPITATED.

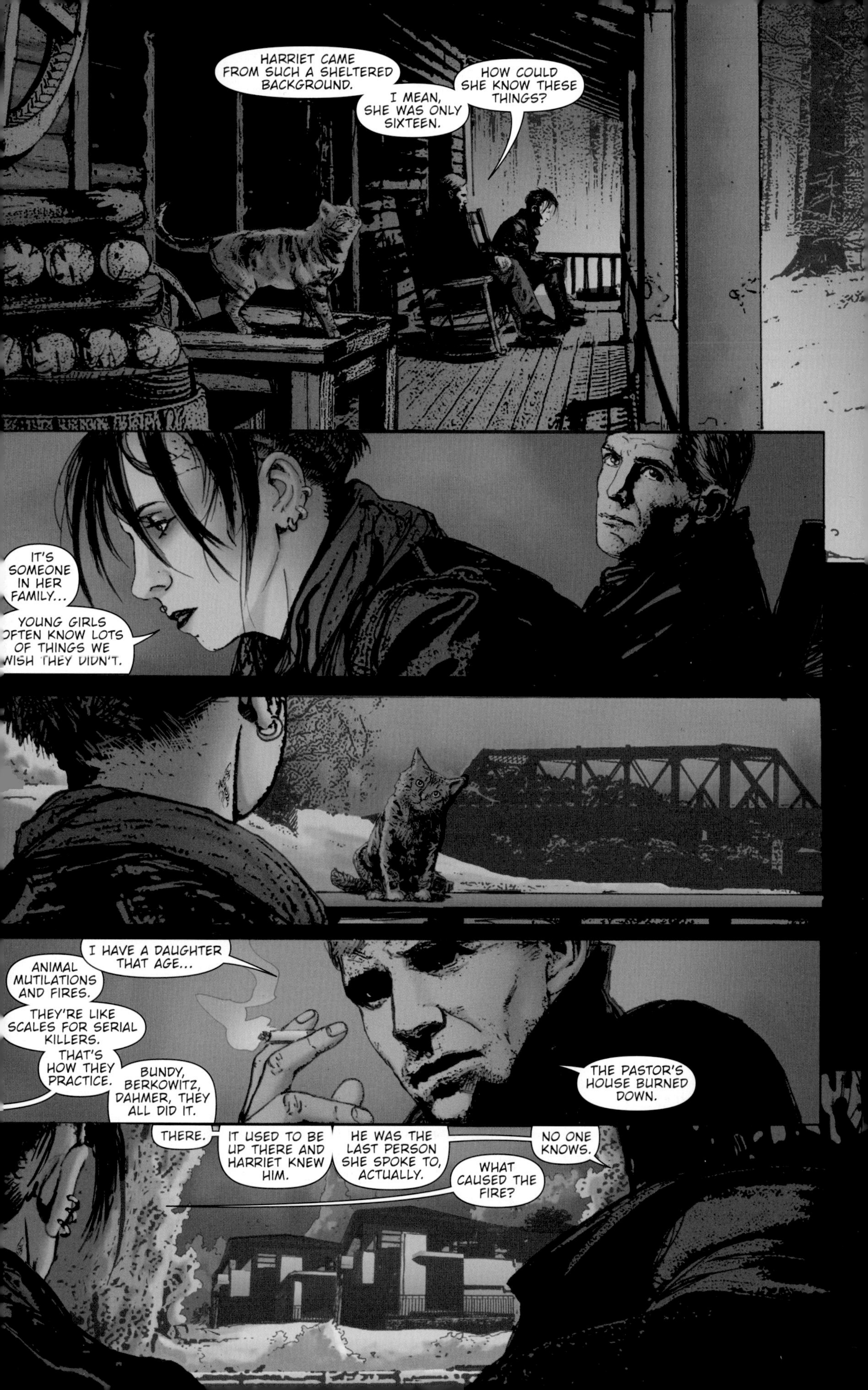
HARRIET CAME FROM SUCH A SHELTERED BACKGROUND.
I MEAN, SHE WAS ONLY SIXTEEN.
HOW COULD SHE KNOW THESE THINGS?
IT'S SOMEONE IN HER FAMILY...
YOUNG GIRLS OFTEN KNOW LOTS OF THINGS WE WISH THEY DIDN'T.
I HAVE A DAUGHTER THAT AGE...
ANIMAL MUTILATIONS AND FIRES.
THEY'RE LIKE SCALES FOR SERIAL KILLERS.
THAT'S HOW THEY PRACTICE.
BUNDY, BERKOWITZ, DAHMER, THEY ALL DID IT.
THE PASTOR'S HOUSE BURNED DOWN.
THERE.
IT USED TO BE UP THERE AND HARRIET KNEW HIM.
HE WAS THE LAST PERSON SHE SPOKE TO, ACTUALLY.
WHAT CAUSED THE FIRE?
NO ONE KNOWS.

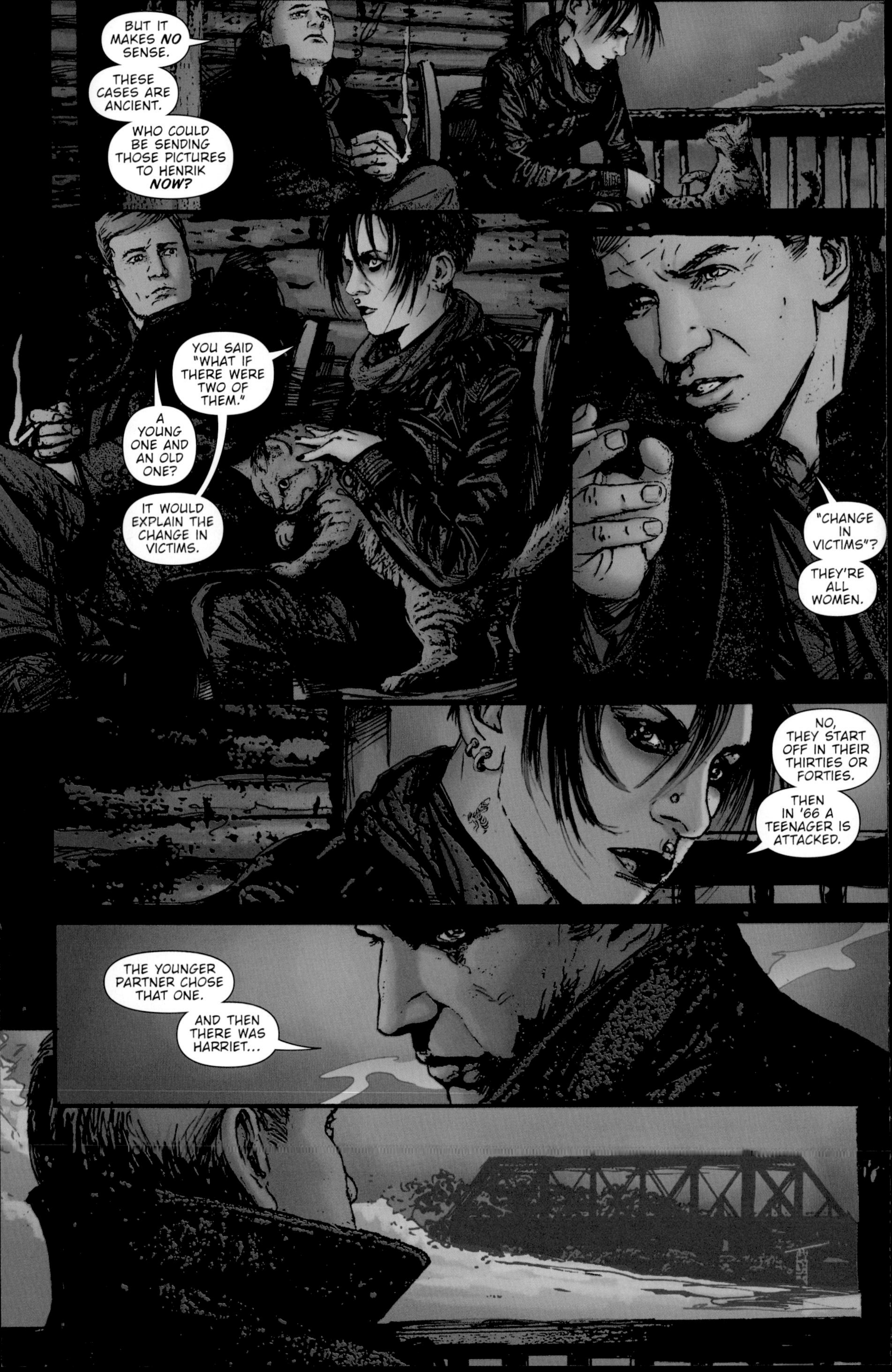
BUT IT MAKES NO SENSE.
THESE CASES ARE ANCIENT.
WHO COULD BE SENDING THOSE PICTURES TO HENRIK NOW?
YOU SAID "WHAT IF THERE WERE TWO OF THEM."
A YOUNG ONE AND AN OLD ONE?
IT WOULD EXPLAIN THE CHANGE IN VICTIMS.
"CHANGE IN VICTIMS"?
THEY'RE ALL WOMEN.
NO, THEY START OFF IN THEIR THIRTIES OR FORTIES.
THEN IN '66 A TEENAGER IS ATTACKED.
THE YOUNGER PARTNER CHOSE THAT ONE.
AND THEN THERE WAS HARRIET...

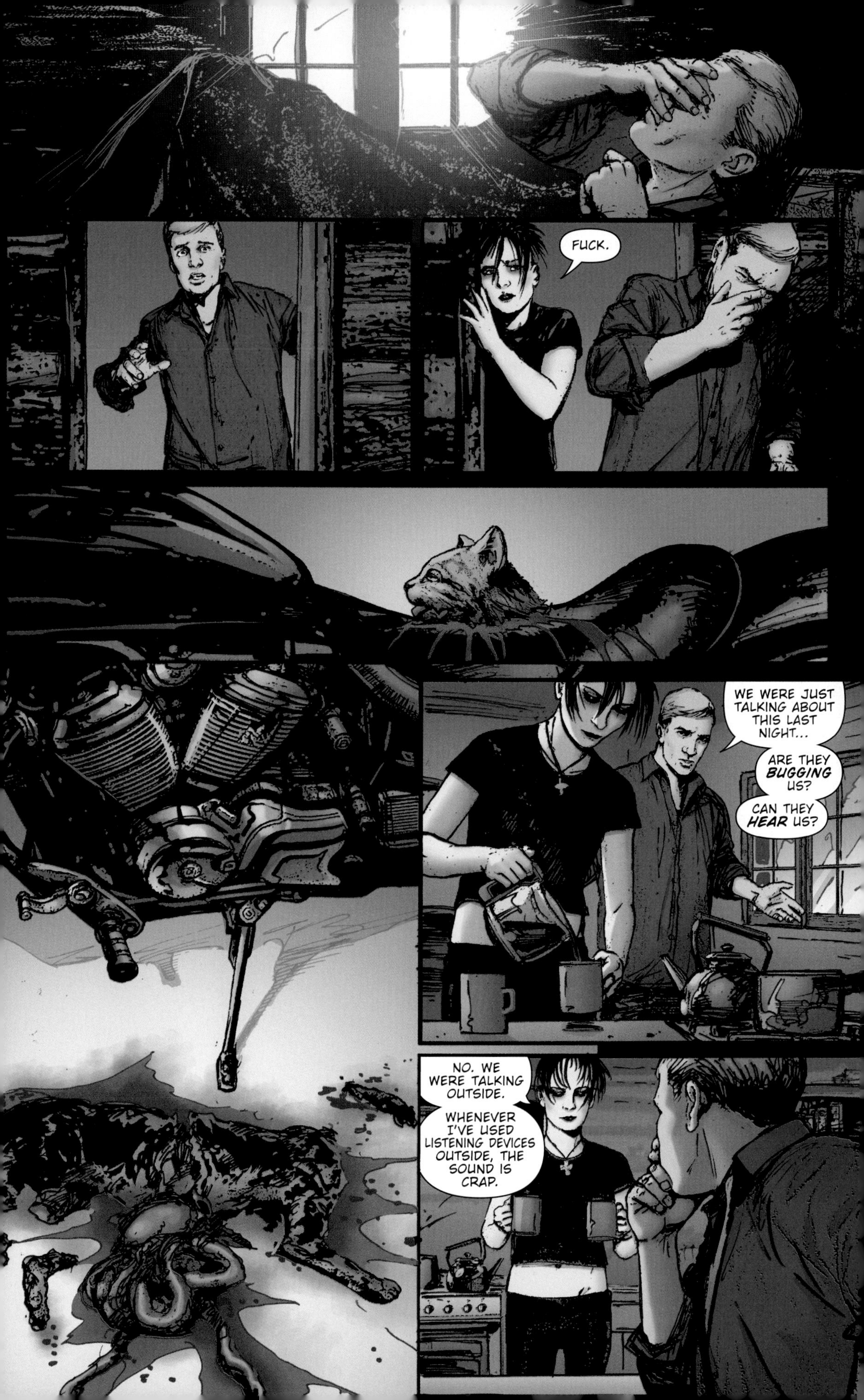
FUCK.
WE WERE JUST TALKING ABOUT THIS LAST NIGHT...
ARE THEY *BUGGING* US?
CAN THEY *HEAR* US?
NO. WE WERE TALKING OUTSIDE.
WHENEVER I'VE USED LISTENING DEVICES OUTSIDE, THE SOUND IS CRAP.

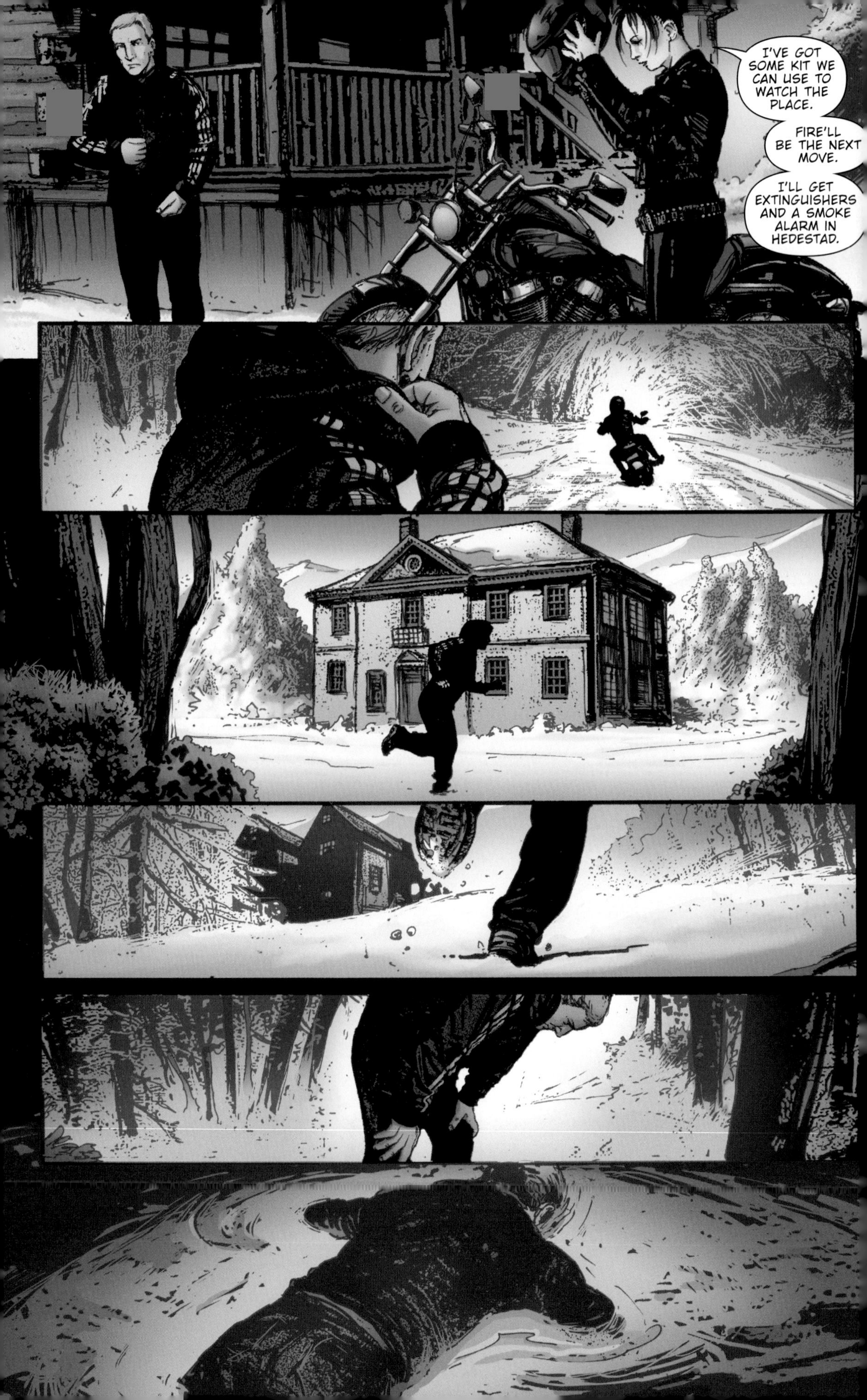
I'VE GOT SOME KIT WE CAN USE TO WATCH THE PLACE.
FIRE'LL BE THE NEXT MOVE.
I'LL GET EXTINGUISHERS AND A SMOKE ALARM IN HEDESTAD.

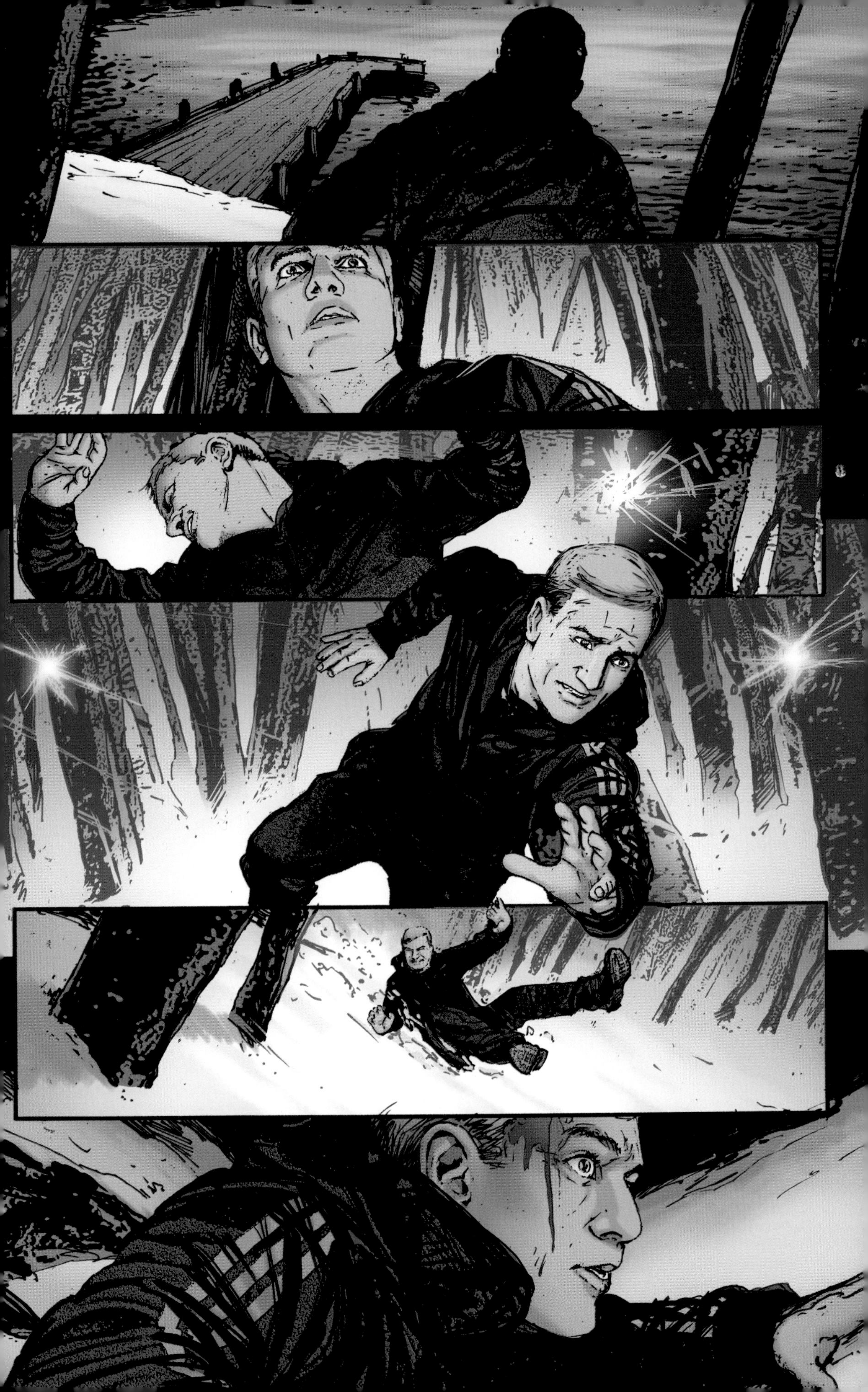

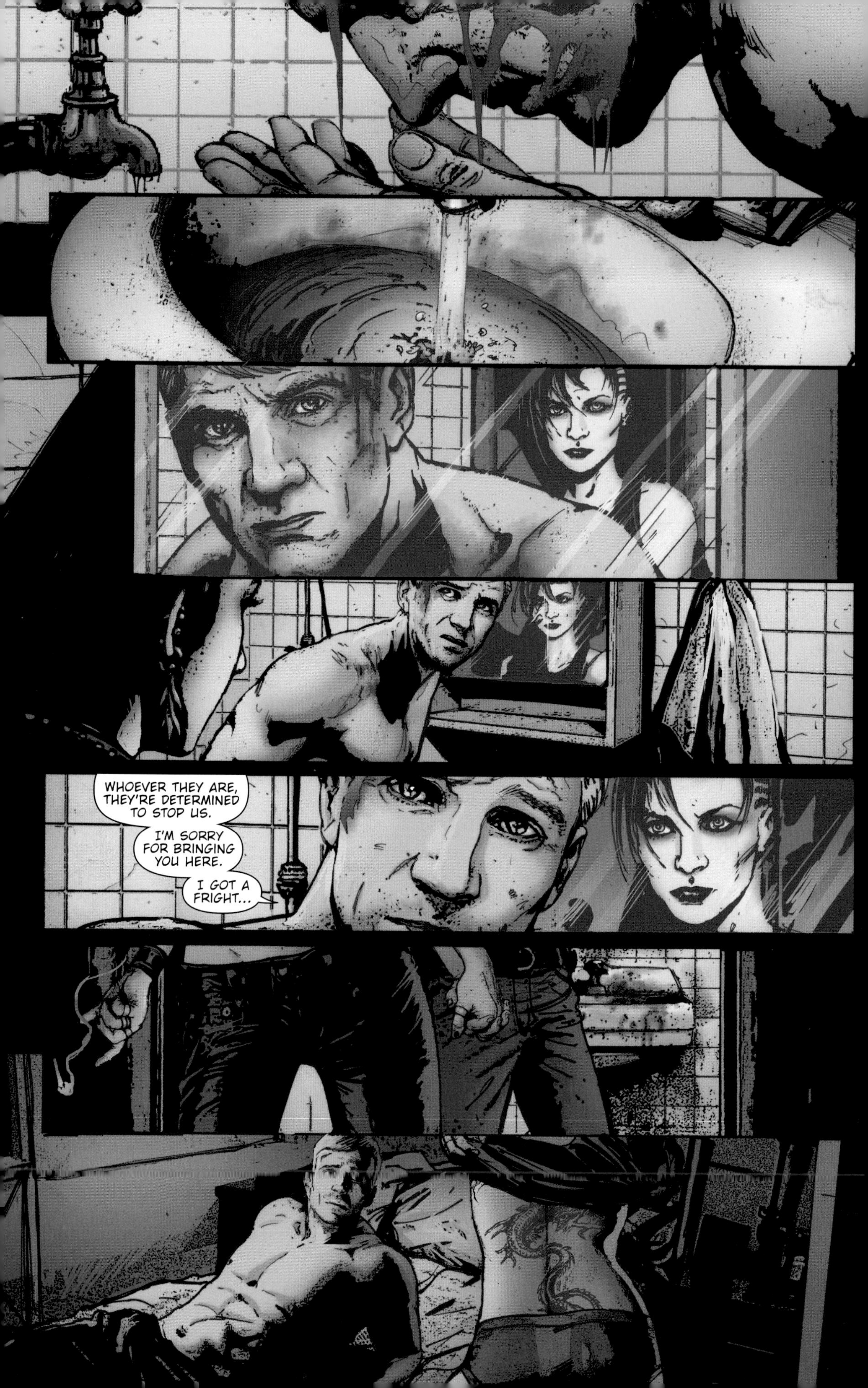
WHOEVER THEY ARE, THEY'RE DETERMINED TO STOP US.
I'M SORRY FOR BRINGING YOU HERE.
I GOT A FRIGHT...

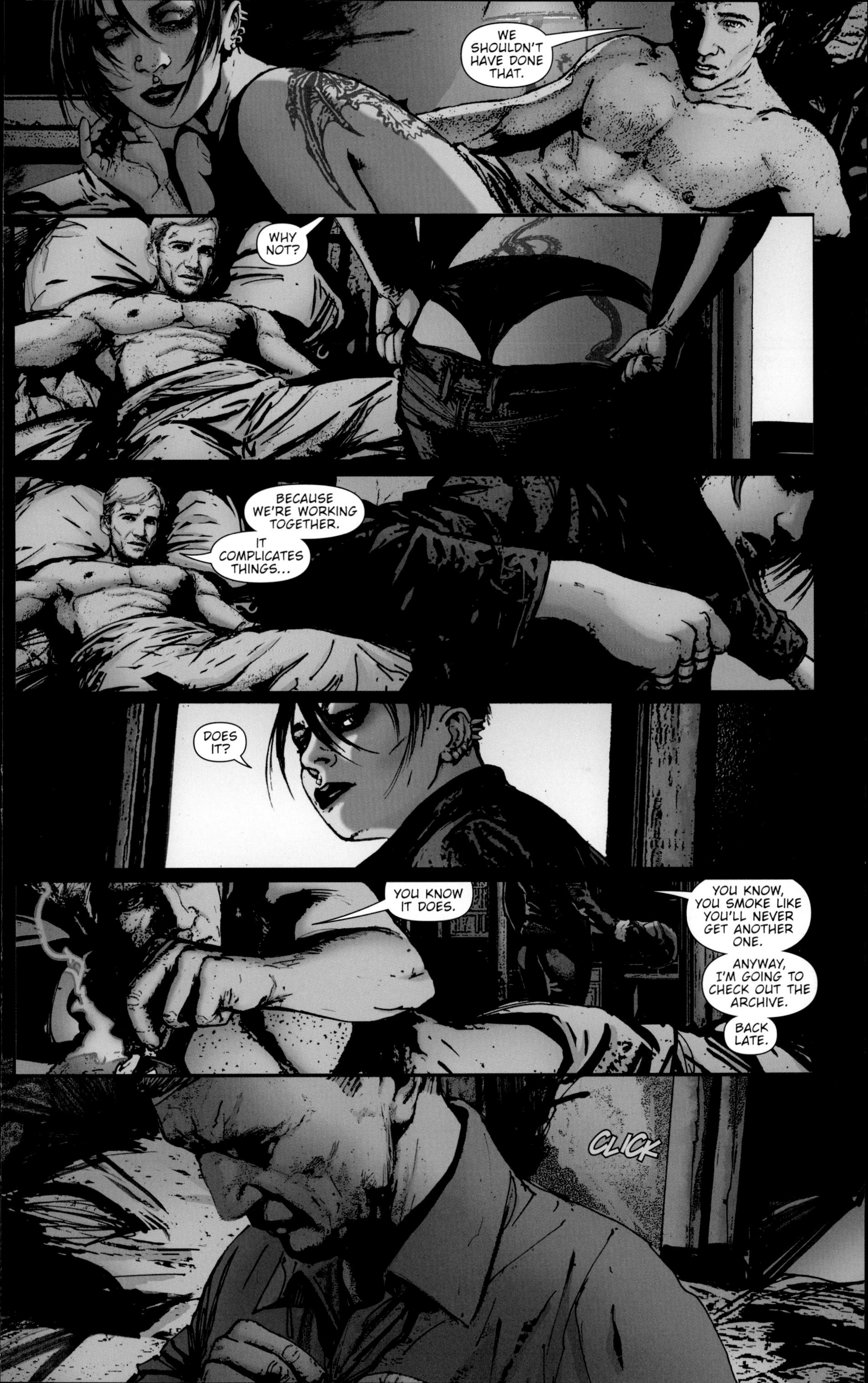
WE SHOULDN'T HAVE DONE THAT.
WHY NOT?
BECAUSE WE'RE WORKING TOGETHER.
IT COMPLICATES THINGS...
DOES IT?
YOU KNOW IT DOES.
YOU KNOW, YOU SMOKE LIKE YOU'LL NEVER GET ANOTHER ONE.
ANYWAY, I'M GOING TO CHECK OUT THE ARCHIVE.
BACK LATE.
CLICK

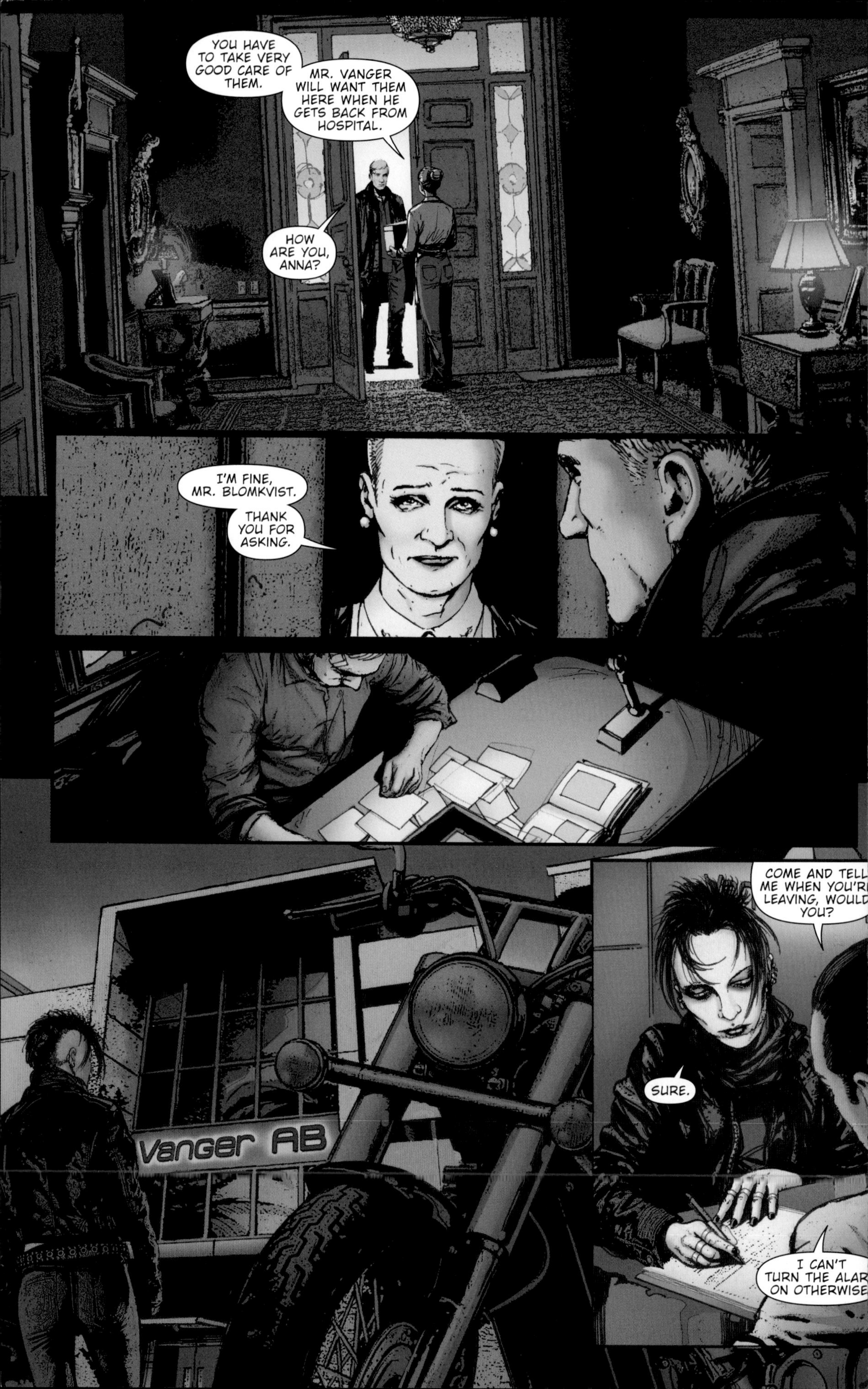
YOU HAVE TO TAKE VERY GOOD CARE OF THEM.
MR. VANGER WILL WANT THEM HERE WHEN HE GETS BACK FROM HOSPITAL.
HOW ARE YOU, ANNA?
I'M FINE, MR. BLOMKVIST.
THANK YOU FOR ASKING.
Vanger AB
COME AND TELL ME WHEN YOU'RE LEAVING, WOULD YOU?
SURE.
I CAN'T TURN THE ALAR ON OTHERWISE

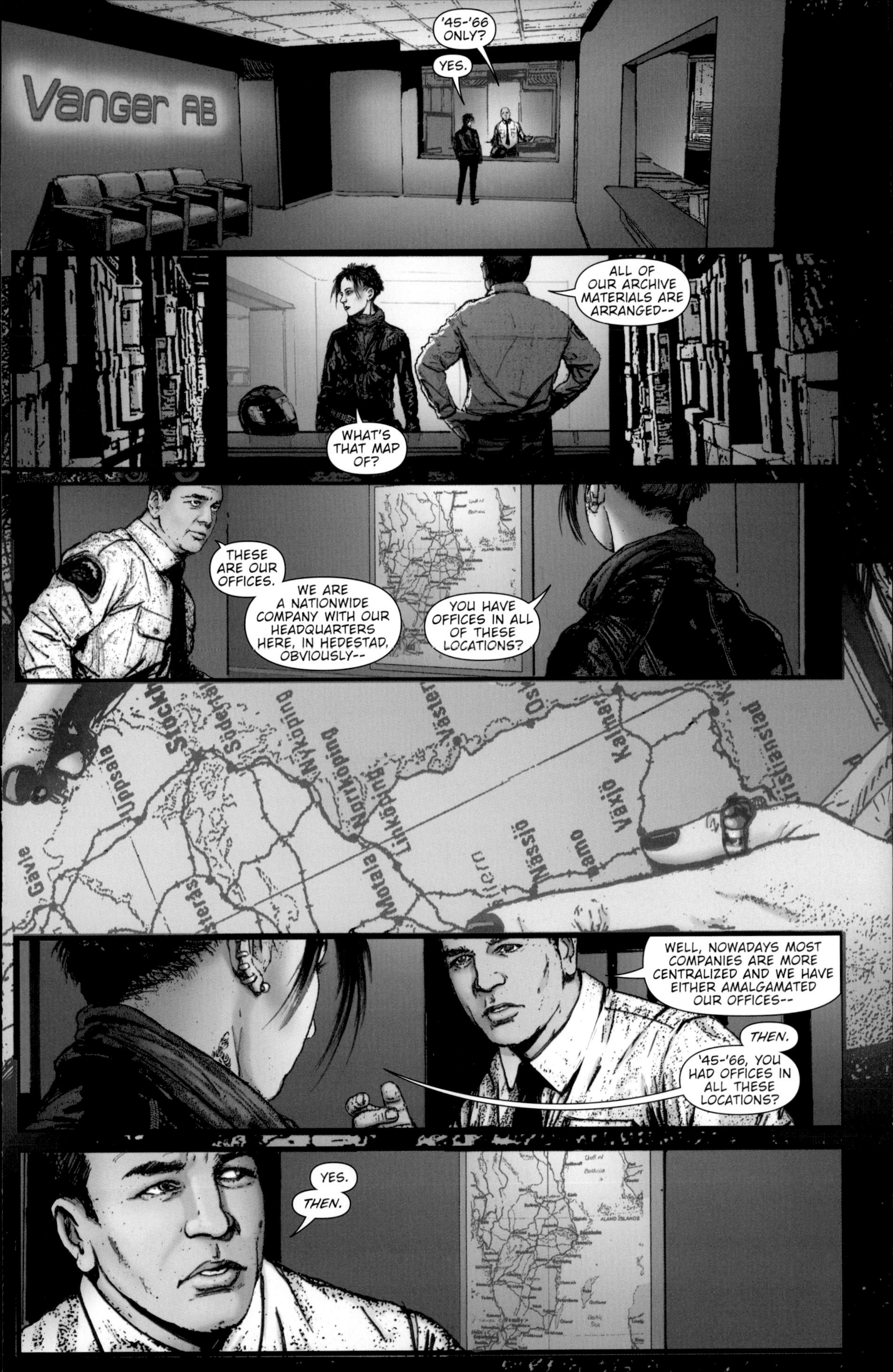
Vanger AB
'45-'66 ONLY?
YES.
ALL OF OUR ARCHIVE MATERIALS ARE ARRANGED--
WHAT'S THAT MAP OF?
THESE ARE OUR OFFICES.
WE ARE A NATIONWIDE COMPANY WITH OUR HEADQUARTERS HERE, IN HEDESTAD, OBVIOUSLY--
YOU HAVE OFFICES IN ALL OF THESE LOCATIONS?
Uppsala
Nyköping
Norrköping
Linköping
Motala
Gävle
Nässjö
Växjö
Kalmar
WELL, NOWADAYS MOST COMPANIES ARE MORE CENTRALIZED AND WE HAVE EITHER AMALGAMATED OUR OFFICES--
THEN.
'45-'66, YOU HAD OFFICES IN ALL THESE LOCATIONS?
YES.
THEN.

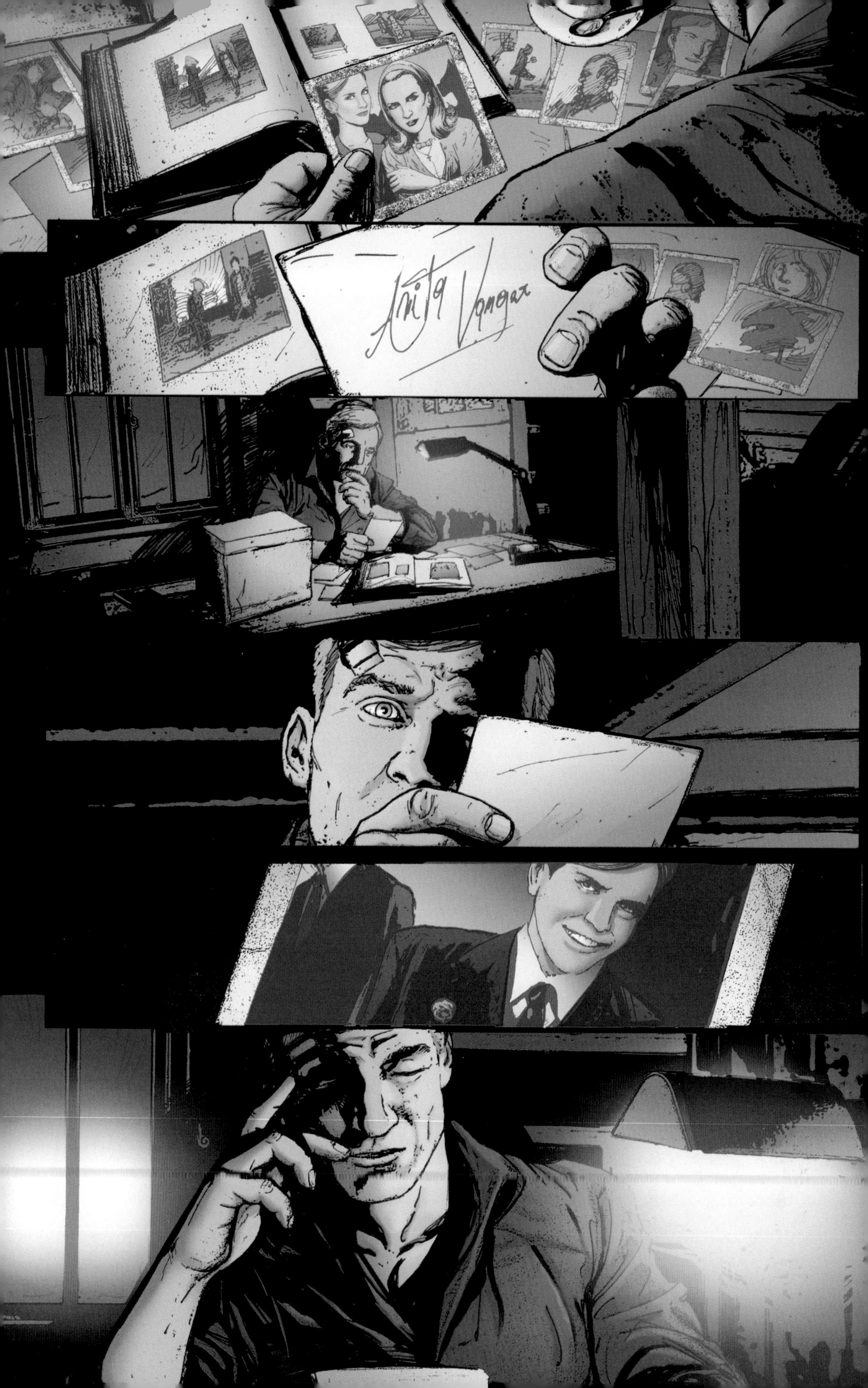
Anita Vanger

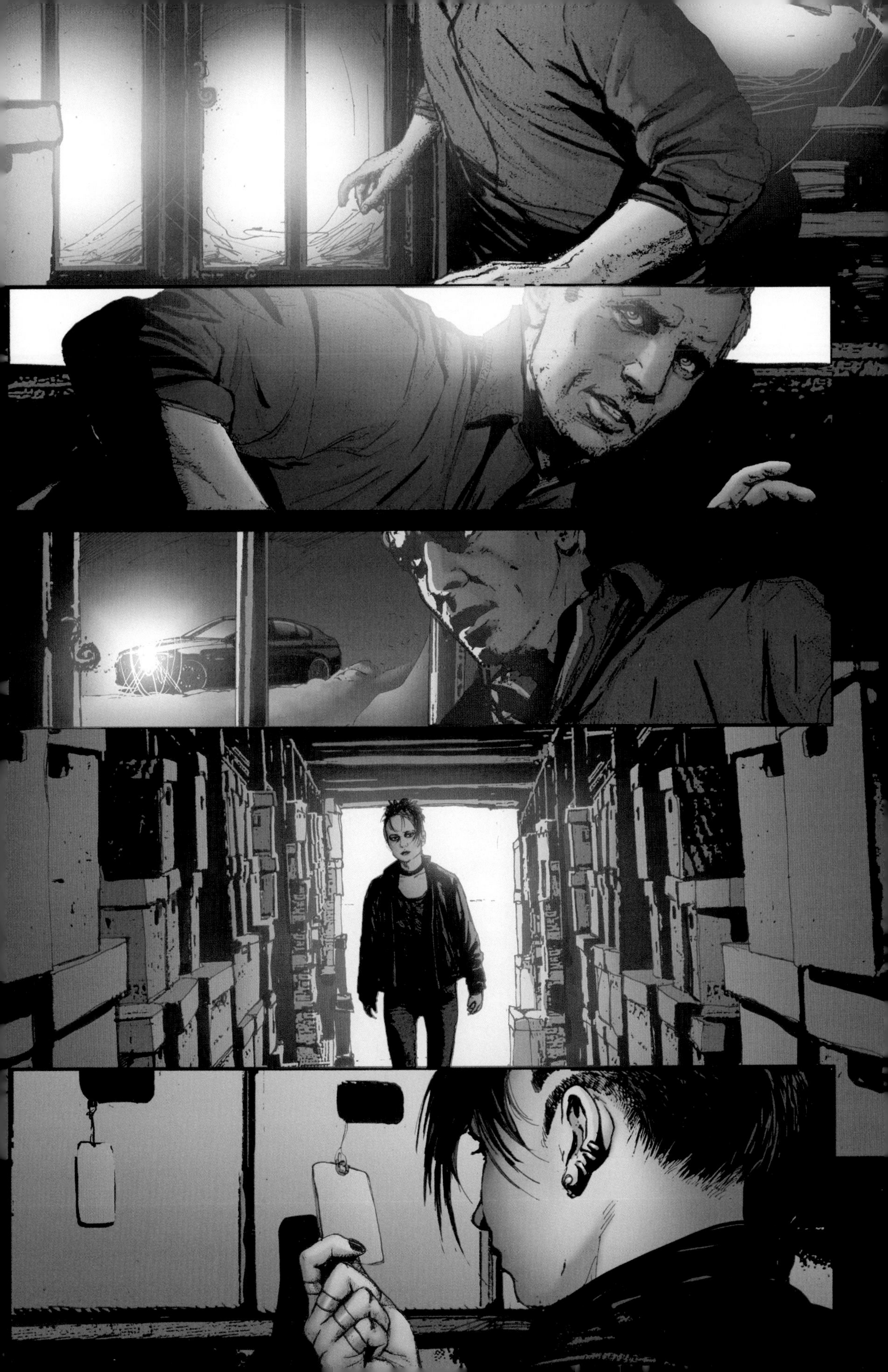

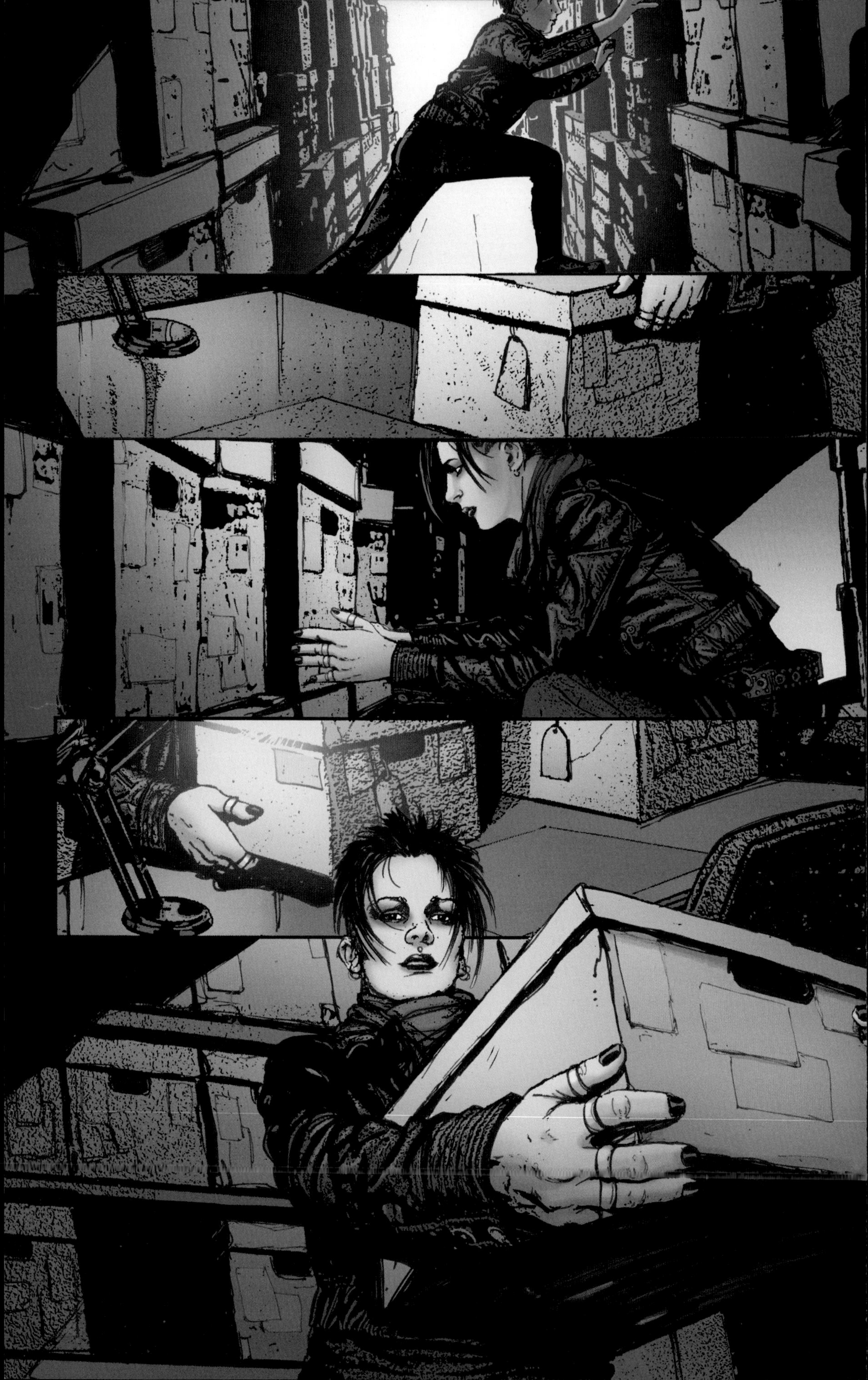

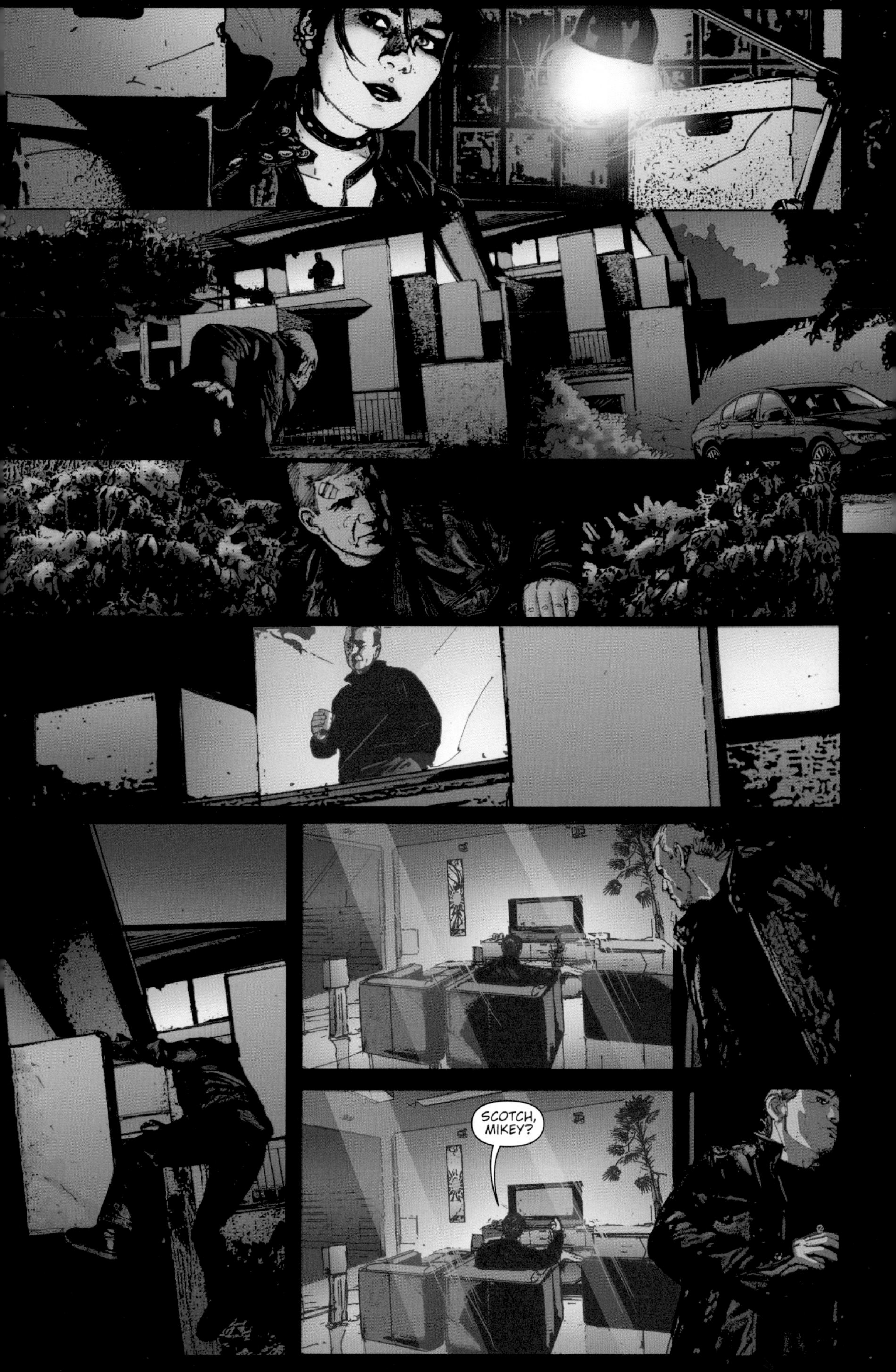
SCOTCH, MIKEY?

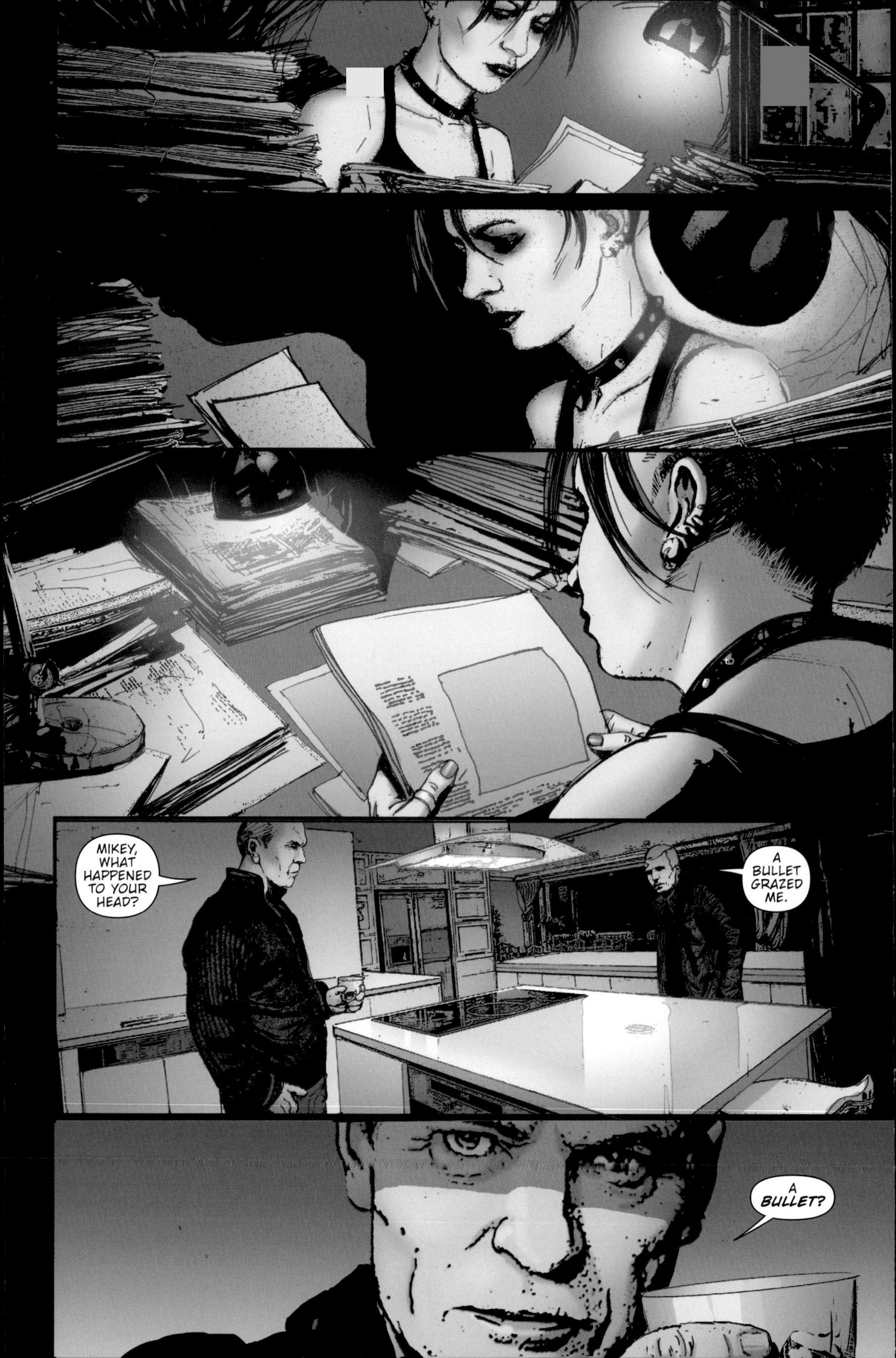
MIKEY, WHAT HAPPENED TO YOUR HEAD?
A BULLET GRAZED ME.
A *BULLET*?

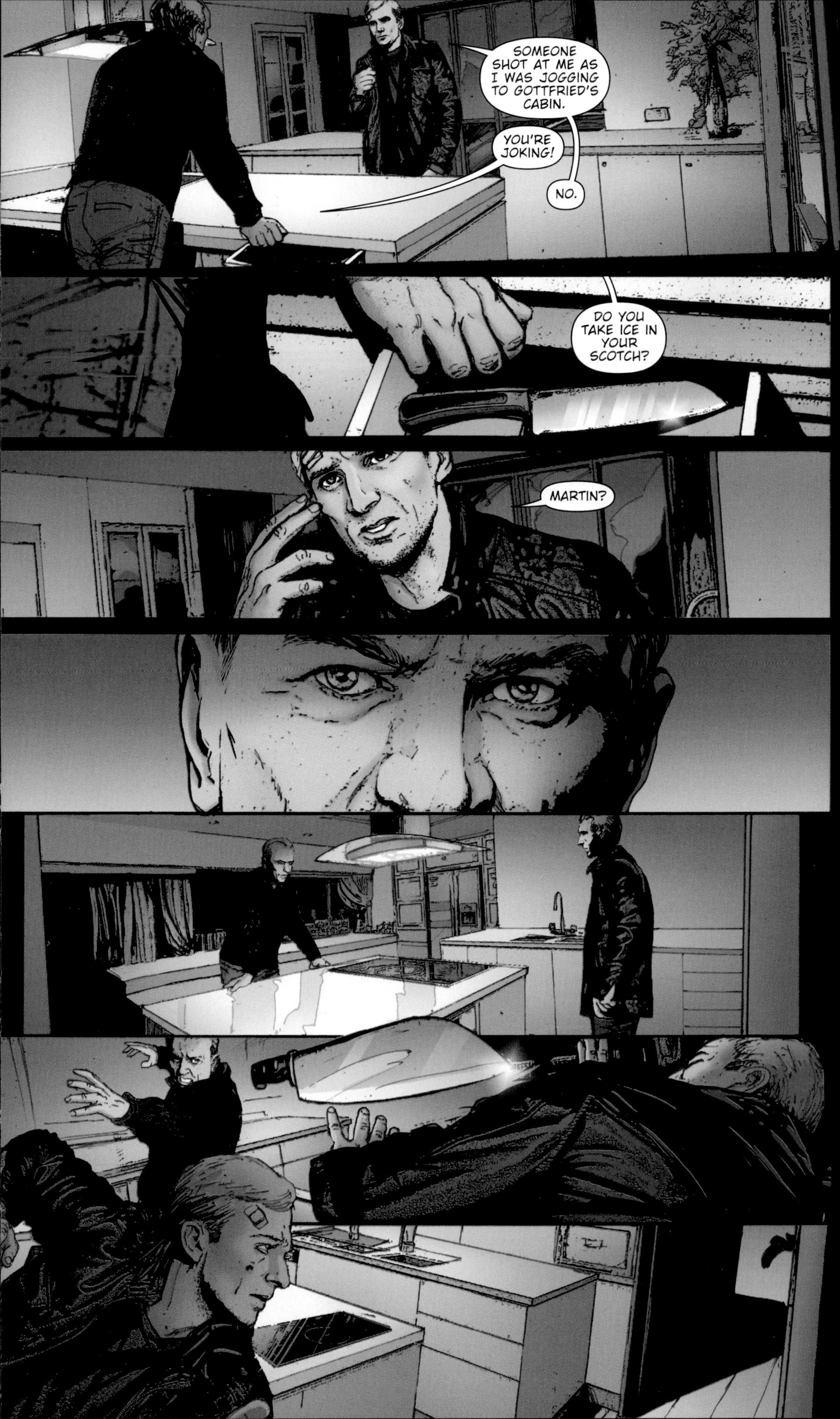
SOMEONE SHOT AT ME AS I WAS JOGGING TO GOTTFRIED'S CABIN.
YOU'RE JOKING!
NO.
DO YOU TAKE ICE IN YOUR SCOTCH?
MARTIN?

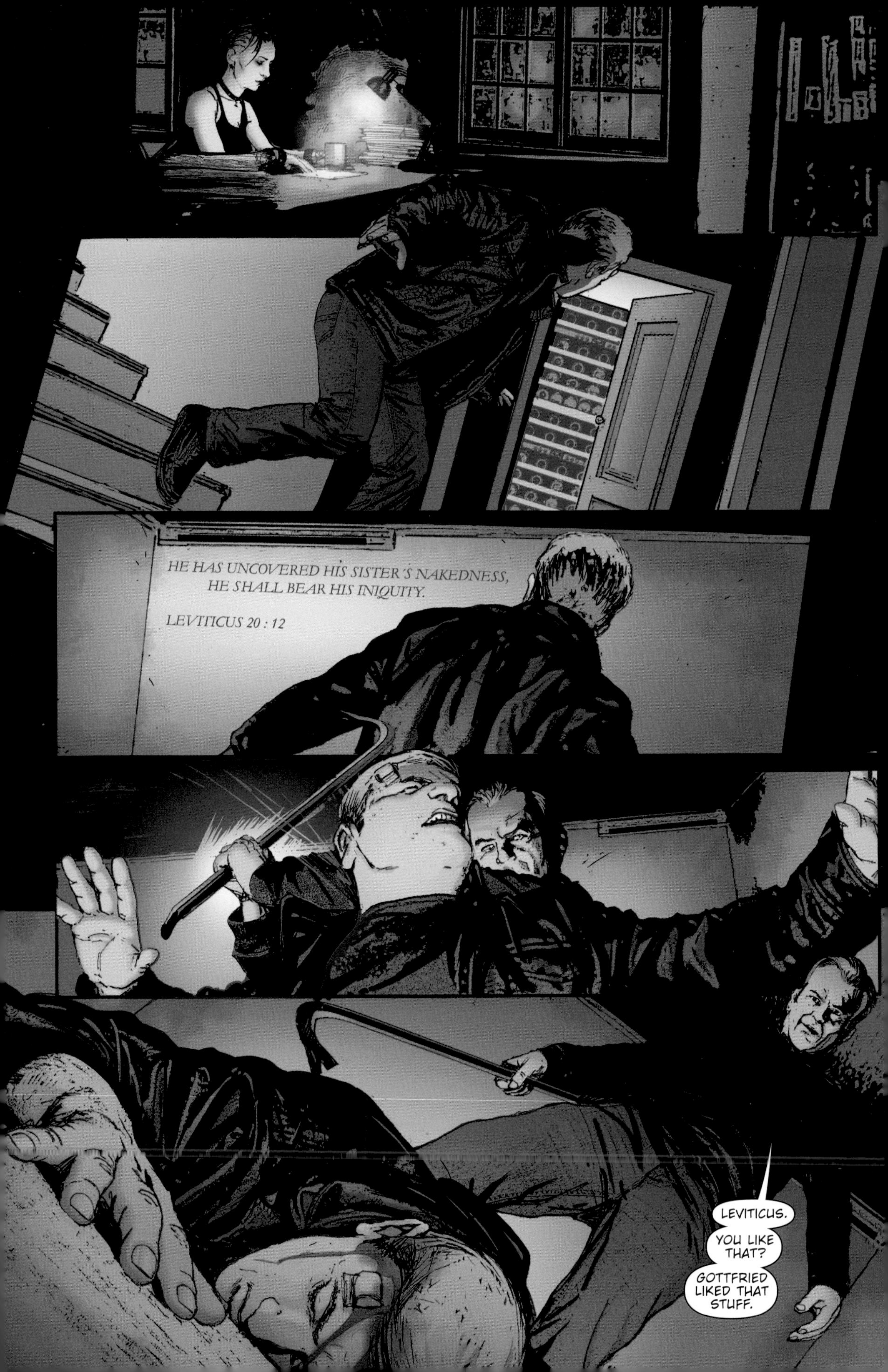

HE HAS UNCOVERED HIS SISTER'S NAKEDNESS, HE SHALL BEAR HIS INIQUITY.
LEVITICUS 20 : 12
LEVITICUS.
YOU LIKE THAT?
GOTTFRIED LIKED THAT STUFF.

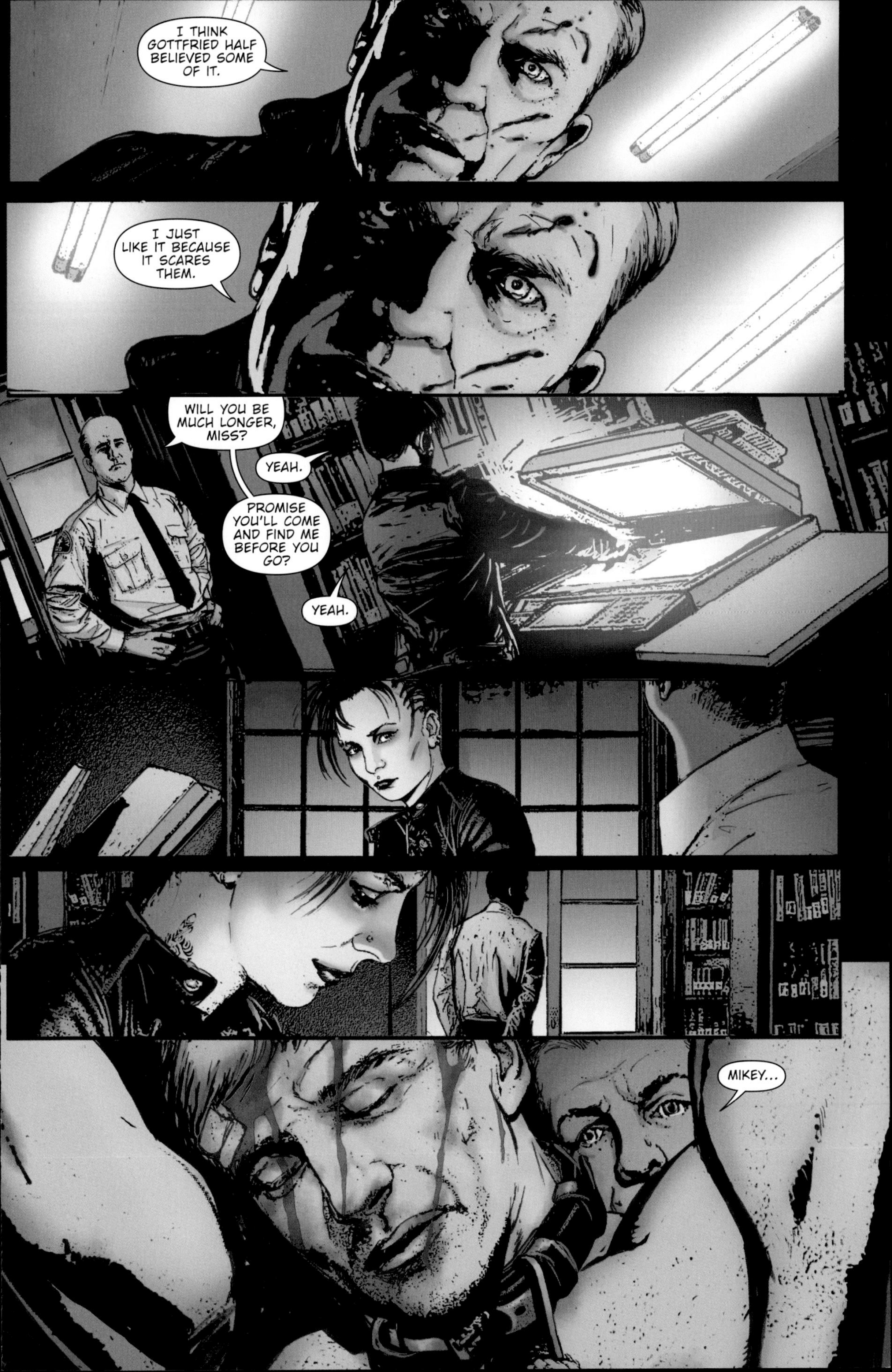
I THINK GOTTFRIED HALF BELIEVED SOME OF IT.
I JUST LIKE IT BECAUSE IT SCARES THEM.
WILL YOU BE MUCH LONGER, MISS?
YEAH.
PROMISE YOU'LL COME AND FIND ME BEFORE YOU GO?
YEAH.
MIKEY...

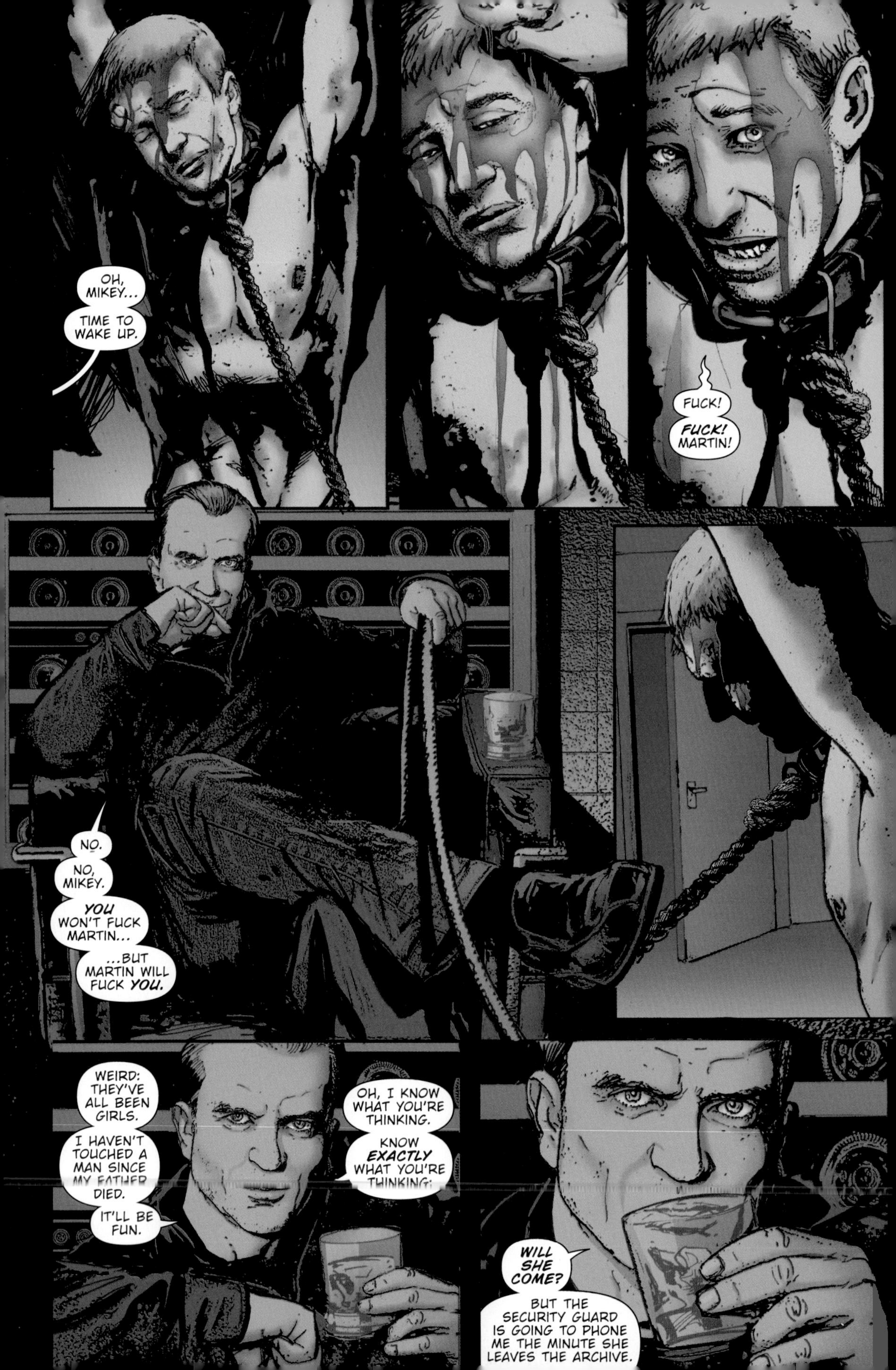
OH, MIKEY...
TIME TO WAKE UP.
FUCK!
FUCK! MARTIN!
NO.
NO, MIKEY.
YOU WON'T FUCK MARTIN...
...BUT MARTIN WILL FUCK YOU.
WEIRD: THEY'VE ALL BEEN GIRLS.
I HAVEN'T TOUCHED A MAN SINCE MY FATHER DIED.
IT'LL BE FUN.
OH, I KNOW WHAT YOU'RE THINKING.
KNOW EXACTLY WHAT YOU'RE THINKING:
WILL SHE COME?
BUT THE SECURITY GUARD IS GOING TO PHONE ME THE MINUTE SHE LEAVES THE ARCHIVE.

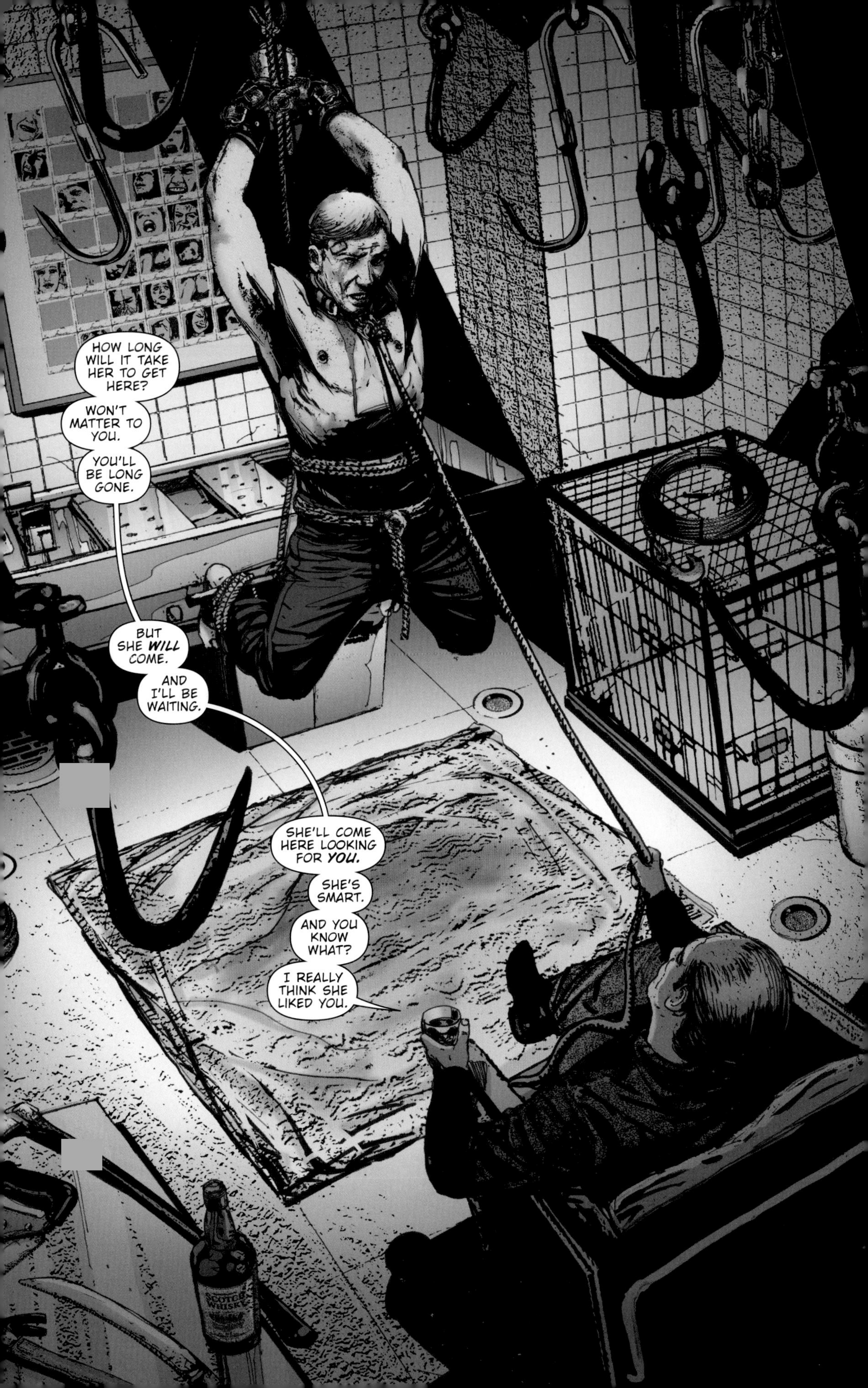
HOW LONG WILL IT TAKE HER TO GET HERE?
WON'T MATTER TO YOU.
YOU'LL BE LONG GONE.
BUT SHE *WILL* COME.
AND I'LL BE WAITING.
SHE'LL COME HERE LOOKING FOR *YOU.*
SHE'S SMART.
AND YOU KNOW WHAT?
I REALLY THINK SHE LIKED YOU.
SCOTCH WHISKY

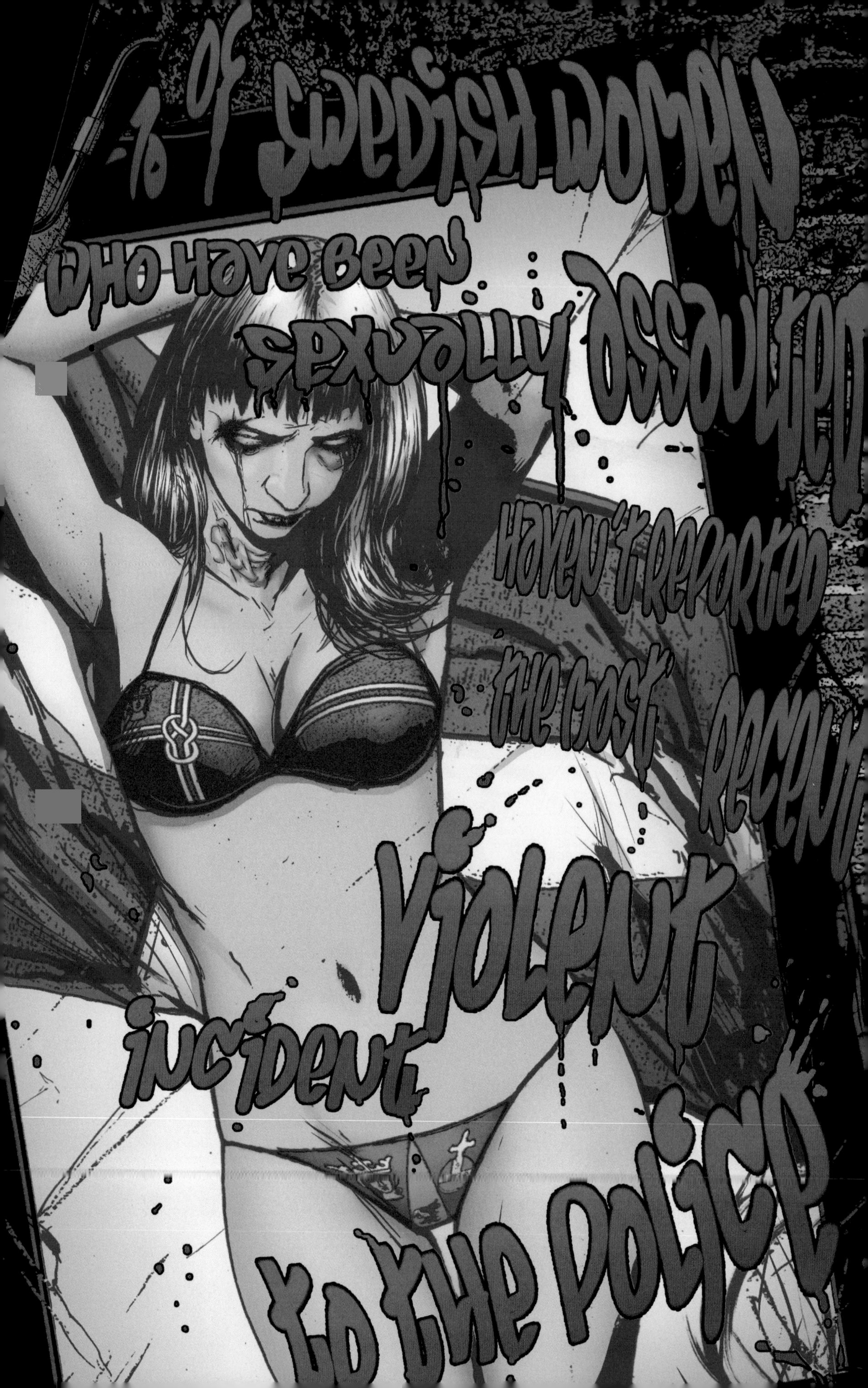

% OF SWEDISH WOMEN
WHO HAVE BEEN
SEXUALLY ASSAULTED
HAVEN'T REPORTED
THE MOST RECENT
VIOLENT
INCIDENT
TO THE POLICE

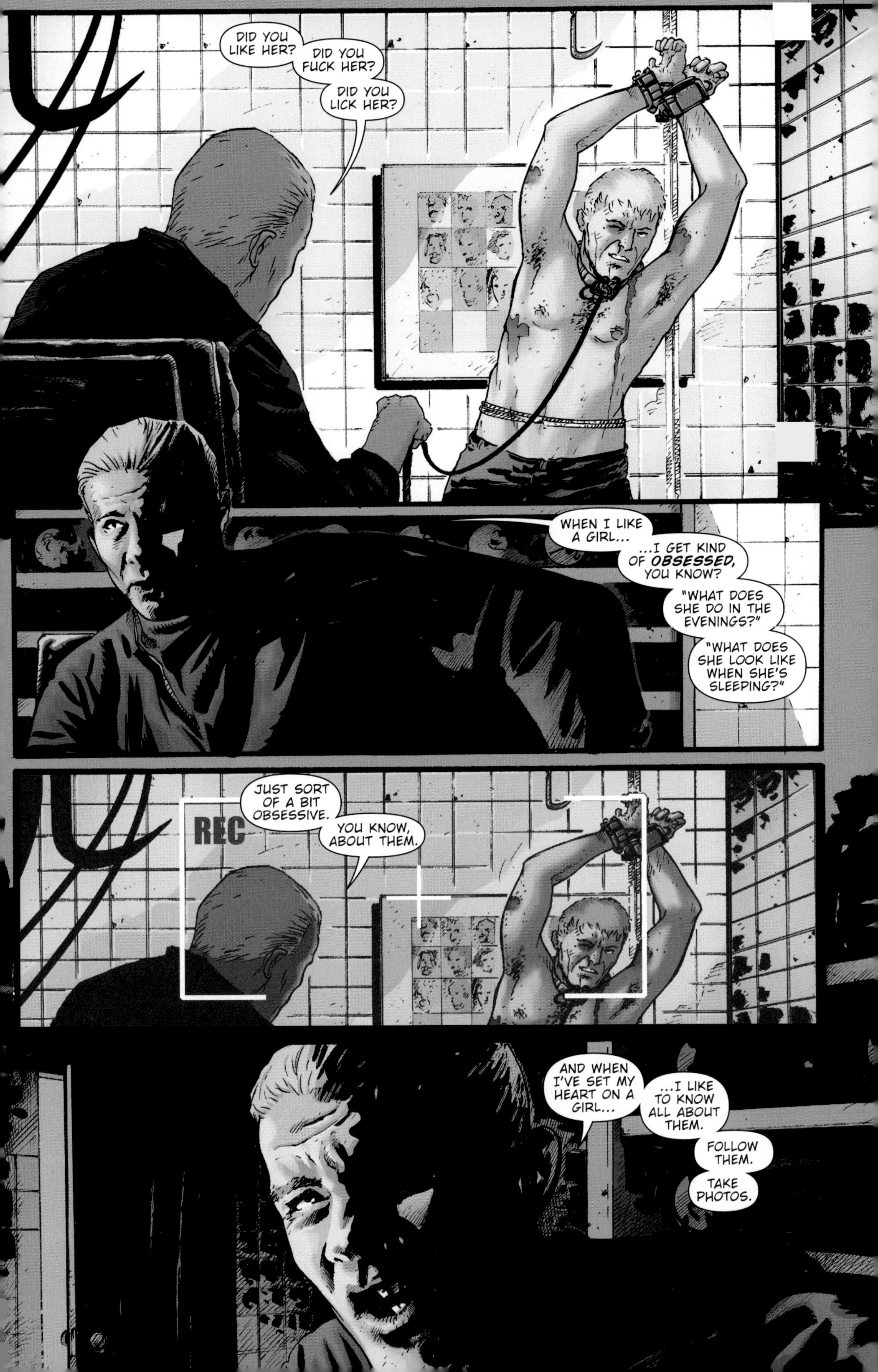
DID YOU LIKE HER?
DID YOU FUCK HER?
DID YOU LICK HER?
WHEN I LIKE A GIRL...
...I GET KIND OF OBSESSED, YOU KNOW?
"WHAT DOES SHE DO IN THE EVENINGS?"
"WHAT DOES SHE LOOK LIKE WHEN SHE'S SLEEPING?"
REC
JUST SORT OF A BIT OBSESSIVE.
YOU KNOW, ABOUT THEM.
AND WHEN I'VE SET MY HEART ON A GIRL...
...I LIKE TO KNOW ALL ABOUT THEM.
FOLLOW THEM.
TAKE PHOTOS.

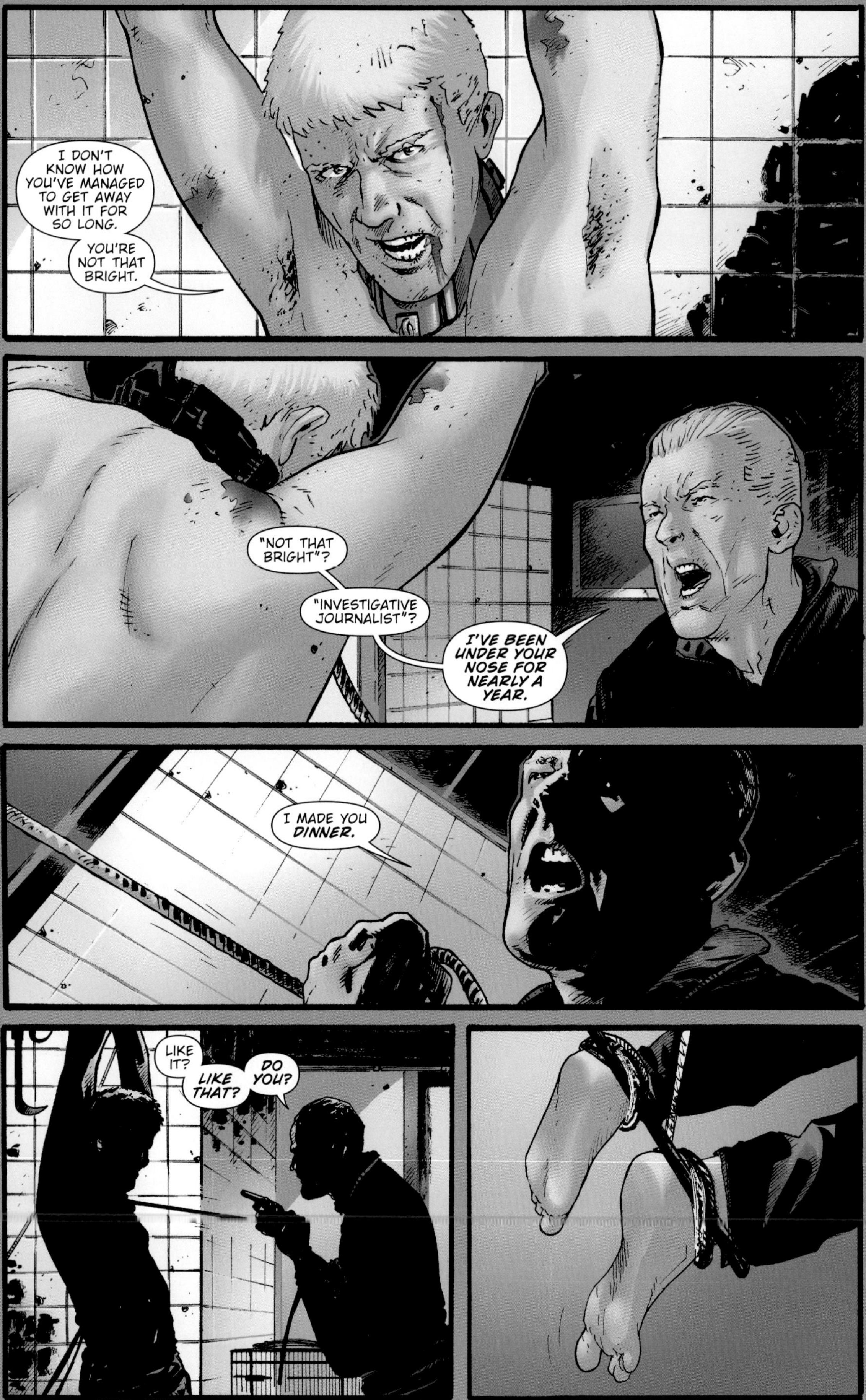
I DON'T KNOW HOW YOU'VE MANAGED TO GET AWAY WITH IT FOR SO LONG.
YOU'RE NOT THAT BRIGHT.
"NOT THAT BRIGHT"?
"INVESTIGATIVE JOURNALIST"?
I'VE BEEN UNDER YOUR NOSE FOR NEARLY A YEAR.
I MADE YOU DINNER.
LIKE IT?
LIKE THAT?
DO YOU?

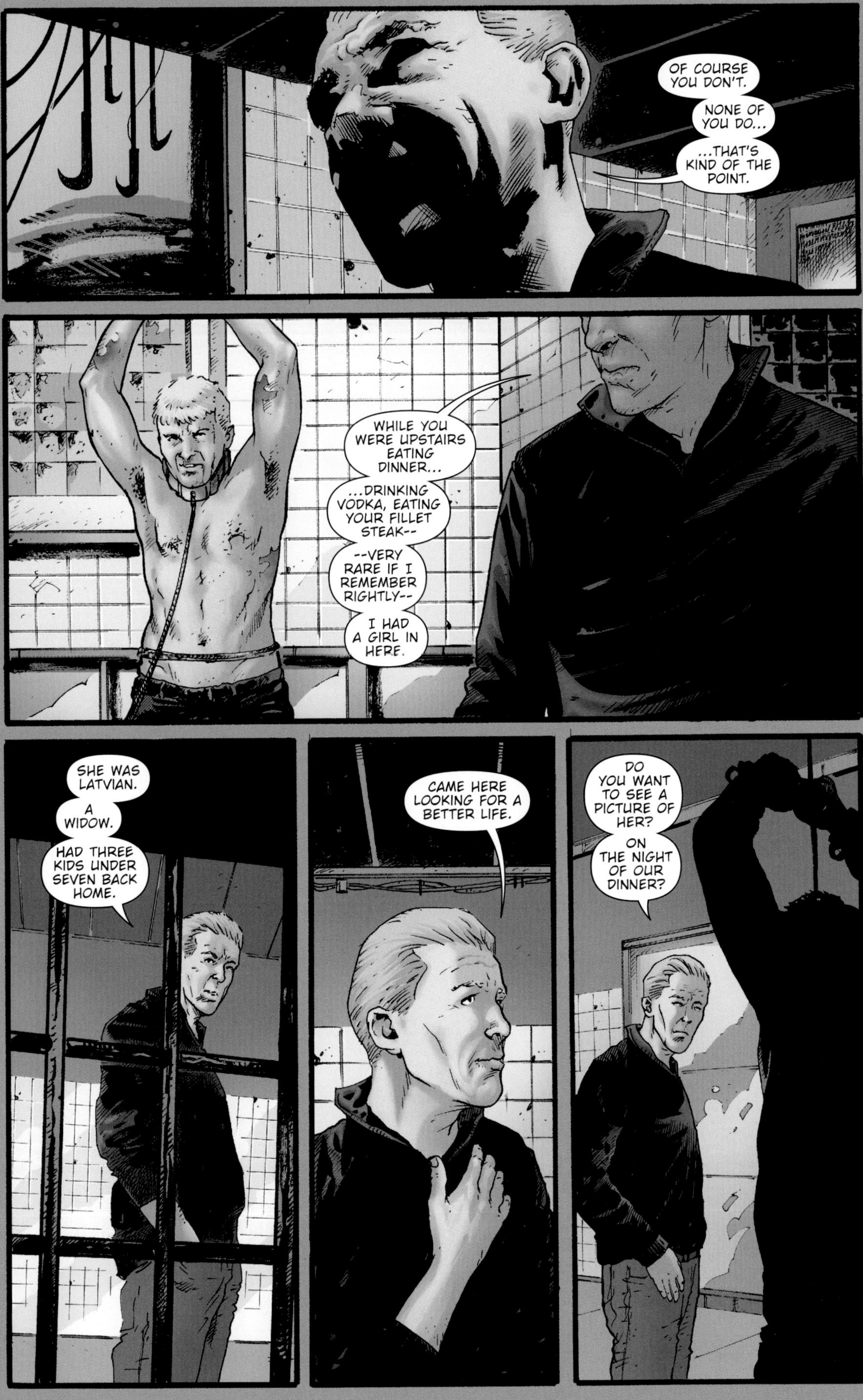
OF COURSE YOU DON'T.
NONE OF YOU DO...
...THAT'S KIND OF THE POINT.
WHILE YOU WERE UPSTAIRS EATING DINNER...
...DRINKING VODKA, EATING YOUR FILLET STEAK--
--VERY RARE IF I REMEMBER RIGHTLY--
I HAD A GIRL IN HERE.
SHE WAS LATVIAN.
A WIDOW.
HAD THREE KIDS UNDER SEVEN BACK HOME.
CAME HERE LOOKING FOR A BETTER LIFE.
DO YOU WANT TO SEE A PICTURE OF HER?
ON THE NIGHT OF OUR DINNER?

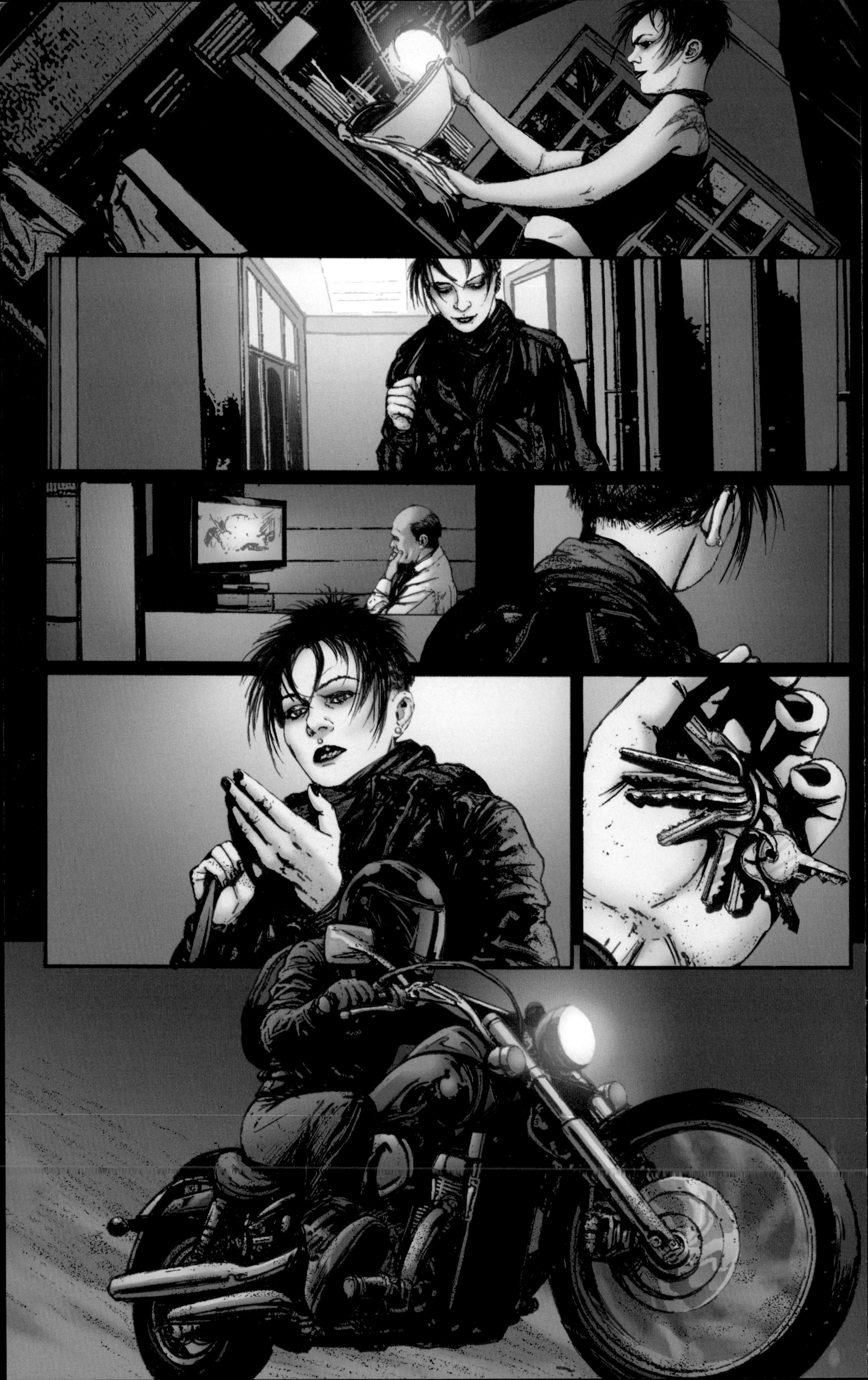

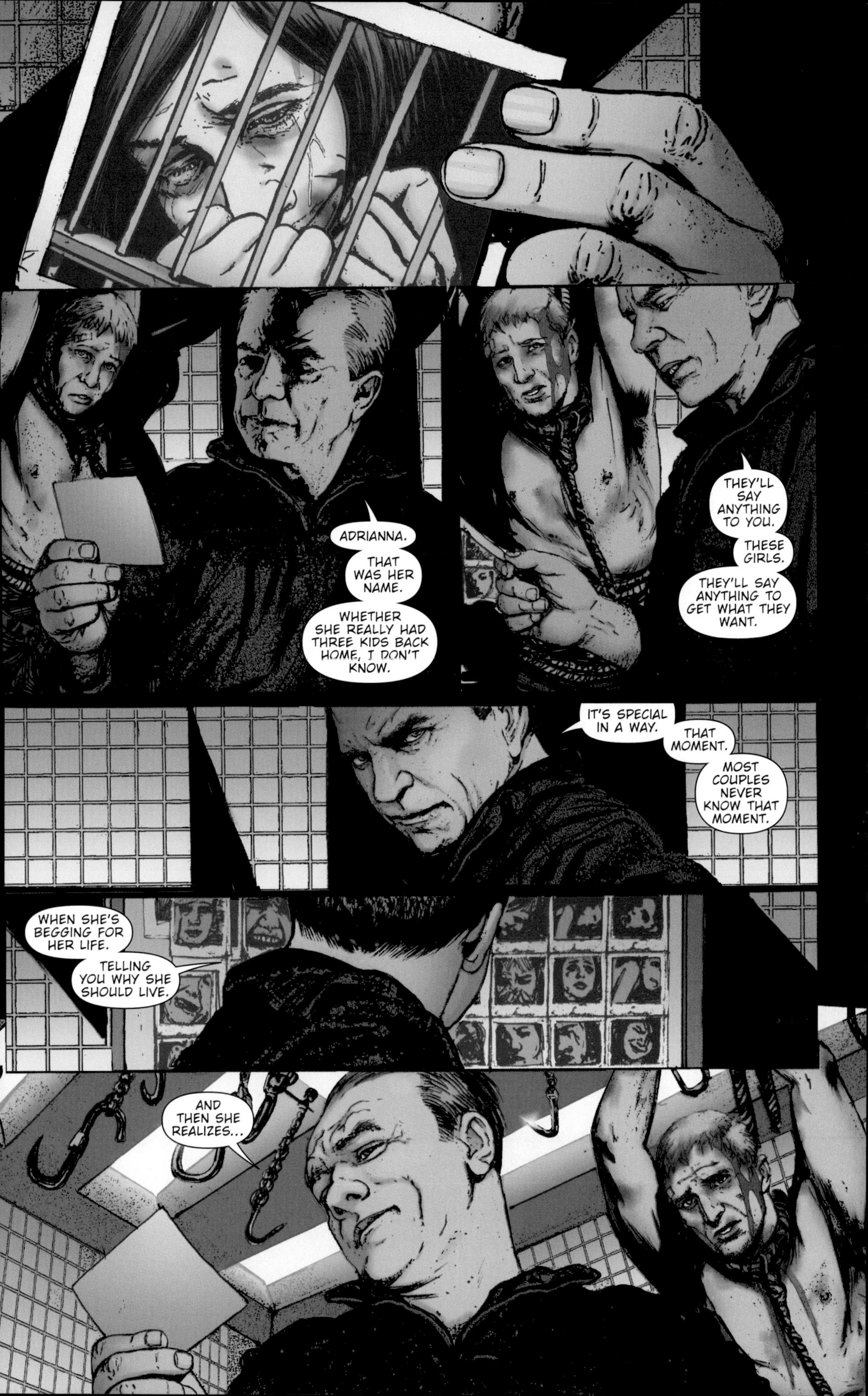
ADRIANNA.
THAT WAS HER NAME.
WHETHER SHE REALLY HAD THREE KIDS BACK HOME, I DON'T KNOW.
THEY'LL SAY ANYTHING TO YOU.
THESE GIRLS.
THEY'LL SAY ANYTHING TO GET WHAT THEY WANT.
IT'S SPECIAL IN A WAY.
THAT MOMENT.
MOST COUPLES NEVER KNOW THAT MOMENT.
WHEN SHE'S BEGGING FOR HER LIFE.
TELLING YOU WHY SHE SHOULD LIVE.
AND THEN SHE REALIZES...

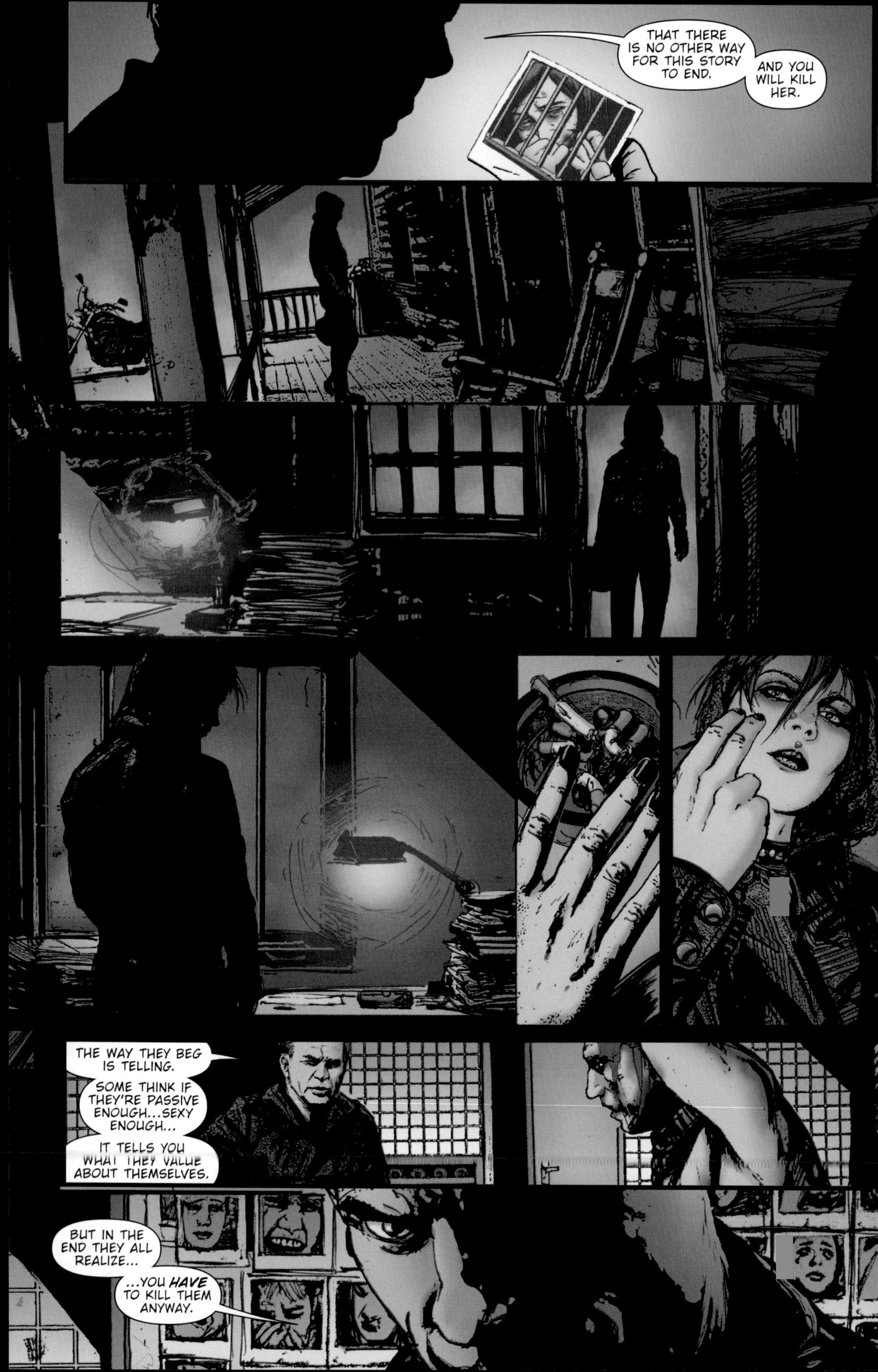

THAT THERE IS NO OTHER WAY FOR THIS STORY TO END.
AND YOU WILL KILL HER.
THE WAY THEY BEG IS TELLING.
SOME THINK IF THEY'RE PASSIVE ENOUGH...SEXY ENOUGH...
IT TELLS YOU WHAT THEY VALUE ABOUT THEMSELVES.
BUT IN THE END THEY ALL REALIZE...
...YOU **HAVE** TO KILL THEM ANYWAY.

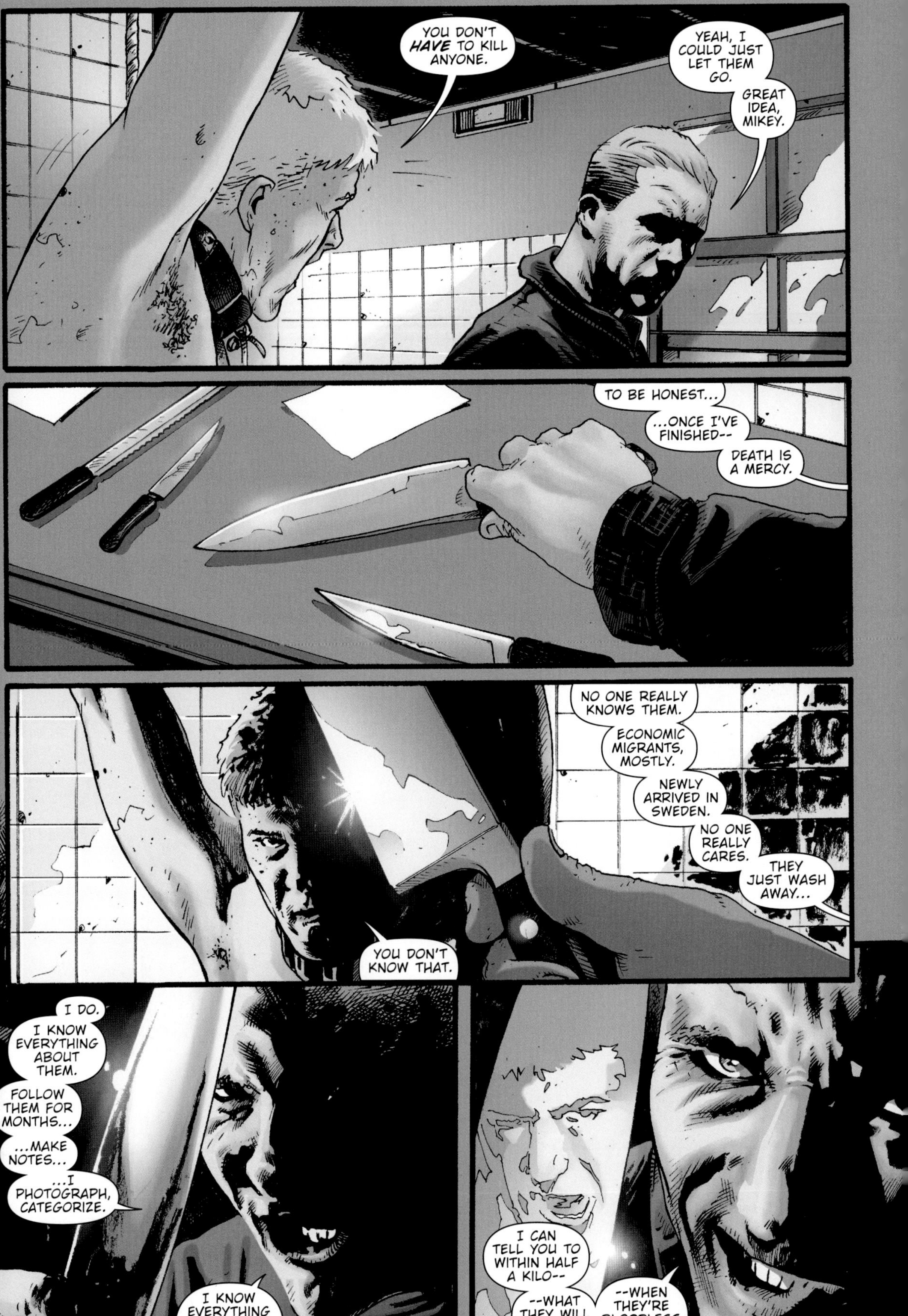
YOU DON'T *HAVE* TO KILL ANYONE.
YEAH, I COULD JUST LET THEM GO.
GREAT IDEA, MIKEY.
TO BE HONEST...
...ONCE I'VE FINISHED--
DEATH IS A MERCY.
NO ONE REALLY KNOWS THEM.
ECONOMIC MIGRANTS, MOSTLY.
NEWLY ARRIVED IN SWEDEN.
NO ONE REALLY CARES.
THEY JUST WASH AWAY...
YOU DON'T KNOW THAT.
I DO.
I KNOW EVERYTHING ABOUT THEM.
FOLLOW THEM FOR MONTHS...
...MAKE NOTES...
...I PHOTOGRAPH, CATEGORIZE.
I KNOW EVERYTHING ABOUT THEM BEFORE I EVER TOUCH THEM.
I CAN TELL YOU TO WITHIN HALF A KILO--
--WHAT THEY WILL WEIGH--
--WHEN THEY'RE BLOODLESS AND IN A SACK.

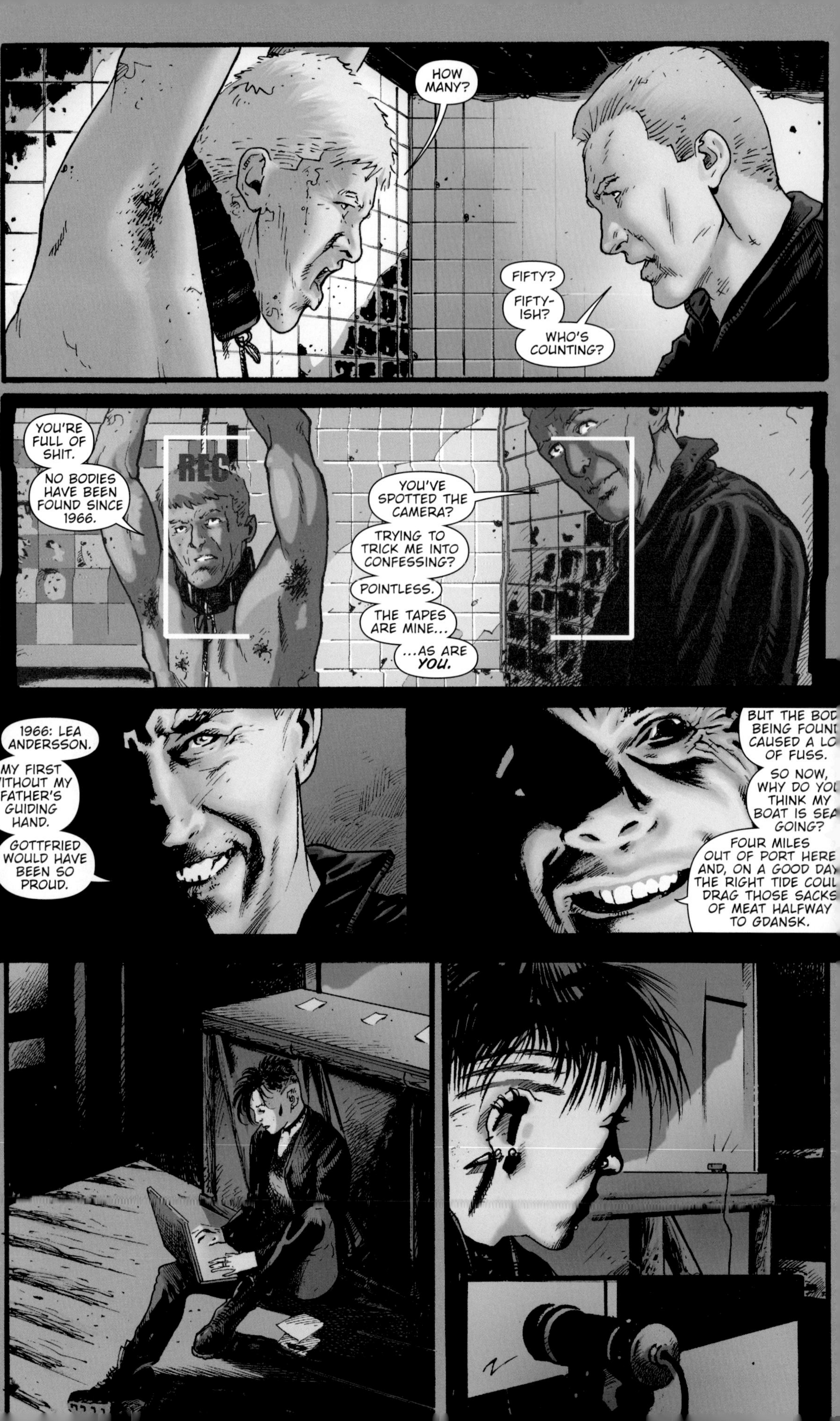
HOW MANY?
FIFTY?
FIFTY-ISH?
WHO'S COUNTING?
YOU'RE FULL OF SHIT.
NO BODIES HAVE BEEN FOUND SINCE 1966.
REC
YOU'VE SPOTTED THE CAMERA?
TRYING TO TRICK ME INTO CONFESSING?
POINTLESS.
THE TAPES ARE MINE...
...AS ARE *YOU.*
1966: LEA ANDERSSON.
MY FIRST WITHOUT MY FATHER'S GUIDING HAND.
GOTTFRIED WOULD HAVE BEEN SO PROUD.
BUT THE BOD BEING FOUNI CAUSED A LO OF FUSS.
SO NOW, WHY DO YOU THINK MY BOAT IS SEA GOING?
FOUR MILES OUT OF PORT HERE AND, ON A GOOD DAY THE RIGHT TIDE COUL DRAG THOSE SACKS OF MEAT HALFWAY TO GDANSK.

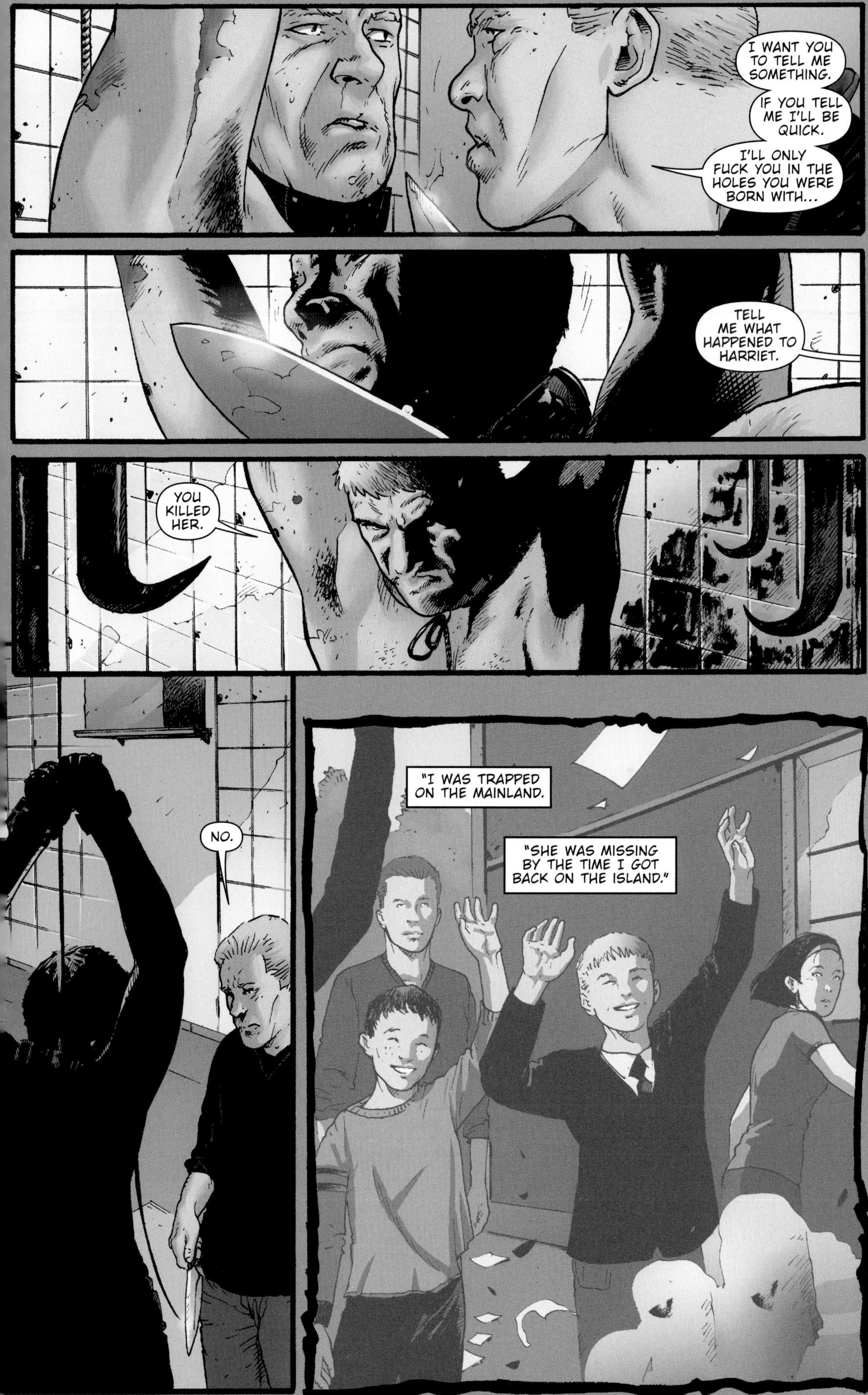

I WANT YOU TO TELL ME SOMETHING.
IF YOU TELL ME I'LL BE QUICK.
I'LL ONLY FUCK YOU IN THE HOLES YOU WERE BORN WITH...
TELL ME WHAT HAPPENED TO HARRIET.
YOU KILLED HER.
NO.
"I WAS TRAPPED ON THE MAINLAND.
"SHE WAS MISSING BY THE TIME I GOT BACK ON THE ISLAND."

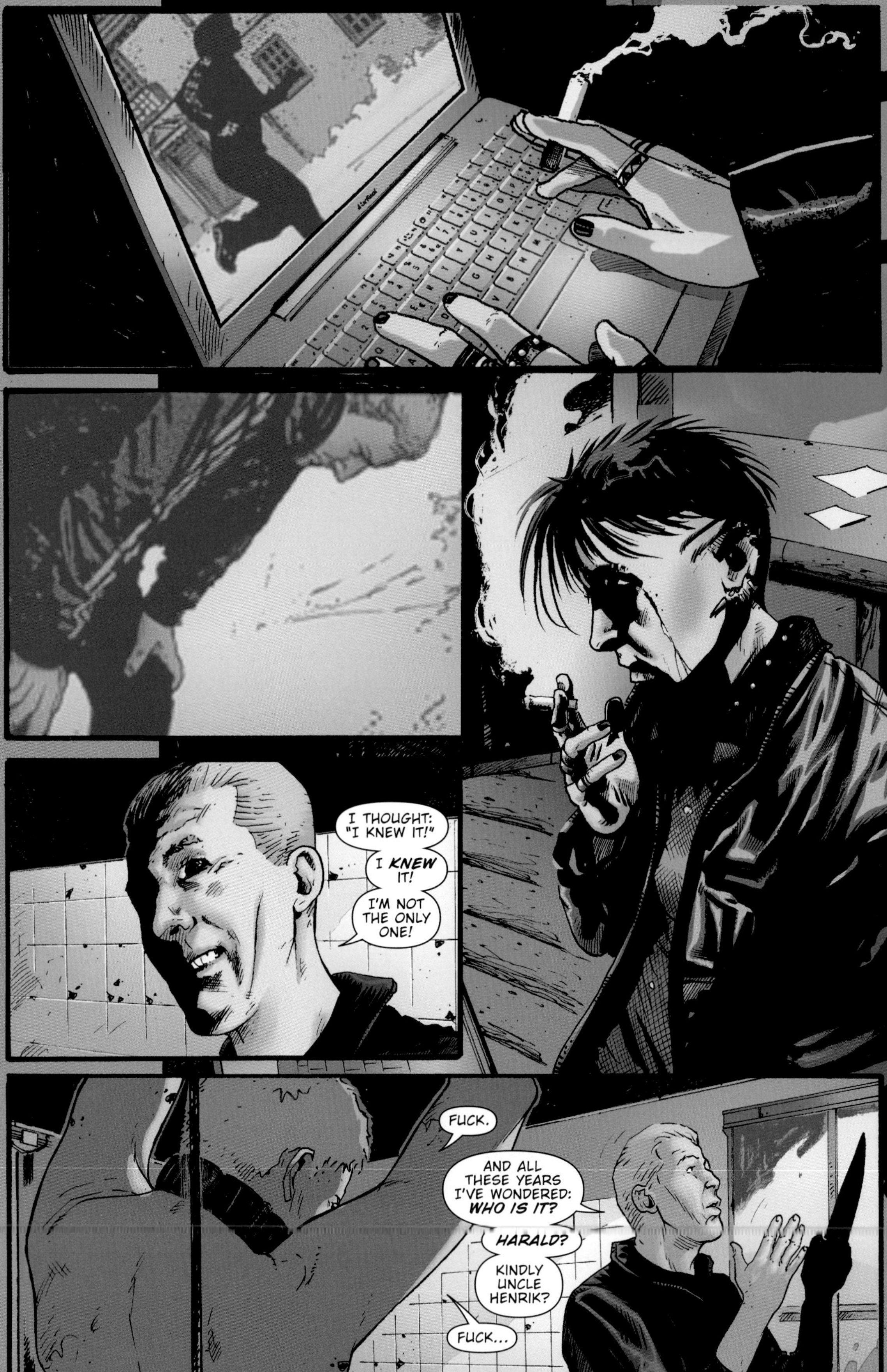
I THOUGHT: "I KNEW IT!"
I KNEW IT!
I'M NOT THE ONLY ONE!
FUCK.
AND ALL THESE YEARS I'VE WONDERED: WHO IS IT?
HARALD?
KINDLY UNCLE HENRIK?
FUCK...

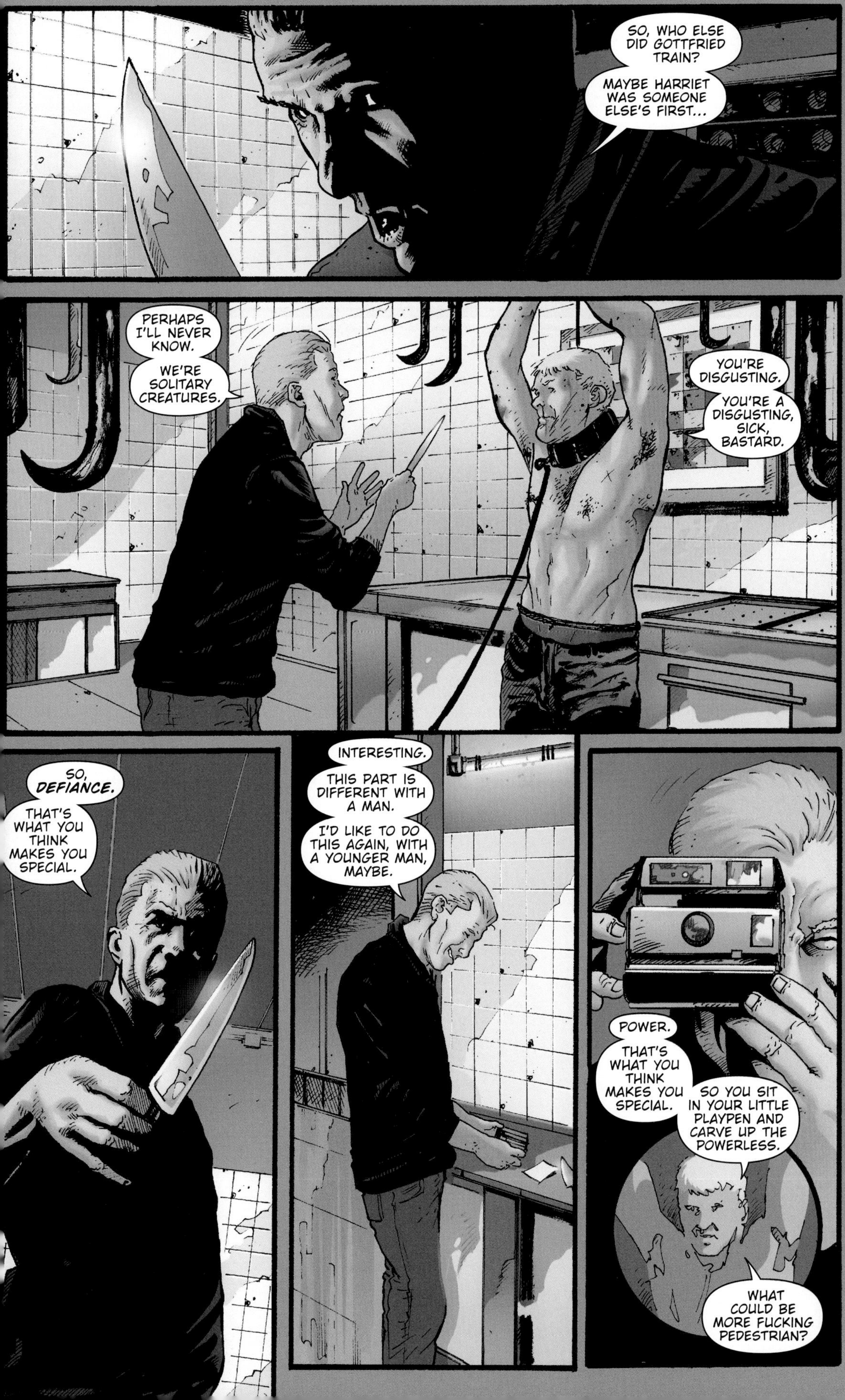
SO, WHO ELSE DID GOTTFRIED TRAIN?
MAYBE HARRIET WAS SOMEONE ELSE'S FIRST...
PERHAPS I'LL NEVER KNOW.
WE'RE SOLITARY CREATURES.
YOU'RE DISGUSTING.
YOU'RE A DISGUSTING, SICK, BASTARD.
SO, *DEFIANCE.*
THAT'S WHAT YOU THINK MAKES YOU SPECIAL.
INTERESTING.
THIS PART IS DIFFERENT WITH A MAN.
I'D LIKE TO DO THIS AGAIN, WITH A YOUNGER MAN, MAYBE.
POWER.
THAT'S WHAT YOU THINK MAKES YOU SPECIAL.
SO YOU SIT IN YOUR LITTLE PLAYPEN AND CARVE UP THE POWERLESS.
WHAT COULD BE MORE FUCKING PEDESTRIAN?

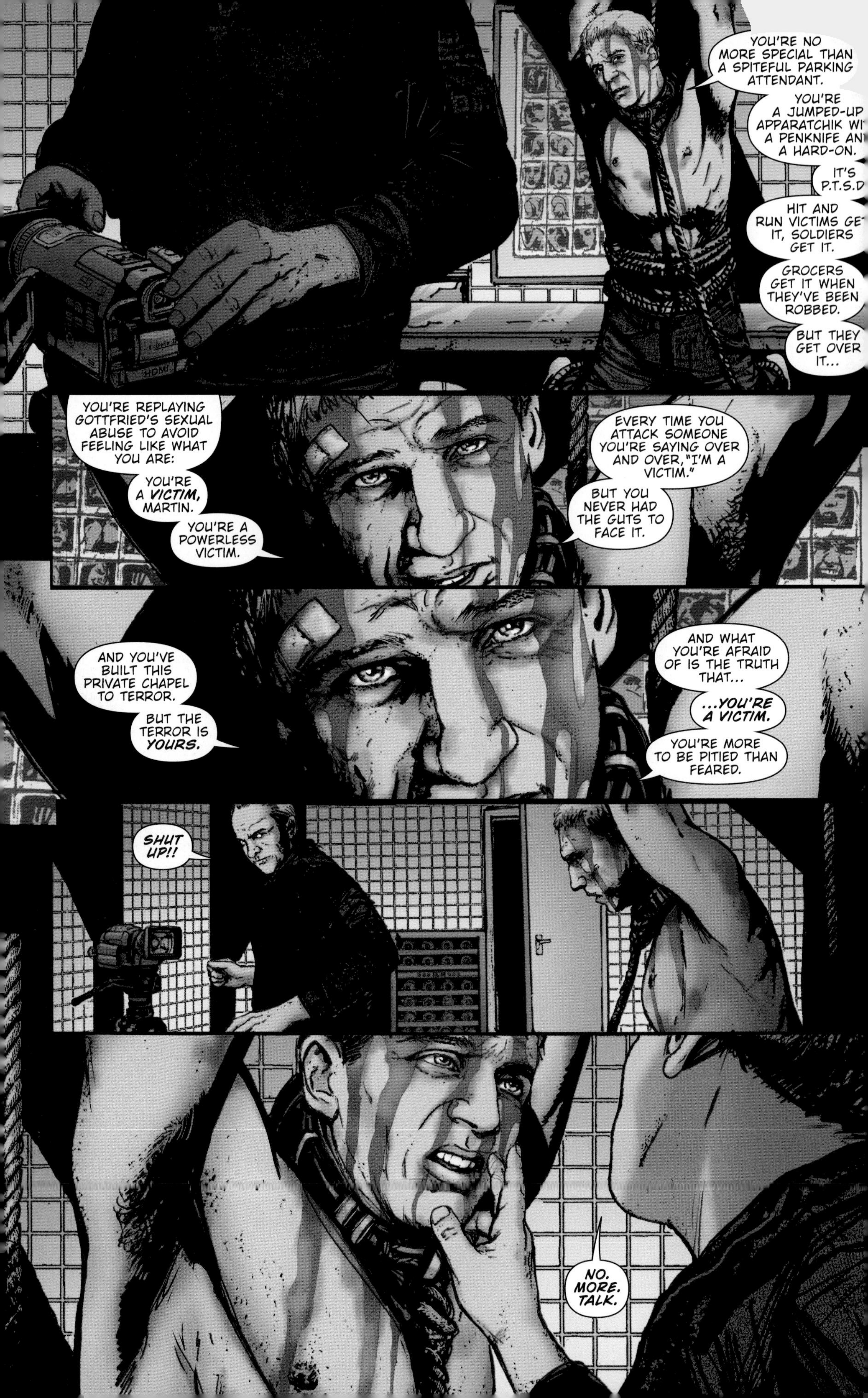
YOU'RE NO MORE SPECIAL THAN A SPITEFUL PARKING ATTENDANT.
YOU'RE A JUMPED-UP APPARATCHIK WI A PENKNIFE AN A HARD-ON.
IT'S P.T.S.D
HIT AND RUN VICTIMS GE IT, SOLDIERS GET IT.
GROCERS GET IT WHEN THEY'VE BEEN ROBBED.
BUT THEY GET OVER IT...
YOU'RE REPLAYING GOTTFRIED'S SEXUAL ABUSE TO AVOID FEELING LIKE WHAT YOU ARE:
YOU'RE A *VICTIM,* MARTIN.
YOU'RE A POWERLESS VICTIM.
EVERY TIME YOU ATTACK SOMEONE YOU'RE SAYING OVER AND OVER, "I'M A VICTIM."
BUT YOU NEVER HAD THE GUTS TO FACE IT.
AND YOU'VE BUILT THIS PRIVATE CHAPEL TO TERROR.
BUT THE TERROR IS *YOURS.*
AND WHAT YOU'RE AFRAID OF IS THE TRUTH THAT...
...YOU'RE A VICTIM.
YOU'RE MORE TO BE PITIED THAN FEARED.
SHUT UP!!
NO. MORE. TALK.

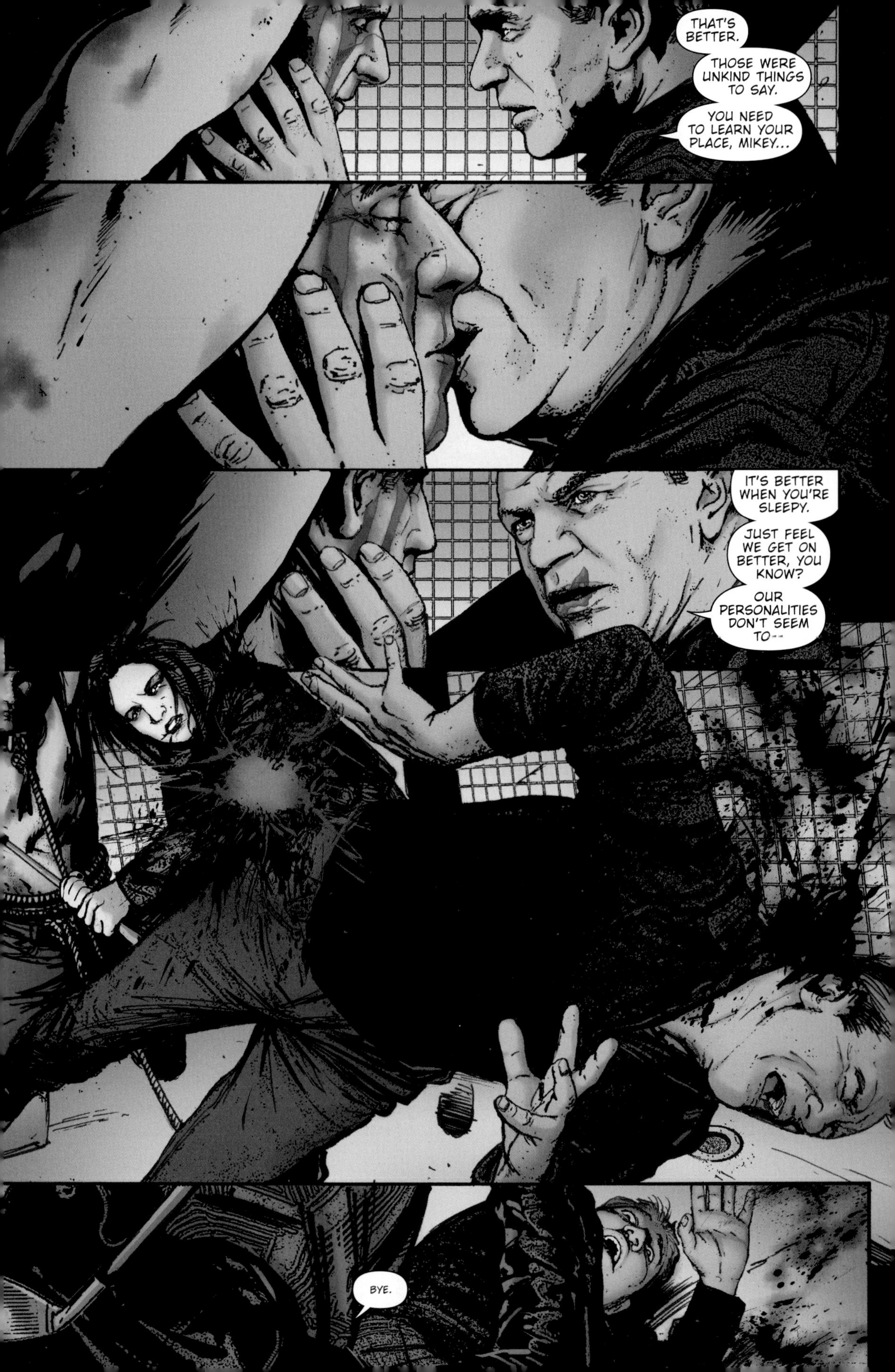
THAT'S BETTER.
THOSE WERE UNKIND THINGS TO SAY.
YOU NEED TO LEARN YOUR PLACE, MIKEY...
IT'S BETTER WHEN YOU'RE SLEEPY.
JUST FEEL WE GET ON BETTER, YOU KNOW?
OUR PERSONALITIES DON'T SEEM TO--
BYE.

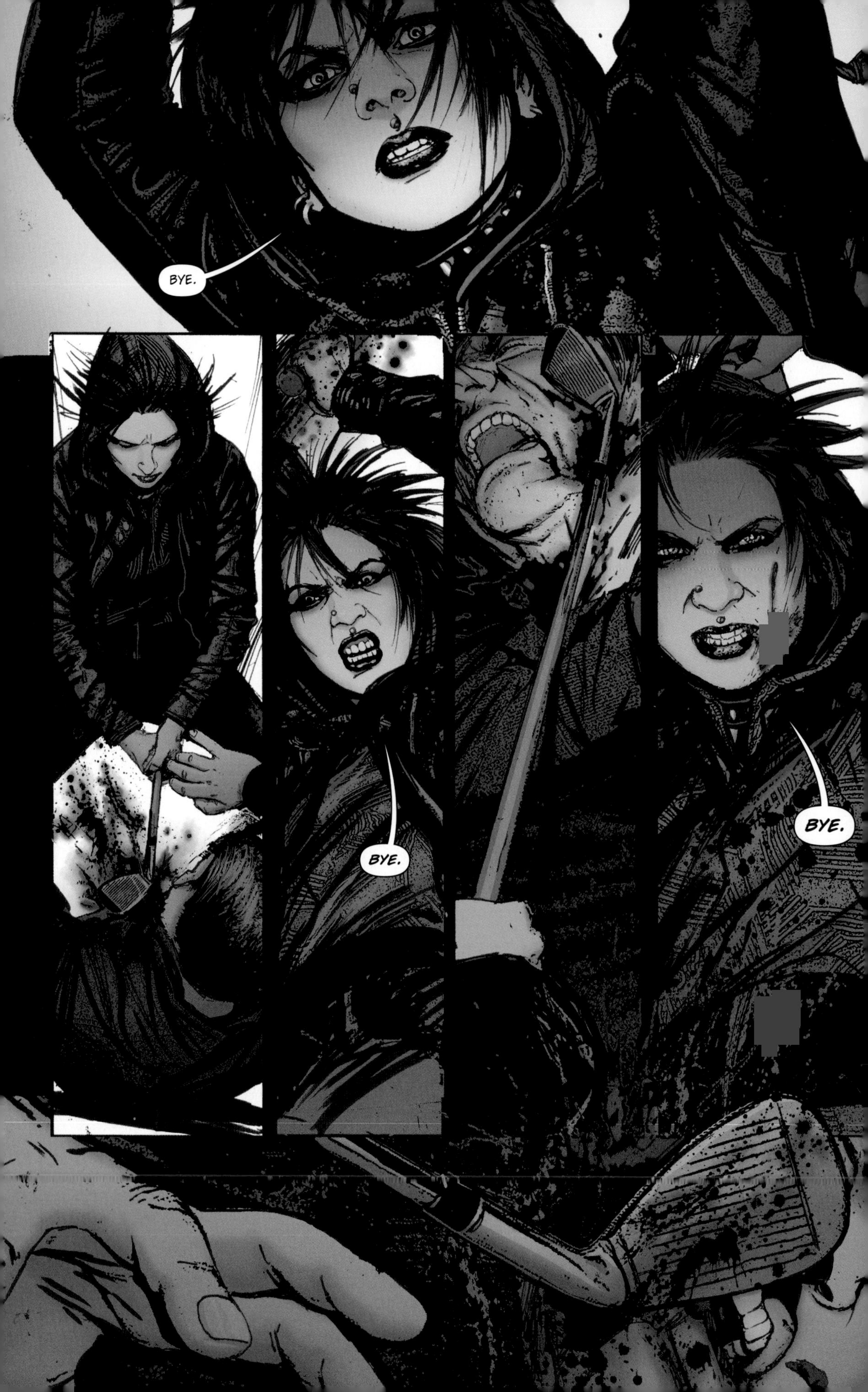
BYE.
BYE.
BYE.

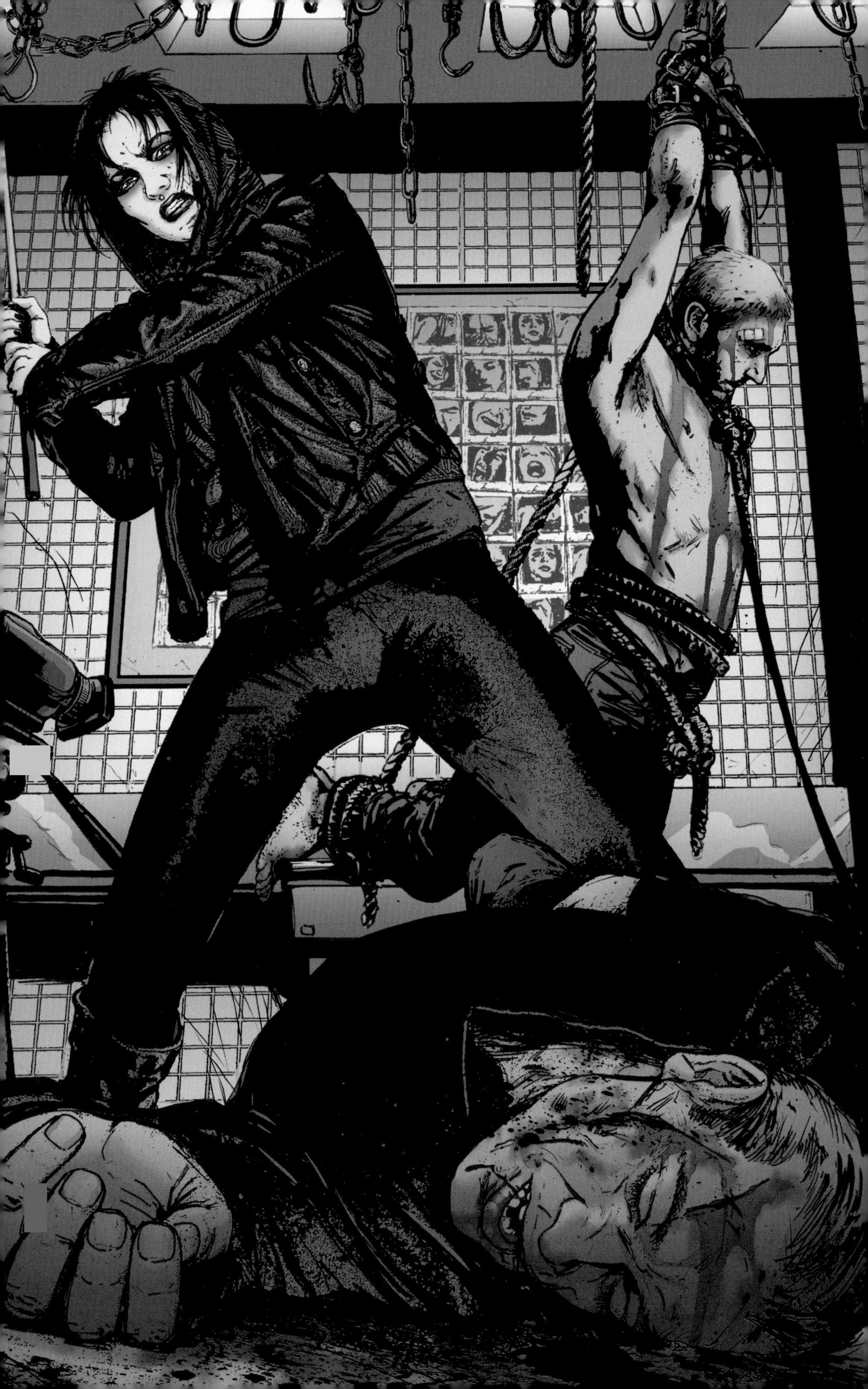

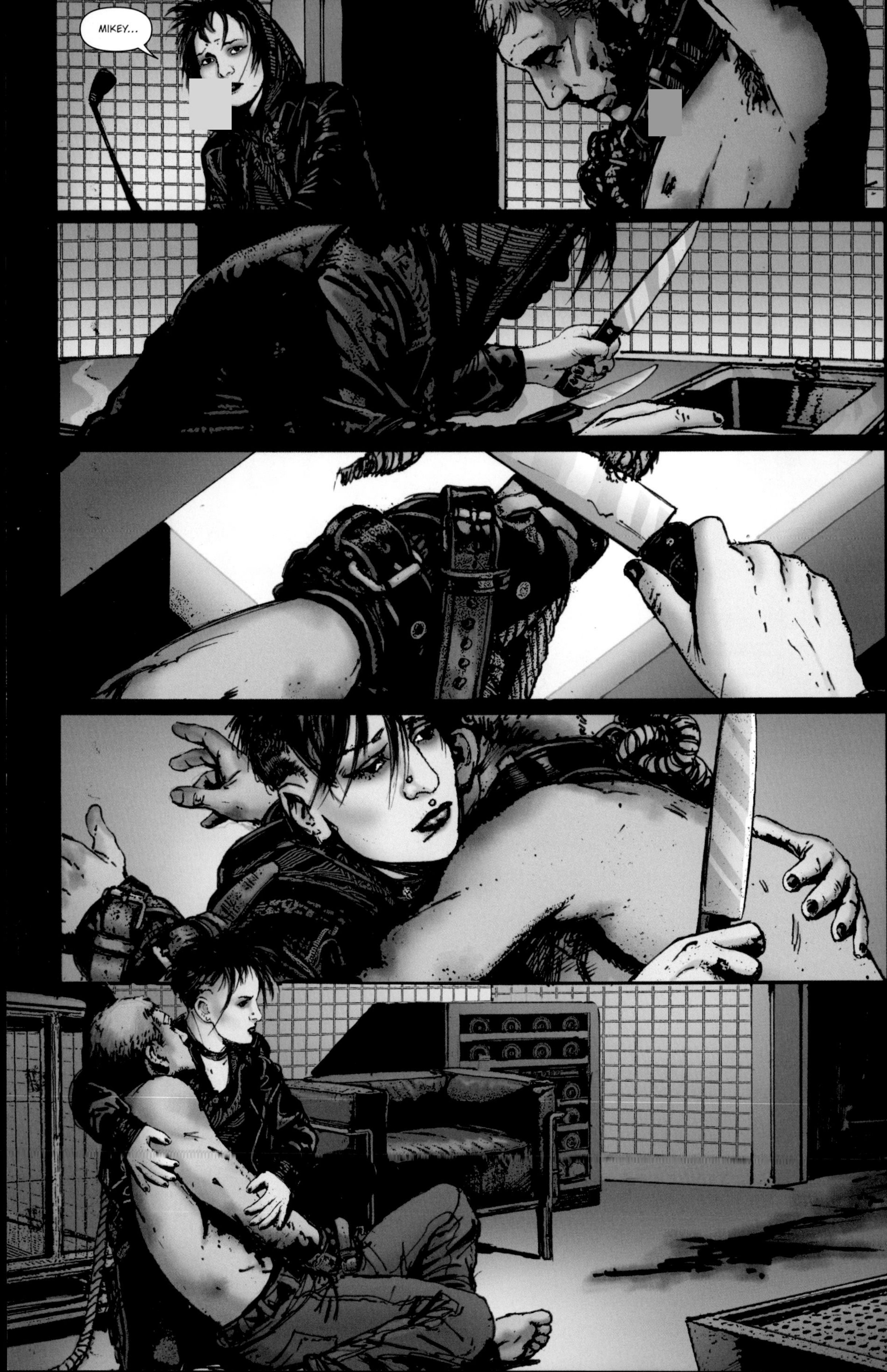
MIKEY...

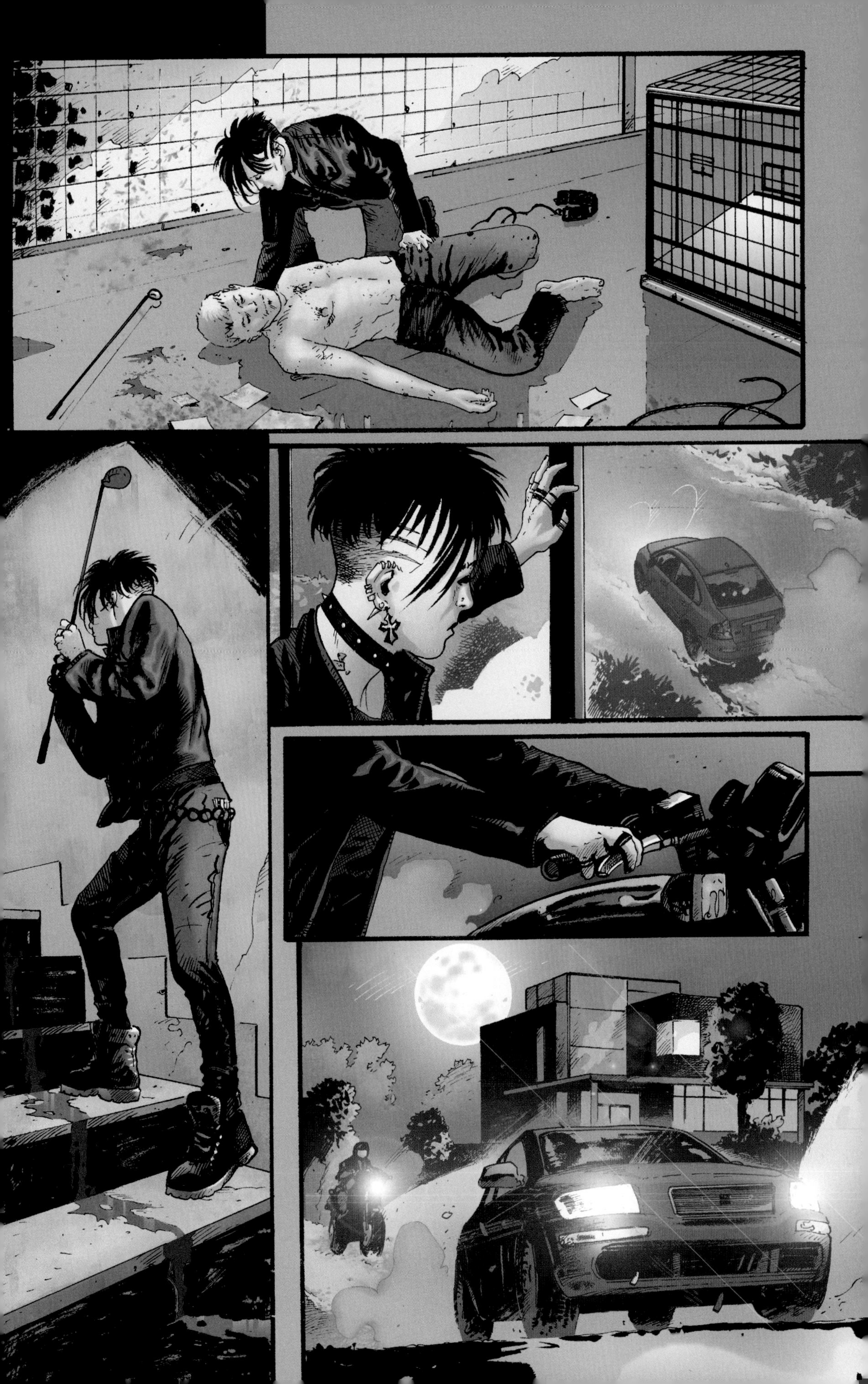

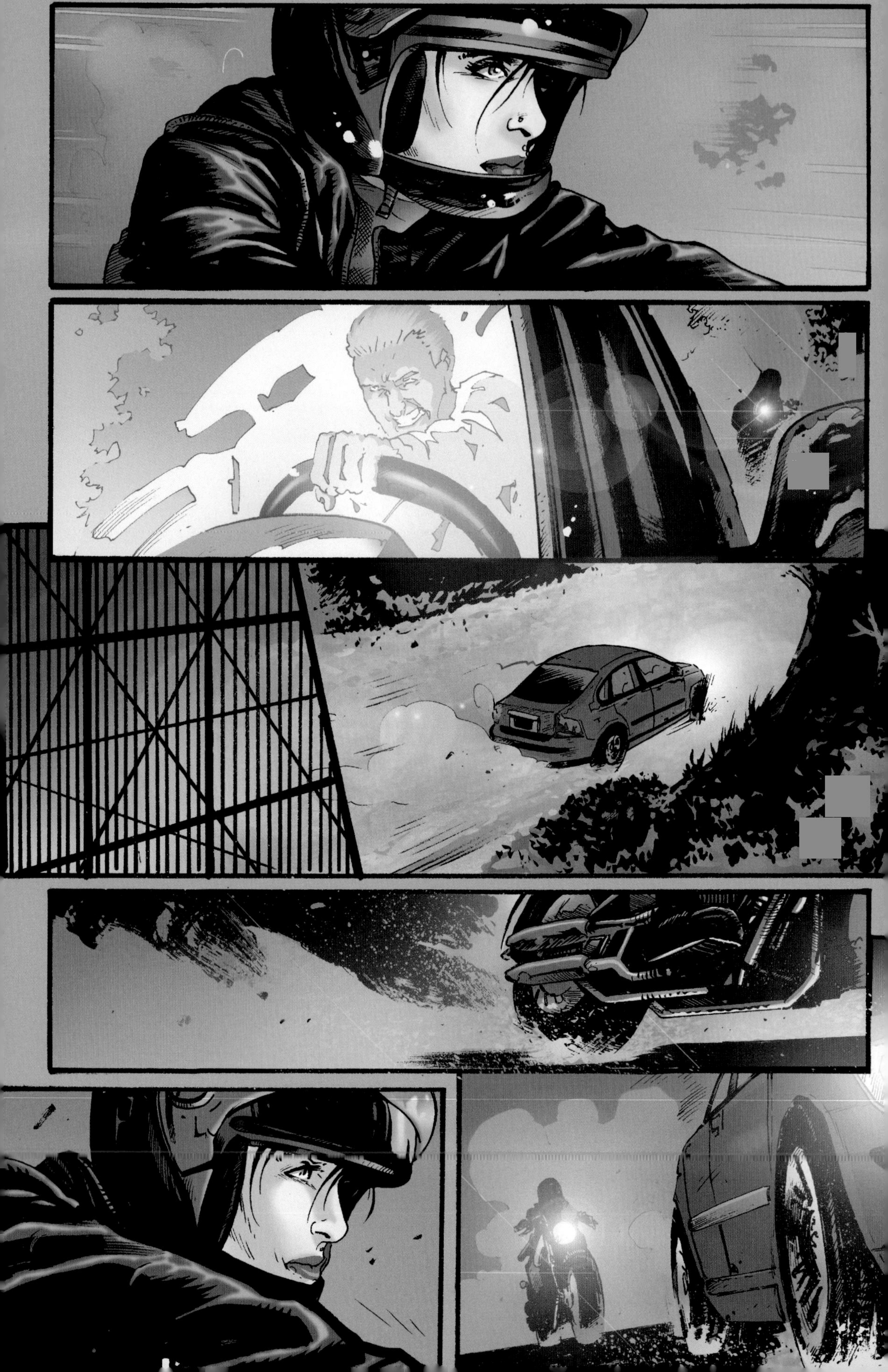

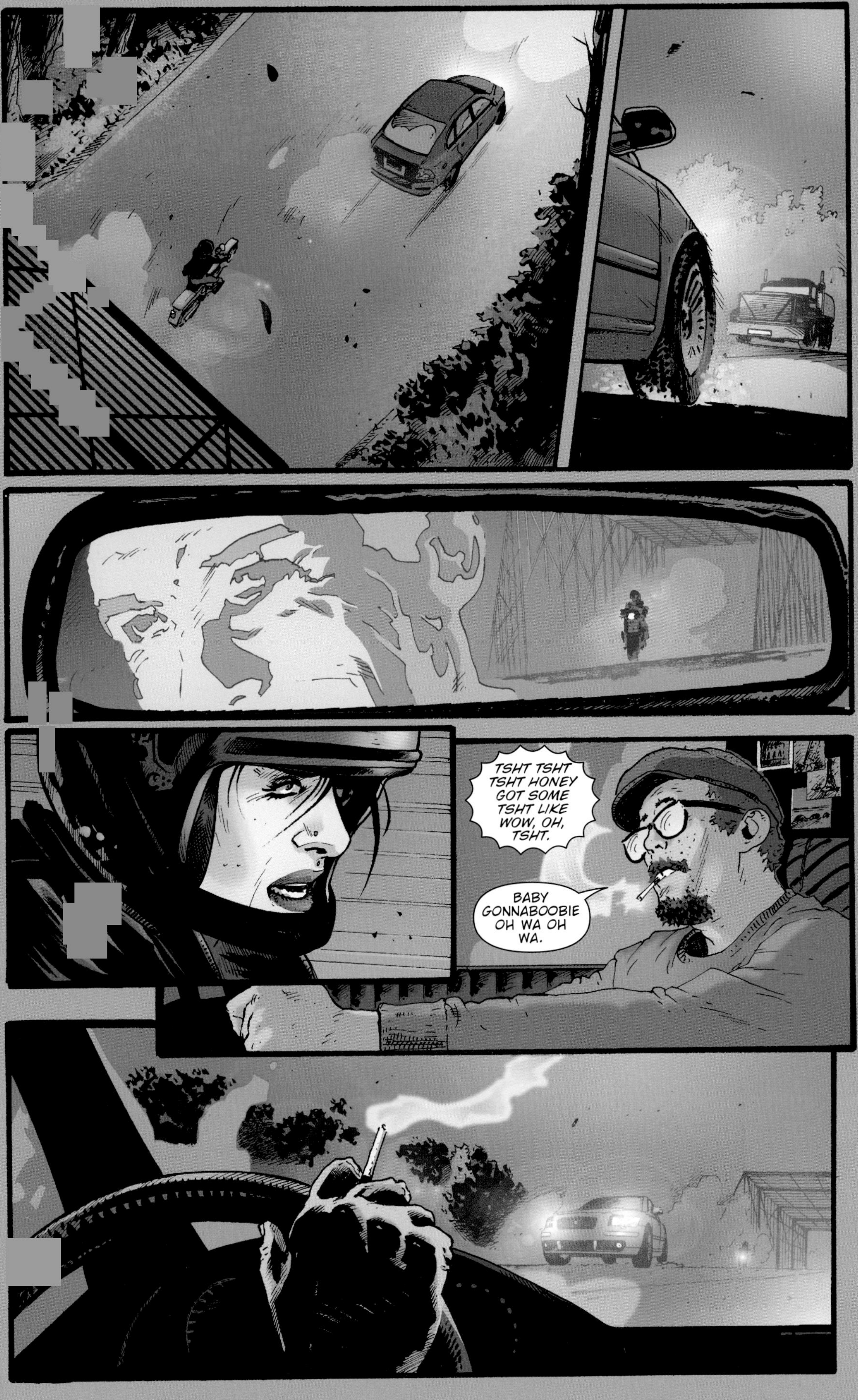
TSHT TSHT TSHT HONEY GOT SOME TSHT LIKE WOW, OH, TSHT.
BABY GONNABOOBIE OH WA OH WA.

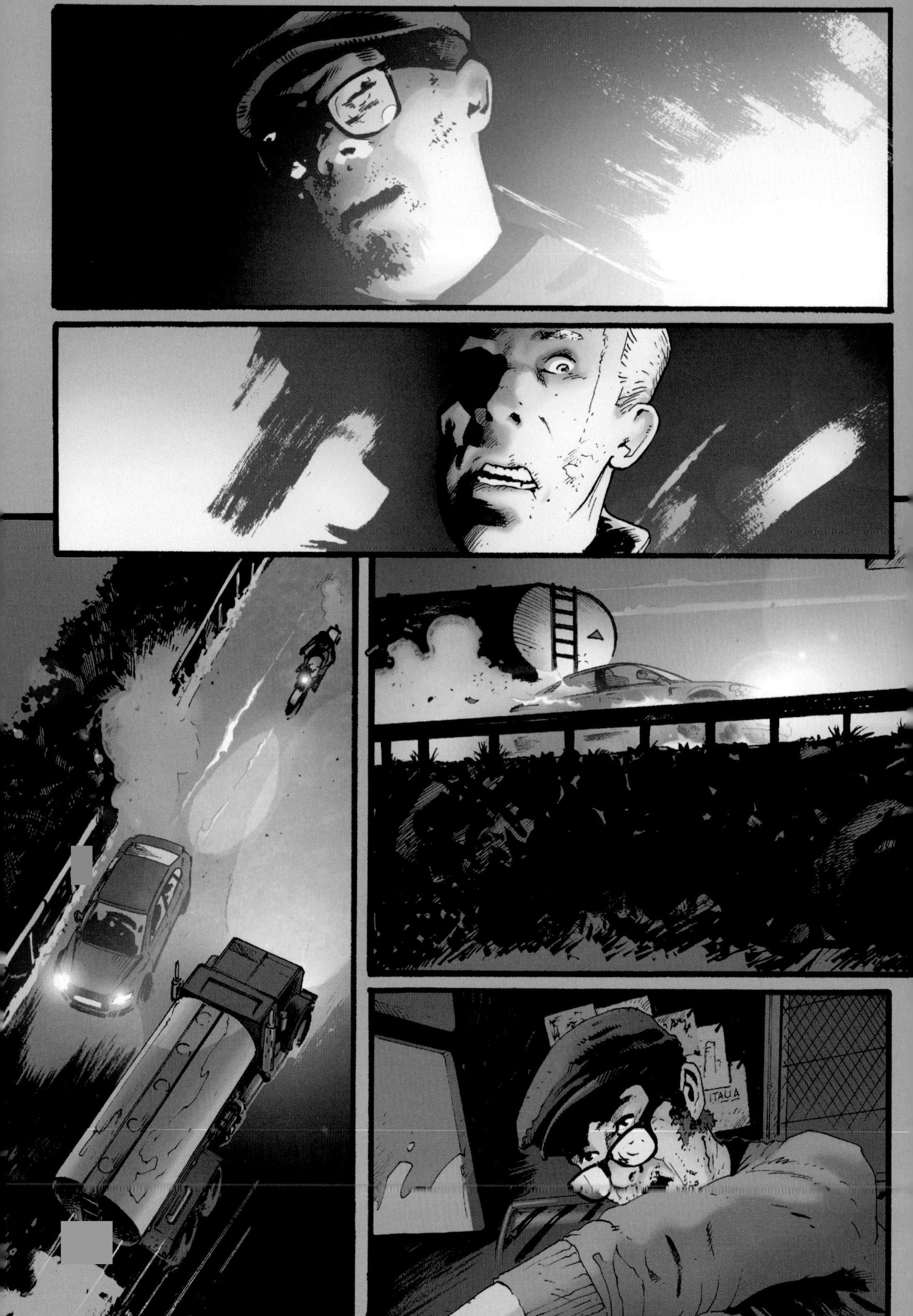
ITALIA

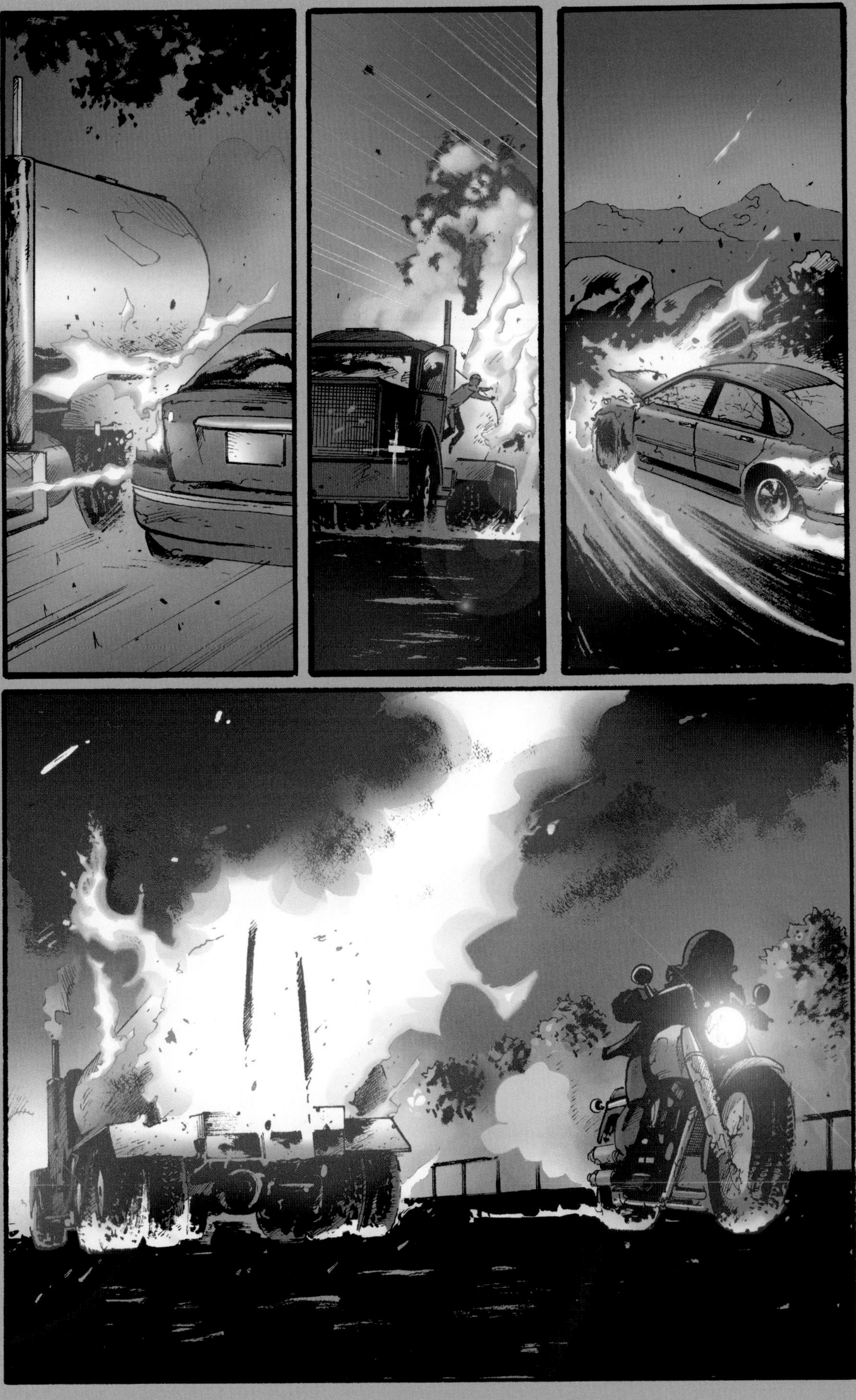

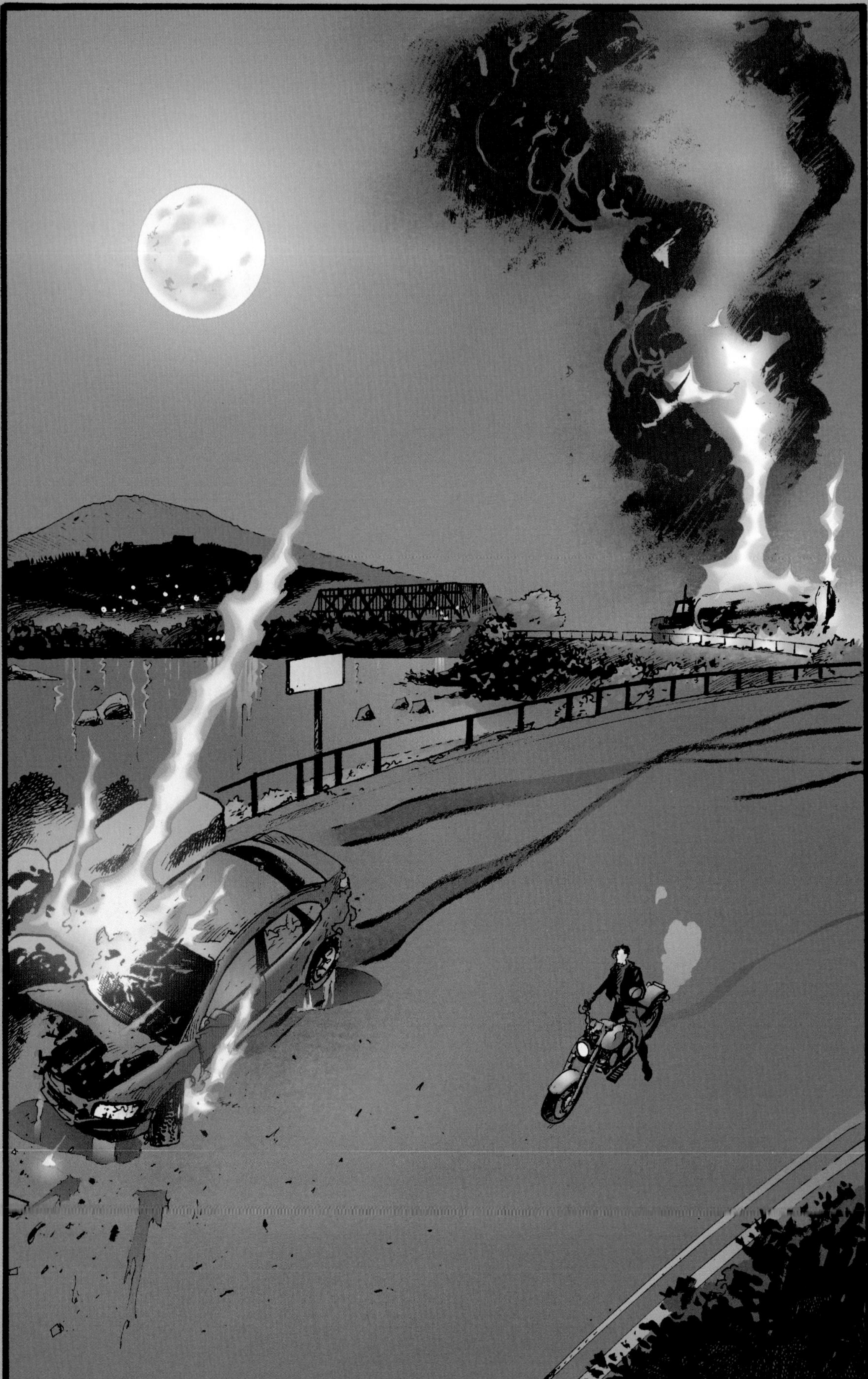

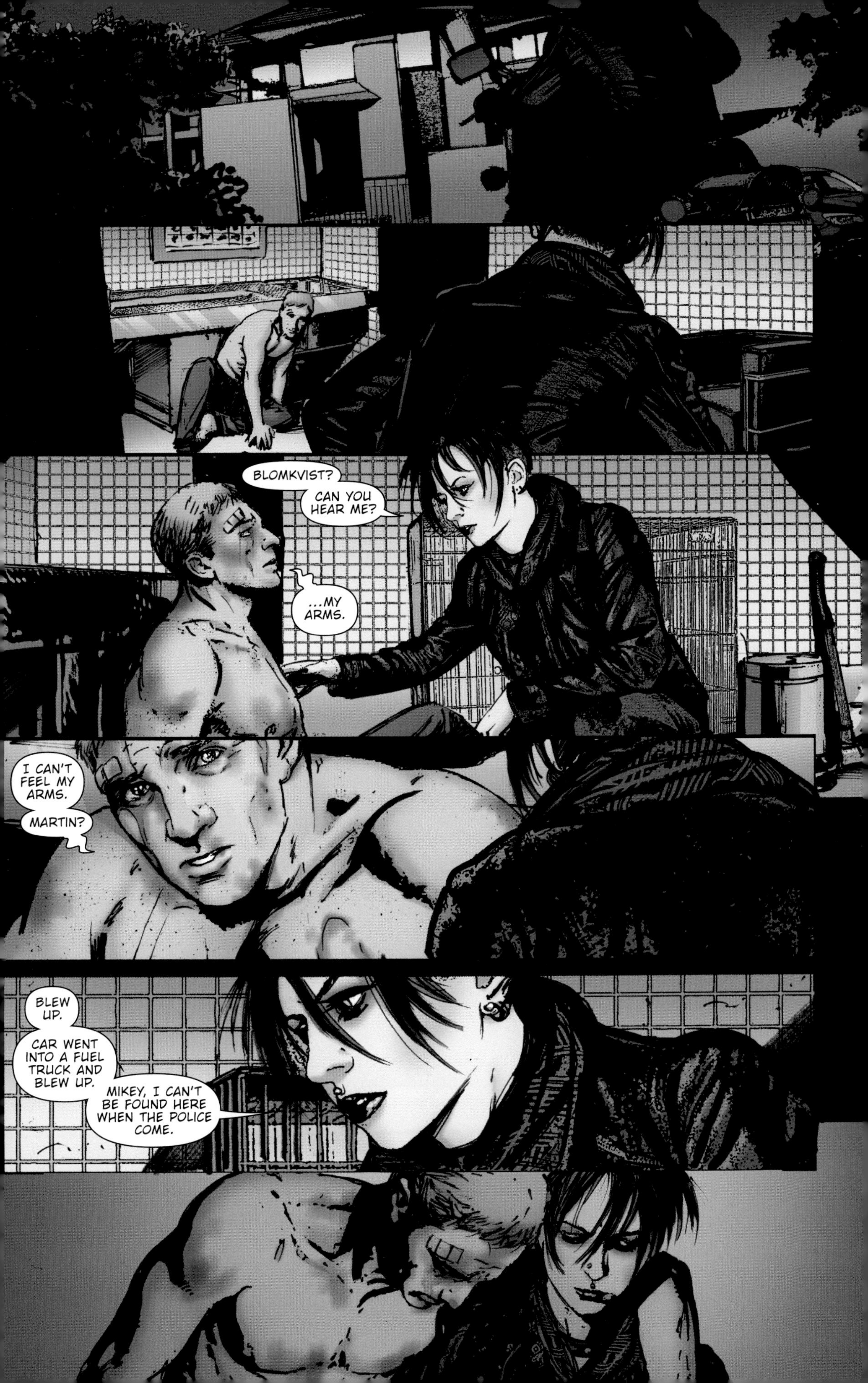
BLOMKVIST?
CAN YOU HEAR ME?
...MY ARMS.
I CAN'T FEEL MY ARMS.
MARTIN?
BLEW UP.
CAR WENT INTO A FUEL TRUCK AND BLEW UP.
MIKEY, I CAN'T BE FOUND HERE WHEN THE POLICE COME.

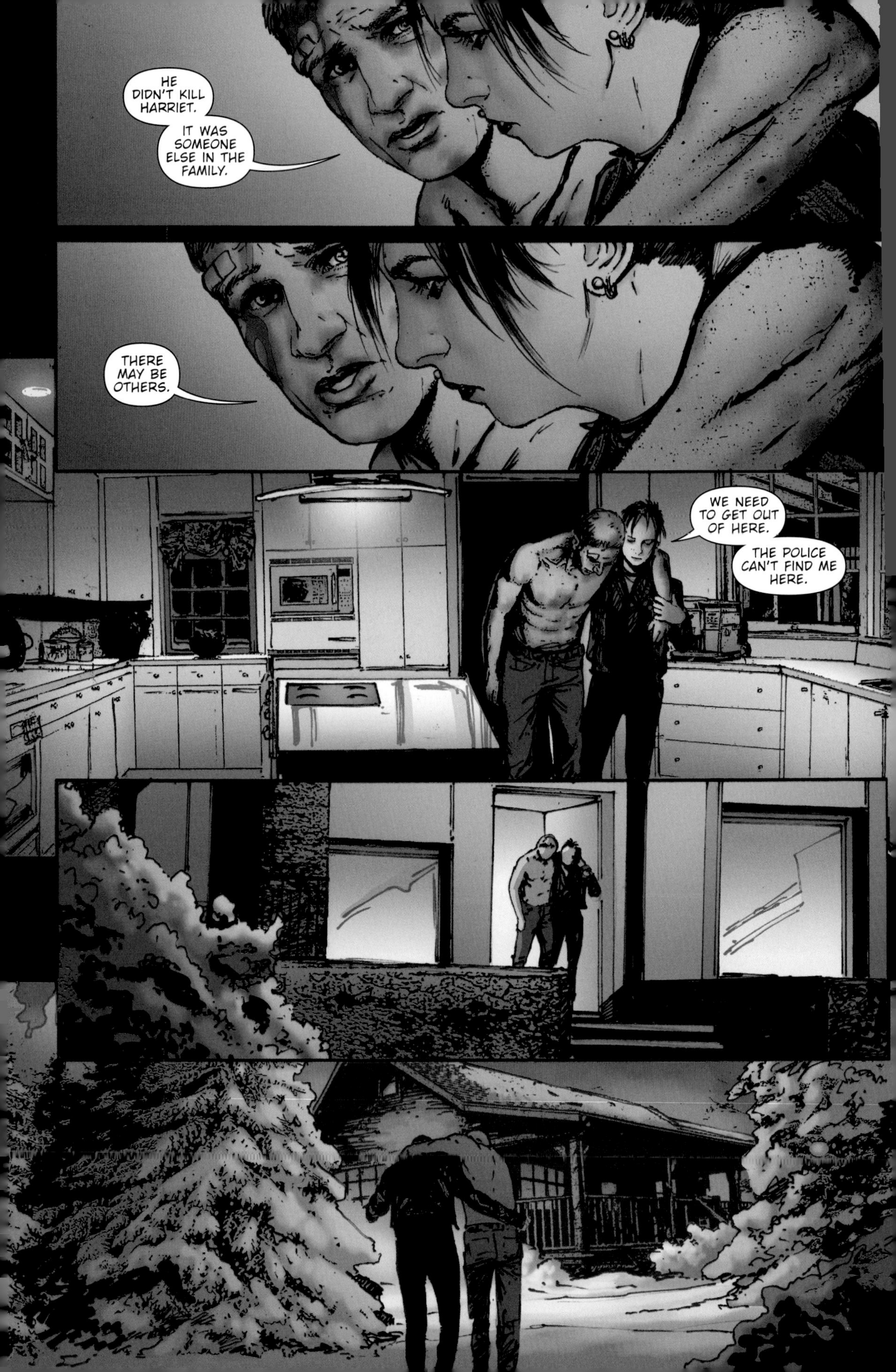
HE DIDN'T KILL HARRIET.
IT WAS SOMEONE ELSE IN THE FAMILY.
THERE MAY BE OTHERS.
WE NEED TO GET OUT OF HERE.
THE POLICE CAN'T FIND ME HERE.

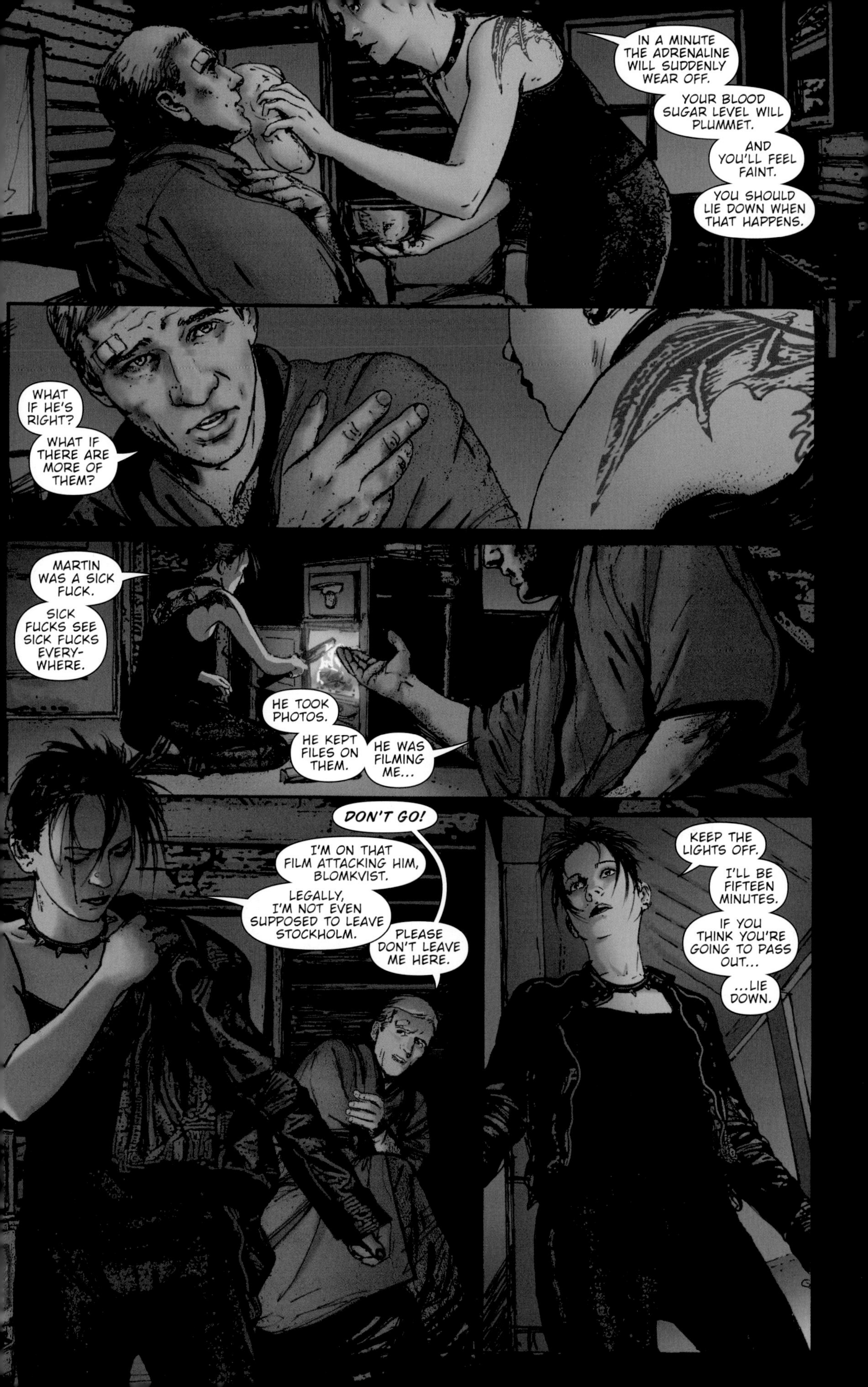
IN A MINUTE THE ADRENALINE WILL SUDDENLY WEAR OFF.
YOUR BLOOD SUGAR LEVEL WILL PLUMMET.
AND YOU'LL FEEL FAINT.
YOU SHOULD LIE DOWN WHEN THAT HAPPENS.
WHAT IF HE'S RIGHT?
WHAT IF THERE ARE MORE OF THEM?
MARTIN WAS A SICK FUCK.
SICK FUCKS SEE SICK FUCKS EVERY-WHERE.
HE TOOK PHOTOS.
HE KEPT FILES ON THEM.
HE WAS FILMING ME...
I'M ON THAT FILM ATTACKING HIM, BLOMKVIST.
LEGALLY, I'M NOT EVEN SUPPOSED TO LEAVE STOCKHOLM.
DON'T GO!
PLEASE DON'T LEAVE ME HERE.
KEEP THE LIGHTS OFF.
I'LL BE FIFTEEN MINUTES.
IF YOU THINK YOU'RE GOING TO PASS OUT...
...LIE DOWN.

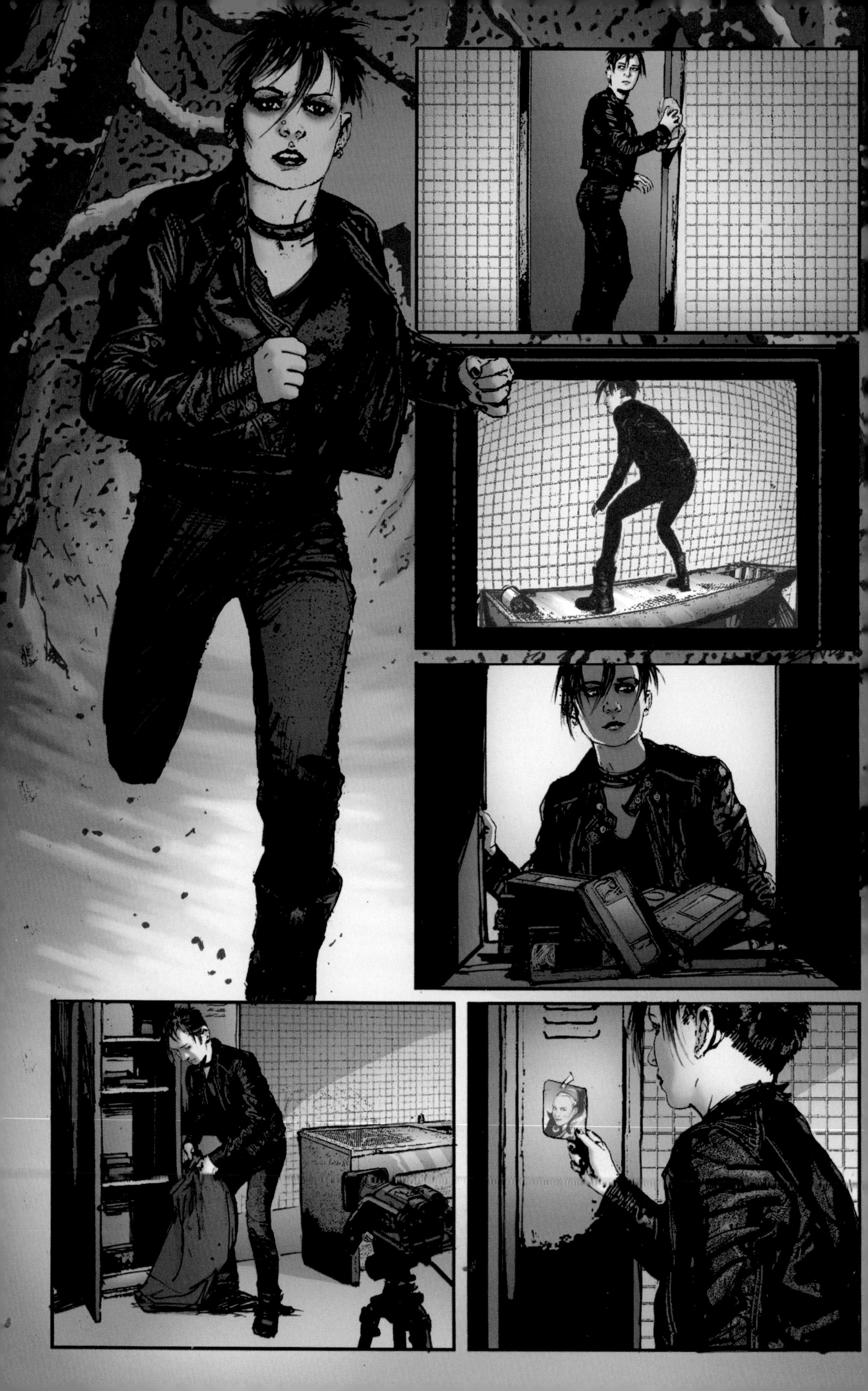

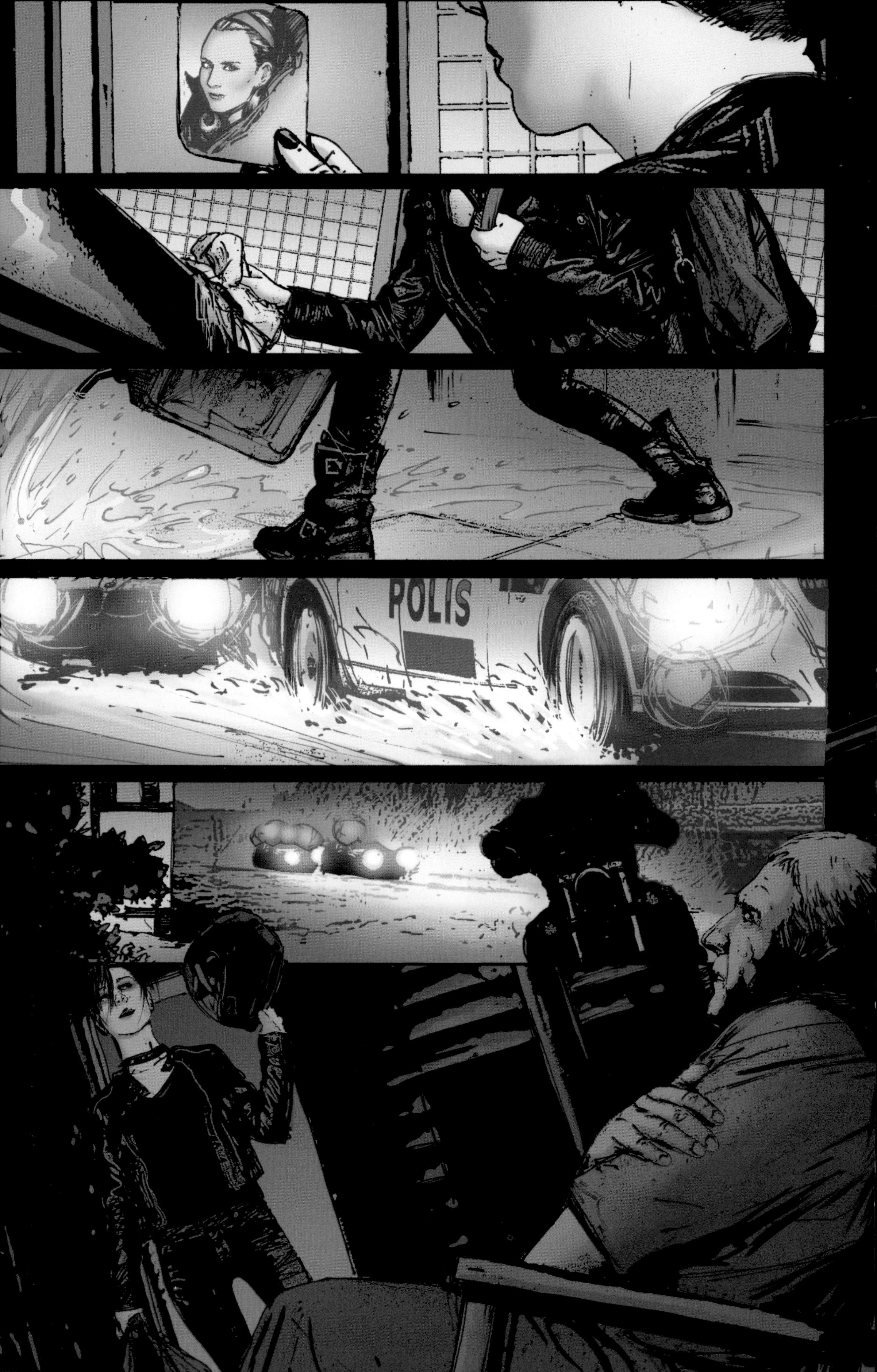
POLIS

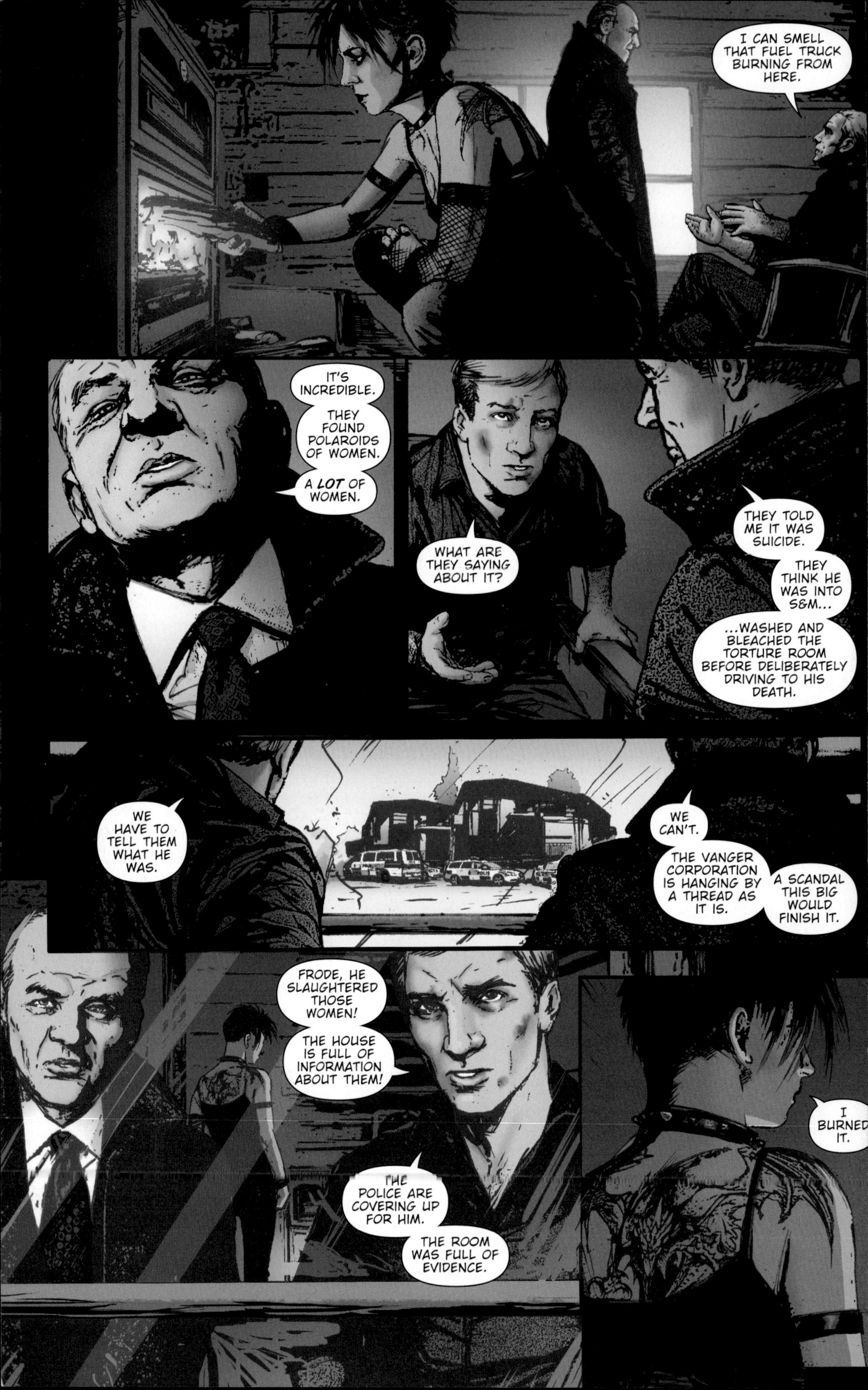
I CAN SMELL THAT FUEL TRUCK BURNING FROM HERE.
IT'S INCREDIBLE.
THEY FOUND POLAROIDS OF WOMEN.
A *LOT* OF WOMEN.
WHAT ARE THEY SAYING ABOUT IT?
THEY TOLD ME IT WAS SUICIDE.
THEY THINK HE WAS INTO S&M...
...WASHED AND BLEACHED THE TORTURE ROOM BEFORE DELIBERATELY DRIVING TO HIS DEATH.
WE HAVE TO TELL THEM WHAT HE WAS.
WE CAN'T.
THE VANGER CORPORATION IS HANGING BY A THREAD AS IT IS.
A SCANDAL THIS BIG WOULD FINISH IT.
FRODE, HE SLAUGHTERED THOSE WOMEN!
THE HOUSE IS FULL OF INFORMATION ABOUT THEM!
THE POLICE ARE COVERING UP FOR HIM.
THE ROOM WAS FULL OF EVIDENCE.
I BURNED IT.

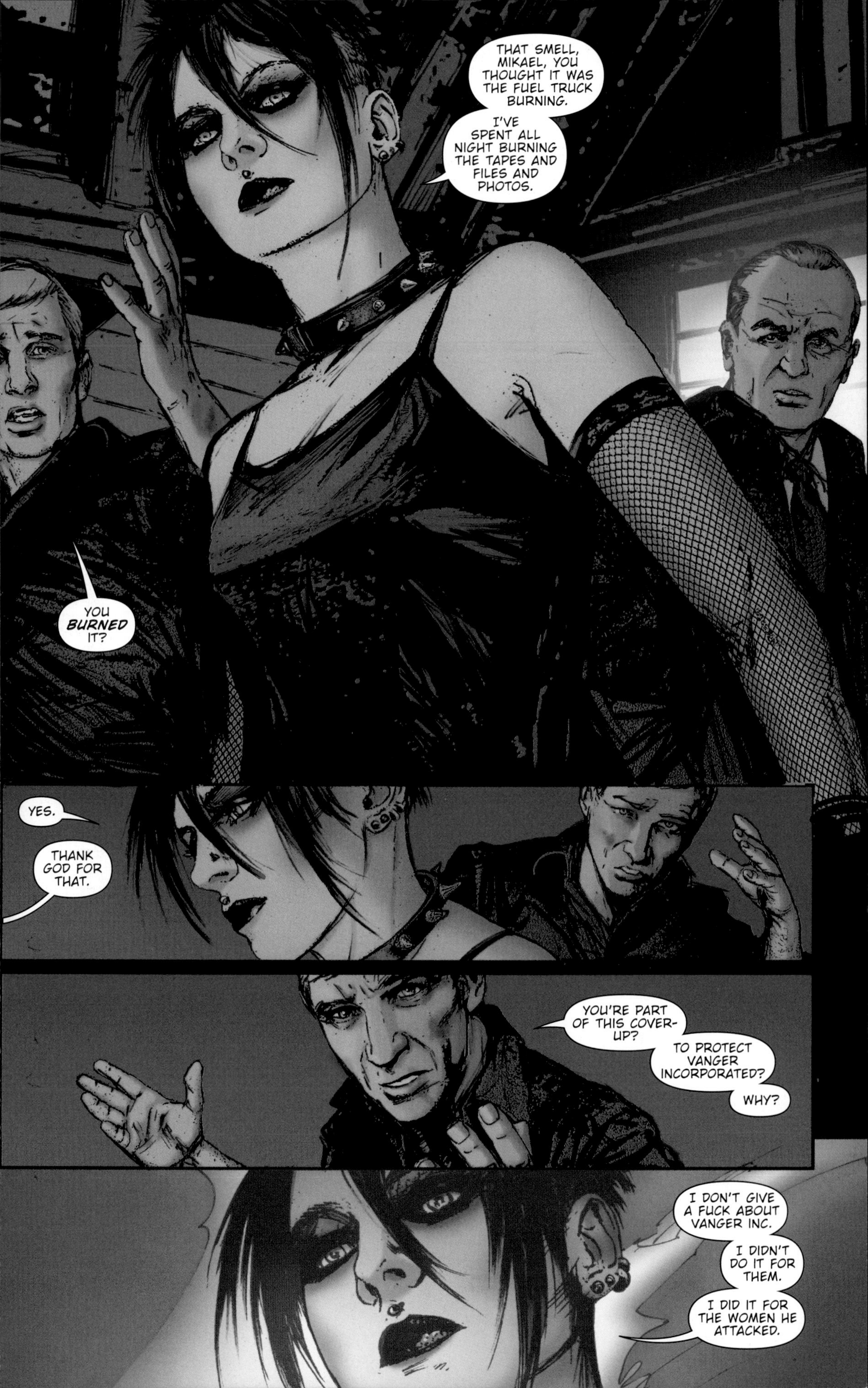
THAT SMELL, MIKAEL, YOU THOUGHT IT WAS THE FUEL TRUCK BURNING.
I'VE SPENT ALL NIGHT BURNING THE TAPES AND FILES AND PHOTOS.
YOU *BURNED* IT?
YES.
THANK GOD FOR THAT.
YOU'RE PART OF THIS COVER-UP?
TO PROTECT VANGER INCORPORATED?
WHY?
I DON'T GIVE A FUCK ABOUT VANGER INC.
I DIDN'T DO IT FOR THEM.
I DID IT FOR THE WOMEN HE ATTACKED.

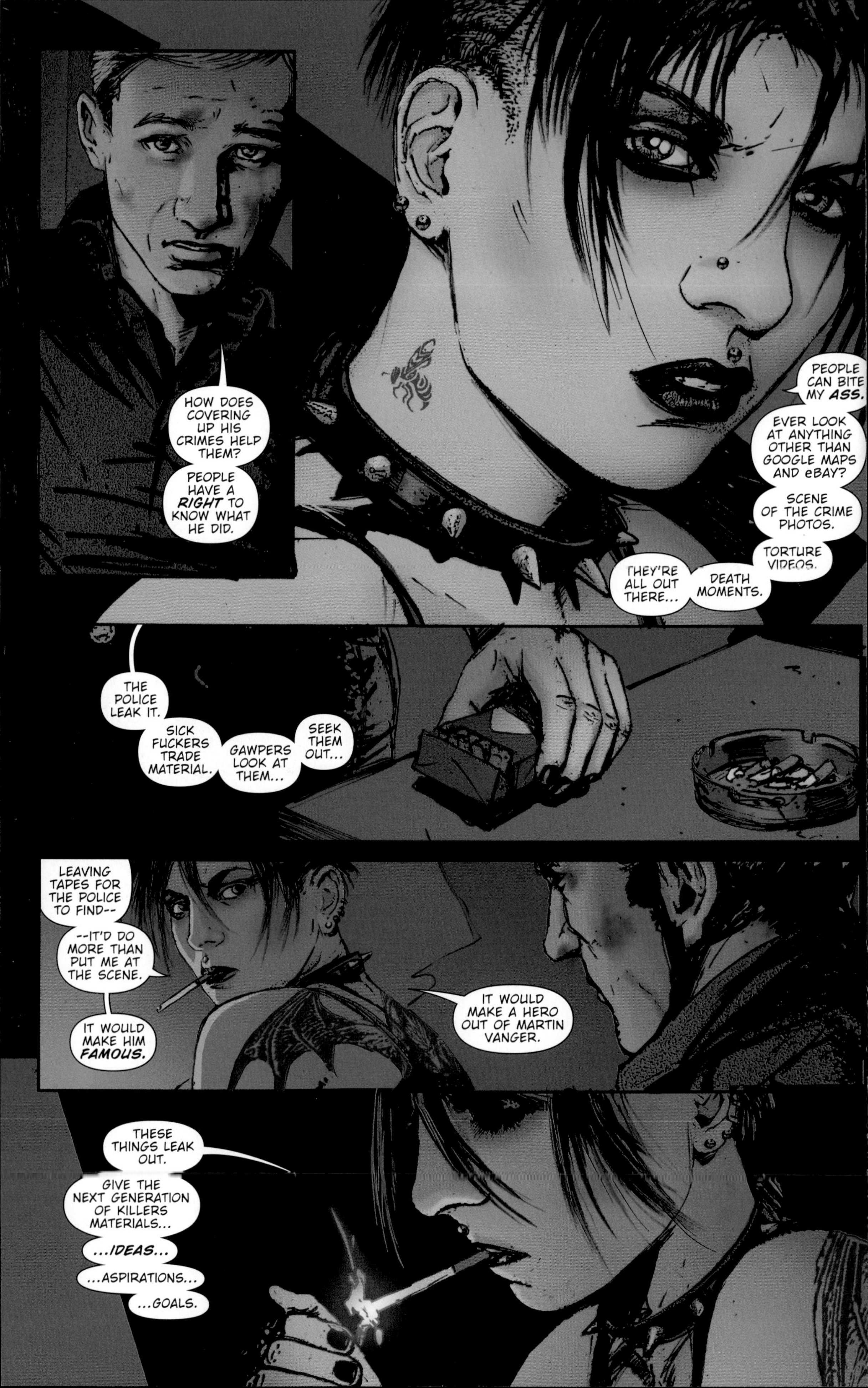
HOW DOES COVERING UP HIS CRIMES HELP THEM?
PEOPLE HAVE A RIGHT TO KNOW WHAT HE DID.
PEOPLE CAN BITE MY ASS.
EVER LOOK AT ANYTHING OTHER THAN GOOGLE MAPS AND eBAY?
SCENE OF THE CRIME PHOTOS.
TORTURE VIDEOS.
DEATH MOMENTS.
THEY'RE ALL OUT THERE...
THE POLICE LEAK IT.
SICK FUCKERS TRADE MATERIAL.
GAWPERS LOOK AT THEM...
SEEK THEM OUT...
LEAVING TAPES FOR THE POLICE TO FIND--
--IT'D DO MORE THAN PUT ME AT THE SCENE.
IT WOULD MAKE HIM FAMOUS.
IT WOULD MAKE A HERO OUT OF MARTIN VANGER.
THESE THINGS LEAK OUT.
GIVE THE NEXT GENERATION OF KILLERS MATERIALS...
...IDEAS...
...ASPIRATIONS...
...GOALS.

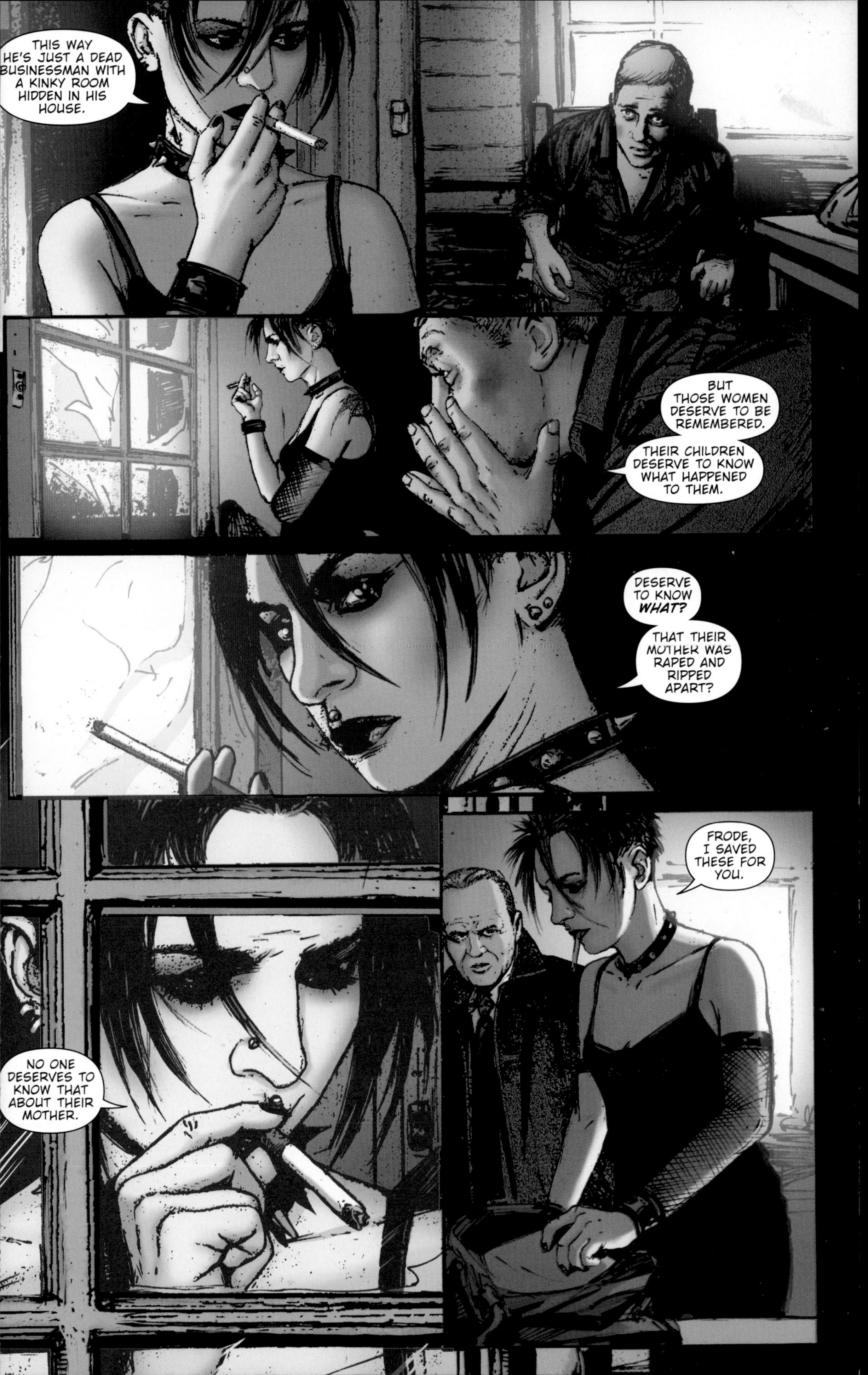
THIS WAY HE'S JUST A DEAD BUSINESSMAN WITH A KINKY ROOM HIDDEN IN HIS HOUSE.
BUT THOSE WOMEN DESERVE TO BE REMEMBERED.
THEIR CHILDREN DESERVE TO KNOW WHAT HAPPENED TO THEM.
DESERVE TO KNOW *WHAT?*
THAT THEIR MOTHER WAS RAPED AND RIPPED APART?
NO ONE DESERVES TO KNOW THAT ABOUT THEIR MOTHER.
FRODE, I SAVED THESE FOR YOU.

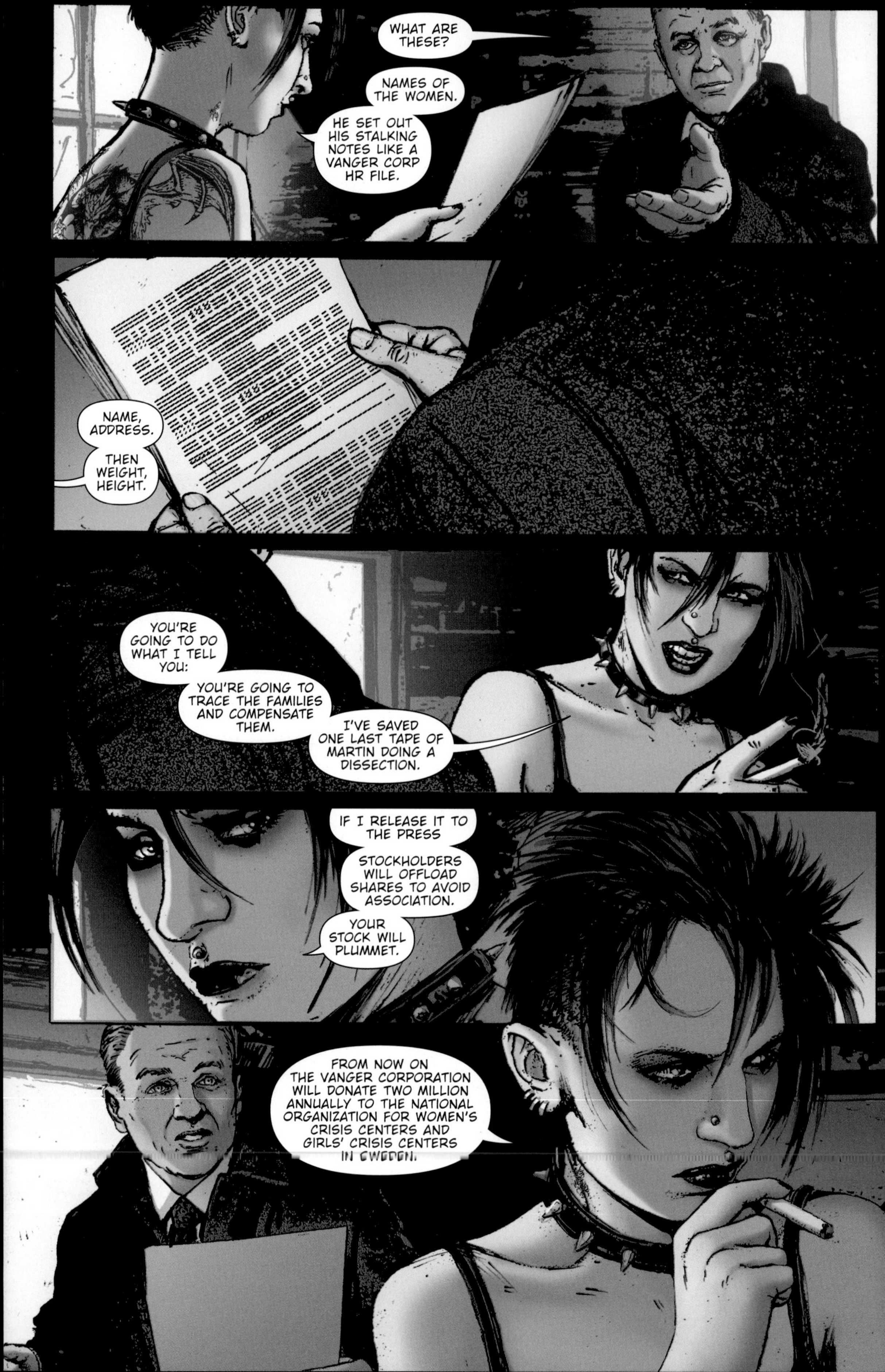
WHAT ARE THESE?
NAMES OF THE WOMEN.
HE SET OUT HIS STALKING NOTES LIKE A VANGER CORP HR FILE.
NAME, ADDRESS.
THEN WEIGHT, HEIGHT.
YOU'RE GOING TO DO WHAT I TELL YOU:
YOU'RE GOING TO TRACE THE FAMILIES AND COMPENSATE THEM.
I'VE SAVED ONE LAST TAPE OF MARTIN DOING A DISSECTION.
IF I RELEASE IT TO THE PRESS
STOCKHOLDERS WILL OFFLOAD SHARES TO AVOID ASSOCIATION.
YOUR STOCK WILL PLUMMET.
FROM NOW ON THE VANGER CORPORATION WILL DONATE TWO MILLION ANNUALLY TO THE NATIONAL ORGANIZATION FOR WOMEN'S CRISIS CENTERS AND GIRLS' CRISIS CENTERS IN SWEDEN.

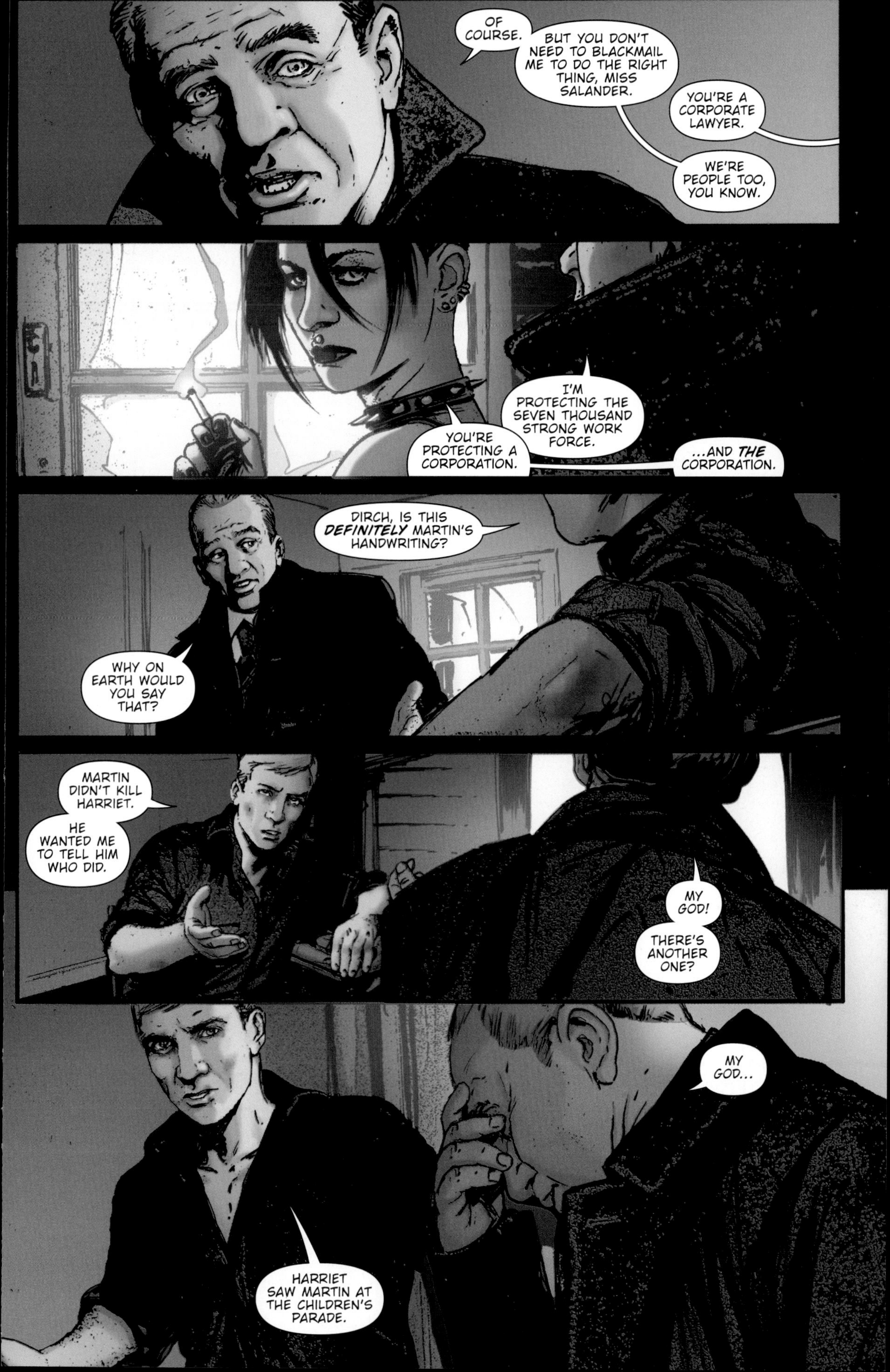

OF COURSE.
BUT YOU DON'T NEED TO BLACKMAIL ME TO DO THE RIGHT THING, MISS SALANDER.
YOU'RE A CORPORATE LAWYER.
WE'RE PEOPLE TOO, YOU KNOW.
I'M PROTECTING THE SEVEN THOUSAND STRONG WORK FORCE.
YOU'RE PROTECTING A CORPORATION.
...AND *THE* CORPORATION.
DIRCH, IS THIS *DEFINITELY* MARTIN'S HANDWRITING?
WHY ON EARTH WOULD YOU SAY THAT?
MARTIN DIDN'T KILL HARRIET.
HE WANTED ME TO TELL HIM WHO DID.
MY GOD!
THERE'S ANOTHER ONE?
MY GOD...
HARRIET SAW MARTIN AT THE CHILDREN'S PARADE.

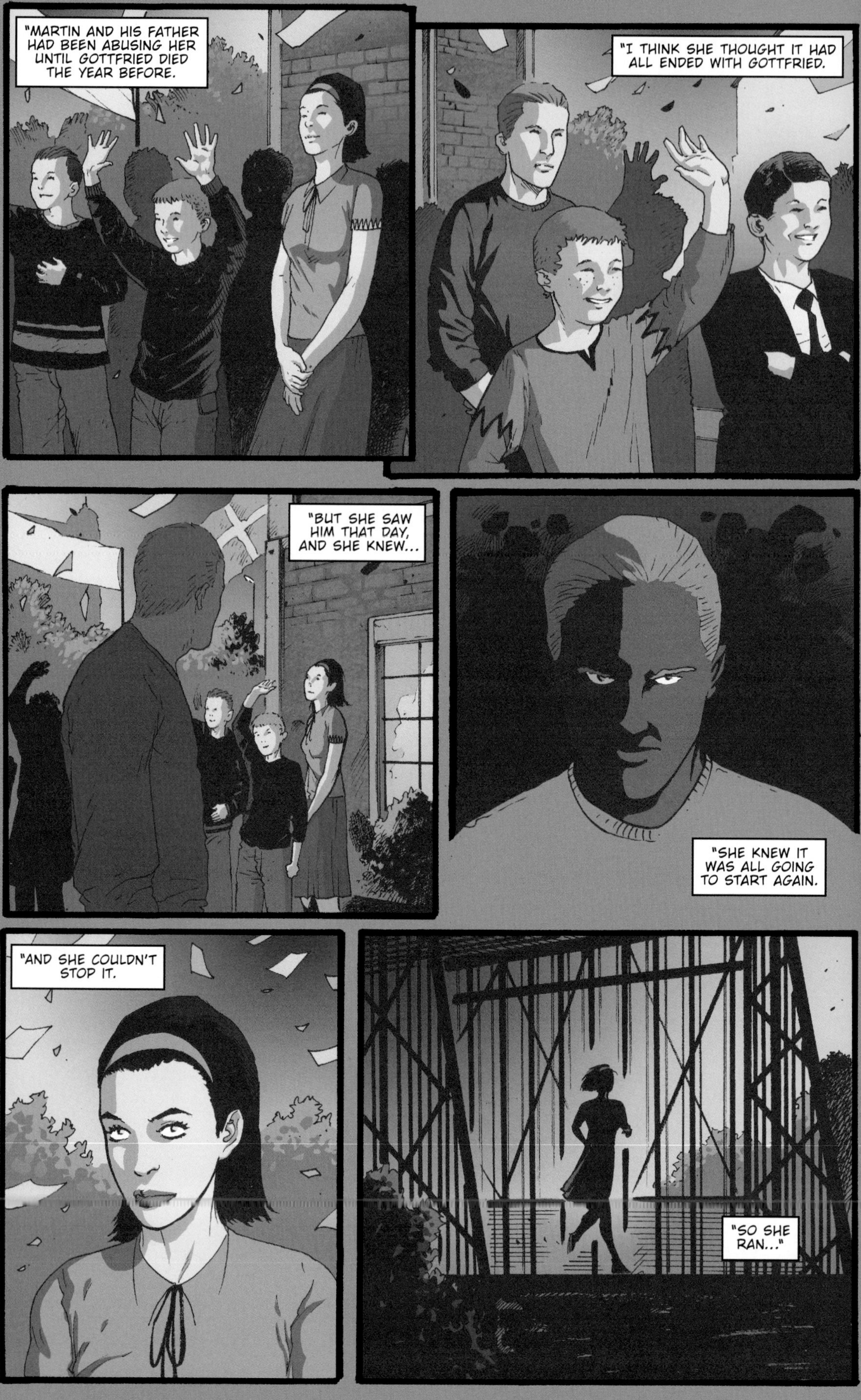
"MARTIN AND HIS FATHER HAD BEEN ABUSING HER UNTIL GOTTFRIED DIED THE YEAR BEFORE.
"I THINK SHE THOUGHT IT HAD ALL ENDED WITH GOTTFRIED.
"BUT SHE SAW HIM THAT DAY, AND SHE KNEW...
"SHE KNEW IT WAS ALL GOING TO START AGAIN.
"AND SHE COULDN'T STOP IT.
"SO SHE RAN..."

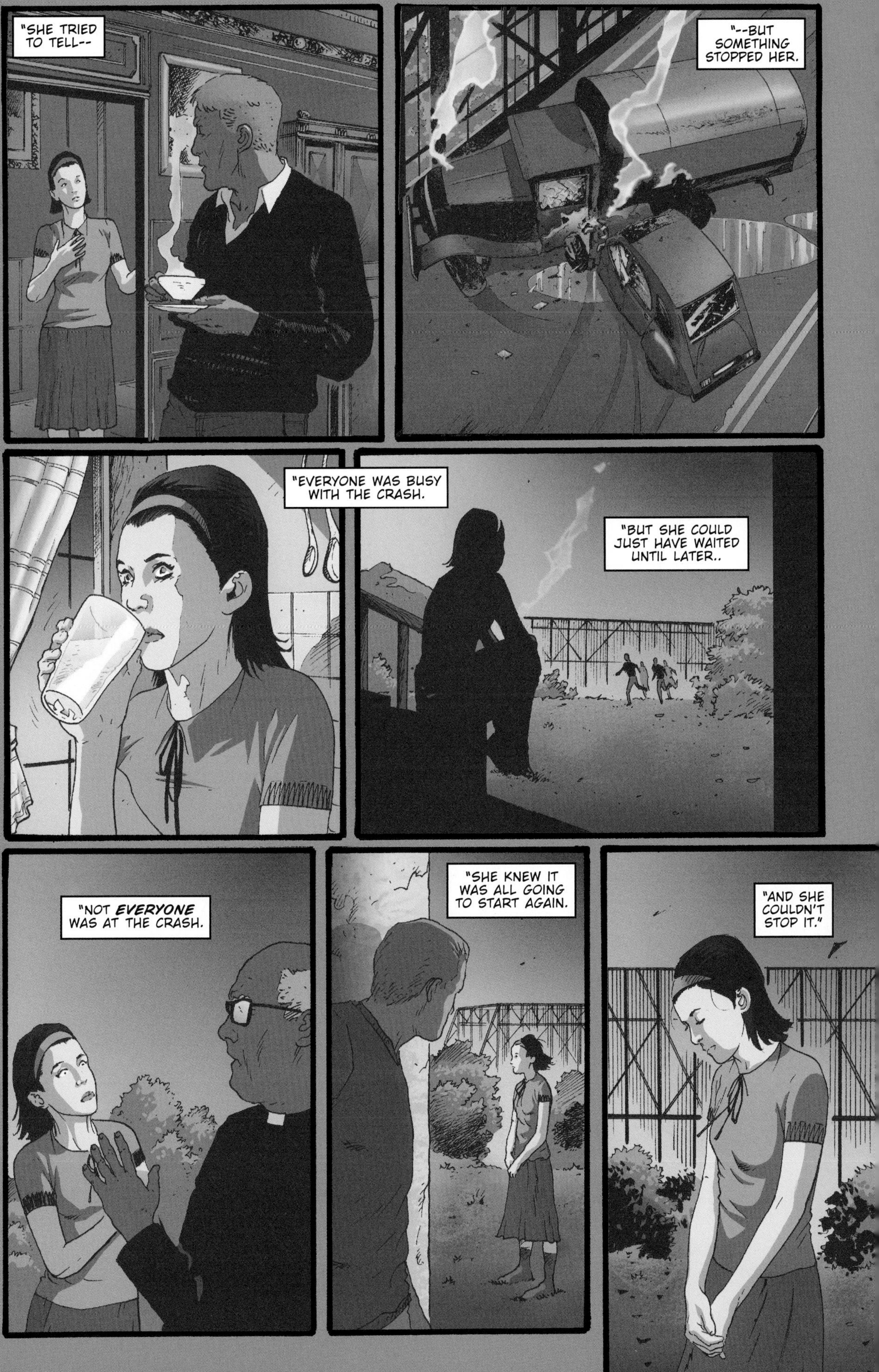
"SHE TRIED TO TELL--
"--BUT SOMETHING STOPPED HER.
"EVERYONE WAS BUSY WITH THE CRASH.
"BUT SHE COULD JUST HAVE WAITED UNTIL LATER..
"NOT *EVERYONE* WAS AT THE CRASH.
"SHE KNEW IT WAS ALL GOING TO START AGAIN.
"AND SHE COULDN'T STOP IT."

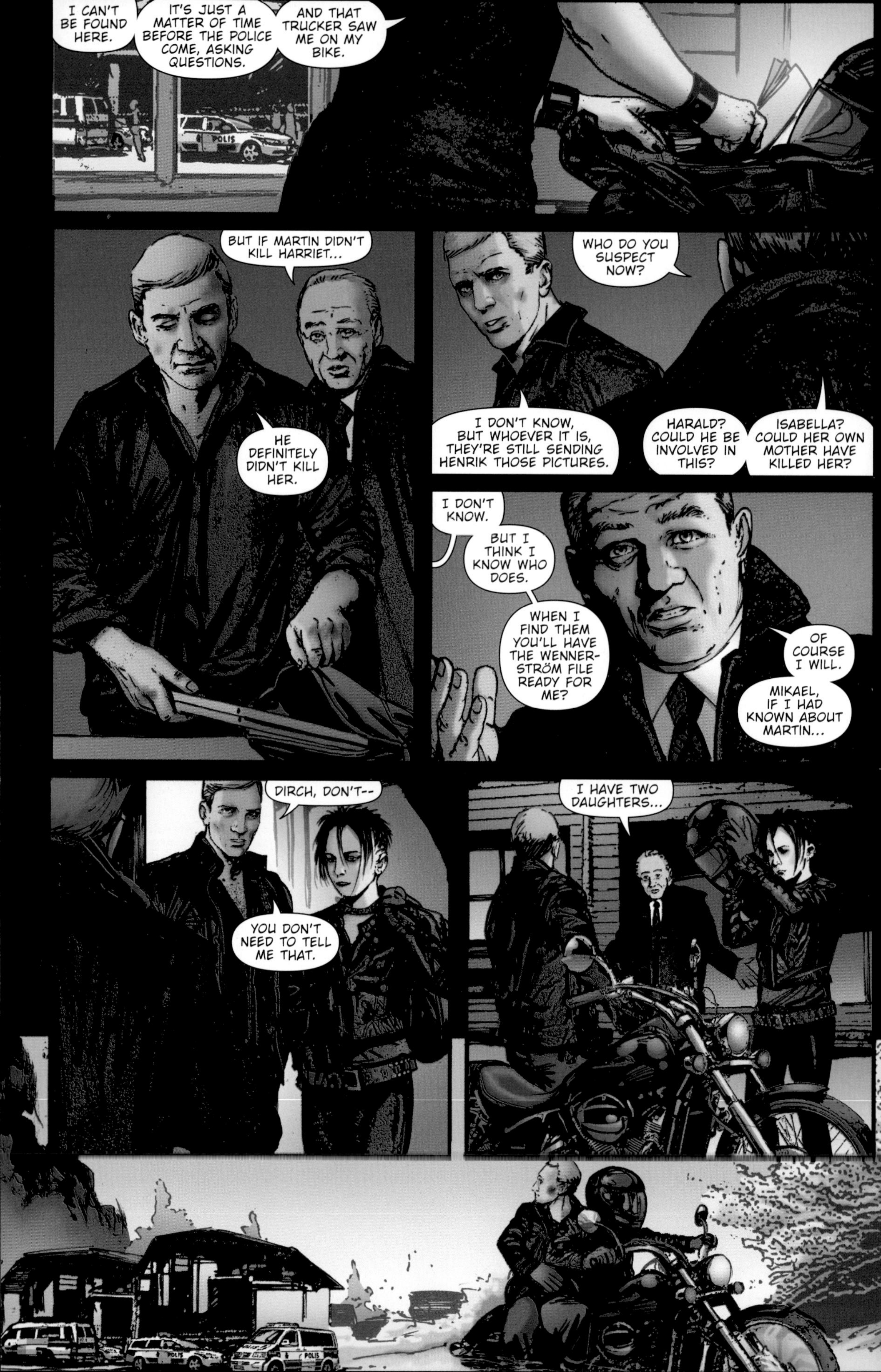
I CAN'T BE FOUND HERE.
IT'S JUST A MATTER OF TIME BEFORE THE POLICE COME, ASKING QUESTIONS.
AND THAT TRUCKER SAW ME ON MY BIKE.
POLIS
BUT IF MARTIN DIDN'T KILL HARRIET...
HE DEFINITELY DIDN'T KILL HER.
WHO DO YOU SUSPECT NOW?
I DON'T KNOW, BUT WHOEVER IT IS, THEY'RE STILL SENDING HENRIK THOSE PICTURES.
HARALD? COULD HE BE INVOLVED IN THIS?
ISABELLA? COULD HER OWN MOTHER HAVE KILLED HER?
I DON'T KNOW.
BUT I THINK I KNOW WHO DOES.
WHEN I FIND THEM YOU'LL HAVE THE WENNER-STRÖM FILE READY FOR ME?
OF COURSE I WILL.
MIKAEL, IF I HAD KNOWN ABOUT MARTIN...
DIRCH, DON'T--
YOU DON'T NEED TO TELL ME THAT.
I HAVE TWO DAUGHTERS...
POLIS
POLIS

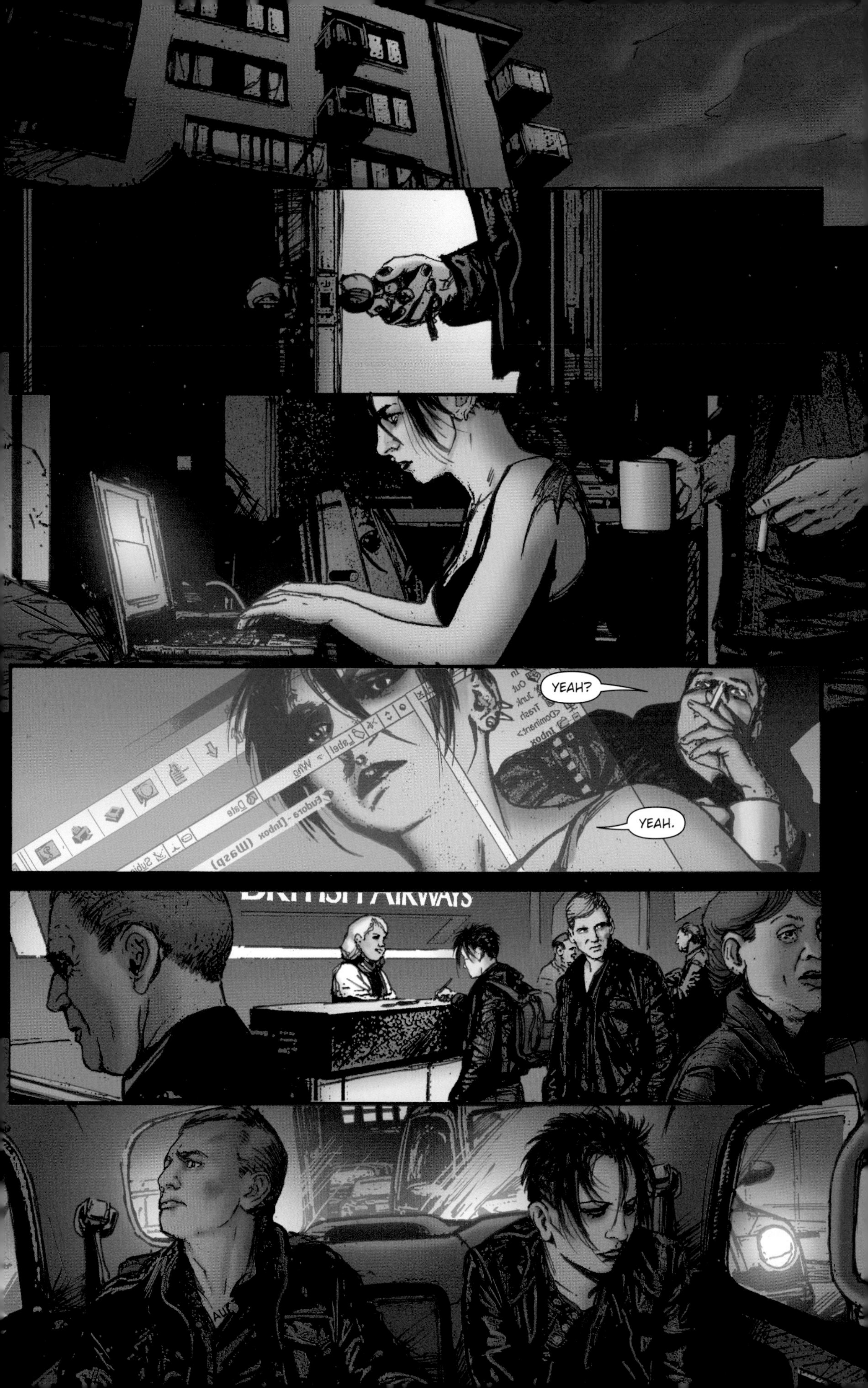
YEAH?
YEAH.
BRITISH AIRWAYS

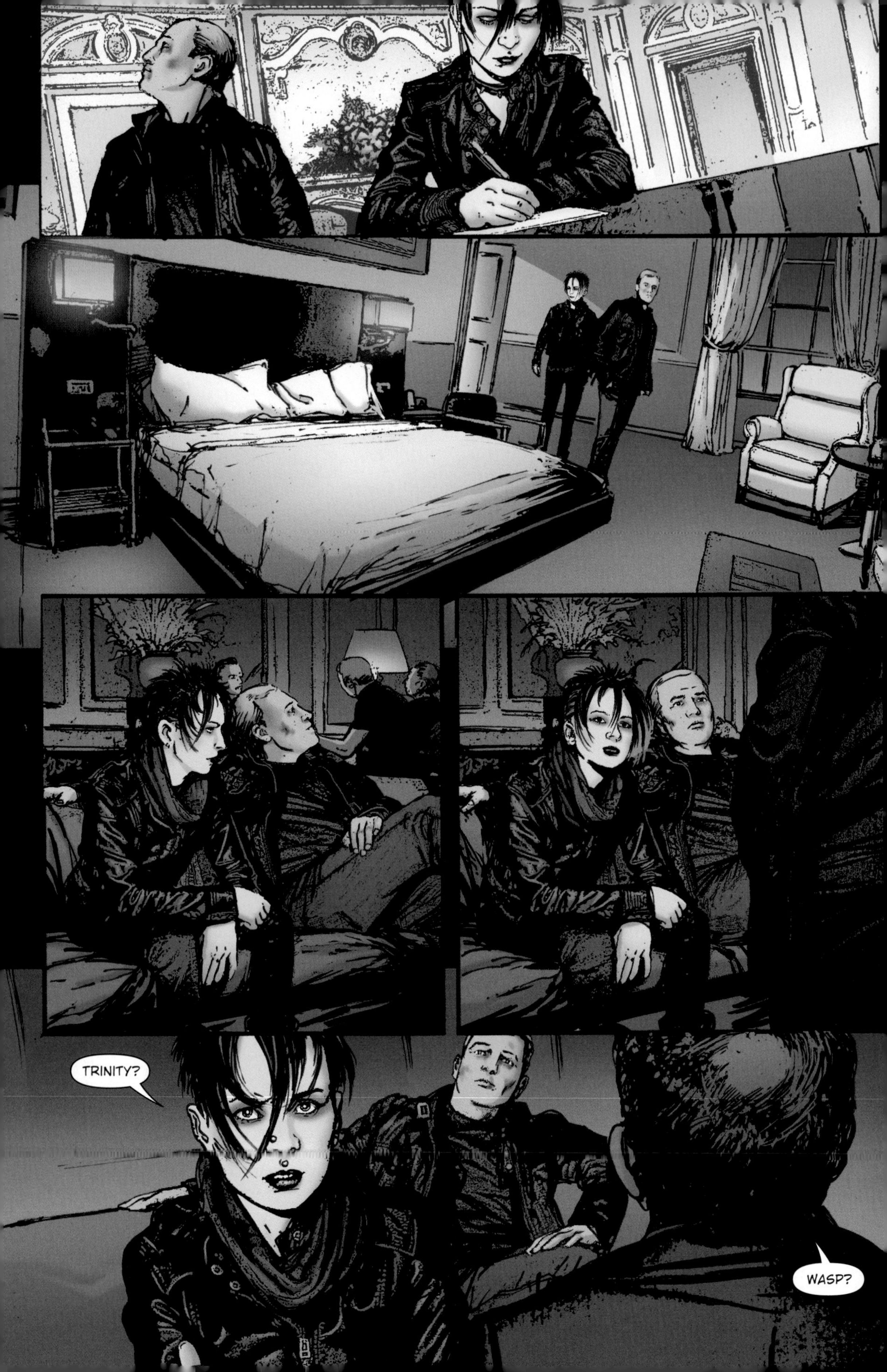
TRINITY?
WASP?

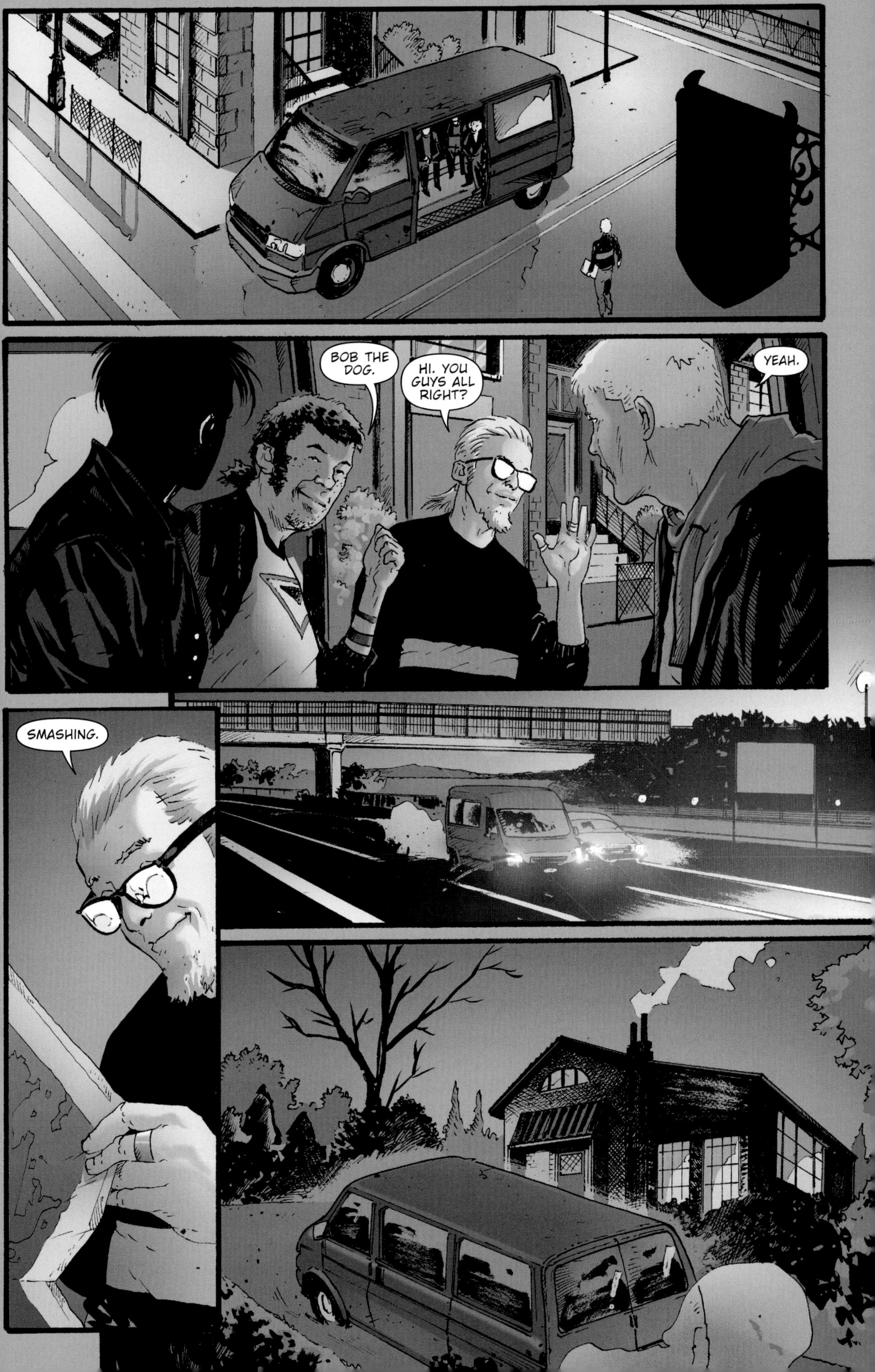
BOB THE DOG.
HI. YOU GUYS ALL RIGHT?
YEAH.
SMASHING.

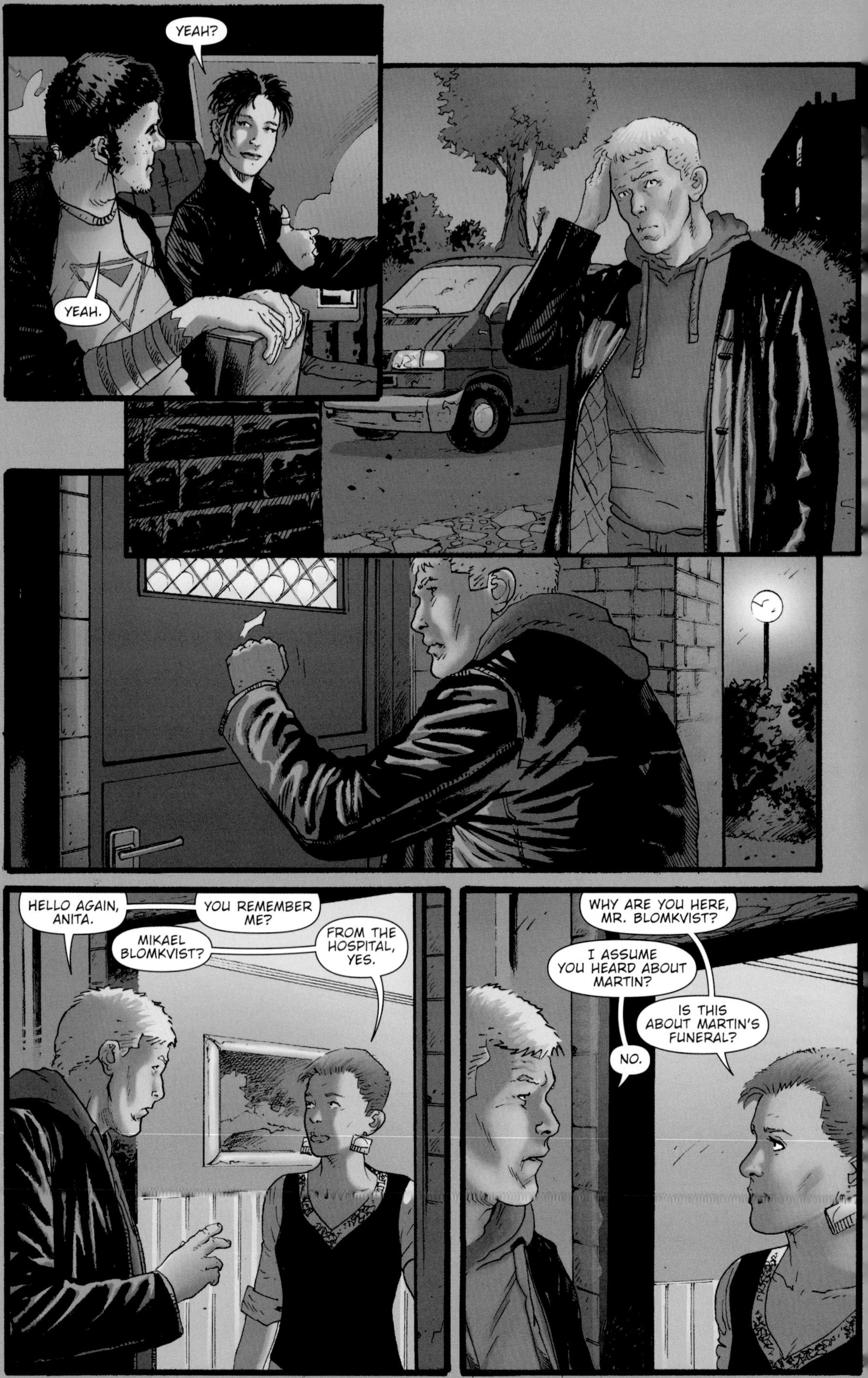
YEAH?
YEAH.
HELLO AGAIN, ANITA.
YOU REMEMBER ME?
MIKAEL BLOMKVIST?
FROM THE HOSPITAL, YES.
WHY ARE YOU HERE, MR. BLOMKVIST?
I ASSUME YOU HEARD ABOUT MARTIN?
IS THIS ABOUT MARTIN'S FUNERAL?
NO.

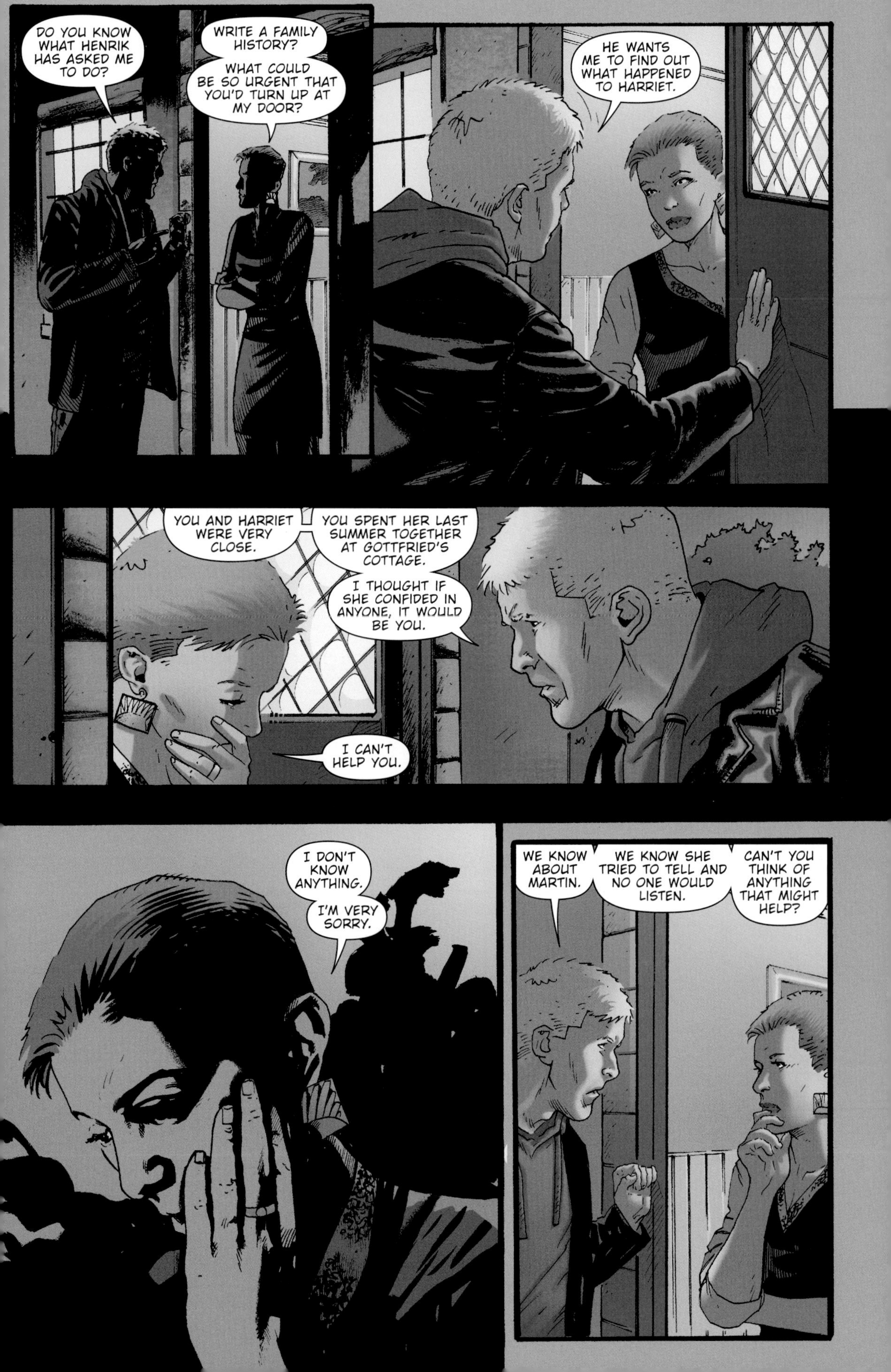
DO YOU KNOW WHAT HENRIK HAS ASKED ME TO DO?
WRITE A FAMILY HISTORY?
WHAT COULD BE SO URGENT THAT YOU'D TURN UP AT MY DOOR?
HE WANTS ME TO FIND OUT WHAT HAPPENED TO HARRIET.
YOU AND HARRIET WERE VERY CLOSE.
YOU SPENT HER LAST SUMMER TOGETHER AT GOTTFRIED'S COTTAGE.
I THOUGHT IF SHE CONFIDED IN ANYONE, IT WOULD BE YOU.
I CAN'T HELP YOU.
I DON'T KNOW ANYTHING.
I'M VERY SORRY.
WE KNOW ABOUT MARTIN.
WE KNOW SHE TRIED TO TELL AND NO ONE WOULD LISTEN.
CAN'T YOU THINK OF ANYTHING THAT MIGHT HELP?

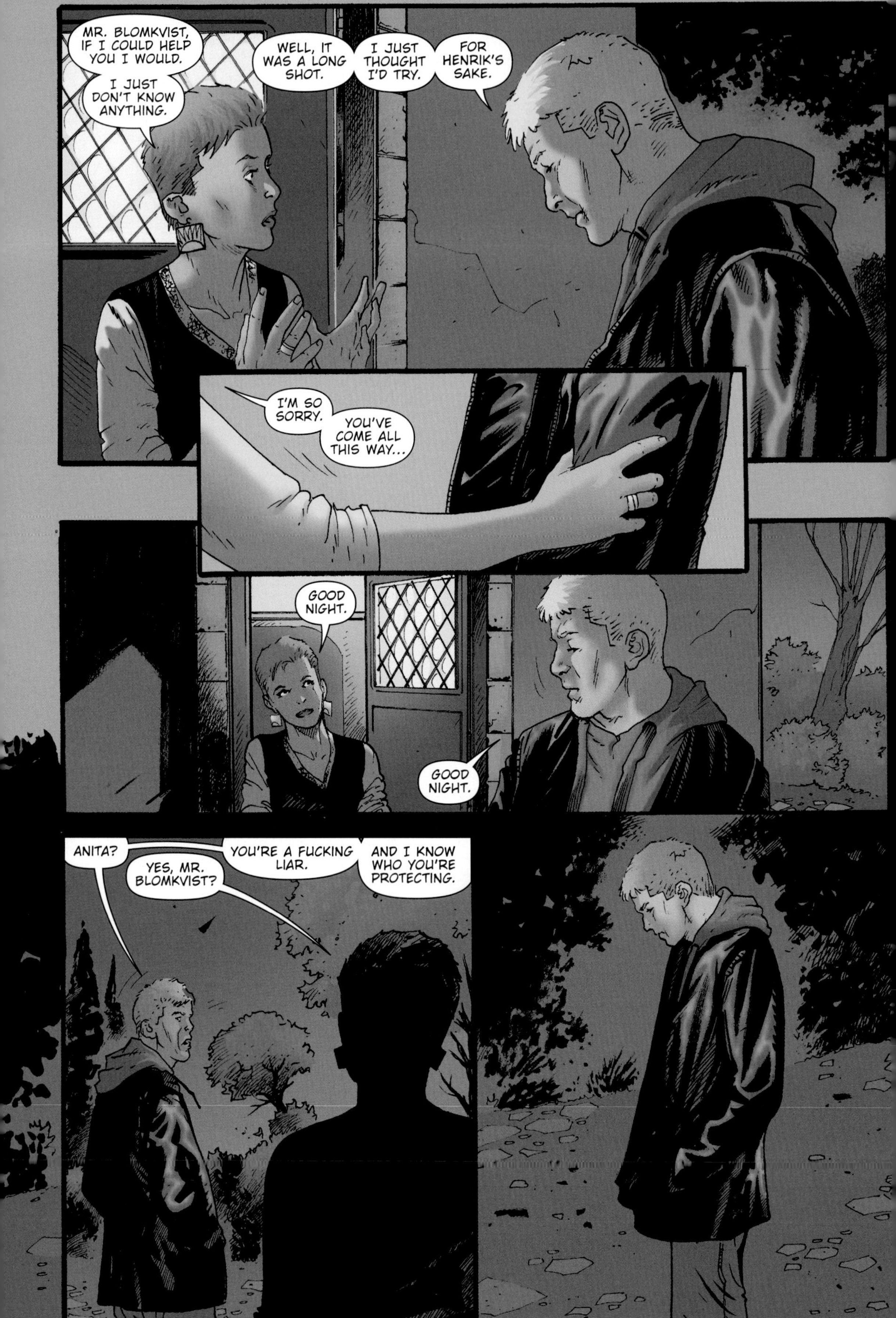

MR. BLOMKVIST, IF I COULD HELP YOU I WOULD.
I JUST DON'T KNOW ANYTHING.
WELL, IT WAS A LONG SHOT.
I JUST THOUGHT I'D TRY.
FOR HENRIK'S SAKE.
I'M SO SORRY.
YOU'VE COME ALL THIS WAY...
GOOD NIGHT.
GOOD NIGHT.
ANITA?
YES, MR. BLOMKVIST?
YOU'RE A FUCKING LIAR.
AND I KNOW WHO YOU'RE PROTECTING.

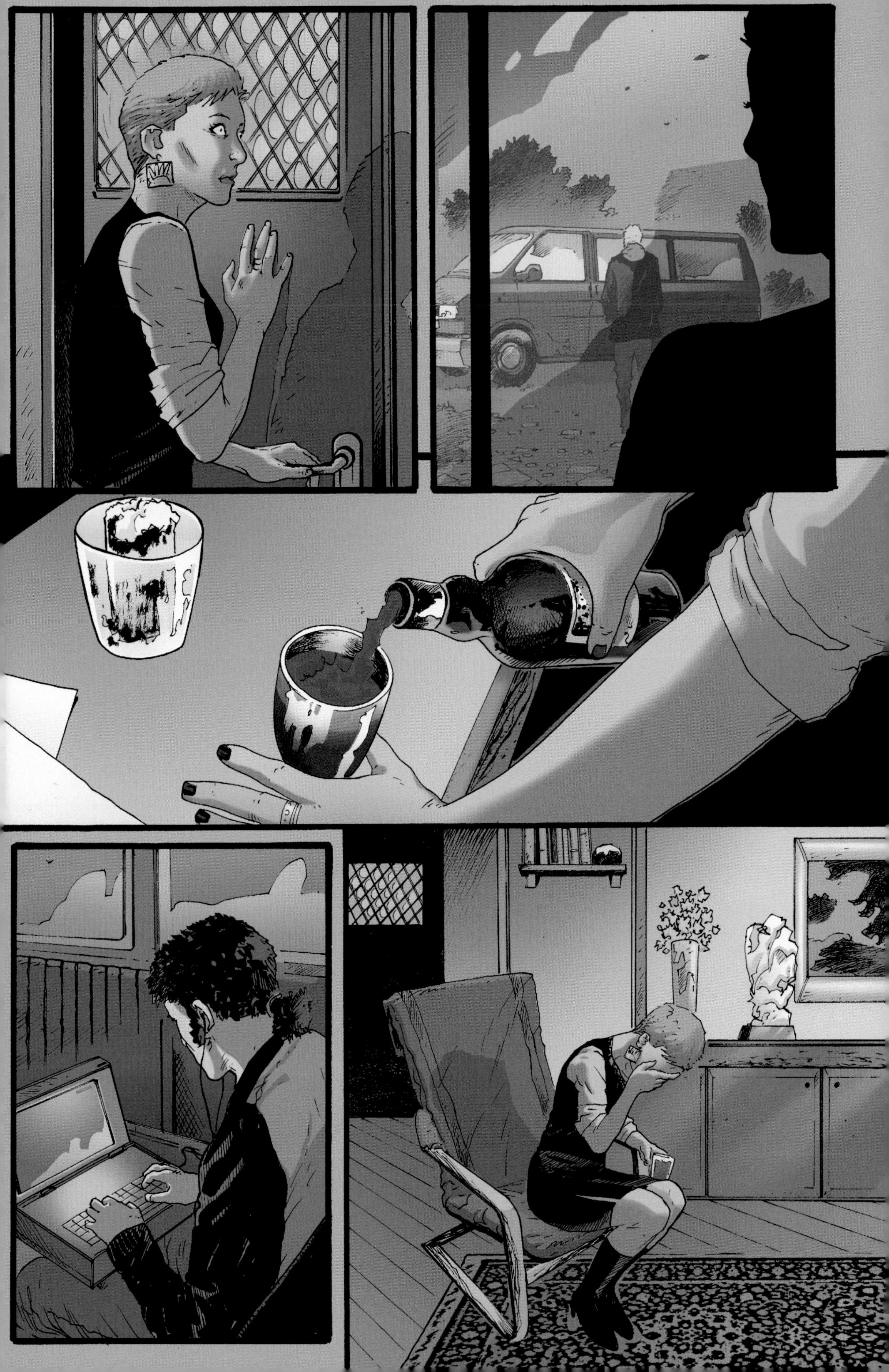

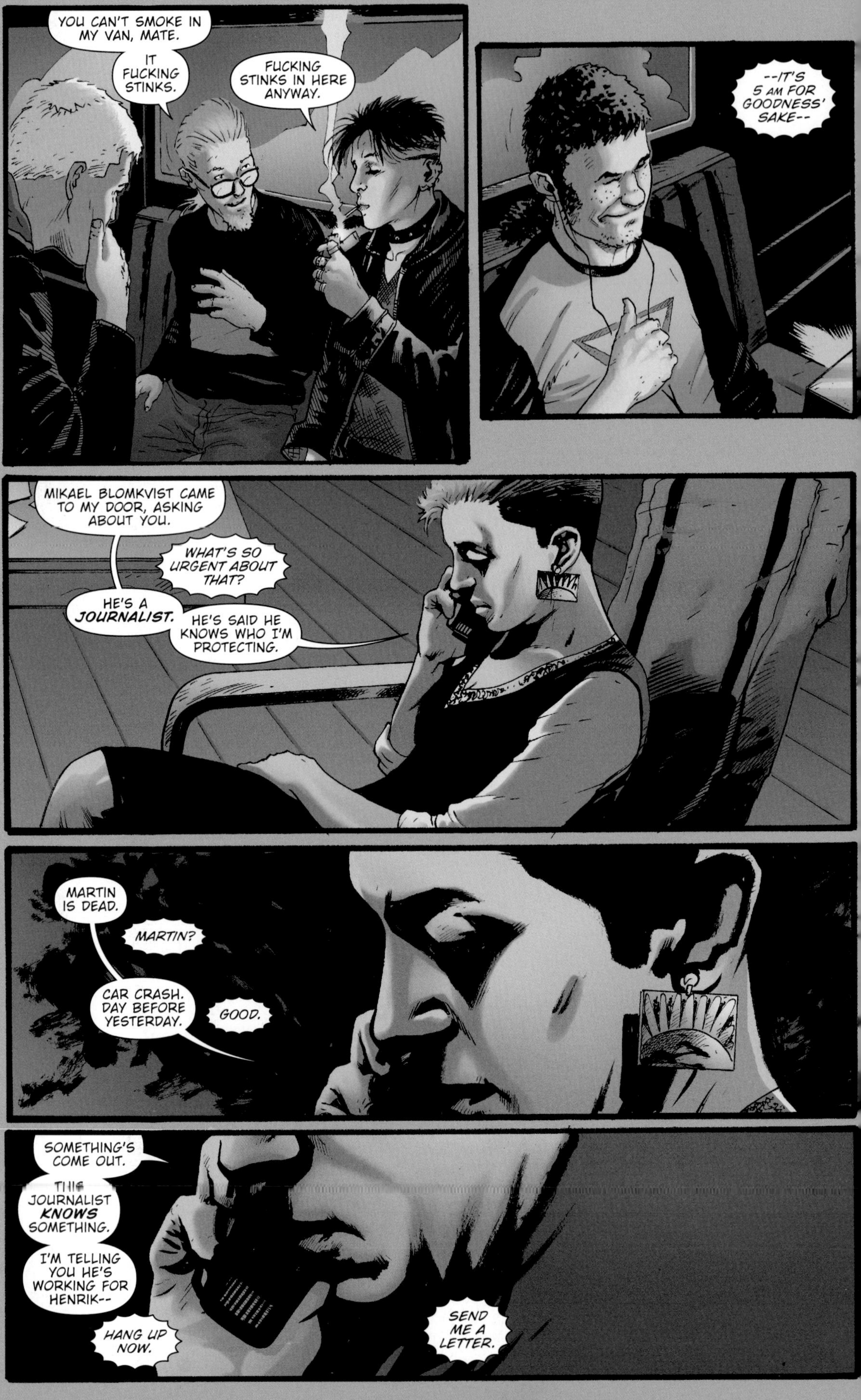
YOU CAN'T SMOKE IN MY VAN, MATE.
IT FUCKING STINKS.
FUCKING STINKS IN HERE ANYWAY.
--IT'S 5 AM FOR GOODNESS' SAKE--
MIKAEL BLOMKVIST CAME TO MY DOOR, ASKING ABOUT YOU.
WHAT'S SO URGENT ABOUT THAT?
HE'S A JOURNALIST.
HE'S SAID HE KNOWS WHO I'M PROTECTING.
MARTIN IS DEAD.
MARTIN?
CAR CRASH. DAY BEFORE YESTERDAY.
GOOD.
SOMETHING'S COME OUT.
THIS JOURNALIST KNOWS SOMETHING.
I'M TELLING YOU HE'S WORKING FOR HENRIK--
HANG UP NOW.
SEND ME A LETTER.

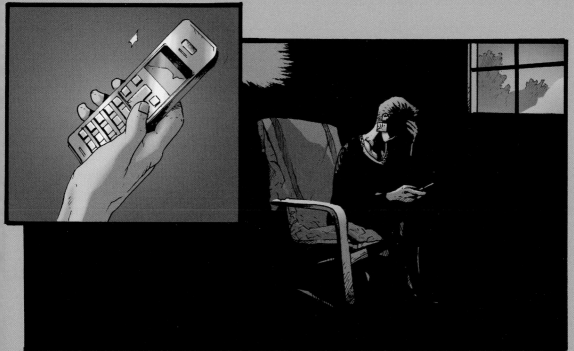

5 AM?

PLUS NINE HOURS!

YAKUTSK, SULAWESI, JAPAN, CENTRAL AUSTRALIA!

"SULAWESI?" WHERE THE HELL IS THAT?

INDONESIA.

I THOUGHT YOU'D KNOW THAT.

I'M A JOURNALIST, I'M NOT GOD.

CENTRAL AUSTRALIA.

QUEENSLAND DIALING CODE.

BRISBANE? LONGREACH.

I HAVE A CONTACT IN BRISBANE.

HE OWES ME.

HE'LL TRACE THE ADDRESS.

STILL HAVE TO KNOW A BIT ABOUT INTER-NATIONAL GEOGRAPHY, THOUGH...

...DON'T YOU, TO BE A JOURNALIST?

'S NOT LIKE INDONESIA IS THE END OF THE FUCKING WORLD.

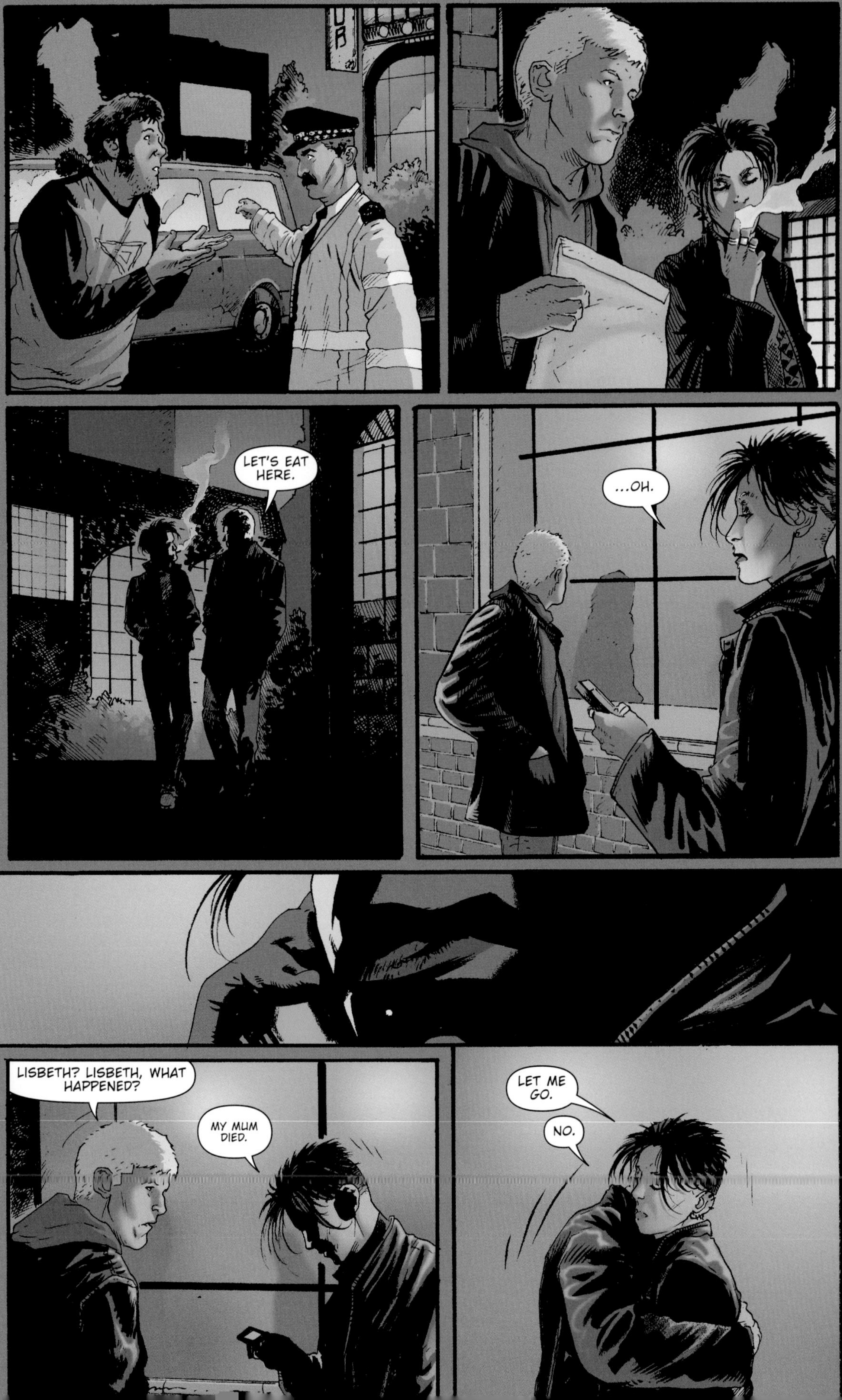
LET'S EAT HERE.
...OH.
LISBETH? LISBETH, WHAT HAPPENED?
MY MUM DIED.
LET ME GO.
NO.

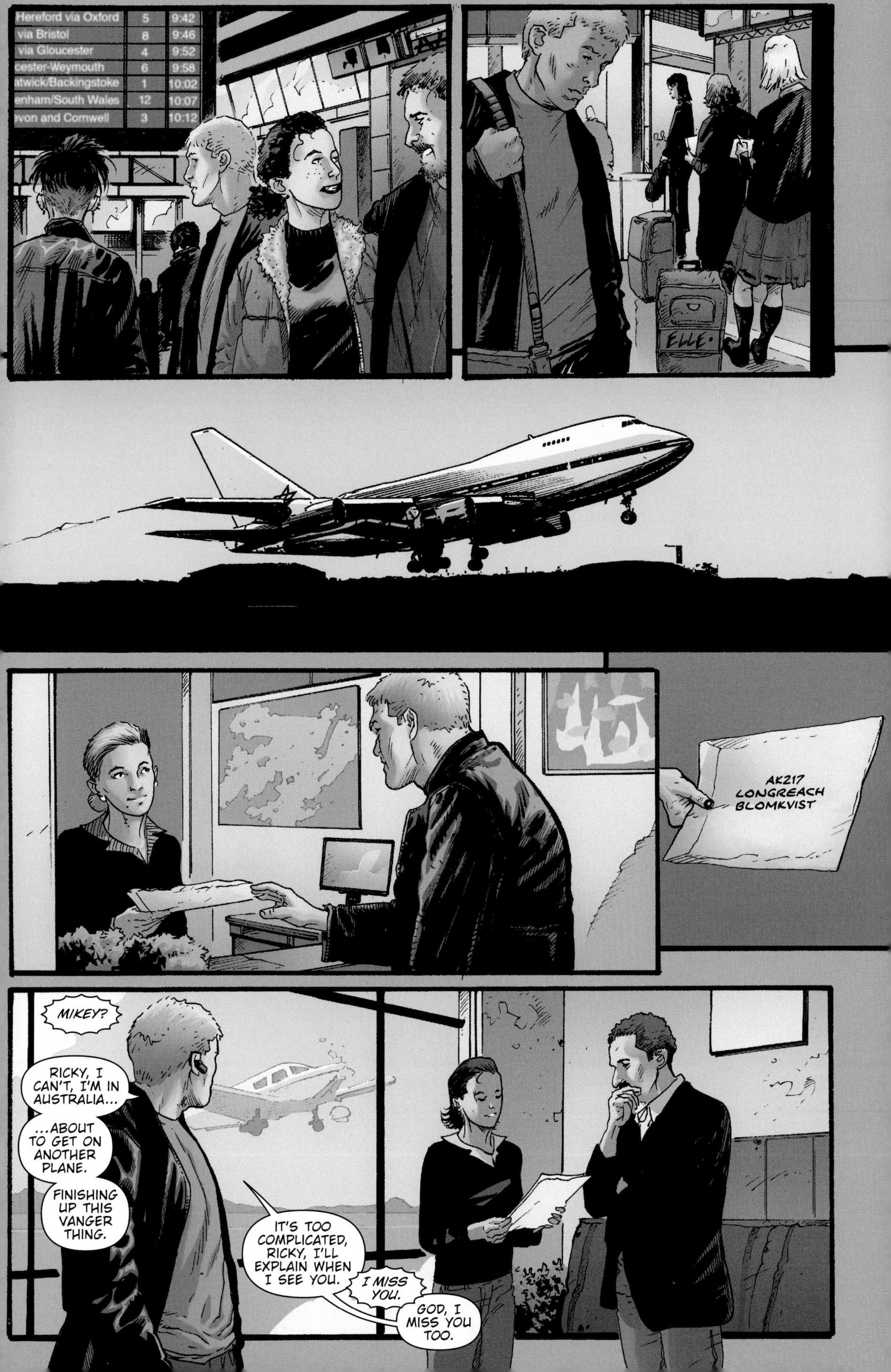
Hereford via Oxford 5 9:42
via Bristol 8 9:46
via Gloucester 4 9:52
cester-Weymouth 6 9:58
atwick/Backingstoke 1 10:02
enham/South Wales 12 10:07
evon and Cornwall 3 10:12
ELLE
AK217
LONGREACH
BLOMKVIST
MIKEY?
RICKY, I CAN'T, I'M IN AUSTRALIA...
...ABOUT TO GET ON ANOTHER PLANE.
FINISHING UP THIS VANGER THING.
IT'S TOO COMPLICATED, RICKY, I'LL EXPLAIN WHEN I SEE YOU.
I MISS YOU.
GOD, I MISS YOU TOO.

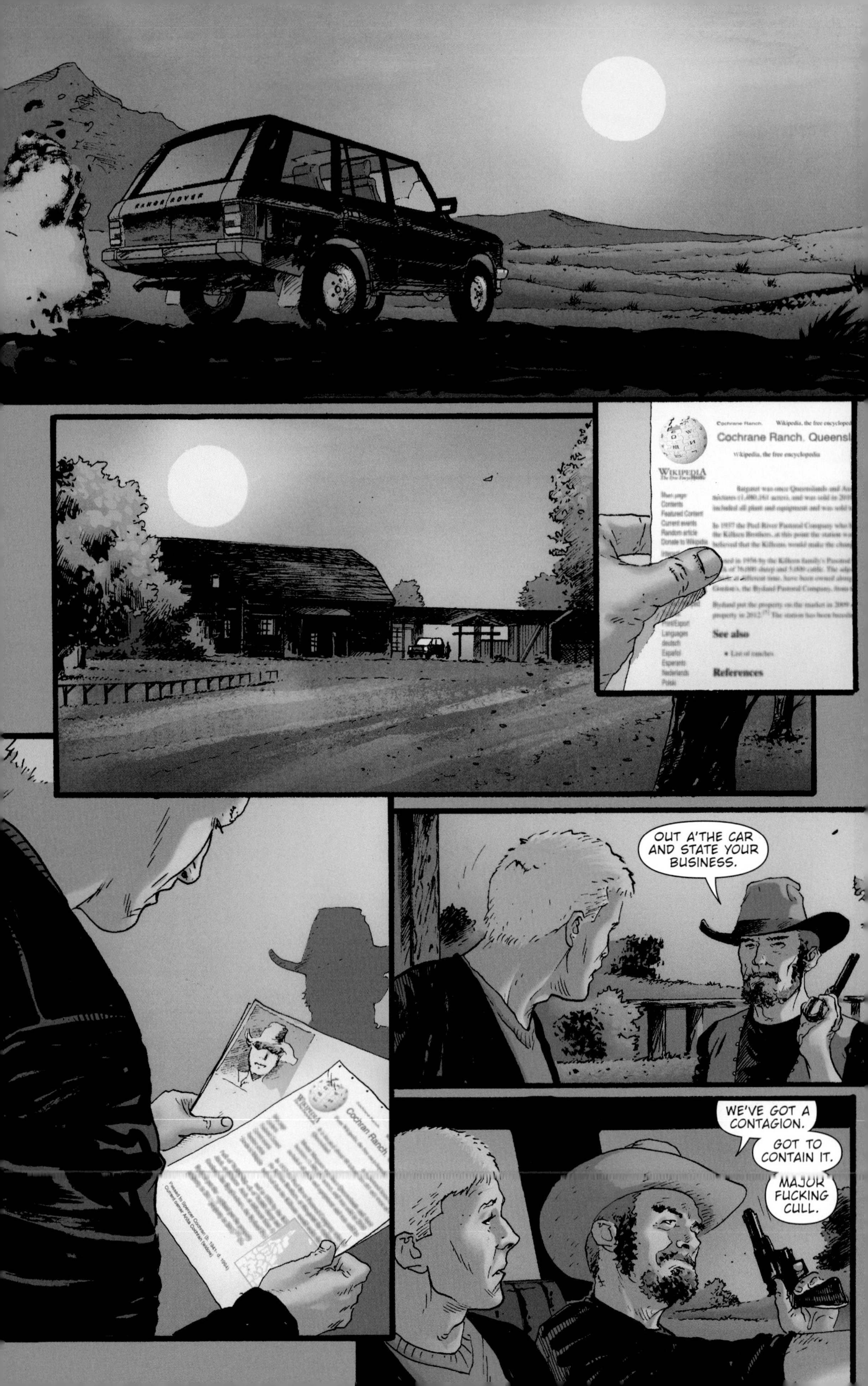
Wikipedia, the free encyclopedia
Wikipedia, the free encyclopedia
See also
References
OUT A'THE CAR AND STATE YOUR BUSINESS.
WE'VE GOT A CONTAGION.
GOT TO CONTAIN IT.
MAJOR FUCKING CULL.

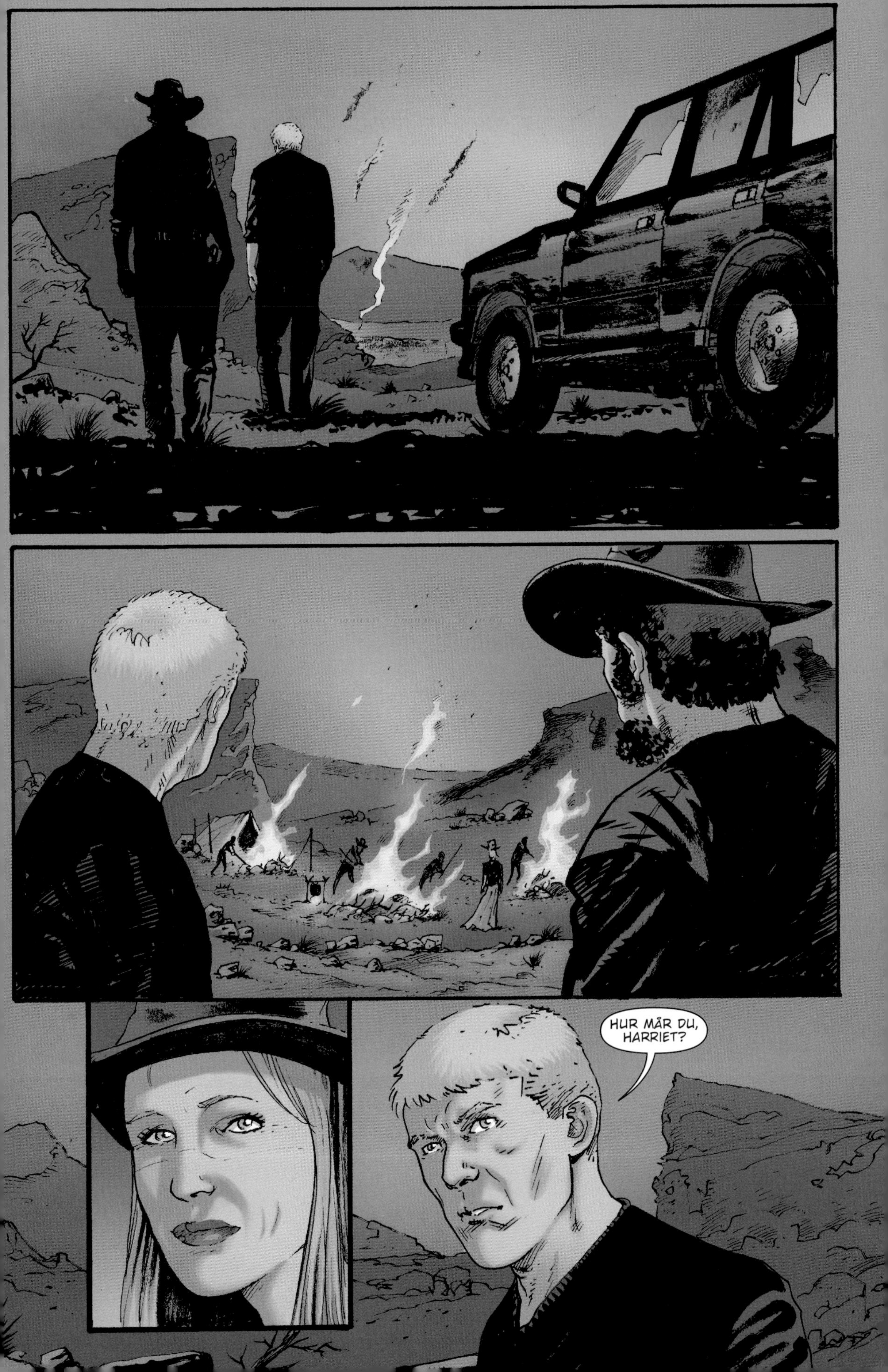
HUR MÅR DU, HARRIET?

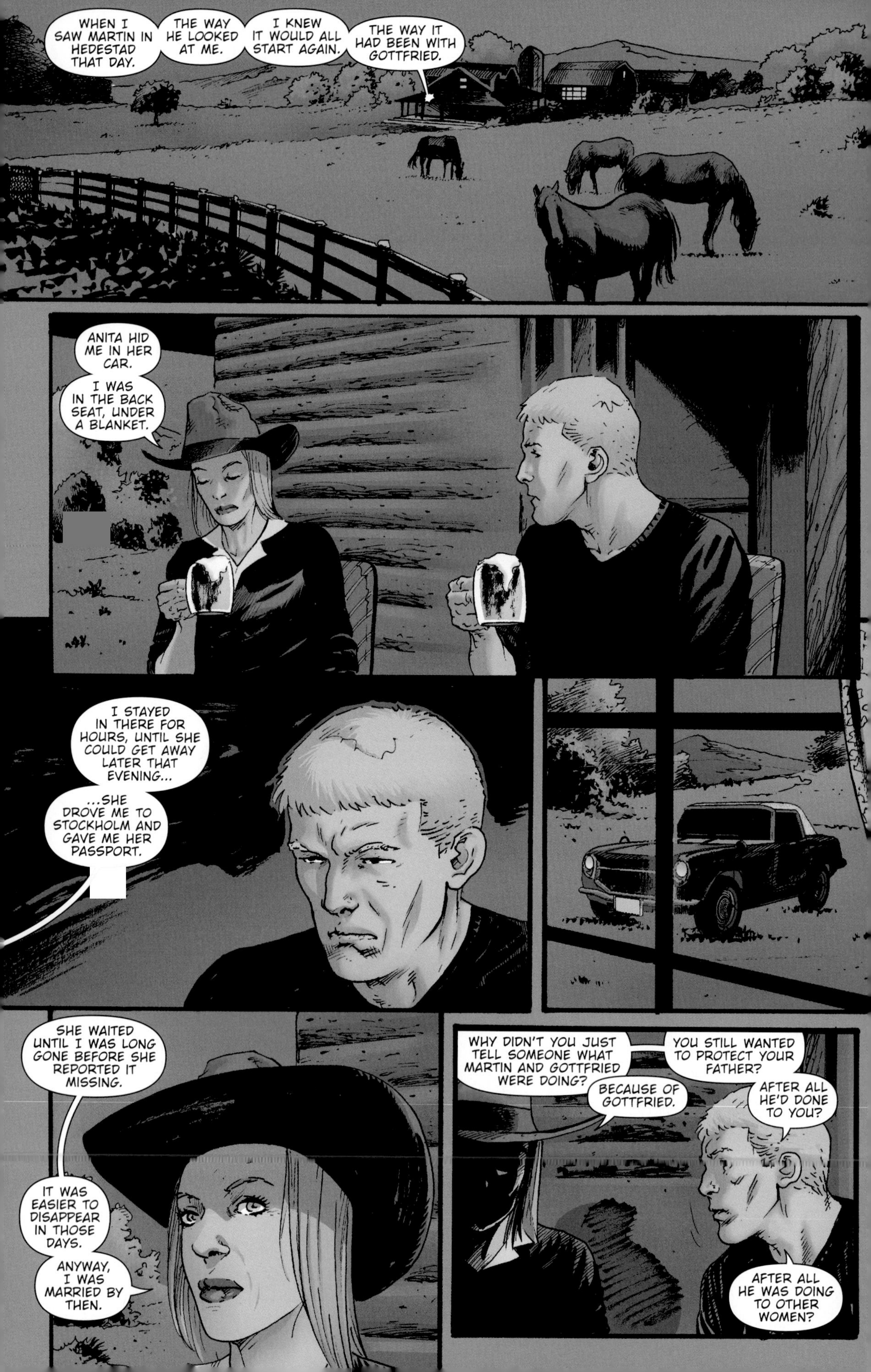
WHEN I SAW MARTIN IN HEDESTAD THAT DAY.
THE WAY HE LOOKED AT ME.
I KNEW IT WOULD ALL START AGAIN.
THE WAY IT HAD BEEN WITH GOTTFRIED.
ANITA HID ME IN HER CAR.
I WAS IN THE BACK SEAT, UNDER A BLANKET.
I STAYED IN THERE FOR HOURS, UNTIL SHE COULD GET AWAY LATER THAT EVENING...
...SHE DROVE ME TO STOCKHOLM AND GAVE ME HER PASSPORT.
SHE WAITED UNTIL I WAS LONG GONE BEFORE SHE REPORTED IT MISSING.
IT WAS EASIER TO DISAPPEAR IN THOSE DAYS.
ANYWAY, I WAS MARRIED BY THEN.
WHY DIDN'T YOU JUST TELL SOMEONE WHAT MARTIN AND GOTTFRIED WERE DOING?
YOU STILL WANTED TO PROTECT YOUR FATHER?
BECAUSE OF GOTTFRIED.
AFTER ALL HE'D DONE TO YOU?
AFTER ALL HE WAS DOING TO OTHER WOMEN?

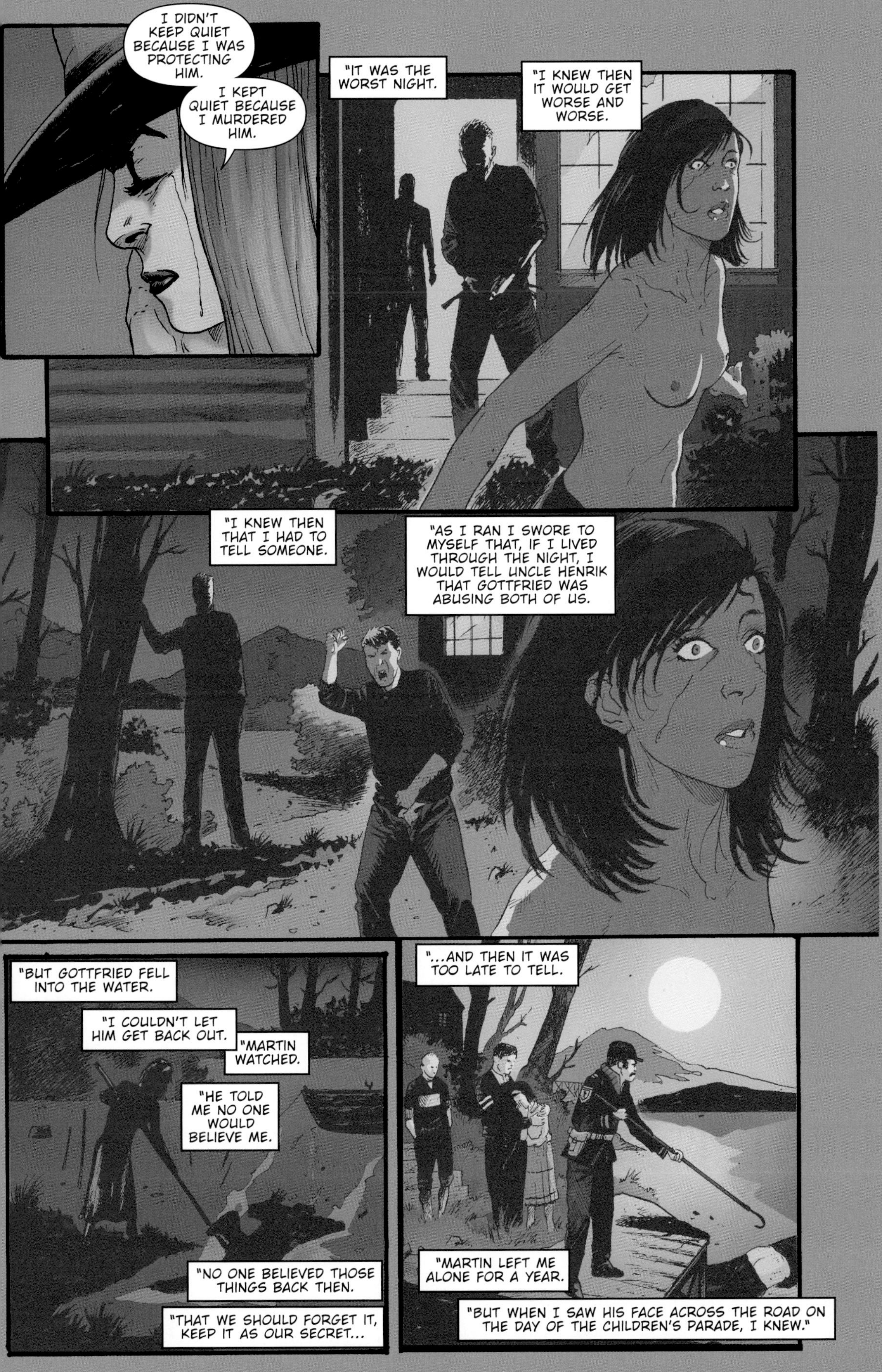
I DIDN'T KEEP QUIET BECAUSE I WAS PROTECTING HIM.
I KEPT QUIET BECAUSE I MURDERED HIM.
"IT WAS THE WORST NIGHT.
"I KNEW THEN IT WOULD GET WORSE AND WORSE.
"I KNEW THEN THAT I HAD TO TELL SOMEONE.
"AS I RAN I SWORE TO MYSELF THAT, IF I LIVED THROUGH THE NIGHT, I WOULD TELL UNCLE HENRIK THAT GOTTFRIED WAS ABUSING BOTH OF US.
"BUT GOTTFRIED FELL INTO THE WATER.
"I COULDN'T LET HIM GET BACK OUT.
"MARTIN WATCHED.
"HE TOLD ME NO ONE WOULD BELIEVE ME.
"NO ONE BELIEVED THOSE THINGS BACK THEN.
"THAT WE SHOULD FORGET IT, KEEP IT AS OUR SECRET...
"...AND THEN IT WAS TOO LATE TO TELL.
"MARTIN LEFT ME ALONE FOR A YEAR.
"BUT WHEN I SAW HIS FACE ACROSS THE ROAD ON THE DAY OF THE CHILDREN'S PARADE, I KNEW."

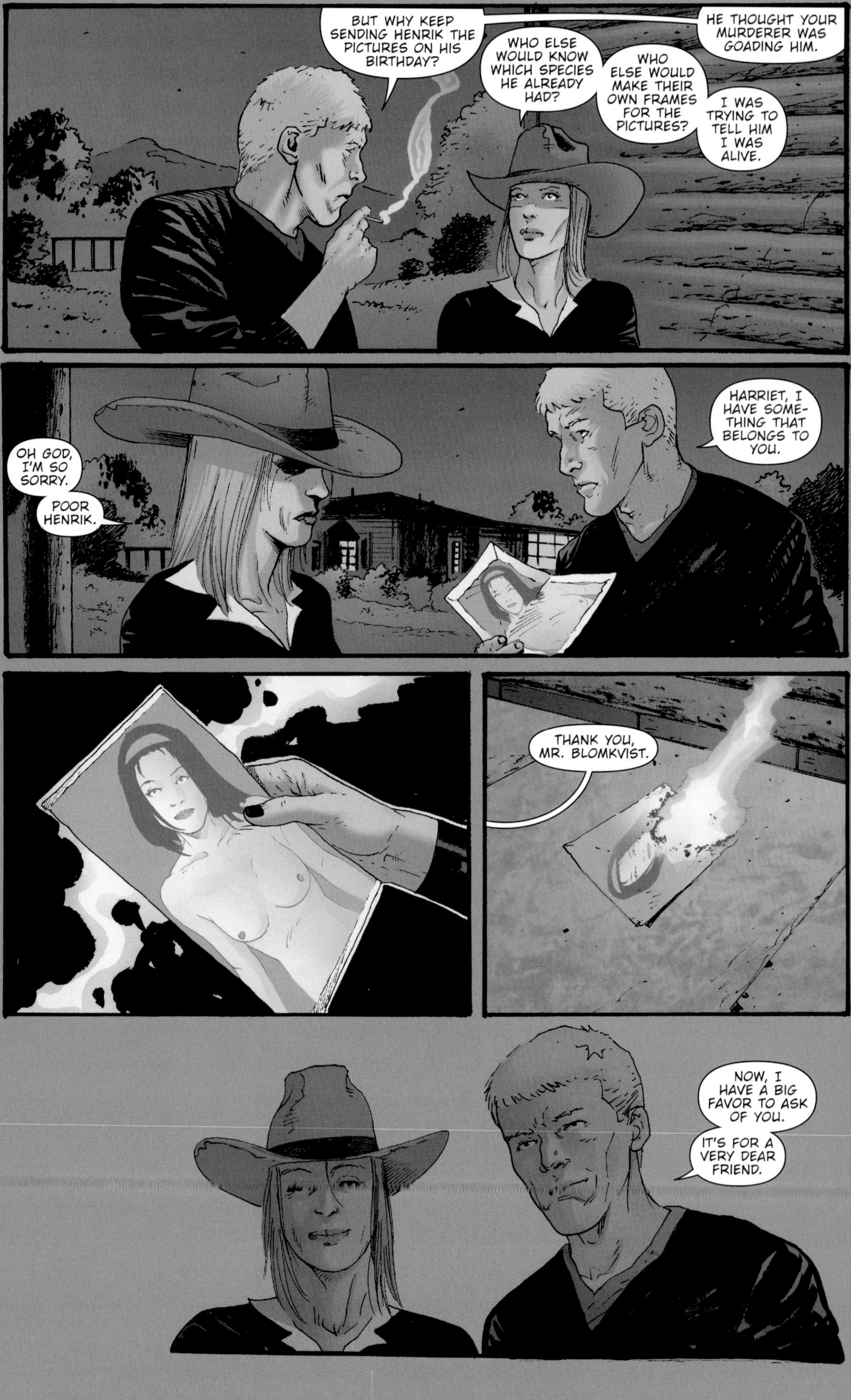
BUT WHY KEEP SENDING HENRIK THE PICTURES ON HIS BIRTHDAY?
WHO ELSE WOULD KNOW WHICH SPECIES HE ALREADY HAD?
WHO ELSE WOULD MAKE THEIR OWN FRAMES FOR THE PICTURES?
HE THOUGHT YOUR MURDERER WAS GOADING HIM.
I WAS TRYING TO TELL HIM I WAS ALIVE.
HARRIET, I HAVE SOMETHING THAT BELONGS TO YOU.
OH GOD, I'M SO SORRY.
POOR HENRIK.
THANK YOU, MR. BLOMKVIST.
NOW, I HAVE A BIG FAVOR TO ASK OF YOU.
IT'S FOR A VERY DEAR FRIEND.

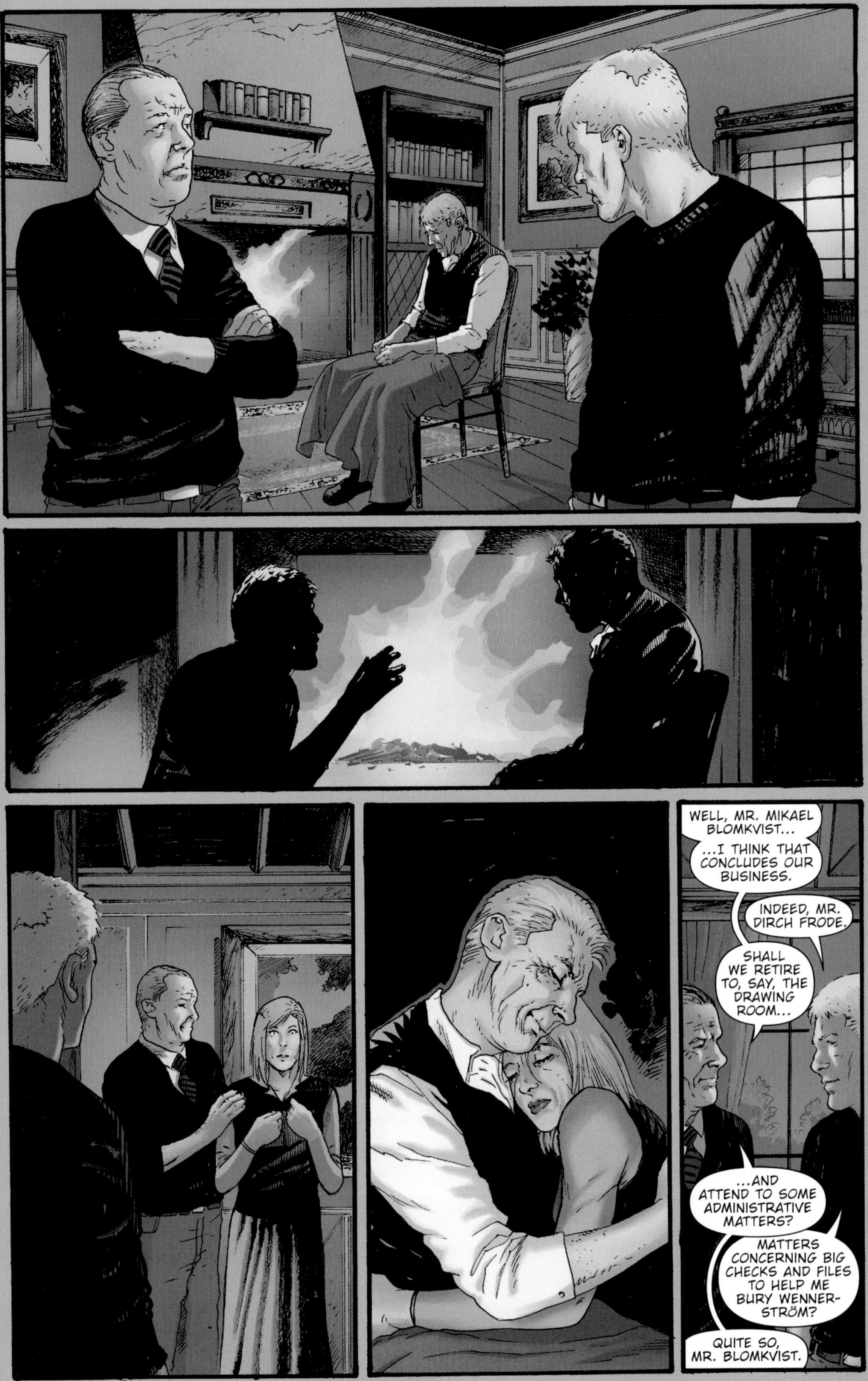
WELL, MR. MIKAEL BLOMKVIST...
...I THINK THAT CONCLUDES OUR BUSINESS.
INDEED, MR. DIRCH FRODE.
SHALL WE RETIRE TO, SAY, THE DRAWING ROOM...
...AND ATTEND TO SOME ADMINISTRATIVE MATTERS?
MATTERS CONCERNING BIG CHECKS AND FILES TO HELP ME BURY WENNER-STRÖM?
QUITE SO, MR. BLOMKVIST.

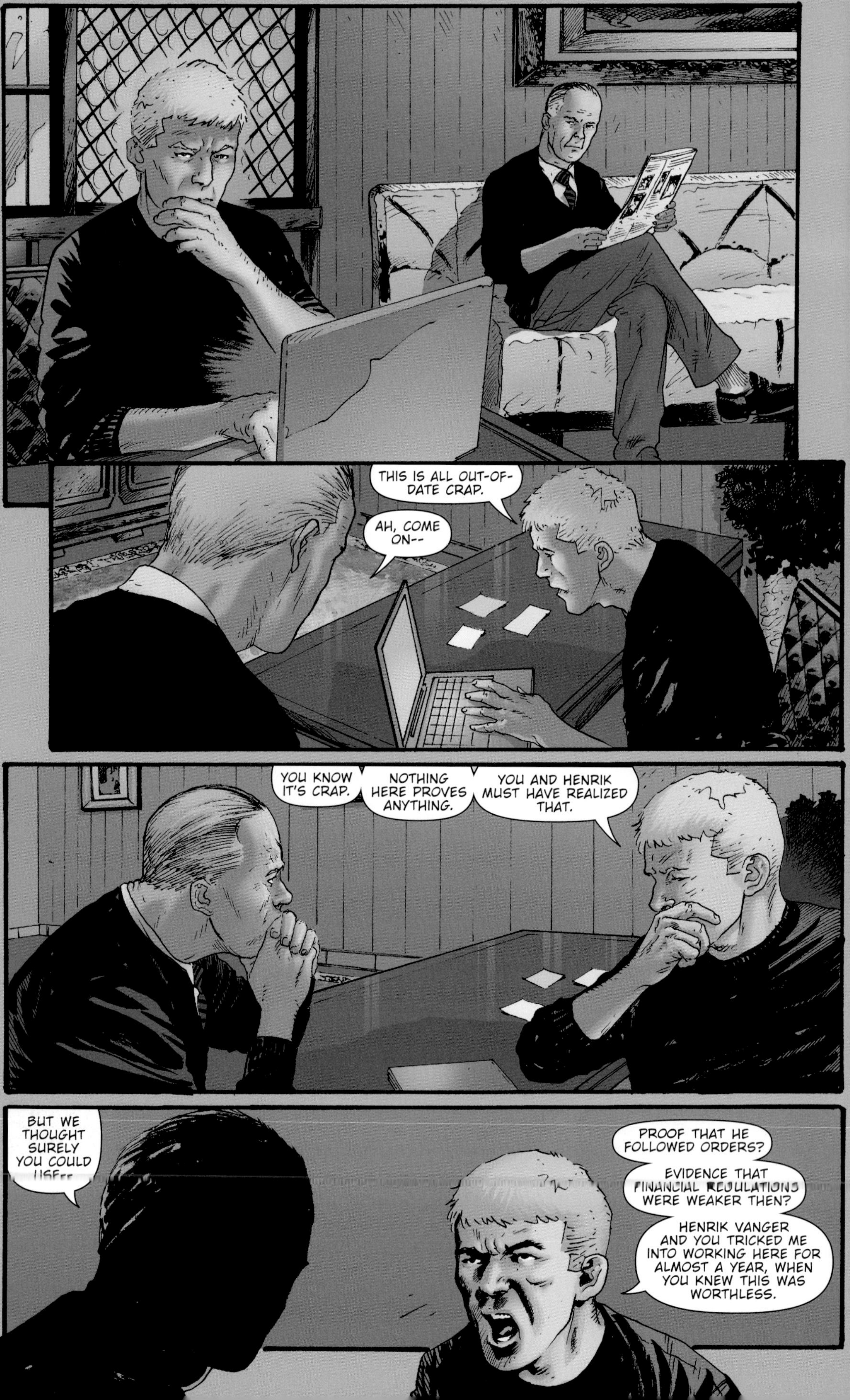
THIS IS ALL OUT-OF-DATE CRAP.
AH, COME ON--
YOU KNOW IT'S CRAP.
NOTHING HERE PROVES ANYTHING.
YOU AND HENRIK MUST HAVE REALIZED THAT.
BUT WE THOUGHT SURELY YOU COULD
PROOF THAT HE FOLLOWED ORDERS?
EVIDENCE THAT FINANCIAL REGULATIONS WERE WEAKER THEN?
HENRIK VANGER AND YOU TRICKED ME INTO WORKING HERE FOR ALMOST A YEAR, WHEN YOU KNEW THIS WAS WORTHLESS.

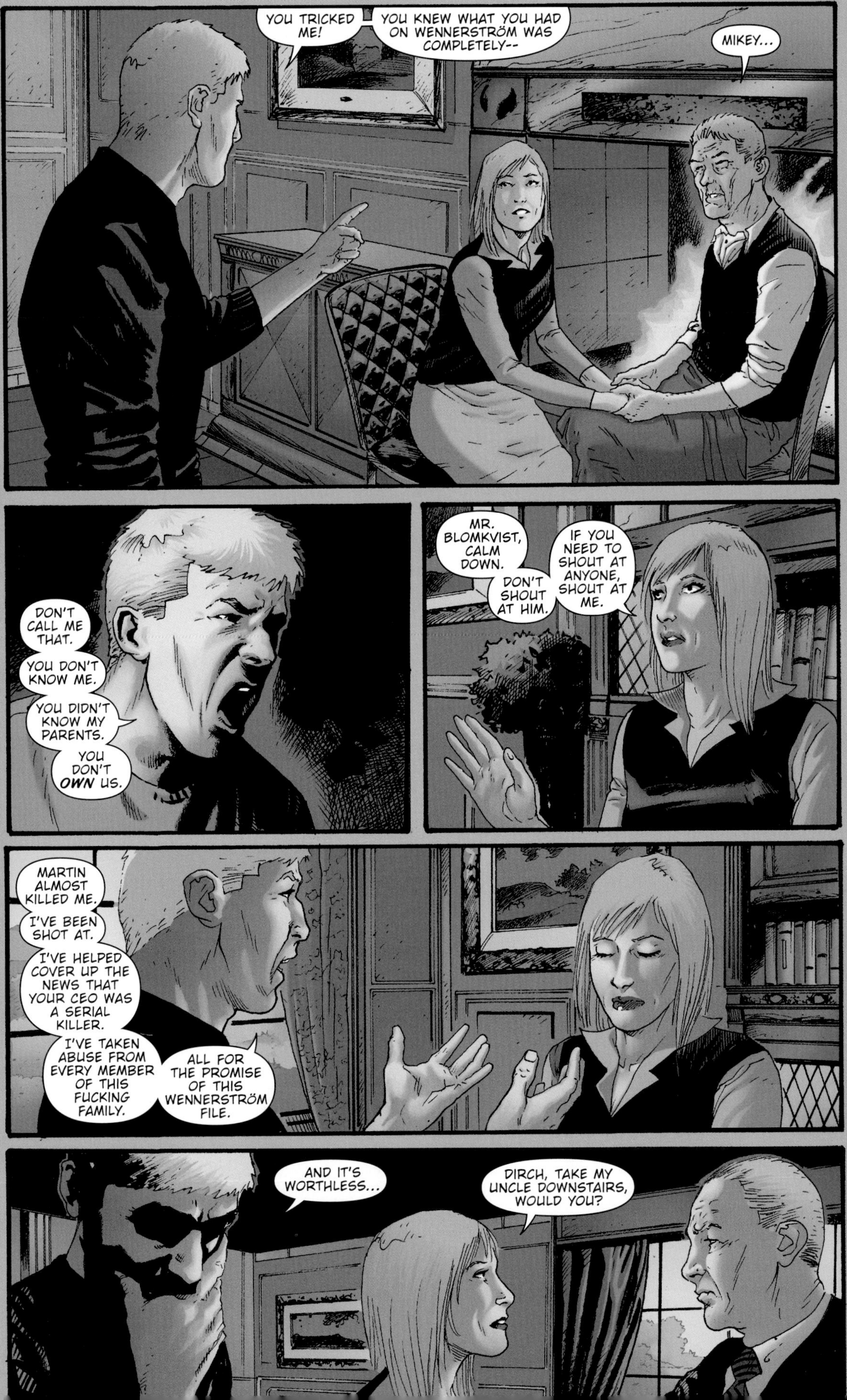
YOU TRICKED ME!
YOU KNEW WHAT YOU HAD ON WENNERSTRÖM WAS COMPLETELY--
MIKEY...
DON'T CALL ME THAT.
YOU DON'T KNOW ME.
YOU DIDN'T KNOW MY PARENTS.
YOU DON'T OWN US.
MR. BLOMKVIST, CALM DOWN.
DON'T SHOUT AT HIM.
IF YOU NEED TO SHOUT AT ANYONE, SHOUT AT ME.
MARTIN ALMOST KILLED ME.
I'VE BEEN SHOT AT.
I'VE HELPED COVER UP THE NEWS THAT YOUR CEO WAS A SERIAL KILLER.
I'VE TAKEN ABUSE FROM EVERY MEMBER OF THIS FUCKING FAMILY.
ALL FOR THE PROMISE OF THIS WENNERSTRÖM FILE.
AND IT'S WORTHLESS...
DIRCH, TAKE MY UNCLE DOWNSTAIRS, WOULD YOU?

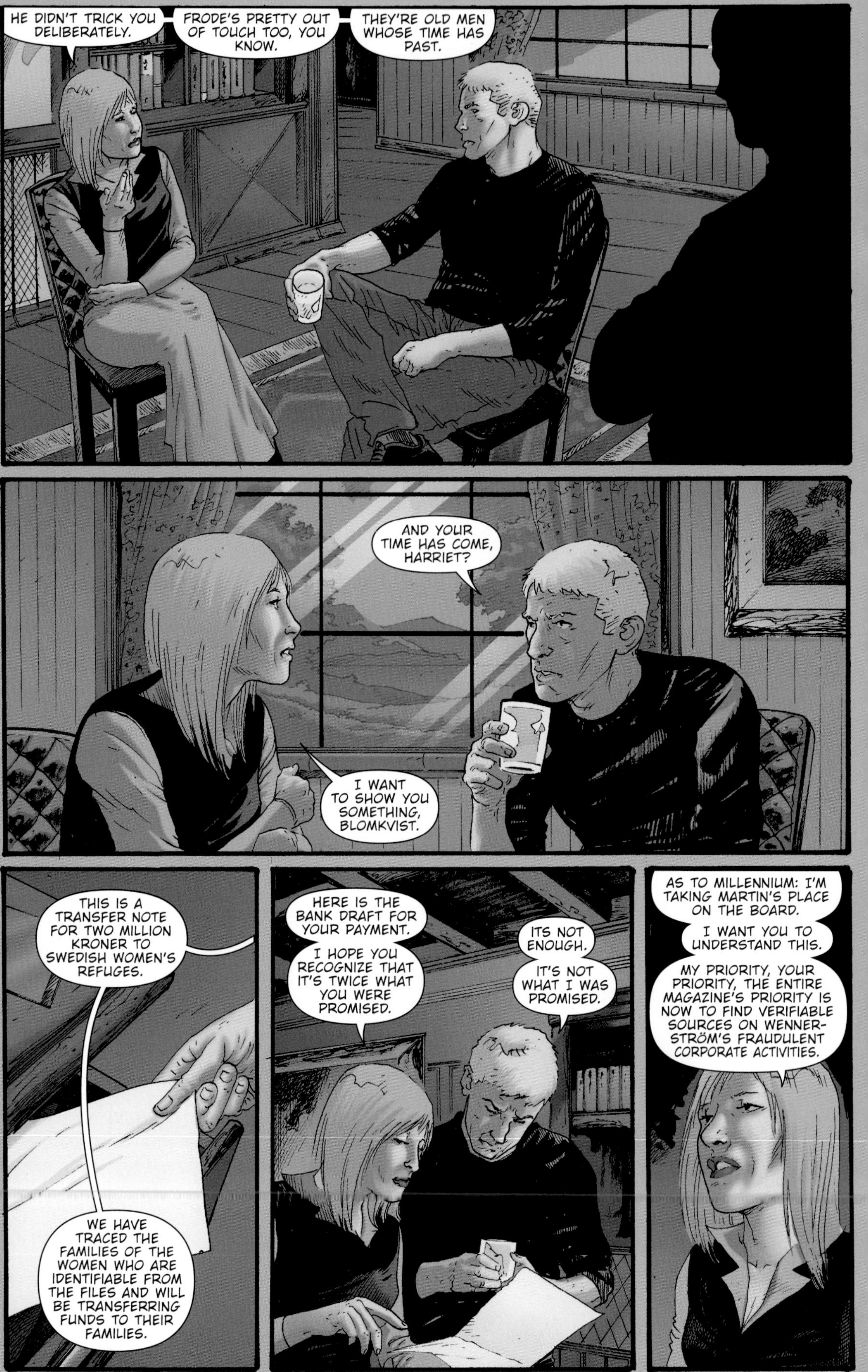
HE DIDN'T TRICK YOU DELIBERATELY.
FRODE'S PRETTY OUT OF TOUCH TOO, YOU KNOW.
THEY'RE OLD MEN WHOSE TIME HAS PAST.
AND YOUR TIME HAS COME, HARRIET?
I WANT TO SHOW YOU SOMETHING, BLOMKVIST.
THIS IS A TRANSFER NOTE FOR TWO MILLION KRONER TO SWEDISH WOMEN'S REFUGES.
WE HAVE TRACED THE FAMILIES OF THE WOMEN WHO ARE IDENTIFIABLE FROM THE FILES AND WILL BE TRANSFERRING FUNDS TO THEIR FAMILIES.
HERE IS THE BANK DRAFT FOR YOUR PAYMENT.
I HOPE YOU RECOGNIZE THAT IT'S TWICE WHAT YOU WERE PROMISED.
ITS NOT ENOUGH.
IT'S NOT WHAT I WAS PROMISED.
AS TO MILLENNIUM: I'M TAKING MARTIN'S PLACE ON THE BOARD.
I WANT YOU TO UNDERSTAND THIS.
MY PRIORITY, YOUR PRIORITY, THE ENTIRE MAGAZINE'S PRIORITY IS NOW TO FIND VERIFIABLE SOURCES ON WENNERSTRÖM'S FRAUDULENT CORPORATE ACTIVITIES.

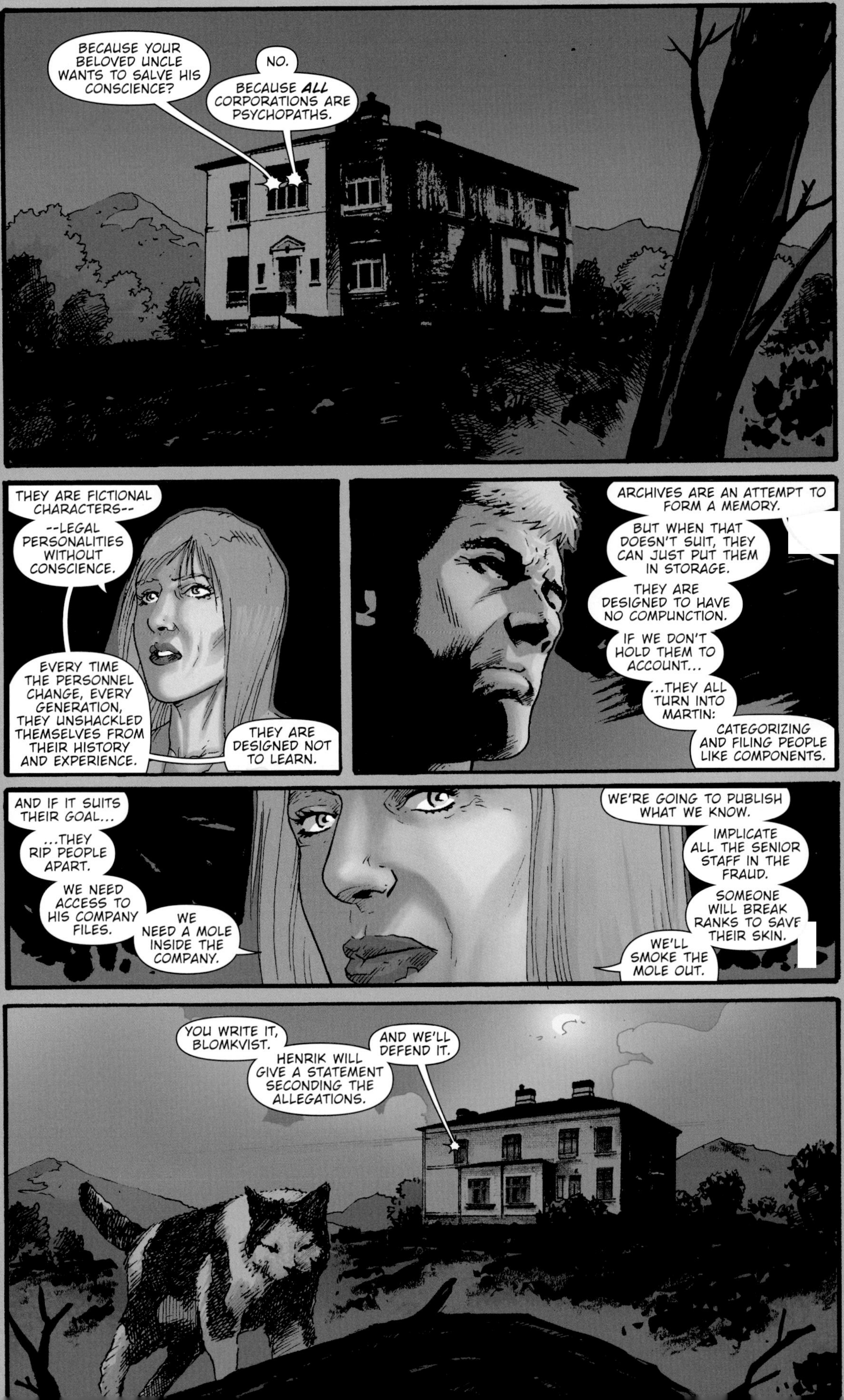
BECAUSE YOUR BELOVED UNCLE WANTS TO SALVE HIS CONSCIENCE?
NO.
BECAUSE ALL CORPORATIONS ARE PSYCHOPATHS.
THEY ARE FICTIONAL CHARACTERS--
--LEGAL PERSONALITIES WITHOUT CONSCIENCE.
EVERY TIME THE PERSONNEL CHANGE, EVERY GENERATION, THEY UNSHACKLED THEMSELVES FROM THEIR HISTORY AND EXPERIENCE.
THEY ARE DESIGNED NOT TO LEARN.
ARCHIVES ARE AN ATTEMPT TO FORM A MEMORY.
BUT WHEN THAT DOESN'T SUIT, THEY CAN JUST PUT THEM IN STORAGE.
THEY ARE DESIGNED TO HAVE NO COMPUNCTION.
IF WE DON'T HOLD THEM TO ACCOUNT...
...THEY ALL TURN INTO MARTIN:
CATEGORIZING AND FILING PEOPLE LIKE COMPONENTS.
AND IF IT SUITS THEIR GOAL...
...THEY RIP PEOPLE APART.
WE NEED ACCESS TO HIS COMPANY FILES.
WE NEED A MOLE INSIDE THE COMPANY.
WE'RE GOING TO PUBLISH WHAT WE KNOW.
IMPLICATE ALL THE SENIOR STAFF IN THE FRAUD.
SOMEONE WILL BREAK RANKS TO SAVE THEIR SKIN.
WE'LL SMOKE THE MOLE OUT.
YOU WRITE IT, BLOMKVIST.
HENRIK WILL GIVE A STATEMENT SECONDING THE ALLEGATIONS.
AND WE'LL DEFEND IT.

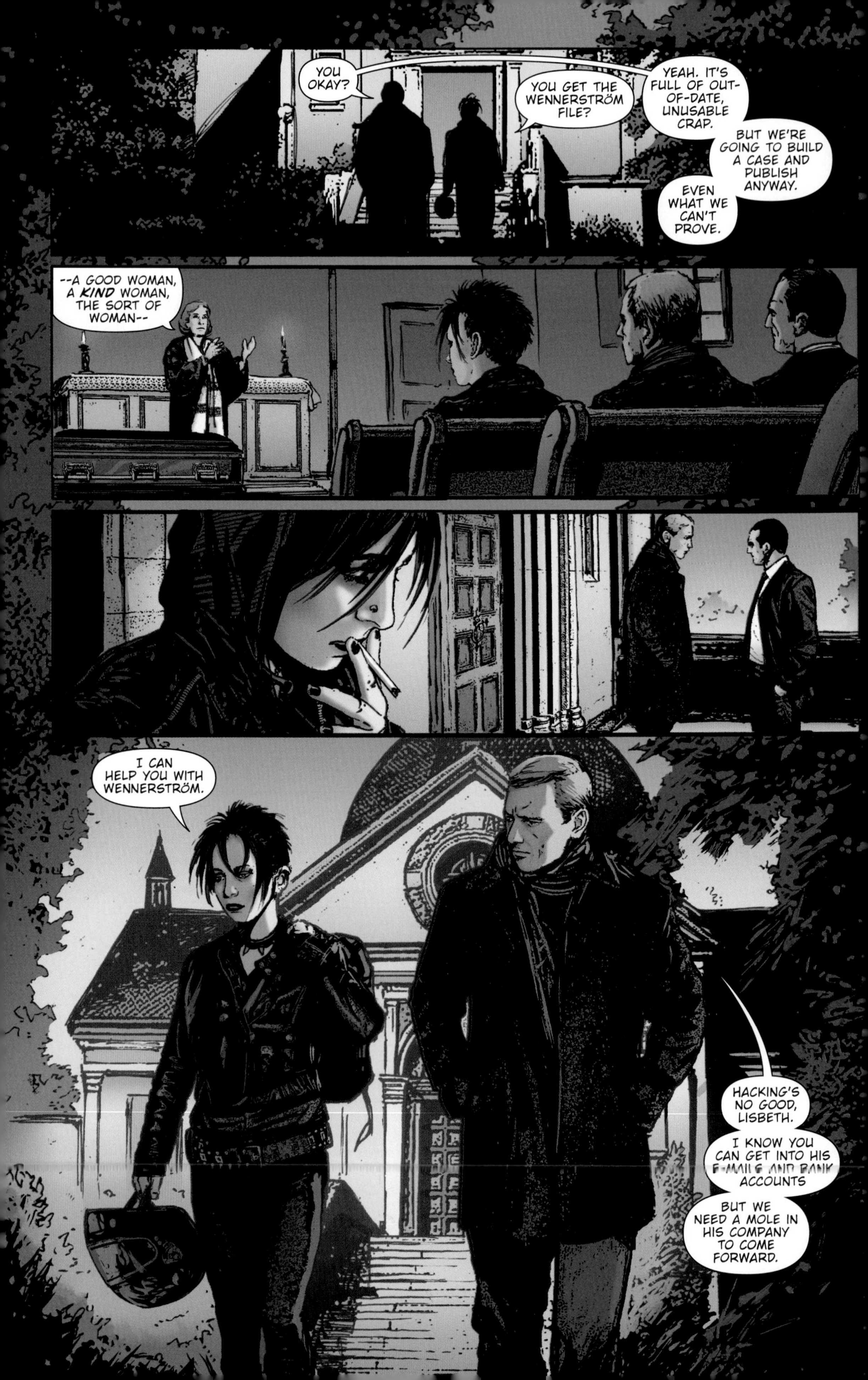
YOU OKAY?
YOU GET THE WENNERSTRÖM FILE?
YEAH. IT'S FULL OF OUT-OF-DATE, UNUSABLE CRAP.
BUT WE'RE GOING TO BUILD A CASE AND PUBLISH ANYWAY.
EVEN WHAT WE CAN'T PROVE.
--A GOOD WOMAN, A *KIND* WOMAN, THE SORT OF WOMAN--
I CAN HELP YOU WITH WENNERSTRÖM.
HACKING'S NO GOOD, LISBETH.
I KNOW YOU CAN GET INTO HIS E-MAILS AND BANK ACCOUNTS
BUT WE NEED A MOLE IN HIS COMPANY TO COME FORWARD.

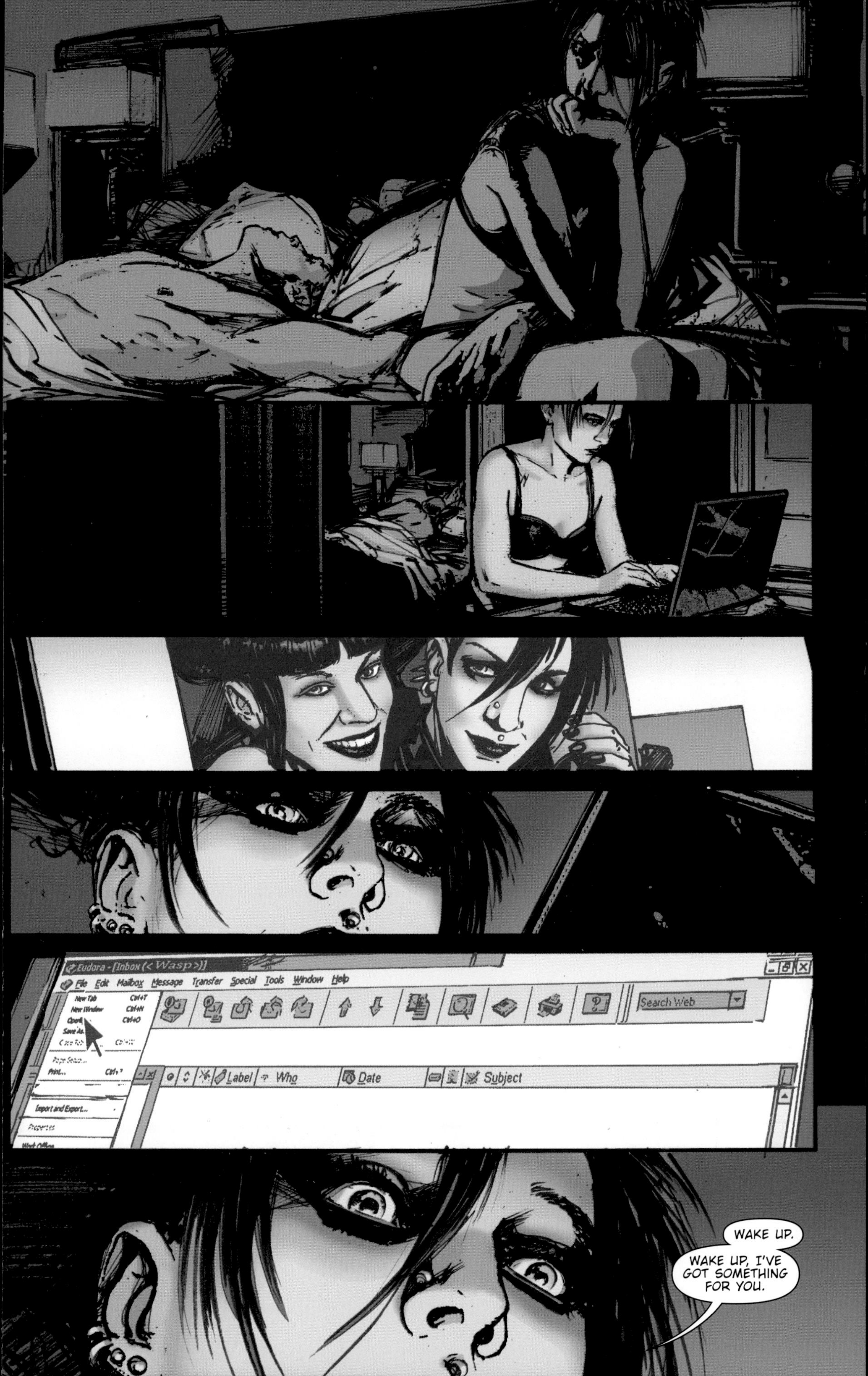
Eudora - [Inbox (<Wasp>)]
File Edit Mailbox Message Transfer Special Tools Window Help
New Tab Ctrl+T
New Window Ctrl+N
Save As...
Import and Export...
Search Web
Label Who Date Subject
WAKE UP.
WAKE UP, I'VE GOT SOMETHING FOR YOU.

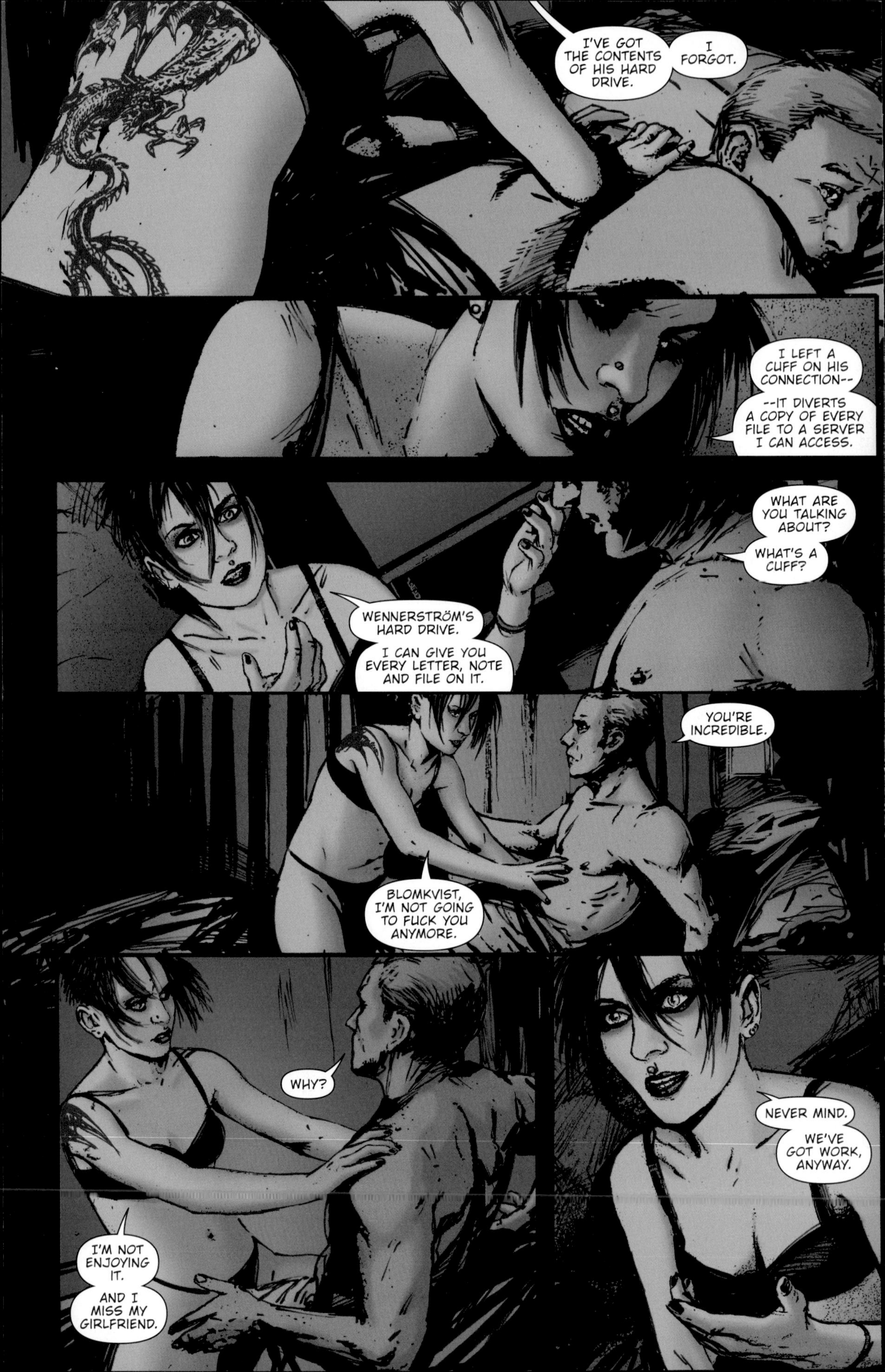
I'VE GOT THE CONTENTS OF HIS HARD DRIVE.
I FORGOT.
I LEFT A CUFF ON HIS CONNECTION--
--IT DIVERTS A COPY OF EVERY FILE TO A SERVER I CAN ACCESS.
WHAT ARE YOU TALKING ABOUT?
WHAT'S A CUFF?
WENNERSTRÖM'S HARD DRIVE.
I CAN GIVE YOU EVERY LETTER, NOTE AND FILE ON IT.
YOU'RE INCREDIBLE.
BLOMKVIST, I'M NOT GOING TO FUCK YOU ANYMORE.
WHY?
I'M NOT ENJOYING IT.
AND I MISS MY GIRLFRIEND.
NEVER MIND.
WE'VE GOT WORK, ANYWAY.

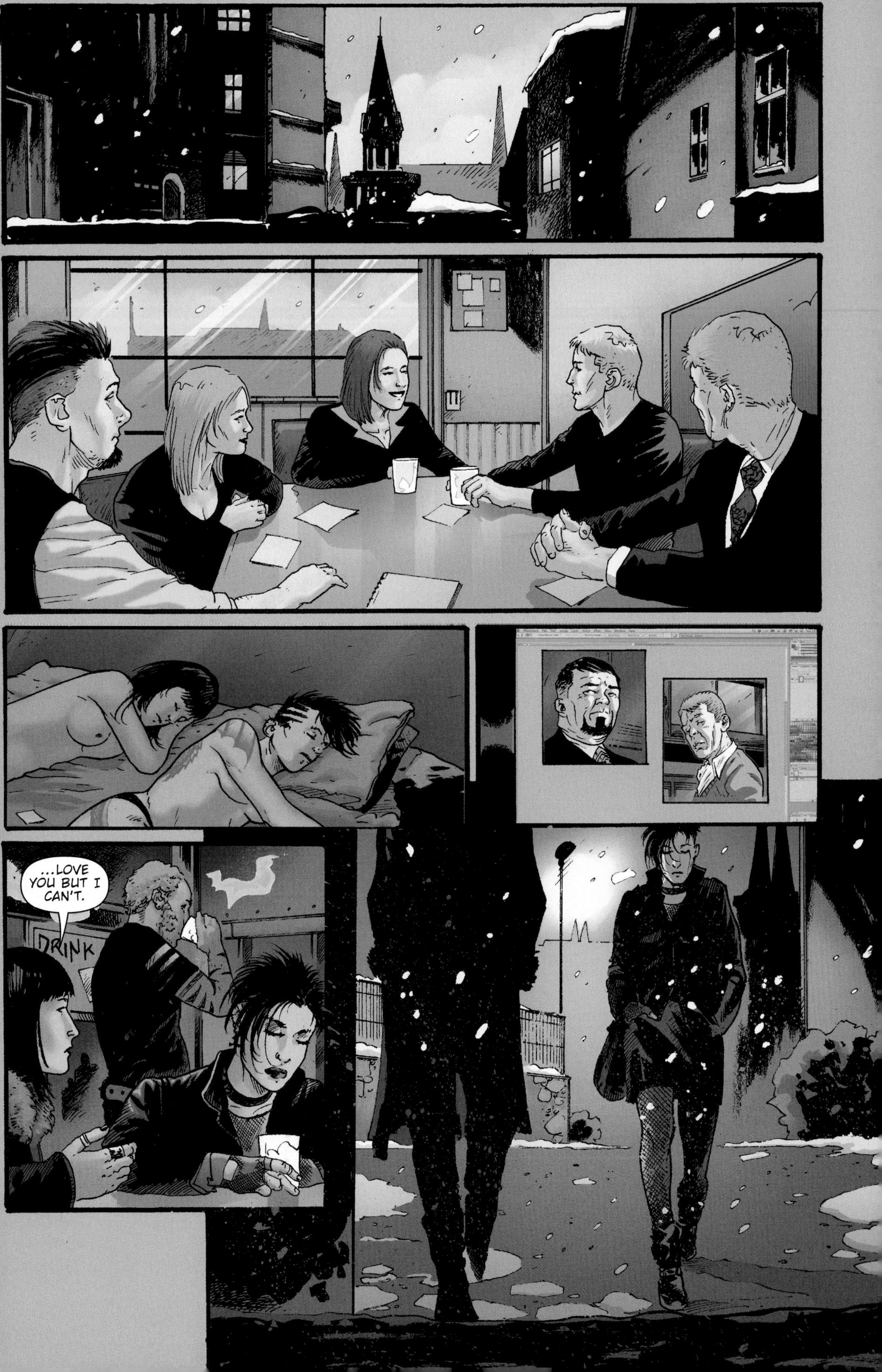
...LOVE YOU BUT I CAN'T.
DRINK

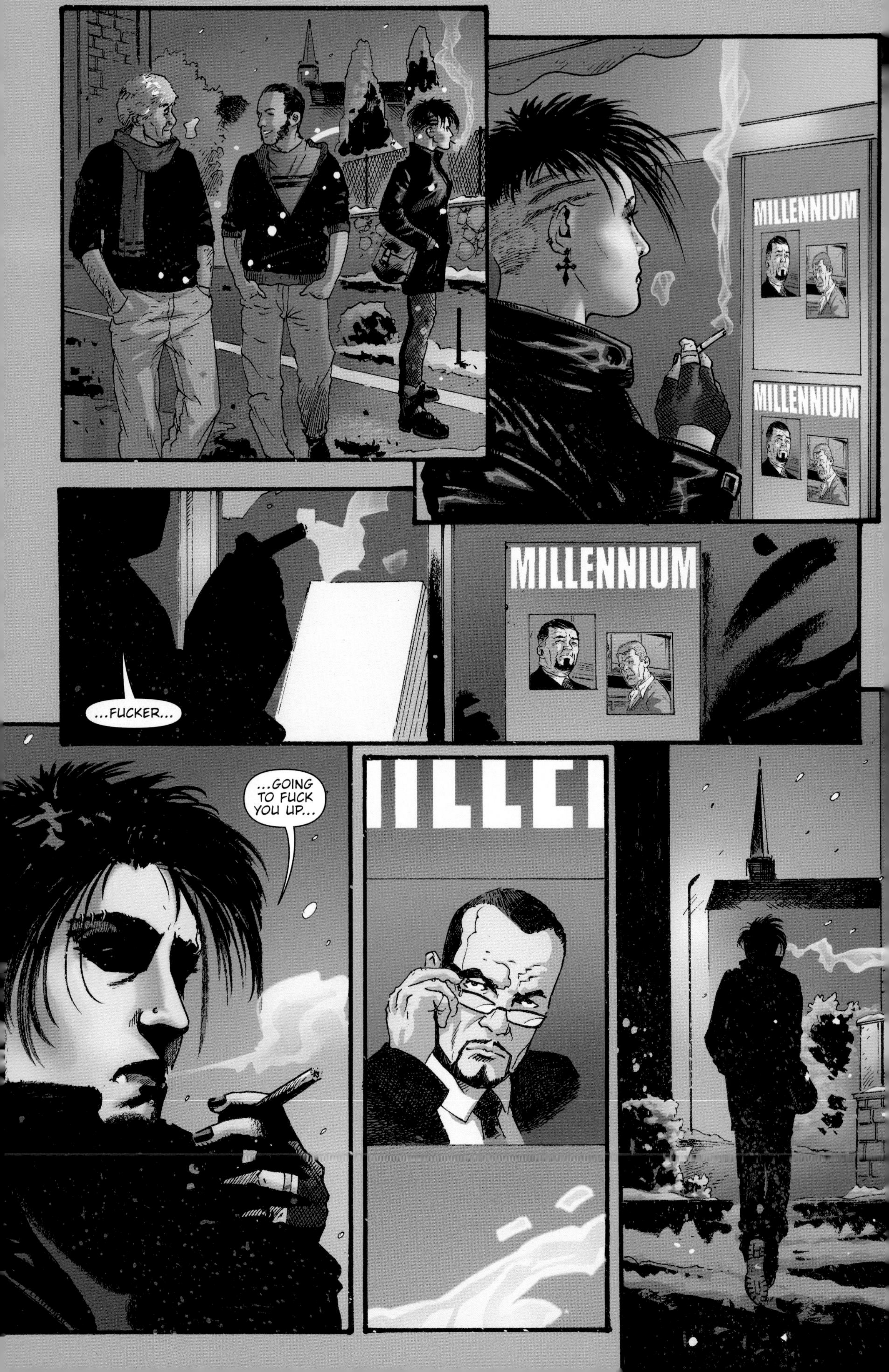
MILLENNIUM
MILLENNIUM
...FUCKER...
MILLENNIUM
...GOING TO FUCK YOU UP...

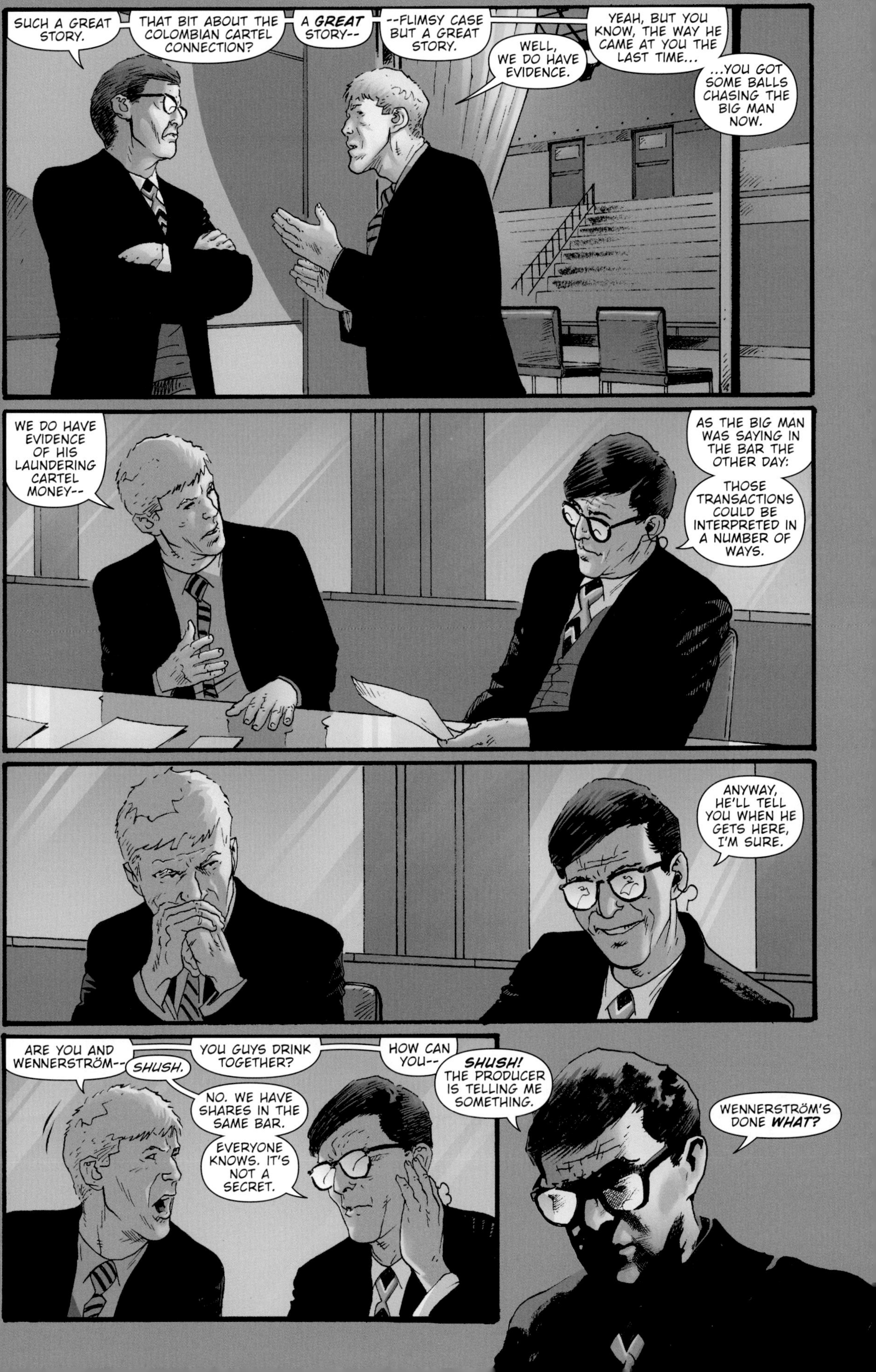
SUCH A GREAT STORY.
THAT BIT ABOUT THE COLOMBIAN CARTEL CONNECTION?
A GREAT STORY--
--FLIMSY CASE BUT A GREAT STORY.
WELL, WE DO HAVE EVIDENCE.
YEAH, BUT YOU KNOW, THE WAY HE CAME AT YOU THE LAST TIME...
...YOU GOT SOME BALLS CHASING THE BIG MAN NOW.
WE DO HAVE EVIDENCE OF HIS LAUNDERING CARTEL MONEY--
AS THE BIG MAN WAS SAYING IN THE BAR THE OTHER DAY:
THOSE TRANSACTIONS COULD BE INTERPRETED IN A NUMBER OF WAYS.
ANYWAY, HE'LL TELL YOU WHEN HE GETS HERE, I'M SURE.
ARE YOU AND WENNERSTRÖM--
SHUSH.
NO. WE HAVE SHARES IN THE SAME BAR.
EVERYONE KNOWS. IT'S NOT A SECRET.
YOU GUYS DRINK TOGETHER?
HOW CAN YOU--
SHUSH! THE PRODUCER IS TELLING ME SOMETHING.
WENNERSTRÖM'S DONE WHAT?

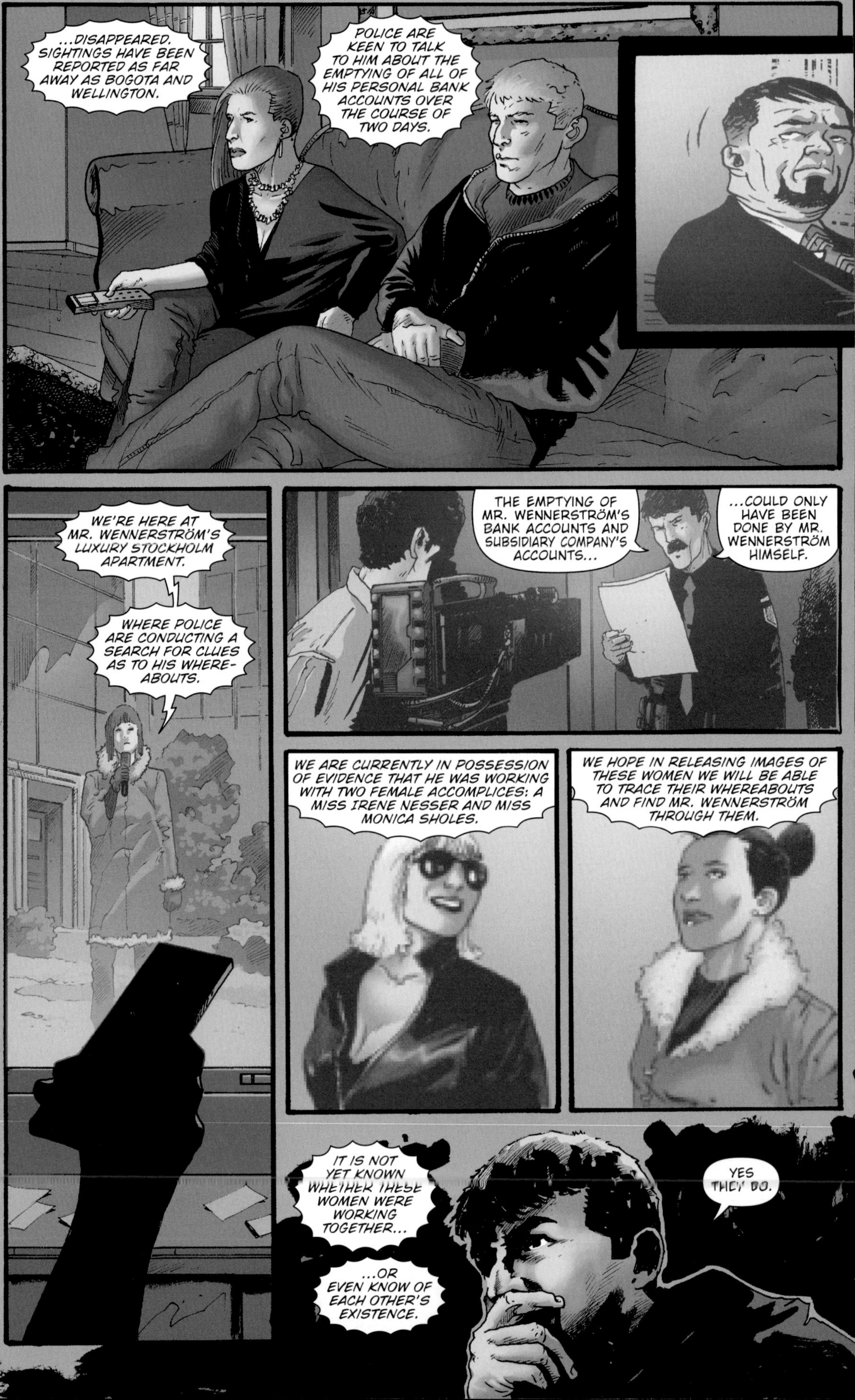
...DISAPPEARED. SIGHTINGS HAVE BEEN REPORTED AS FAR AWAY AS BOGOTA AND WELLINGTON.
POLICE ARE KEEN TO TALK TO HIM ABOUT THE EMPTYING OF ALL OF HIS PERSONAL BANK ACCOUNTS OVER THE COURSE OF TWO DAYS.
WE'RE HERE AT MR. WENNERSTRÖM'S LUXURY STOCKHOLM APARTMENT.
WHERE POLICE ARE CONDUCTING A SEARCH FOR CLUES AS TO HIS WHERE-ABOUTS.
THE EMPTYING OF MR. WENNERSTRÖM'S BANK ACCOUNTS AND SUBSIDIARY COMPANY'S ACCOUNTS...
...COULD ONLY HAVE BEEN DONE BY MR. WENNERSTRÖM HIMSELF.
WE ARE CURRENTLY IN POSSESSION OF EVIDENCE THAT HE WAS WORKING WITH TWO FEMALE ACCOMPLICES: A MISS IRENE NESSER AND MISS MONICA SHOLES.
WE HOPE IN RELEASING IMAGES OF THESE WOMEN WE WILL BE ABLE TO TRACE THEIR WHEREABOUTS AND FIND MR. WENNERSTRÖM THROUGH THEM.
IT IS NOT YET KNOWN WHETHER THESE WOMEN WERE WORKING TOGETHER...
...OR EVEN KNOW OF EACH OTHER'S EXISTENCE.
YES THEY DO.

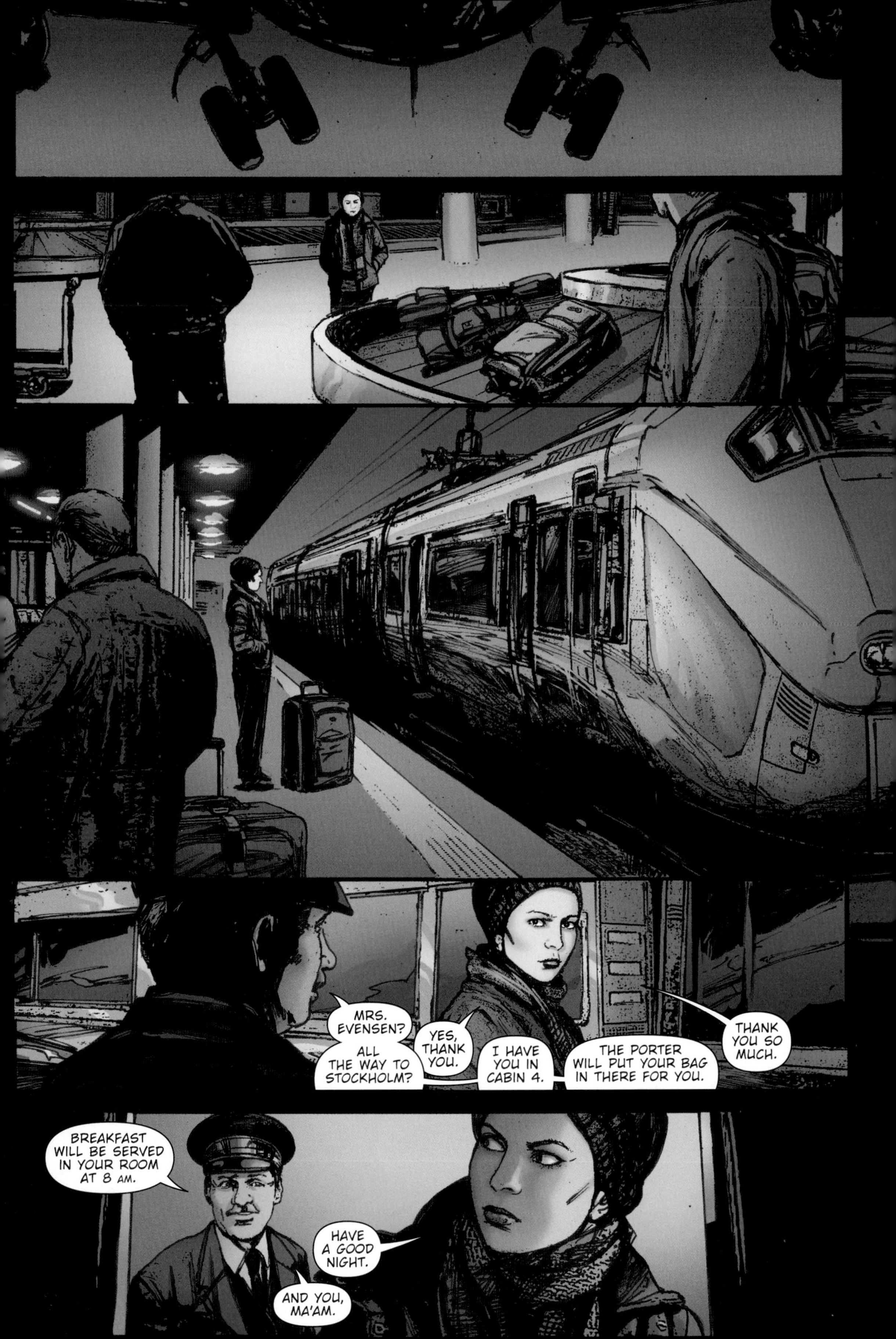
MRS. EVENSEN?
ALL THE WAY TO STOCKHOLM?
YES, THANK YOU.
I HAVE YOU IN CABIN 4.
THE PORTER WILL PUT YOUR BAG IN THERE FOR YOU.
THANK YOU SO MUCH.
BREAKFAST WILL BE SERVED IN YOUR ROOM AT 8 AM.
HAVE A GOOD NIGHT.
AND YOU, MA'AM.

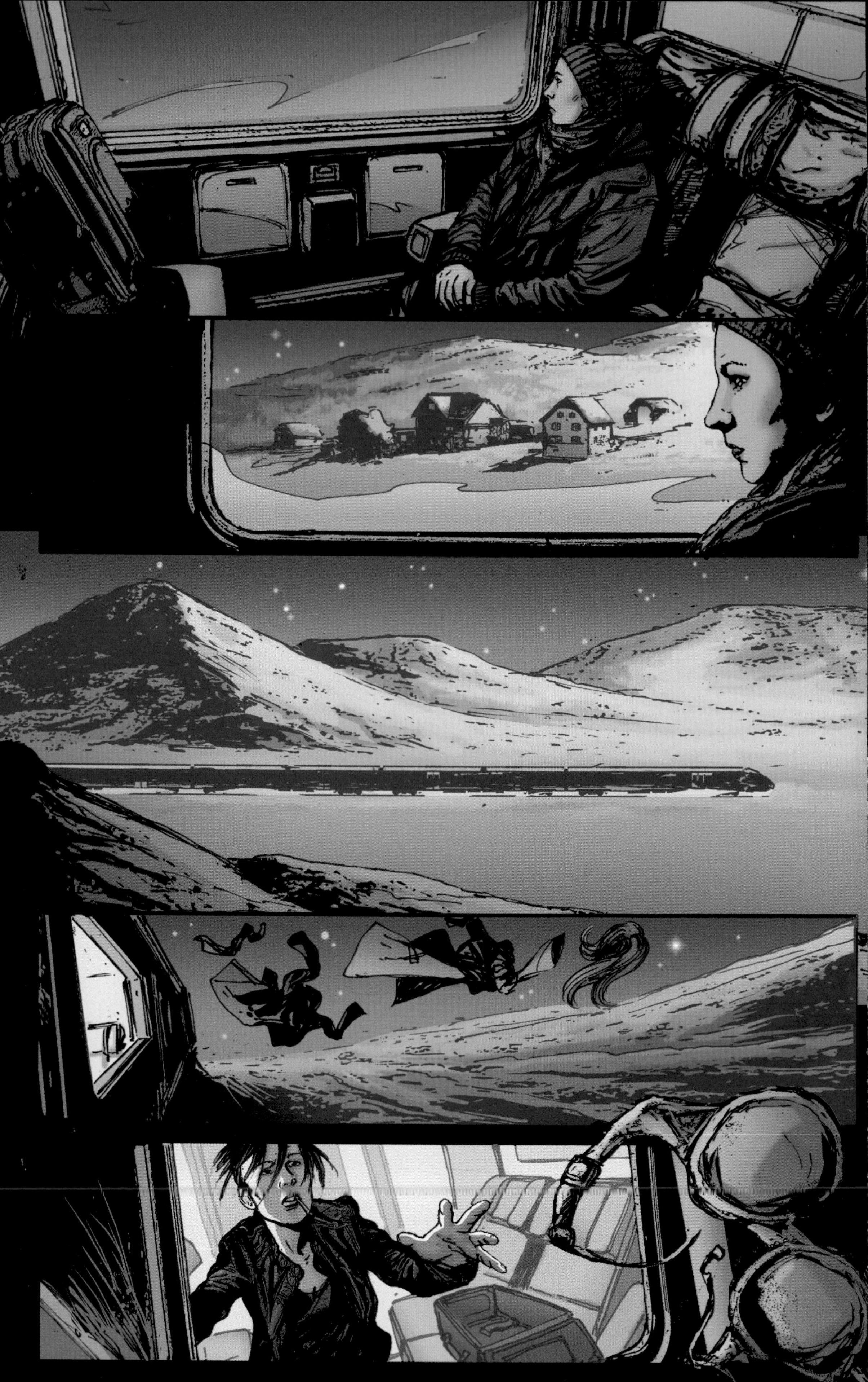

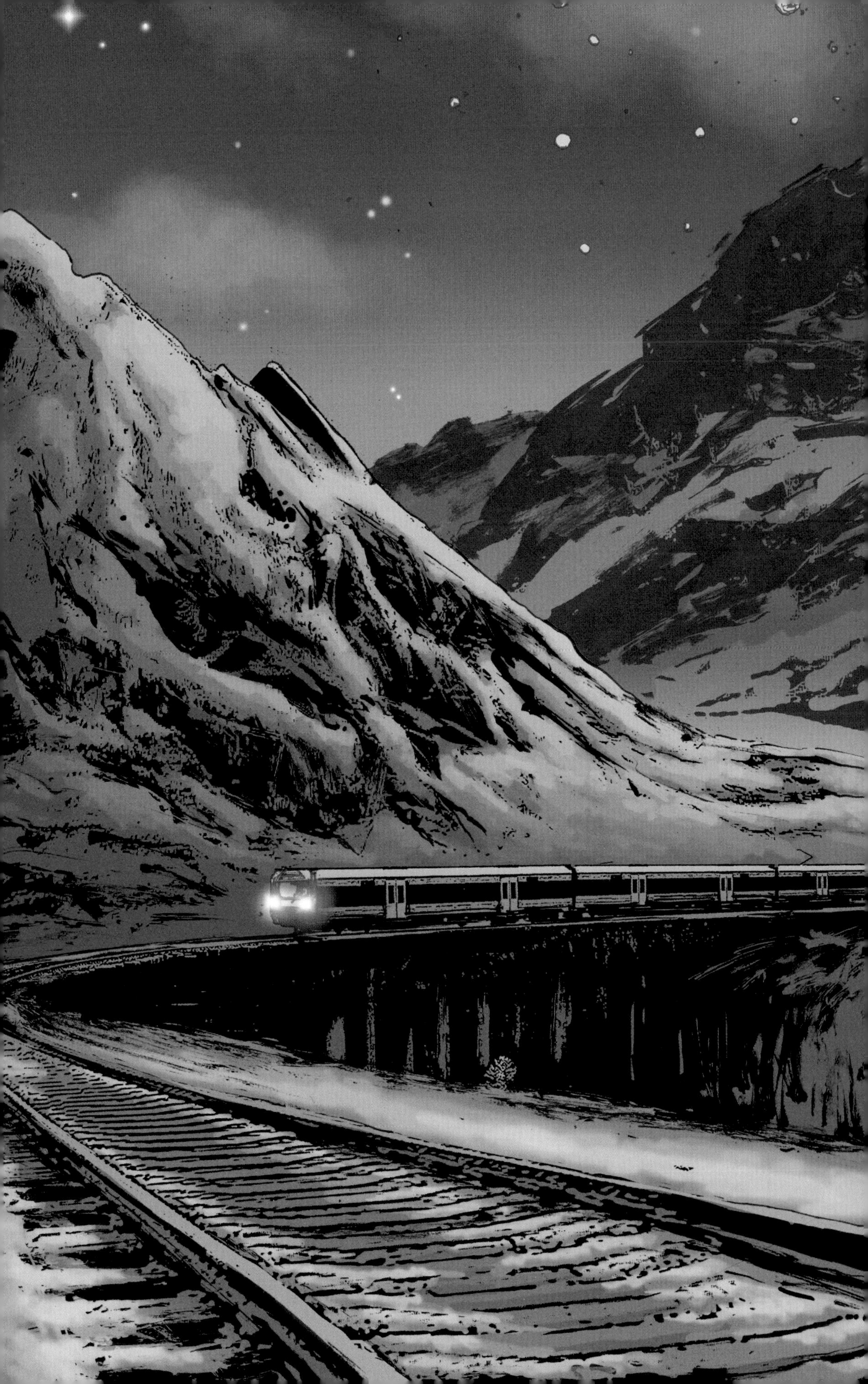

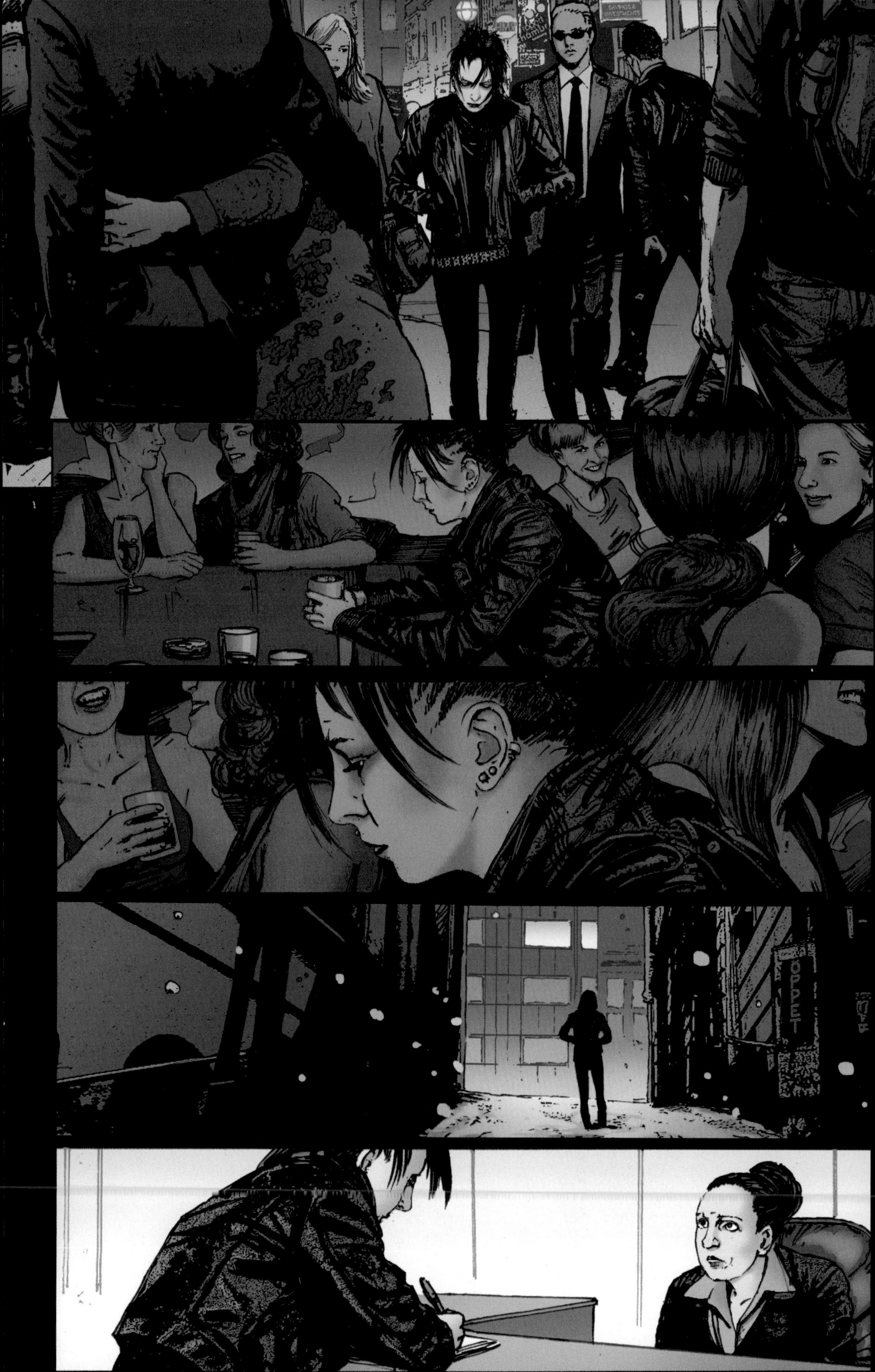
OPPET

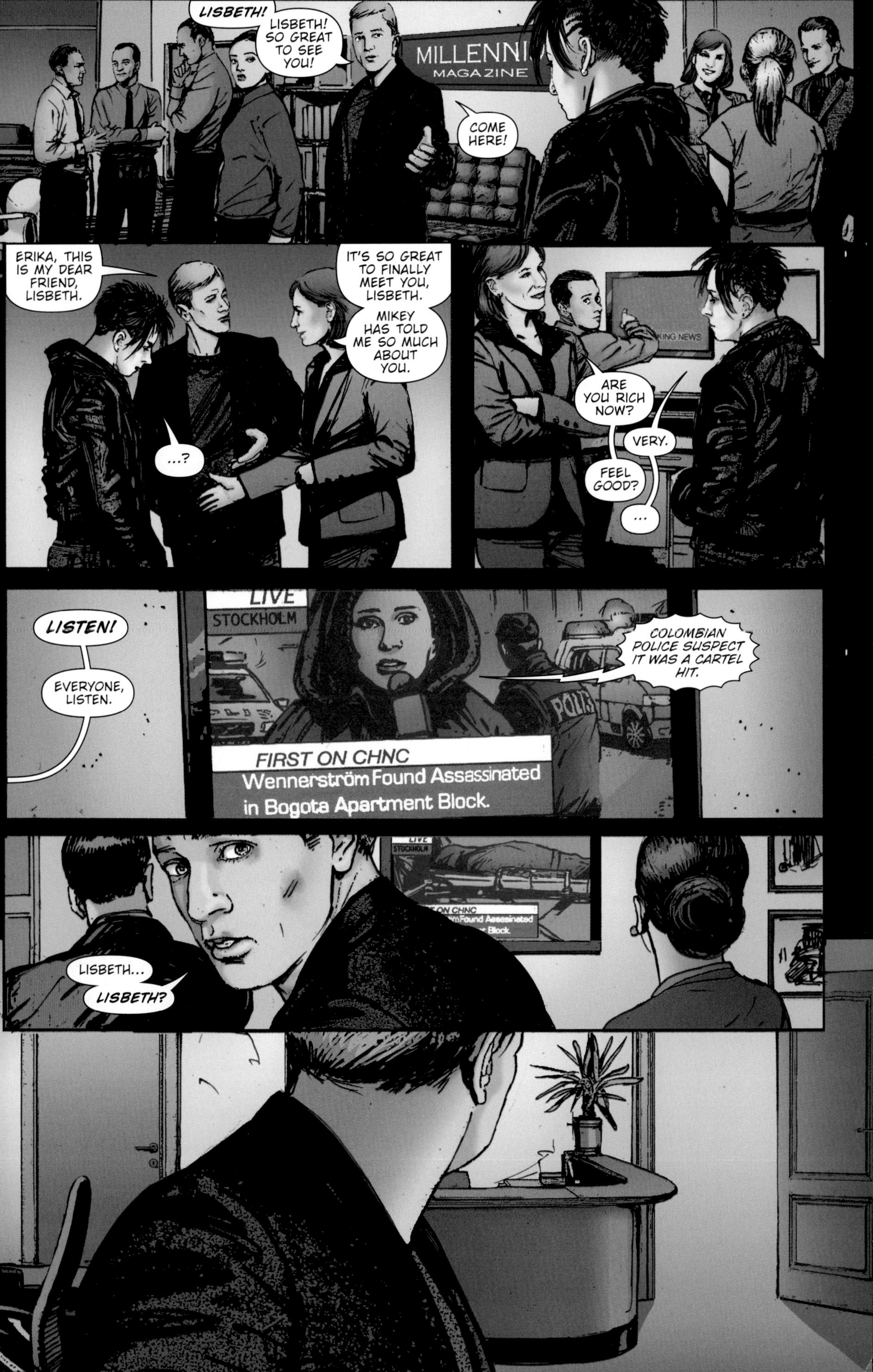

LISBETH!
LISBETH! SO GREAT TO SEE YOU!
MILLENNI
MAGAZINE
COME HERE!
ERIKA, THIS IS MY DEAR FRIEND, LISBETH.
IT'S SO GREAT TO FINALLY MEET YOU, LISBETH.
MIKEY HAS TOLD ME SO MUCH ABOUT YOU.
...?
KING NEWS
ARE YOU RICH NOW?
VERY.
FEEL GOOD?
...
LISTEN!
EVERYONE, LISTEN.
LIVE
STOCKHOLM
COLOMBIAN POLICE SUSPECT IT WAS A CARTEL HIT.
POLIS
FIRST ON CHNC
Wennerström Found Assassinated in Bogota Apartment Block.
LISBETH...
LISBETH?

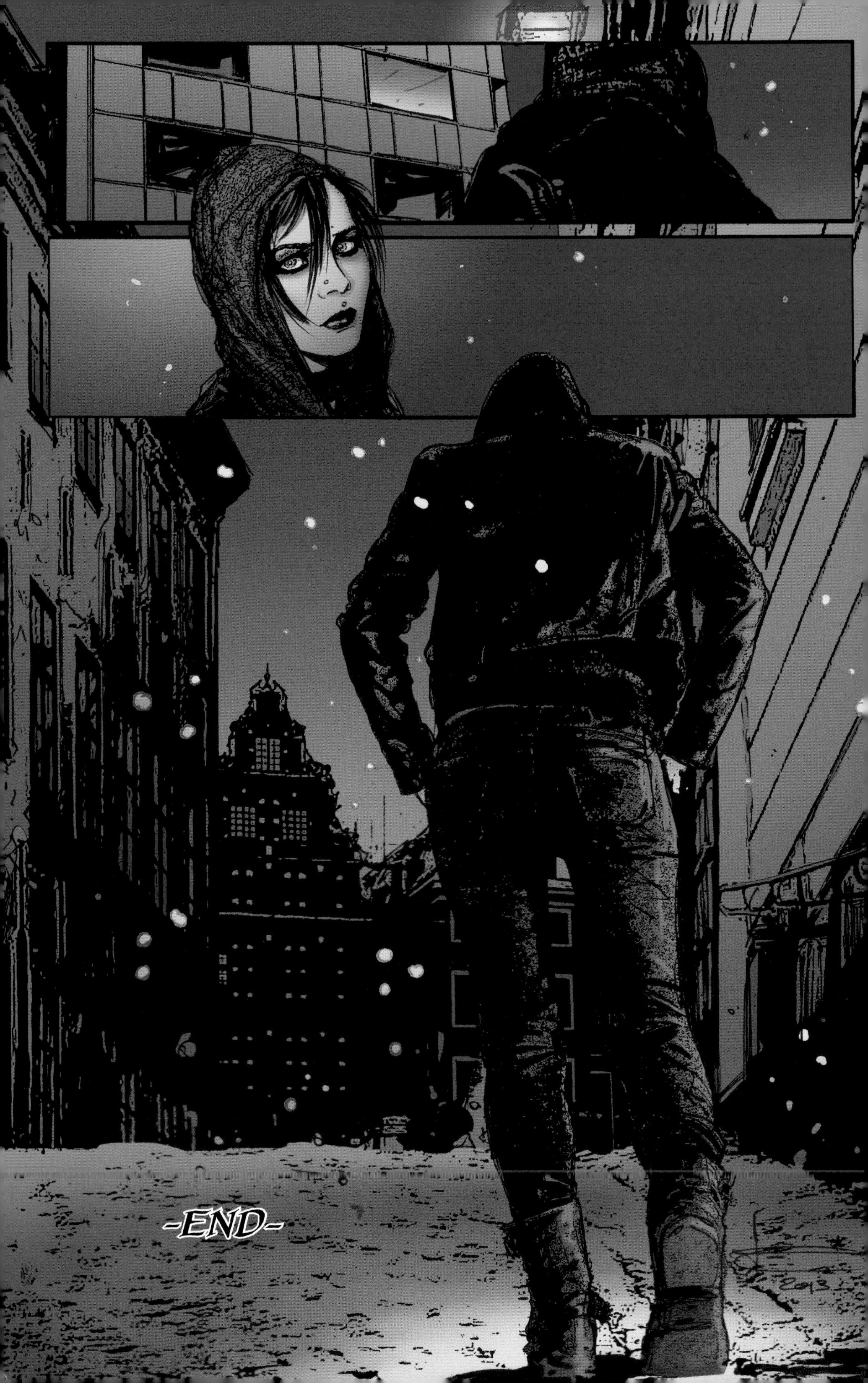
-END-

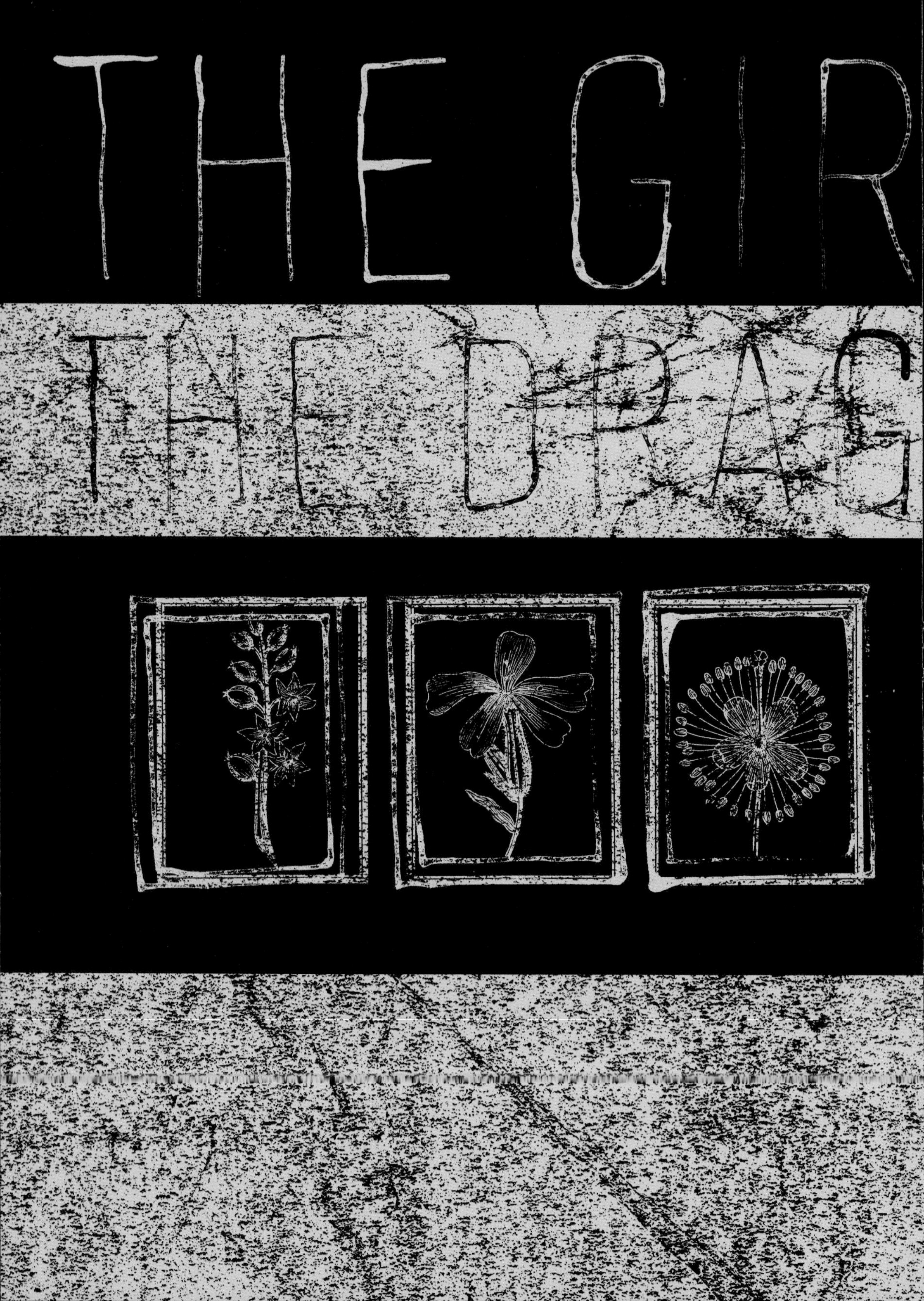
THE GIR
THE DRAG

Denise Mina is a Scottish crime writer and playwright. Her first novel, *Garnethill*, won the Crime Writers' Association John Creasy Dagger for the best first crime novel. She is also known for writing the DC Comics series HELLBLAZER and the graphic novel A SICKNESS IN THE FAMILY.

Leonardo Manco is an Argentine comic book artist and penciller best known for his dark and gritty style. He's worked on titles including Blaze of Glory, Apache Skies, Deathlok, and HELLBLAZER.

Andrea Mutti attended the International School of Comics in Brescia. He has worked extensively for the French market and is known for his work on the DC/Vertigo series DMZ and THE EXECUTOR.

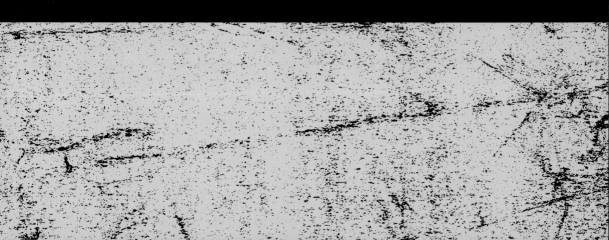

TO BE CONTINUED IN...

A GRAPHIC NOVEL BOOK ONE

DENISE **MINA** LEONARDO **MANCO** ANDREA **MUTTI**

STIEG LARSSON'S
THE GIRL WHO PLAYED WITH FIRE

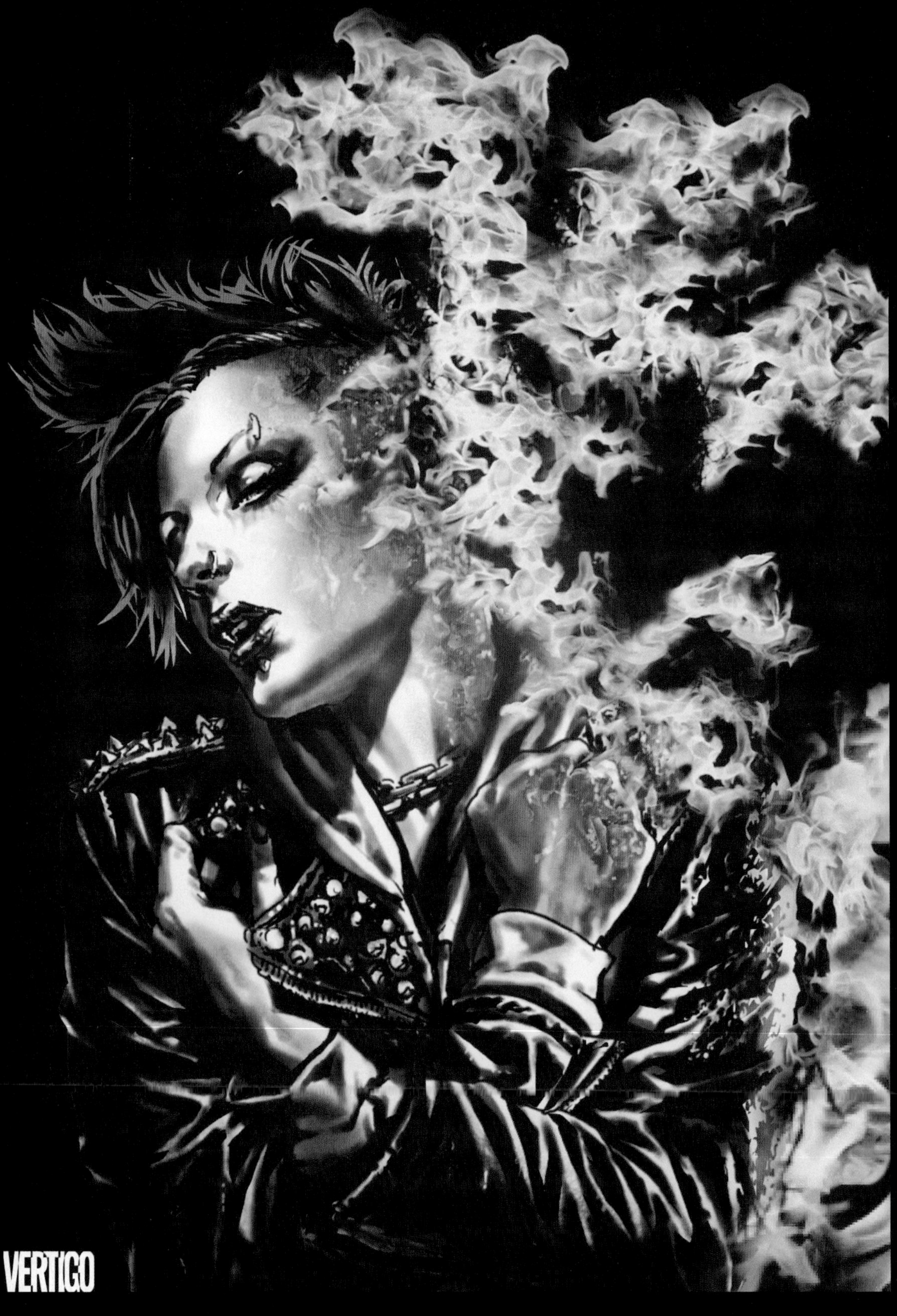
VERTIGO

The Phenomenal
#1 Bestselling Thrillers
NOW A MAJOR MOTION PICTURE
THE GIRL WITH THE DRAGON TATTOO
#1 NATIONAL BESTSELLER
"Wildly suspenseful." —The Washington Post
STIEG LARSSON
"THE HOTTEST BOOKS ON THE PLANET."
—Entertainment Weekly
#1 NATIONAL BESTSELLER
THE GIRL WHO PLAYED WITH FIRE
A NOVEL
STIEG LARSSON
"BELIEVE THE HYPE. THIS IS GRIPPING STUFF...
#1 NATIONAL BESTSELLER
THE GIRL WHO KICKED THE HORNET'S NEST
A NOVEL
STIEG LARSSON
...LISBETH IS ONE OF CRIME FICTION'S MOST UNFORGETTABLE CHARACTERS." —People
Available everywhere books are sold, in trade paperback, mass market, and eBook editions
www.StiegLarsson.net
Vintage Crime / Black Lizard

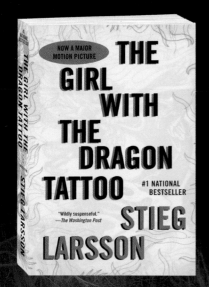

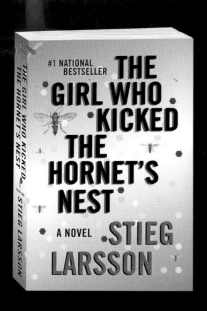

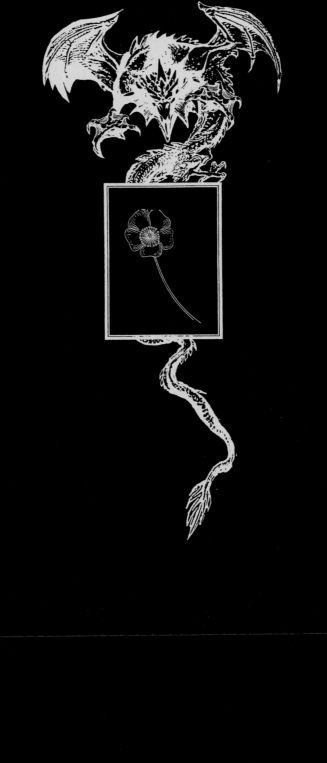